Mark V. Redmond

Social Decentering

A Theory of Other-Orientation Encompassing Empathy
and Perspective-Taking

DE GRUYTER
OLDENBOURG

ISBN 978-3-11-051565-7
e-ISBN (PDF) 978-3-11-051566-4
e-ISBN (EPUB) 978-3-11-051580-0

Library of Congress Cataloging-in-Publication Data
Names: Redmond, Mark V., 1949- author.
Title: Social decentering : a theory of other-orientation encompassing
  empathy and perspective-taking / Mark Redmond.
Description: Berlin ; Boston : Walter de Gruyter, [2018] | Includes
  bibliographical references and index.
Identifiers: LCCN 2018008279 | ISBN 9783110515657 (softcover)
Subjects: LCSH: Social perception. | Empathy. | Social interaction.
Classification: LCC HM1041 .R43 2018 | DDC 302--dc23 LC record available at
https://lccn.loc.gov/2018008279

Bibliographic Information Published by the Deutsche Nationalbibliothek
The Deutsche Nationalbibliothek lists this publication in the Deutsche Nationalbibliografie;
detailed bibliographic data are available on the Internet at http://dnb.dnb.de.

© 2018 Walter de Gruyter GmbH, Berlin/Boston
Cover illustration: Mark V. Redmond
Typesetting: Integra Software Services Pvt. Ltd.
Printing and binding: CPI books GmbH, Leck

MIX
Papier aus verantwor-
tungsvollen Quellen
FSC® C083411

www.degruyter.com

Dedicated to Dr. Frank Dance, Dr. Carl Larson, and the late Dr. Alton Barbour and Dr. Al Goldberg. It's been a long journey since each of them guided my dissertation on empathy and communication competence, but the influence of their wisdom never wanes. Also, in remembrance of fellow students who began that journey with me but who are no longer here to see the finale: Dr. Norm Watson, Dr. Jim Toulhuizen, and Dr. Marc Routhier.

This book is also dedicated to all those who seek to make this a better world with their willingness to consider the perspectives, values, beliefs, thoughts, feelings, and experiences of those who provide them love and support, and those who challenge and confront them.

Acknowledgments

I owe a very large debt of gratitude to Lori Peterson, who edited several of my chapters. Her attention to detail and wordsmithing often turned my gibberish into meaningful prose. Thank you Lori. My thanks also to Dr. Phil Backlund and Dr. Katherine Rafferty for reading some of the chapters and providing constructive feedback. I am indebted to my colleague, Dr. Denise Vrchota, for providing her moral support and a kind ear throughout the development and writing of this book. Thanks to my wife, Peggy, for her understanding and patience while I whiled away the hours writing. A special thanks to Anja Cheong, acquisitions editor of De Gruyter for her enthusiastic support, encouragement, and guidance. I particularly appreciated her openness to even my most trivial questions and her helpful responses. And finally, my gratitude to Frauke Schafft and Janine Conrad at De Gruyter for helping me through the production process.

https://doi.org/10.1515/9783110515664-201

Contents

Preface/Introduction

The following comments are intended to align your expectations as a reader with those of mine as the writer by primarily explaining what is not included in this book. If you have elected to read this book of your own accord (versus an assigned reading for a class), you might be expecting a thorough, detailed discussion of empathy and perspective-taking, but you will not find that. Many years ago, after considerable time reviewing the literature on empathy, perspective-taking, and role-taking, I wrote a convention paper where I detailed the confusion surrounding the meaning and measurement of those concepts. As a solution, I decided to erase the board and start with a blank slate and a new term. Since that time, others have also languished over the confusion of the meaning of the terms empathy and perspective-taking, often merging them together in attempts to more clearly identify boundaries and meaning resulting in such terms as empathic perspective-taking, affective perspective-taking, and cognitive empathy. Other scholars have also discussed these issues of conceptual confusion, so there is no need to rehash those issues here.

Instead, the focus of this book is to explain and expand on the theory of social decentering, though I will review research and theory on empathy and perspective-taking, insofar as they provide support and clarity to social decentering. I originally published an abbreviated description of social decentering and a measure of social decentering in the *Journal of Research in Personality* (Redmond, 1995). This book includes a comprehensive discussion of social decentering theory which I argue is a multidimensional theory that encompasses empathy and perspective-taking. Among the goals of the theory is to provide a framework that solves many of the issues that have confronted research and theory in empathy and perspective-taking. But the social decentering theory goes beyond simply combining knowledge about empathy and perspective-taking, to provide an innovative model that explains the process people use when analyzing another person's thoughts, feelings, and dispositions.

Initially, I drew from the work of Jean Piaget (1950, 1974) in using the term decentering, but I came to realize the use of that term would prove too limiting, since for Piaget, decentering focused on children's recognition of physical perspectives. My interest was in how people apply the same general process, not just to their physical world, but to their entire social world – more specifically, to seeing the world from another person's perspective. Thus, I added the term social to decentering to more accurately reflect the phenomenon I wished to study – social decentering.

I believe that social decentering theory is the theory that would emerge after you shake together all of the main conceptual components associated with empathy, perspective-taking, and role-taking and then pour them out into a single mold. The theory of social decentering reflects a way of organizing the most significant elements of other-oriented concepts to create a unified theory. But more importantly, my goal was to create a theory that is a true reflection of the social cognitive process that takes place when a

https://doi.org/10.1515/9783110515664-001

person considers another person's dispositions within a given situation. I use the term disposition as a catchall term because I got tired of listing the multitude of elements a person might review when considering another person's world – their perspectives, thoughts, feelings, attitudes, needs, world view, beliefs, values, biases, education, experiences, race, sex, age, and so on. Nonetheless, when explaining social decentering, I refer to efforts to consider another person's thoughts, feelings, and other dispositions. I explicitly identify thoughts and feelings in addition to disposition to emphasize two of the major elements that constitute other-orientation – the cognitive and the affective.

In choosing to focus on social decentering as a form of social cognition, other areas of theory and research related to empathy and perspective-taking are excluded. For example, I do not review or include theory and research related to empathy from a neurological perspective. The reason for excluding this material is again to differentiate a conscientious process from a neurological reaction such as motor mimicry. A significant amount of research that involves mapping neurological responses to perceptions of others has resulted in identifying mirror neurons. On the most basic level, mirror neurons occur when the same neuron that is triggered in one animal is triggered in another animal who observes the first. I use this to explain to my wife why I grunt when I'm watching football on TV and grunt when a player is tackled – my physiological reaction or motor mimicry is mildly similar to what the player experienced – my neurons are mirroring his. One can argue that my neurological response then provides me with information about what the player must have experienced which provides a basis for empathizing with him. Bayne and Hays (2017) point out that knowing what neural pathways are illuminated in response to another's emotions does not provide a "full realization of empathy in an interpersonal context" (p. 33). In addition, discovering shared neuropathways fails to reflect the other thoughts that occur as observers experience emotions. The social cognitive aspects of social decentering go beyond neuro-emotional responses as individuals think about the person, the situation, and themselves as they make sense of the emotional response. Thus, to maintain the focus on the deliberative process that surrounds being other oriented, the research and theory related to the neurological perspective is not included.

Another reaction that is somewhat akin to unconscious motor mimicry that is associated strongly with empathy is altruism. A considerable amount of research has been devoted to understand people's tendency to be altruistic and the affect that empathy has on altruistic behavior. Batson's empathy-altruism hypothesis posits that empathic concern for another elicits altruistic motivation (Batson & Shaw, 1991). The hypothesis was generated to counter the claims that altruism actually stems from egotistic concern. Inherent in the ongoing study of the relationship between empathy and altruism are issues of definition and assessment. The confusion that exists regarding empathy that I mentioned above also interferes with efforts to understand empathy and altruism. Focusing only on the application of empathy to altruism results in failing to appreciate the many other ways that being other-oriented affects our behaviors and relationships. Rather than getting somewhat sidelined in my efforts to present a comprehensive introduction to social decentering, this text does not directly examine altruism. But I have included discussion about social decentering producing efforts to help others.

Just as Piaget was interested in how children's cognitive development allows them to recognize differences in physical perspectives through decentering, other scholars have examined the development of empathy in children to determine at what age children sense the feelings of others. A considerable amount of theory and research on empathy, perspective-taking, and role-taking focuses on their development, particularly in children and adolescents. But the focus of this book is on the role other-orientation plays in adult interactions and interpersonal relationships.

There is little doubt that our social experiences in childhood through adolescence establish the foundation on which other-orientation builds as we become adults. When we reach adulthood, our use of empathy, perspective-taking, and social decentering takes on an important role that was not present during childhood – developing and maintaining intimate relationships. That use requires refinement and expansion of the skills associated with being empathic in childhood. For the most part, I avoided incorporating into my discussion, the results of research on empathy and perspective-taking that centered on samples of children or teens because of the uncertainty as to how validly those results apply to adults. In recognition of the unique ways in which adults develop and apply other-oriented processes and to provide a central focus to this text, social decentering is discussed in terms of how adults use it in their daily interactions and relationships with other adults.

Whether you are convinced after reading this monograph about the validity of social decentering theory or not, I hope you will have gained at least some innovative ways to think about how people make sense of their social world and the significant role that taking into consideration another person's thoughts, feelings, and dispositions plays in our lives. I also hope that this monograph answers some of the extant questions concerning other-oriented processes, and that I have raised a few worthy questions of my own that might inspire your own journey.

References

Batson, C. D., & Shaw, L. L. (1991). Evidence for altruism: Toward a pluralism of prosocial motives. *Psychological Inquiry, 2*, 107–122.

Bayne, H. B., & Hays, D. G. (2017). Examining conditions for empathy in counseling: An exploratory model. *Journal of Humanistic Counseling, 56*, 32–52.

Piaget, J. (1950). *The psychology of intelligence*. New York: Harcourt, Brace.

Piaget, J. (1974). *The language and thought of the child*. New York: New American Library.

Redmond, M. V. (1995). A multidimensional theory and measure of social decentering. *Journal of Research in Personality, 29*, 35–58.

1 Theory of Social Decentering Part 1: Activation, Input, and Analysis

A husband and wife are sitting down for dinner together. The husband is thinking about whether he should tell his wife about the clerk who flirted with him earlier in the day when he went to the store. He decides not to share the story because he believes it will make his wife feel jealous and insecure. At work, the boss snapped at several of the employees about their shoddy work and lack of professionalism before returning to her office and slamming the door. One employee who knows the boss well attributes this behavior to the boss's recent conflicts with higher management and pressure to improve productivity. A teacher has a student who is struggling in his course. The student is exasperated because she is unable to understand the material adequately enough to do well on the tests and assignments. Though the instructor doesn't know the student well, his own experience as an undergraduate in a course that exasperated him provides a basis for understanding some of the student's feelings. In each of the three scenarios, a person is able to consider the situation at hand from another person's perspective. This ability to consider another person's perspective, to be other-centered (an effort that enhances our ability to effectively communicate, to manage relationships, and to achieve personal goals), is the focus of the social decentering theory.

1.1 Defining Social Decentering

Social decentering was coined as a term to encompass being other-oriented in the broadest sense. Piaget (Piaget & Inhelder, 1969) used the term *decentering* to describe the ability of children to see the physical world from another person's perspective. For Higgins (1981), role-taking represents movement from egocentrism to decentration. Higgins describes decentration as "the ability to interrelate two or more mental elements in active memory" (p. 131) with that ability continuing to develop, thus increasing the number of mental elements that can be interrelated. Social decentering shares the same basic cognitive processes that are represented in these initial conceptualizations of decentering. However, rather than being limited to a visually oriented perspective as with Piaget, I've added the modifier "social" to emphasize an orientation centered on another person – of seeing and feeling the world as another person does. *Social decentering* is introduced as a new term to represent this other-oriented process because other terms like *empathy*, *perspective-taking*, and *role-taking* are used in a myriad of inconsistent ways or are restrictive in their treatment of other-orientation. However, much of the foundation for social decentering is by necessity drawn from the theory and research generated under the rubrics of empathy, perspective-taking, and role-taking.

https://doi.org/10.1515/9783110515664-002

Social decentering is a multidimensional social cognitive process that involves taking into account another person's feelings, thoughts, perspectives, and other dispositions in a given situation (Redmond, 1995). Social decentering is considering or experiencing the world as if you are the other person – becoming an ephemeral other. Before presenting a model of social decentering, examining each of the elements in the definition of social decentering provides a clearer understanding of the meaning and boundaries of the concept.

1.1.1 Social Decentering as Multidimensional

A conceptual chaos surrounds the definitions of empathy, perspective-taking, and role-taking (see reviews by Cuff, Brown, Taylor, & Howat, 2016; Hojat, 2016; or the debate between Zaki, 2017 and Bloom, 2017). One significant problem relates to treating being other-centered as a unidimensional concept, for example, focusing only on the cognitive aspect or the affective aspect rather than on both. Gehlbach (2004) recognized this problem when he developed a multidimensional alternative to perspective-taking that he labeled "social perspective-taking." In a similar vein, social decentering is conceptualized as a *multidimensional* process, with four distinct stages: activation, input (information retrieval, seeking, or creation), analysis (information processing), and response (output). The input consists of two dimensions: observed and recalled experience-based information, and imagination-based information. The analysis stage has three options: use of information and analysis based on the self, use of information and analysis based on the specific-other person, and use of information and analysis based on generalized others (similar to implicit personality theory). Two internal responses occur in the next stage: a cognitive response (understanding and analysis) and an affective response (sympathy, empathy, or other emotions). Each of the stages and their constituent parts are discussed in detail later in this chapter.

1.1.2 Social Decentering as Social Cognition

In as much as social cognition concerns itself with "the mental processes involved in perceiving, attending to, remembering, thinking about, and making sense of the people in our social world" (Moskowitz, 2005, p. 3), social decentering is a *social cognitive process*. Social decentering involves people thinking about and feeling the world from other people's perspectives – processing what they perceive, remember, and imagine about other people. Then, as a social cognitive process, social decentering relies on person perception, impression formation, schemas, dispositional inferences, and stereotypes while being subject to biases, priming, processing errors, and inaccuracies. Social decentering also facilitates other social cognition processes, such as attribution, which involves generating explanations for another person's behavior (Heider, 1958). Social decentering can be used to produce and evaluate possible explanations. But while attribution seeks to identify the reason or cause for an observed behavior (Moskowitz, 2005), social decentering can be used to anticipate behavior and reactions and to develop and adapt strategies to effectively achieve goals when interacting with others. And, unlike attribution which is conducted only from the attributor's vantage point, social decentering focuses on trying to understand what has occurred or will occur from the perspective of the other person. One attribution phenomenon, fundamental attribution bias, actually represents an antithesis of social decentering. Because of fundamental attribution bias, individuals fail to consider the impact of circumstance when generating explanations for other people's actions. In contrast, the social decenterer specifically takes into consideration the given situation.

Social decentering is also a social cognitive ability or skill. The process of taking into consideration another person's dispositions involves conscious effort, and as such, making effort can be learned, developed, and improved. However, successful social decentering depends on other social cognitive abilities, such as person perception, attribution, decision-making, deduction, strategic planning, emotional intelligence, and general social information processing. Some people are better social decenterers than others, and this variation can be measured. As with any skill, social decentering changes over time and from situation to situation. The skill can begin to develop early in childhood, continue to develop throughout life, stagnate in development, or even deteriorate. Changes in social decentering affect a person's self-concept, interpersonal relationships, and success in meeting social goals.

1.1.3 Social Decentering as a Taking into Account

The *taking into account* part of social decentering involves the cognitive process of managing information and is a critical component of the overall theory and model of social decentering. In some instances, such taking into account occurs as a predictive process in which individuals' anticipation of interactions leads them to analyze the person or people they expect to encounter. In developing and considering their interaction strategies, individuals might take into account the other people involved to enhance their selection of the most effective strategy. Then during interactions, individuals might take into account the behaviors of the other interactants when considering how to act and respond. Obviously, time is a critical factor in the amount of deliberation and processing that can occur. For example, a manager approaches a computer programmer and asks the programmer to work over the weekend, which the programmer would prefer not to do (any similarity to *Office Space* is purely accidental). The programmer has only a brief moment of time to take into account the manager while creating a reply to both save face and keep the weekend free.

While such taking into account generates understanding, usually an explanation of another person's behavior (attribution), it also contributes to the general impression formation process by aiding in the establishment of constructs about a particular person. Unexpected behaviors can stimulate the search for an explanation of the behavior (this is elaborated on further in the chapter). Explanations can be generated by this process of taking into account, specifically about the person who has behaved unexpectedly. Causal attribution theory identifies three potential causes for a person's behavior: the circumstance, the stimulus, and the person. Taking into account the person involves analyzing the person as the cause of the behavior. Traditionally, determination of cause is related to the consensus, consistency, and distinctiveness of information. However, the information is often insufficient to make a complete analysis of these three factors, and researchers blame errors in such processing to attributional biases or experimental shortcomings (Försterling, 2001). Social decentering offers another way that individuals can determine the cause of another person's behavior – by taking into account the other person's behavior from the other person's perspective. In essence, is the behavior consistent with how one expects another person to behave based on what is known about that person? The halo and horn effects represent a broad, though biased, application of this process. Such analyses might lead to the conclusion that the behavior does not fit the existing schema resulting in an attribution of cause to circumstance or stimulus, which might explain why such attributions are found in research even without the covariance associated with consensus, consistency, or distinctiveness.

Taking into account can produce constructs that become part of a schema. In forming impressions of other people, individuals observe a person's behavior, attribute a cause to the behavior, and then, if the cause is attributed to a person, they add that to the schema they develop of the other person. When observed behaviors result in new attributions about an individual, they become fodder for subsequent social decentering. In this way, social decentering has a reciprocal relationship with attribution, in that social decentering contributes to attributions and attributions contribute to social decentering.

1.1.4 Social Decentering as a Focus on Dispositions Held by Others

A person's feelings, thoughts, perspectives, and other dispositions are what get taken into account through social decentering. The phrase *feelings, thoughts, perspectives, and other dispositions* is used as shorthand for taking into account as much as possible about what constitutes the other person – becoming an ephemeral other. In essence, social decentering involves considering another person's cognitive and affective dispositions. Feelings, thoughts, and perspectives represent three significant dispositions to which other-oriented processes are attuned. Recognition that considering another person's feelings differs from considering another person's thoughts has resulted in distinguishing affective empathy from cognitive empathy. Davis (2005) sees six aims of perspective-taking (in its broadest definition); determining the thoughts, emotions, perceptual points of view, motives, goals, and intentions of other people. Krauss and Fussell (1996) see perspective-taking as considering the other person's background knowledge, beliefs, and attitudes; current interpretations of stimuli and events; plans, goals, and attitudes; social context; physical context, speech style, emotional state, and current state of message comprehension. They conclude that "virtually any aspect of a person might be thought of part of his/her perspective, and something that at least potentially should be taken into consideration when formulating a message" (p. 674). Similarly, social decentering has a broad set of goals and draws upon the full breadth of information people might garner if they experience the world as another person does. Social decentering involves considering the other person's feelings, thoughts, values, beliefs, background, experiences, knowledge, needs, motives, relationships, and more. At the extreme, social decenterers might temporarily become the other person. Popular media has reflected this extreme with shows about law enforcement profilers who take on a criminal's persona to better understand and anticipate the criminal's next move. In some ways, everyday people are also profilers. Just as professional profilers gather as much information as they can about their targets, everyday people gather as much information as they can about the people with whom they interact to enhance their social decentering.

1.1.5 Social Decentering as Contextually Bound

Finally, social decentering occurs relative to a *given situation*; that is, individuals take into consideration the context surrounding the target of their decentering. We are generally motivated to engage in social decentering because something about a given situation triggers our need to consider the other. We become concerned with why a person has reacted to a given situation or stimulus or how that other person might react to an anticipated situation or stimulus. Why did our friend suddenly hang up on us? Why was our boss in such a good mood today? How will my spouse react if I end up being an hour late for dinner tonight? Answering these questions involves considering a particular person in a particular situation. Thus, social decentering means analyzing another person within a specific context rather than simply forming an impression in general. Participants in Gerace, Day, Casey, and Mohr's (2013) study reported that their perspective-taking efforts involved consideration of personal information about the other and information about the situation or context. A manager might have an impression of an employee as hardworking and mild mannered. In considering whether to promote the employee to shift supervisor, the manager can use social decentering to apply that impression in considering how well the employee could handle the given situation – managing others.

The ability to consider a given situation further extends the complexity of social decentering, which requires awareness and knowledge of the qualities and nuances that make up a given situation. Individuals not only need a variety of social cognitive skills, they need to be aware of and sensitive to the interplay between the external circumstances and the internal states of other people. For example, if the manager promoted an employee to shift supervisor, but failed to consider the dynamics and relationships that existed among the other employees, the manager might be surprised when the employee fails to successfully manage the shift. Such a problem was part of the reason Fiedler (1968) developed a contingency model of leadership which recognized that just because a person is a good leader in one situation, does not automatically mean that the person will be successful in a different situation. Fiedler focused on identifying the elements that make up a given situation relative to particular leadership styles. In essence, his approach considers a person's leadership qualities in a given situation.

The cognitive activity that occurs in attending to the context or situation, which has been labeled event schemas, scripts, event prototypes, and event stereotypes, produces generalizations about how people act in a given situation. These event generalizations provide another basis for both understanding and evaluating a person's behavior in a given situation. For example, an individual might hold a set of expectations about how people act at funerals, which are applied in inferring what behaviors a friend displayed while recently attending a funeral. These event generalizations, like the behavioral scripts studied by Schank and Abelson (1977), provide a framework for analyzing another person's behavior. Understanding the actions of the other person is likely to require greater effort if the script or expectations associated with a given situation are violated. Not having a script or expectations associated with a given situation creates greater ambiguity and undermines an individual's ability to socially decenter. Just as individuals develop repertoires of expectations associated with roles or group memberships (stereotypes), they also develop repertoires of scripts, prototypes, and schemas that are specifically linked to given situations.

1.1.6 Accuracy, Depth, and Breadth of Social Decentering

One issue often raised about other-oriented processes centers on the production of accurate understanding. Accuracy is one way to assess how well a person has analyzed another person's dispositions; however, being inaccurate does not mean an individual has not engaged in being other-oriented or social decentering. Three possible conditions exist: (1) not engaging in social decentering and being inaccurate (except by chance), (2) engaging in social decentering and being inaccurate, and (3) engaging in social decentering and being accurate. The second condition is important to recognize and study; it represents situations in which an individual socially decenters, but in which errors occur within the process. Research on empathic accuracy by Ickes and his colleagues has emphasized the ability to accurately read another person's mind in reporting the thoughts that occurred during a given interaction; suffice it to say, it represents a very specific other-oriented process. An individual might be very accurate in considering a partner's reaction to a proposed course of action when planning an encounter, yet be unable to surmise that partner's immediate thoughts during a conversation. Given that empathy can be affective and cognitive, an individual might empathically share the same emotional response as another person to a given situation, yet be unable to articulate an understanding of what that other person was thinking. In this situation, the individual appears not to be empathic because of a failure to correctly identify another person's thoughts, despite sharing the same emotional disposition. On the other hand, social decentering theory has been developed to take into account the accuracy and inaccuracy of analysis as well as affective and cognitive responses.

Social decentering is a process that varies in depth from a cursory analysis of the other person to complex and sophisticated analysis of the individual and situation. Such analyses produce variations in the level of understanding and feelings, and the complexity of the adaptation and responses. Compared to complex analyses, cursory social decentering is likely to include more errors. Although cursory analysis can produce a degree of accurate understanding, a lack of analytical depth could result in inappropriate adaptation and response. Social decentering is an interval variable – individuals vary in their ability to apply social decentering, and social decentering can be employed to varying degrees of depth. A given individual might also vary in applying social decentering; thus, social decentering can be both a state variable and a trait variable.

As a state, social decentering varies within any given individual as he or she exerts more or less effort to engage the process. As a trait, however, social decentering varies between individuals because some individuals regularly engage in more in-depth analyses than do others. A variety of factors affect the depth of analysis, such as the motivation to consider another person's dispositions and the amount of information available about another person. The available information affects the breadth of social decentering as well. That is, it affects the number of factors about a person or a given situation that an individual can take into consideration while decentering. Social decentering also varies in the variety of another person's dispositions that individuals consider. One of the most basic issues of breadth is the degree to which individuals consider the cognitive or affective dispositions of another person. Focusing on only one obviously reduces the breadth of social decentering. In the following sections and throughout this book, I explore the factors that affect the depth and breadth of social decentering in more detail.

1.2 The Theory and Model of Social Decentering

I have derived this theory and model of social decentering from a synthesis of scholarship in social cognition, social information processing, attribution theory, role-taking, perspective-taking, and empathy. More specifically, this theory merges various perspectives and integrates confounding findings into a cohesive model. For example, the model addresses the issue whether empathy is a cognitive or affective process by including both as conjoint processes that contribute to social decentering. Figure 1.1 shows the complete model of social decentering, identifying the various stages and the relationships between them. Overall, social decentering is a process which is externally or internally activated, involving the input of information, analysis of information, and some internal responses, potentially leading to development and implementation of specific strategies and actions.

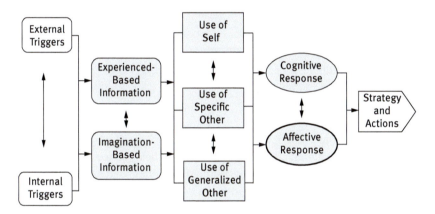

Figure 1.1: Model of social decentering.

1.2.1 Activation

Social decentering occurs in response to a stimulus – something activates the process. That stimulation can be either external or internal. In discussing a situation-oriented theory of personality, Mischel and Shoda (2010) identified both external situations of the social world and internal sources such as thought, planning, and imagination as triggers of cognitive processing (see Figure 1.2). External triggers stimulate spontaneous social decentering, such as considering a friend's feelings when, during a conversation, the friend expresses distress over a recent romantic breakup. Analysis of interviews regarding participants' recall of a perspective-taking occurrence found that a lack of understanding motivated them to perspective take (Gerace et al., 2013). Not all external social stimuli trigger social decentering; they must pass a threshold which then causes people to attend to and attempt to interpret other people's behaviors. In this way, social decentering contributes to attribution. External stimuli direct our attention to some human phenomenon in a way that compels us to try to explain or understand it. One such phenomenon occurs when relational or behavioral expectations are violated. Burgoon's (1978) theory of expectancy violation posits that behaviors happen within a given range of acceptability for which there are thresholds, which when crossed, arouse our attention. This arousal triggers interpretation, explanation, and evaluation of those violations (Burgoon, 1978). Dunning (2001) identifies expectancy violations and "surprising information" as conditions which create curiosity and efforts to explain. Such a disconfirmation of expectations or predictions "demands deeper and more careful analysis of relevant information, aimed at explaining and understanding the predictive failure" (Roese & Sherman, 2007, p. 102). Social decentering is one tool employed in this analysis.

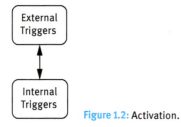

Figure 1.2: Activation.

Besides violations of expectations, social decentering can be triggered by other external stimuli. For example, looking at a young mother interacting with her children in a playground might lead us to begin considering the mother's feelings and thoughts or those of the children. Although no expectancy violation has taken place, we engage in taking on the perspective of the other people to make sense of what we observe. This example illustrates that we can engage in social decentering without having any intention of using the information to facilitate interactions with the people whose dispositions we are considering.

Indeed, we apply social decentering in response to characters we observe in movies, watch on TV, or read about in books. While such mediated characters act as external stimuli, social decentering with characters is a way of expanding our cognitive and affective experiences. We socially decenter for the fun of it. Identifying with, being transported into, or even "becoming" a character in a novel, TV show, movie, or video game enhances our experience. Without a significant investment of resources, we can enact social decentering to "become" the character with whom we identify and experience that character's emotions. Some responses to characters are not the product of social decentering, but instead are neurological responses caused by neuron mirrors or motor mimicry, such as a person involuntarily jerking or moaning in response to a movie character being hit.

Besides enabling us to experience a character's emotional responses, social decentering positions us to understand and predict that character's behavior. Interestingly, such an application turns the decenterer into a critic when the subsequent actions of the character don't match the predicted behavior. The decenterer either dismisses the character as unrealistic and unbelievable, or dismisses the behavior as out of character. Fisher (1984) identified a narrative paradigm in conceptualizing humans as storytellers who also judge the quality of other people's stories. According to Fisher, one quality a listener/reader/viewer judges in a story is its "characterological coherence," that is, the degree to which the characters act in the way that the person believes that they should act given that person's knowledge about the character and situation. The understanding of characters a person develops through social decentering can lead that person to reject a story in which the characters lack coherence by behaving in ways that do not fit the listener/reader/viewer's expectations.

People's own thoughts act as internal triggers of social decentering as they develop and act on personal goals that require planning for future interactions or reviewing past interactions. These thoughts then evoke social decentering as a tool for analyzing, planning, and strategizing. For example, a person's thoughts about ending a romantic relationship might activate the social decentering process as a tool for developing and evaluating possible exit strategies. Thus, people's social goals motivate them to engage in planning, and they use social decentering as a part of the process. Dunning (2001) sees social cognition processes giving people the ability to predict and control social situations, "such predictability and control allows people to adapt their behavior toward ways that provide the most pleasure and avoid the most pain" (p. 351). I explain the specific role of social decentering in planning later in my discussion of strategies and actions (Stage 5).

Besides being a tool used for planning future interactions, social decentering can also be applied in a review of past interactions. People are motivated to use social decentering when reflecting on prior experiences in order to make sense of them. They employ social decentering as they review a specific past social situation by drawing on their knowledge of the people involved, the context, and information about similar situations, interactions, and occurrences. For example, at the end of the day a person might reflect on a coworker who stormed out of a meeting earlier in the day during an argument, using social decentering to interpret the reason for the coworker's behavior.

An external or internal stimulus does not always trigger social decentering. The failure to activate the mental process is one factor cited by Epley and Caruso (2009) that limits the accuracy of perspective-taking. Individuals must be motivated to act on the stimulus. For instance, an individual who hears about a former friend in distress might not be motivated to consider the ex-friend's feelings (i.e., to socially decenter). The level of motivation is one factor that differentiates people's predilection to socially decenter. Some people might intrinsically be other-oriented because of their personality, culture (being from a collectivistic or feminine culture), or experience (for example, trained counselors), and thus more motivated to socially decenter.

At the relational level, Harvey and Omarzu (1999) linked minding of close relationships to relationship success and satisfaction. They identified "wanting to know about one's partner" as a key component of such minding that depends on a person's "great motivation to know about the other's background, hopes, fears, uncertainties, and what keeps him or her awake at night" (p. 12). Motivation is needed because, as Myers and Hodges (2009) explained, "taking the perspective of another person is a mentally taxing task that requires more than just keen observational skills; it requires considerable motivation and intelligence to construct an understanding of the other person" (p. 285). Zaki and Cikara (2015) observed that "people's emotions and beliefs prior to entering empathy-inducing situations can predispose them to experience or avoid empathy within those situations" (p. 472). Our feelings and thoughts entering an interaction provide motive to turn social decentering on or off.

Carpenter, Green, and Vacharkulksemsuk (2016) recognized the distinction between having an ability to consider other people's perspectives and the motivation to do so. They argued that some people view perspective-taking as "annoying, unimportant, or dull" (p. 372). They developed a measure of mind-reading motivation and found that motivational differences explained variations in people's perspective-taking that were not accounted for by such measures as Davis' measure of empathic concern or perspective-taking. Many of the items that constitute the measure of social decentering presented in Chapter 2 include wording that captures the motivation of the respondents to engage in other-orientation similar to Carpenter et al.'s measure.

Mustering the resources and motivation to engage in social decentering can emanate from a person's desire to develop or maintain an intimate relationship. In a previous study (Redmond, 2006, discussed further in Chapter 4), I found that while individuals might lack a general tendency to socially decenter, both men and women tended to develop social decentering in intimate relationships in response to a specific partner. The more intimate and important relationships are to people, the greater their motivation appears to be to use skills and strategies such as social decentering to sustain the relationship. Long (1994) found that couples in low-adjustment marriages reported taking the perspective of their spouses significantly less than those in high adjustment marriages. Long speculated that the lower perspective-taking in low-adjustment marriages might be due to such couples having less motivation to understand their partners. Long's speculation suggests that liking one's partner would impact motivation. Results of another study provide some support for this speculation. Respondents who examined scenarios of interpersonal conflicts, respondents' motivation to take a character's perspective related to their liking of that character (Frantz & Janoff-Bulman, 2000).

Confidence and effort are two factors that affect the motivation to engage in systematic social cognitive processing. Motivation to engage in systematic social cognitive processing (e.g., social decentering) is tied to the level of confidence that individuals have in the results of their heuristic processing (Moskowitz, 2005). As a social cognitive process, the extent to which individuals employ social decentering is dependent on their confidence in their heuristic conclusions. Individuals set the acceptable level of confidence, and if they decide that they want greater confidence, they then are likely to engage in more systematic processing (Moskowitz, 2005). Moskowitz explained that people set thresholds of confidence for their use of heuristic or systematic processing, and the more important a goal is to them, the greater the level of confidence they set. Thus, in social decentering, the more important it is to people to have confidence in their own assessment of other people's dispositions, the more effort they will put into decentering. For example, the more important a personal relationship is to an individual, the greater the likelihood is that the individual will put time and effort into applying social decentering.

Originally, Ickes and his colleagues (Graham & Ickes, 1997; Ickes, Gesn, & Graham, 2000) found no significant difference in empathic accuracy between men and women. However, after changing the measure so that respondents indicated how accurate they felt each prediction was, Ickes et al. found that female respondents had higher empathic accuracy than did the male respondents. The researchers attributed the newly found difference to women being motivated to match the gender stereotype that women have greater empathy than men. Implicit in this hypothesis is that men are not motivated when they are questioned about the confidence of their responses – apparently because they do not consider having empathic accuracy as a part of the male role. In essence, when the measure was changed to make salient the respondents' confidence in their empathic assessment, women put more effort than men did into producing accurate responses.

Social decentering thus takes effort and time – general costs to the decenterer. Application of social exchange principles suggests that individuals weigh the cost associated with social decentering against the reward or benefit it produces. An individual is likely to engage in only limited other-oriented analysis when walking by a stranger who is in tears because there is limited reward for doing so. But an individual is likely to engage in a more concerted effort to understand and adapt to a tearful friend. That effort is made because doing so can enhance the relationship, validate the individual's role as a friend, and provide the support and comfort that is expected from a friend. Such efforts can also stem from outcome dependency; Dunning (2001) observes that a person exerts more effort to think about others when his or her outcomes depend upon those others. However, taking time to socially decenter creates a cost because it takes time away from other activities. Talbert (2017) argued that there is not a lot of conscious deliberation or inferential processing when people interact because they interfere with the conversational flow. Time can also restrict the depth of analysis. During an ongoing conversation, time limits the participants' abilities to take inventory of available information, collect additional information, make imaginative considerations, and process and analyze information. Reeder's (2009) extension of attribution into mindreading leads to his multiple inference model. His model includes somewhat an immediate and automatic processing of another person and the situation in creating a rudimentary understanding of the other's behavior and

evokes spontaneous inferences. The model also recognizes an analytic and deliberative process that takes time and effort while creating a coherent explanation of what
occurred. In a similar way, social decentering provides limited analysis during interactions, but can be used before or after to develop more in-depth understanding.

While such limitations suggest that the participants should apply heuristics or even
mindless scripts, interpersonal interactions, by nature, require that the participants
constantly adapt their responses to each other and thus engage in at least a limited
form of social decentering (Redmond, 2005). The role that effort plays in collecting and
analyzing information is reflected in the full model of social decentering presented
later. In general, social exchange theory predicts that the more important or potentially
rewarding the outcome of social decentering is to an individual, the more time and
effort the individual is likely to expend decentering. But sometimes the effort can be
undermined by distractions or competing tasks. Lin, Keysar, and Epley (2010) argued
that using theory of mind as the basis of knowledge of another's beliefs and mental
states requires effort. And when that effort is undermined by competing demands,
respondents are more likely to be engage in a less effortful process, simply using themselves as the basis of interpreting others' actions – that is, they interpret egocentrically.

Motivations are general inclinations that lead to the development of goals or specific objectives. Social motivation produces a variety of goals in social interactions
such as accomplishing tasks (task goals), developing and maintaining relationships
(social relationship goals), managing self-image (face goals), and constructing a
shared social world (social reality goals) (Krauss & Fussell, 1996). Social decentering
is a tool that can be used by individuals to accomplish these social goals. Redmond
(1989) identified functions associated with social decentering and empathy. Much
like goals, these functions represent what individuals can accomplish through the
use of social decentering. Peoples' ability to understand, predict, and adapt to others
through empathy contributes to their communication competence, increases their
ability to persuade or gain compliance from others, enhances their decision-making,
helps them develop interpersonal relationships, and serves as a foundation for providing confirming and comforting responses (Redmond, 1989). Individuals might use
social decentering as one strategy toward achieving these goals, with some of the
goals benefiting more from social decentering than others. As such, social decentering provides one path an individual might take in response to triggers (see Figure 1.3).

Figure 1.3: The activation process.

While external and internal triggers act to prompt the use of social decentering, other factors exist that suppress its use. Some everyday interactions may actually involve little adaptation because of their scripted, mindlessness, and egocentric nature (Berger & Bradac, 1982; Dickson, 1982; Gudykunst & Hall, 1994; Keysar, 2007; Keysar, Barr, & Horton, 1998; Langer, 1978; Redmond, 1989). Therefore, when enacting a script for routine or mindless interactions, people have little need or motivation to socially decenter; rather they simply follow the routine or script that they have developed for the given situation. Scripted or mindless interactions increase the likelihood for egocentric communication where a participant creates messages that make sense to himself or herself without considering or adapting to the recipient. Since most interactions take place between partners with similar cultural and personal backgrounds, such egocentric messages are generally understood by the receivers (Redmond, 1989). But disruptions in scripted or egocentric exchanges might require individuals to adapt. For example, listeners might display confused or blank expressions or provide incongruous responses when they don't understand an egocentric message. Such responses can trigger social decentering and adaptation. Thus, an adapted conversational exchange might go like this: "Who is this Uncle Joe you are mentioning?" "Oh that's right; you've never met Uncle Joe. He really wasn't an uncle, just a close friend of my father's. You would have liked him. He had your same sense of dry humor." The question from the listener about the unknown referent, Uncle Joe, triggers social decentering process which results in the speaker recognizing the absence of information the partner has while also incorporating knowledge of the partner in the reply.

Another factor that suppresses the use of social decentering is fundamental attribution bias which has the same impact as egocentrism. Fundamental attribution bias is the antithesis of social decentering because individuals fail to examine situations from other people's viewpoints; they fail to take the perspective of others (Moskowitz, 2005). As Moskowitz (2005) observed, "[...] that although perspective-taking is an important ingredient in forming accurate attributions, taking the perspective of others is not something perceivers do quite naturally or spontaneously" (p. 280).

Other cognitive and emotional processes can also interfere with social decentering. Negative emotions might hamper individuals' abilities to engage in other-orientation (Gehlbach, 2004). For example, studies suggest that couples' interpersonal conflicts appear to create distorted perceptions and undermine their perspective-taking (Sillars & Scott, 1983; Sillars, Roberts, Leonard, & Dun, 2000). At times, we are actually motivated not to engage in other-orientation. Simpson, Ickes, and Blackstone (1995) found that close but insecure dating couples exhibited less empathic accuracy (ability to identify their partner's thoughts) when the thoughts that they were judging were related to perceived external threats (the attractiveness and sexual appeal of slide images). Simpson et al. argued that the conditions of threat, insecurity, and closeness motivate inaccuracy; that is, when these three conditions are present, individuals are likely to distort their perception of their partner in order to preserve their relationships. Following this argument, people using social decentering might be motivated to reach inaccurate but comforting conclusions. Individuals might also choose to avoid social decentering all together, if they feel that engaging in social decentering will lead to predictions of negative or hurtful outcomes. Uncertainty becomes preferable to the certainty of a negative outcome. For example, if you are afraid what a partner might want out of the relationship, you might restrain from considering your partner's thoughts and feelings as a way of maintaining the status quo.

In an examination of empathy as emotional engagement, Zaki (2014) identified factors that motivated people to avoid or seek engagement. Interestingly, several of his factors depend upon a cognitive appraisal of the person and situation which is essentially engaging in the cognitive process of social decentering. In explaining the results of their study, Park and Raile (2010) posited that the cognitive process of perspective-taking might initiate empathy. Thus, the result of cognitive appraisal predicts emotional reactions for the decenterer. Zaki argued that people might avoid empathy and shift their attention because of predicted affective costs – feeling bad. People might also avoid empathy to avoid material costs; that is, if they let themselves get emotionally connected, they will feel compelled to provide material help, such as giving to a charity. Avoidance gets used to avoid empathizing; for example, changing the channel from video showing distressed people in need of charitable help. Finally, Zaki argues that in competitive situations where empathy might interfere with winning, people avoid empathizing with the other. Such behavior can be seen in negotiations and conflicts where people are not motivated to emotionally connect. Zaki sees motivation to empathize occurring when it involves sharing a positive affect, serves as a source for creating affiliation and strengthening a relationship, and confirms an individual's identity as empathic.

In summary, other-orientation and specifically social decentering is activated by external and internal triggers. Once this process is activated, people begin a survey of the information they have stored, are observing, or can envision. They begin the next stage – the input stage of social decentering.

1.2.2 Input (Information Sources)

Suppose your friend has been moody lately and turns down your invitation for lunch. How do you go about understanding, explaining, and adapting to your friend's behavior? The first thing you'll probably do is take an inventory of what you know about your friend and see if any of that information explains the behavior. Perhaps you remember that it's the one-year anniversary of your friend's divorce, or that your friend acts this way at the beginning of each new school semester. If you cannot determine an explanation based on recall of specific historical information of your friend, you might begin generating hypotheses based on general knowledge of the friend. You use your imagination along with your own implicit personality theories and other

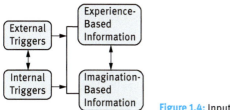

Figure 1.4: Input.

attribution processes to explore "what-if" scenarios in order to find a hypothesis that best fits the information that you do have about your friend.

The preceding example illustrates that once social decentering is triggered, it requires input or information on which to build analyses and strategies (see Figure 1.4). Information is the fundamental building block on which individuals build social decentering. An extensive body of research and theory has been generated (for example, social judgment theory, attribution theory, social or person perception, impression formation, and stereotyping and bias) on how individuals process social information. Considerable research has been devoted to the mechanisms and processes involved in accessing information about other people (for example, see reviews in Devine, Hamilton, & Ostrom, 1994). Of particular concern is that the objectivity of these processes is influenced by biases, priming, goals and motives, availability heuristics, and dissonance. Unfortunately, much of the research in this area fails to adequately take into account the transactional and interpersonal nature of social decentering and instead primarily focuses on the recall or processing of controlled information. Wyer and Gruenfeld (1995) noted that social cognition research has "been performed under conditions in which the information is presented out of its social context" (p.8). Rather than reviewing in detail this body of literature, I focus on the principles and findings most relevant to social decentering.

Wyer and Gruenfeld (1995) likened information processing to the creation of numerous storage bins in the mind into which information is placed. They identified two qualities that affect information retrieval from these bins: relevance (salience or representativeness) and recency. Previously stored judgments and information are relevant when they share the same objectives as the current situation. And, the most recently acquired relevant information tends to be retrieved. However, older information might be retrieved in the absence of relevant recently acquired information, but is hampered by a third information processing quality – accessibility (Förster & Liberman, 2007). Individuals might have information that is relevant to their analysis, but because they did not acquire the information recently, they are unable to access the information. Bias also limits access when individuals' preexisting goals, norms, values, and expectations restrict their ability to perceive or access information. In addition, priming through pre-exposure to stimuli can activate some "associated memory structures" (Förster & Liberman, 2007, p. 201) that influence subsequent perceptions and interpretations, and thus limit access to other relevant information.

The speed with which people process information while socially decentering requires cognitive efficiency. Some scholars have suggested that people act as "cognitive misers" when processing social information, and rather than gathering all the available relevant information, they "rely on preexisting expectations and theories to select a sample of potentially relevant information" (Howard & Renfrow, 2003, p. 266). Thus, people turn to stereotypes, heuristics, schemas, and other associative representations. According to this perspective of social cognition, particularly social information processing, the efficient mind, working to minimize effort, is prone to shortcuts and heuristics that can create inaccurate interpretations and conclusions. The realization that an interpretation is in error (fails to support goal attainment), is likely to trigger another round of analysis devoted to a more accurate assessment. In other words, errors can occur when schemata fail, which leads to more active cognitive analyses (Howard & Renfro, 2003). Unfortunately, the methodology used in researching such shortcomings relies primarily on the participants' reading and writing accounts and interpretations, and thus fails to account for the dynamics and feedback that occurs during transactional, face-to-face interpersonal interactions. In such interactions, individuals are cognitively busy and don't have the time or resources for a second round of making dispositional inferences, though they might do so later when they have time (Fiske, 1993).

Fiske (1993) suggested an alternative metaphor to the energy conserving conceptualization of a cognitive miser; that people are motivated tacticians, choosing among possible strategies depending on their goals. She and other social cognitive scholars emphasize the role that goals play in activating deliberative social information processing. The goals perspective helps explain why individuals break away from their dependence on heuristics and instead, engage in systematic social information processing. Besides goals, the social situation or context might also prompt the motivated tactician (Schwarz, 1998). Schwarz explained that while there are times when people rely on cognitive shortcuts, "they pay close attention to complex information and engage in systematic and effortful processing strategies when required" (p. 258). Martin and Achee (1992), reaching a similar conclusion after reviewing research on concept priming, offered a two-stage model of information use. In the first stage, individuals retrieve the most accessible information (as heuristics and priming would suggest, but in the second stage, individuals test for situational constraints associated with the information and, if they detect constraints, they access new information that is more congruent with their goals.

Apparently, the more important the goal or outcome is to people, the greater the effort they will expend in systematically processing the information. For example, Thompson, Roman, Moskowitz, Chaiken, and Bargh (1994) found that participants exerted effortful processing of ambiguous information when they had motivation, access (memory), and opportunity (attentional resources). To socially decenter then, people must be motivated to engage in the process, have access to information, and have the ability to select, attend to, and process information. As with other social information processes, social decentering can be conducted with varying degrees of effort, thus producing variations in analysis, completeness, and accuracy. A casual observer of a mother in a park with her children will put little, if any, effort into social decentering because of low motivation. This lack of effort is likely to produce a more general and superficial interpretation of the mother's situation than the interpretation made by a close friend who knows that because of a divorce settlement, the mother has limited visitation time with her children.

Motivation to effectively and accurately engage in social decentering is necessary to overcome information-processing pitfalls. Priming is one such pitfall because it can create biased information processing by preventing access to information that might lead to alternative interpretations or decisions. Despite significant evidence of the occurrence of priming, people form more accurate impressions and minimize some of the effects of priming, negative expectations (Neuberg, 1989), or bias when they are simply instructed to form an accurate impression. In activating social decentering, an individual is likely to be inclined to inherently recognize the need to make an accurate assessment and thus reduce priming effects. But what distinguishes effective social decenterers from ineffective ones is their ability to objectively retrieve and analyze information. Ford and Kruglanski (1995) found that when perceivers were motivated to generate alternative explanations for some other person's behavior, they avoided the primed and most easily recalled explanation. Paramount to such information processing, then, is the motivation to generate alternative (Ford & Kruglanski, 1995) and accurate explanations. Research links the motivation to form accurate judgments to: abandoning unwarranted expectations, more complex and correct attributions, recalling information that is inconsistent with expectations, and searching for diagnostic information (Thompson et al., 1994).

The previous discussion provides a framework for understanding the manner in which information is generated for use in social decentering. Social decentering depends on two sources of information as fodder for analysis: experience-based information and imagination-based information. These two sources of information parallel those identified by Myers and Hodges (2009) in observing that people depend on mental representations and imagination to infer what is in another person's mind.

1.2.2.1 Experience-Based Information

Experience-based information comes from immediate observations or memory. Sometimes the immediate context both triggers social decentering and provides information on which to base this social decentering. Again, seeing a woman in a park with her children might cause us to think about how that woman sees the world, and in developing those thoughts, we might incorporate information directly from the immediate situation. Her age, attire, race, body size, personal accessories, makeup, and behavior toward her children all provide information that could prove germane to understanding her view of the world. Our ability to collect observational information is enhanced by our skills in, for example, listening and person perception, as well as our interpersonal and nonverbal sensitivity. Underlying such observational information is the ability to avoid perceptual barriers and biases. Thus, people's ability to effectively socially decenter varies with their ability to effectively collect experience-based information.

People's ability to socially decenter also varies with people's ability to store and recall information. As discussed earlier, social information processing involves sorting, storing, and retrieving social information, and consequently social decentering depends on effective and efficient social information management. Social information processing leads to the creation of schemas for the people with whom we interact. The complexity of the schemas is dictated by the importance of the relationship, frequency and depth of interactions, and level of information gained. Schemas represent our knowledge base for the people around us. We tap into the information stored in these schemas when we engage in social decentering. We also tap into our impressions, feelings, previous analyses, and understanding of our partners.

While part of social information processing occurs automatically, other aspects are deliberative, and thus are affected by the skills individuals apply to process information. Wyer (2006), in reviewing three models of information processing and reflecting on the model that he developed with T. K. Srull, made the following observation:

> [...] we considered it self-evident that several different cognitive processes come into play in the course of making a judgment, some of which were automatic and some of which were deliberative, and that the nature of these processes depended on the type of goal in question, the type of information available, and constraints of the situation in which the processing occurred. (Wyer, 2006, p. 193)

The automatic parts of information processing are particularly prone to bias and error because of such factors as priming. The deliberative process can also be biased by the types of goals established, impact of the situation, inability to remain objective, and the failure to adequately analyze and process the various interpretations. Other factors that diminish effective information processing include the failure to store relevant information, mis-organization or mismanagement of the information, and inability to recall information.

What happens when individuals have little or no information to recall, or are unable to access stored information? Are they unable to tap into social decentering? In such cases, they have two immediate options: either to seek additional information through active perception and engagement as well as other information-gathering methods; or to create new information by using their imagination. Talbert (2017) argued that knowledge of others cannot be created only through intentional and rational cognition. She wrote, "Getting to know another person requires interaction, which by definition is a joint enterprise and requires something different than a one-sided, conscious deliberative attitude" (p. 552). Experience-based information does indeed depend on shared experiences with others whereby we gather information that can then be later accessed in social decentering. The more we interact, the greater the potential for more information, for maintaining information, and for correcting errors in inferences and beliefs. One claim made by Talbert that is particularly relevant to social decentering is knowing how to interact. We need communication skills to manage interactions, and thus gain information. Social decentering is dependent on a variety of interpersonal skills such as listening, probing, nonverbal sensitivity and expressiveness, and confirming responses. Such skills help to establish and maintain relationships and facilitate self-disclosure. Those disclosures are needed to provide an information base for social decentering.

1.2.2.2 Imagination-Based Information

In considering another person's worldview, people can use the information they have to extrapolate new information through the use of imagination, fantasy, and creativity. That is, the human mind is capable of seeing things that are not apparent to the brain; there is an ability to go beyond their actual observations and use their imaginations to create information. In a qualitative analysis of conversational partners, one method to achieve understanding of the other's experience was to fantasize about the other's experience and visualize the situation (Meneses & Larkin, 2017). In discussing creativity and imagination, Berys Gaut (2003) noted that imagination allows us to

> try out different views and approaches by imagining them, without being committed either to the truth of the claims or to acting on one's imagings. Imagination allows one to be playful, to play with different hypotheses, and to play with different ways of making objects. (pp. 160–161)

In discussing the purpose or aim of imagination, Gaut (2003) coincidentally described the process of empathizing and social decentering as

> [...] imagination can aim at learning something: here truth governs the imaginative project, but it is an extrinsic, adopted, aim of imagining, not its intrinsic aim. I may imagine myself in someone else's position *in order* to discover what she is feeling: but I do not believe that I am in her position. (p. 161)

Just as our planning depends on our ability to imagine the future or alternative contexts, our social decentering draws on our ability to imagine the unknown and create potential knowns from which to select information. Such a process occurs in counterfactual thinking, in which individuals assess the possible through "if-then" cognitions (Kahneman & Miller, 1986; Miller, Turnball, & McFarland, 1990). Counterfactual thinking provides a good example of how observation-based information stored in memory serves as a foundation for imagination-based information. Counterfactual thinking primarily considers past events and imagines different outcomes if some element were changed; for example, "If I had stayed in college, I'd probably own my own store by now," or "If I had married John instead of Henry, then I would have had a life of luxury." Such thinking can occur in the social decentering process as an individual imagines various if-then scenarios while considering another particular person's behavior in each scenario; for example, "If I had married Henry's best friend, John, then Henry would have felt betrayed and angry and probably done something rash." Byrne (2005) uses the terms *counterfactual imagination* and *rational imagination* to emphasize rational imagining as more than just creative musings about the world, but imagining with direction and structure bounded by facts and logic. Thus, one principle of counterfactual thinking is that people consider "true possibilities" (Byrne, 2005). Using imagination-based information in social decentering helps us to determine the best or truest alternative representation of another person's cognitive and affective disposition (thoughts, feelings, perspectives, etc.).

Imagination or fantasy is also a key element to some conceptualizations of empathy (Dymond, 1945; Stotland, Mathews, Sherman, Hansson, & Richardson, 1978) and perspective-taking (Batson, 2009). In developing their Fantasy-Empathy scale, Stotland et al. (1978) found that "the tendency to fantasize vividly the experience of others was shown here to be a fundamental part of the empathy process [...]" (p. 44). Research on perspective-taking and empathy often operationalizes these concepts in terms of imagination by asking participants to imagine another person's situation and respond to various measures.

The use of imagination in considering other's perspective is evident in the work of James Honeycutt and others on imagined interactions. Honeycutt, Zagaki, and Edwards (1990) defined *imagined interactions* as "a process of social cognition, whereby actors imagine and therefore indirectly experience themselves in interaction with others" (p. 1). Such imagined interactions "afford actors the opportunity to envision the act of discoursing with others, anticipating their responses, and even adjusting to their roles" (p. 1). In anticipating responses, individuals engage in social decentering, using what they know to imagine possible responses and then how to adapt accordingly.

Imagination and creativity are also elements of other communication theories such as interactive conversational planning (Waldron, 1997). Waldron identified three types of planning during conversation: knowledge-based planning (experience-based information) which involves applying recalled prefabricated plans; accommodative planning which involves prefabricated plans that are situation specific and adapted to the context; and creative, proactive planning which involves creating novel and hypothetical action sequences (imagination-based information).

Our imaginations provide us with a means to fill in missing information, envision the unknown, and plan for the future. Sakellaropoulo and Baldwin (2006) contended that since we can never truly reach a shared reality with another person, we depend on imagined information, but uncertainty about the accuracy of such information leads to unavoidable dialogical misunderstandings. The accuracy of imagination-based information depends on a variety of factors: the quality of the foundational information; contextual sensitivity; the ability to imagine, fantasize, or be creative; the completeness of the imagining; and bias. For example, how will a close friend react to the news that you've gotten a new job and will have to move away? What do you already know about your friend that allows you to imagine the response? If you don't know that this friend depends on you as a sole source of validation and friendship, then you are unlikely to correctly imagine the response. A cursory analysis might lead you to expect your friend to be excited for you, failing to consider your friend's loss of validation. And like experience-based information, imagination-based information can be biased by such factors as priming. Indeed, research on priming often involves asking participants to imagine a situation or response after having been primed, resulting in narrower or biased outcomes.

Interaction between Experience-based and Imagination-Based Information

In reviewing the connection between planning and imagined interactions, Berger (2002) wrote that

> [i]maging an interaction either before or after it has occurred requires that relevant knowledge be activated and assessed from long-term memory. That is, the imagining process itself requires that relevant knowledge about people and interaction processes be consulted for imagination to occur. (p. 197)

Imagination-based information is grounded in experience-based information – our experiences, observations, and stored memories. Thus, the two sources of information have a somewhat symbiotic relationship. The more experience-based information people have, the more potential they have for generating accurate imagination-based information, but having experience-based information also means people have less need for generating such imagination-based information. Conversely, the less experience-based information an individual has, the greater the need people have for imagination-based information, but the less effective they are likely to be in generating accurate and useful imagination-based information. And, imagination-based information is likely to be inaccurate to the degree that it is derived from inaccurate experience-based information. But the development and evaluation of imagination-based information can lead to a reconsideration of the accuracy of held beliefs – of experience-based information. Discrepancies between imagination-based information and experience-based information can stimulate either the collection of more experience-based information or more complex imagining. For instance, hearing that a friend behaved at a party in a manner we can't imagine might lead us to seek more details or to imagine under what circumstances the friend might act that way.

We process experience-based and imagination-based information about both individuals and contexts or situations. Besides using our imagination to fill in for missing information about a specific individual or a situation, we can also place the individual into an imagined situation or imagine that individual in a situation we have experienced. That is, we can draw from our own experiences (observed or recalled) in a given context to imagine how a given individual (including ourselves) might react or behave within that context. This process is epitomized by the wristband that displays the acronym, WWJD (What would Jesus do?), which reminds wearers to imagine how this religious figure would respond to a given situation. People often ask themselves how some other person they know and often admire, like a parent, friend, or boss, would handle a given issue.

We can also use our experience-based knowledge of other people to deliberate on how those people would behave or respond to imaginary contexts (i.e., imagined interactions) or to imagined variations in a context (i.e., counterfactual thinking). For example, after watching a friend's reaction of disappointment after getting a C on a test, we might imagine how that friend would have reacted to getting an F. Or we might imagine how another person will react to several behavioral options we are contemplating. Again, our experience-based knowledge of these people serves as the foundation for determining the validity of their potential responses to such imagined variations.

Imagining both the person and situation is a fundamental activity for novelists as they develop a character study and then imagine how that character would behave in a given situation. Evaluation of how well this is done is the basis of Fisher's (1984) argument for characterological coherence. As I discussed earlier, part of the validity of a narrative is based on the degree to which people act in a manner that is consistent with what is known about them. Stories in which the players "act out of character" are seen as less credible than those with characterological coherence. Social decentering can be used to evaluate characterological coherence. Through social decentering, a person can imagine various alternative reactions and behaviors and decide which are most in character with the person under consideration. Good novelists and storytellers are likely to be strong social decenterers.

The effectiveness of using both experience-based and imagination-based information depends upon having the motivation and skills to use both. While science seeks grace in empirical objectivity where variables are available to the senses, little progress would be made in science without the application of imagination. Seeing beyond that which is experienced leads to new knowledge and a keener ability to socially decenter. Such knowledge serves only as the raw material on which social decentering builds; how that information is interpreted, organized, and analyzed represents the most significant stage of social decentering.

1.2.3 Analysis (Information Processing)

Unlike other theories and approaches to other-orientation, social decentering theory is built on the premise that there are three different methods of analyzing the input information: use of self, use of specific-other, and use of generalized-other (see

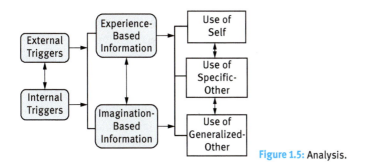

Figure 1.5: Analysis.

Figure 1.5). *Use of self* means that the decenterers attribute their own perspective and responses to a given situation to their target of social decentering. That is, decenterers can attribute their own affective and cognitive dispositions to another person or use their own dispositions to identify potential differences with others. Use of self can be highly effective to the degree that the decenterer and the other person are similar and to the degree their situations are similar. *Use of specific-other* means that the decenterers use information that they observed, recalled, or imagined about a particular person as the foundation for their analysis of that person or to people who are perceived to be similar to that person. Knowledge that is specific to the person being considered varies in depth, thus causing variation in the quality of analysis. *Use of generalized-other* means that the decenterers use their personal theories of how people think, act, and feel (implicit personality theories, stereotypes, and general schemas) as the foundation for understanding another person's cognitive and affective disposition. The degree to which these personal theories apply to the person under consideration determines the effectiveness of this method of social decentering. Figure 1.6

Method	Definition	Examples
Use of Self	Decenterers attribute their own perspectives and responses in a given situation to their target of social decentering.	"I'll bet you're feeling excited and a little nervous; I know I did when I graduated." "If I my child was missing, I'd devastated. I'm bet they are too."
Use of Specific-Other	Decenterers use information they observed, recalled, or imagined about a particular person as the foundation for analyzing that person.	"Joe was upset when I was 10 minutes late; he's going to be real peeved that I'm 30 minutes late." "Mary reminds me of my laid-back sister, so she probably won't be upset when I'm late."
Use of Generalized-Other	Decenterers uses their own personal theories of how people think, act, and feel as the foundation for understanding another person.	"College freshman have lousy study skills, so I'd better pass out a study guide for this class." "I don't want to wait on this table of teenagers; teenagers never leave a very good tip."

Figure 1.6: Three analysis methods for analyzing information.

provides examples for each of these three methods. Gerace et al.'s (2013) analysis of participants' discussions of perspective-taking conversations identified three themes regarding how participants tried to understand the other's perspective: use of self-information, use of other-information, and use of general information.

Each of these three methods draws on both experience and imagination-based information. We can recall information we have stored about ourselves, specific others, or people in general and use it to analyze a particular situation. We can also use our observations of our own reactions, the reactions of specific others, and those of people in general. And, we can imagine ourselves in situations that we have not experienced firsthand, applying those results to our analysis of a particular person's response to that situation. Similarly, we can imagine specific others or generalized others in situations for which we have no direct experience based information. Thus, we can utilize both experience-based and imagination-based information to arrive at the strongest pool of information on which to base social decentering.

The three methods are not novel, and the foundation for each is peppered throughout previous theory and research in social cognition. I review some of that research in the following sections, providing evidence of each method's existence and insights into factors that influence each method.

1.2.3.1 Use of Self

In applying use of self analysis, people draw on their recall or imaginings of their own experiences, perspectives, thoughts, feelings, and other self-dispositions associated with a previous, current, or anticipated situation and use that information to analyze another person's dispositions. Van Boven and Loewenstein (2005) contended that people naturally use the self as starting point in making predictions about others because we usually have well-developed mental models of ourselves which are easily accessible. But when people impose their own dispositions onto another person, they engage in projection (that is, I assume the feelings I'm having are the feelings you're having) which can create biased and inaccurate predictions about others. Van Boven and Loewenstein concluded that cross-situational projection can be an accurate and efficient way to make social judgments particularly when little is known about the others, but it can be limited by biases and inaccuracies.

The use of self method can also be used to create contrasting references for someone perceived as significantly different. As Beer and Ochsner (2006) observed, "[...] the self can be used as a reference to organize representations of other people (i.e., we are similar because we both like reading but we differ on extraversion)" (p. 99). Biernat (2005) in discussing standards for judging others writes, "[...] self is a highly familiar, accessible, salient, and *emotionally charged* standard that leads us to judge individuals and groups as both like us and not" (p. 72). The degree to which the use of self generates accurate information depends on the similarity and relevance of the qualities used to consider the other person's cognitive and affective disposition.

Two college roommates who are similar in their desire to succeed in college and in their academic skills and successes might be well positioned to employ the use of self in understanding each other's reaction to failing an important midterm exam. If one roommate is 18 and the other is a 30-year-old non-traditional returning student, the 18-year-old might imagine what it would be like if she were a 30-year-old nontraditional student finding out about failing an exam. In this use of the imagined self, the degree of similarity between the roommates along with the younger roommate's imagination skills would determine the quality of her resulting analysis. Finally, recognizing the difference, the younger roommate might not know how the older roommate would react, but might assume that her roommate would react in the same way that she would.

Research in neuroscience has demonstrated that people do indeed use their own thoughts and feelings as "proxies for other minds" (Mitchell, 2009, p. 1039), particularly when the other person is perceived as similar. Research by Ames (2004) provides evidence that when individuals perceive the targets of their analysis to be similar to themselves, they turn to projection, and when they perceive the target to be dissimilar to themselves, they turn more to stereotyping. Gnepp (1989) contended that one way children understand another person's feelings in a given situation is that children imagine themselves in the same situation and then project their own feelings onto the other person. Gnepp saw this particularly effective when the situation is familiar and the other person similar. Tamir and Mitchell (2013) conducted a series of experiments involving participants' assessment of their likes, dislikes, and habits, read descriptions of two people, one similar to them and one different, and assessed the two people. They hypothesized that people would use themselves as an anchor and then adjust their assessment of others away from that anchor. Tamir and Mitchell concluded that "individuals indeed naturally and spontaneously recruit self-knowledge during social inferences about similar others and then correct away from such anchors" (p. 160), but that was not true when judging someone different. We can expect then that when we believe someone is similar to us, we incorporate use of self as a starting point and then adjust our view of them relative to additional information we gain. But when we see someone as particularly different, we don't evoke the use of self. An inclination not to use the self because another is seen as different could actually hamper the ability to socially decenter when the other person is actually more similar than realize. An assumption of difference is one factor that inhibits effective intercultural communication and understanding (Beebe, Beebe, & Redmond, 2017).

In studying empathic accuracy in married couples, Thomas, Fletcher and Lange (1997) found that "women who assumed more similarity produced significantly higher levels of empathic accuracy than women who assumed less similarity" (p. 848), where similarity was the degree to which a woman's reported thoughts and feelings were similar to what she assumed her husband was thinking or feeling. In discussing this finding, they surmise that the high level of reciprocity and interdependence of married couples makes use of self a valued heuristic. In a study on egocentrism in dating and married couples, Murray, Holmes, Bellavia, Griffin, and Dolderman (2002), found egocentric women understood their partners better than less egocentric women and were more satisfied. The researchers suggest that assimilating the partner into self can lead to correct predictions about the partner. Part of their findings might be due to higher levels of similarity between the partners, in which case, egocentric use of self serves as an effective base for understanding.

Use of self might be implemented because it is quick and requires minimal effort in analyzing the other person's thoughts, feelings, and perspective in a given situation. However, use of self can also operate as part of a complex social decentering process in which decenterers assess the similarities and differences between themselves and their targets, imagine and reflect on their own responses to various scenarios, and finally, assess the reliability of their conclusions.

The use of self, as a factor in social information processing and perception, is found in inference theory of empathy (Berlo, 1960), in vicarious responding (Aronfreed, 1968), in the conceptualization of projection (Deutsch & Madle, 1975), and in situational role-taking (Higgins, 1981). In explaining the inclusion of self as a component of social cognition, Beer and Ochsner (2006) argued that "[...] the self may serve as a cognitive filter through which other people are perceived. For example, introspections and personal experiences may be used to make inferences about the intentions and emotions of others, either consciously or unconsciously" (p. 99). They also observe that "considering one's own feelings in a similar situation is one source of information for making inferences about others. Additionally, people might project their own beliefs onto others" (p. 99).

In applying inference theory to empathy, Berlo (1960) explained that a man's (that is, a person's) self-concept works in conjunction with his observations of others:

> On the basis of his prior interpretations of himself, he makes inferences about the internal states of others. In other words, he argues to himself that if behavior on his part represented such and such a feeling, a similar behavior produced by somebody else would represent a similar feeling.

> This view of empathy assumes that man has first-hand knowledge of himself and second-hand knowledge of other people. It argues that man has the ability to understand himself, through analysis of his own behaviors. From this analysis, man can make inferences about other people based on the similarities between their behavior and his own. (p. 122)

While that is a fairly narrow perspective of how people take into consideration another person's state, it explains well how individuals use their own experiences as the foundation for interpreting other people's dispositions. However, since people's experiences vary greatly in similarity, this approach fails to adequately explain what happens when there is little similarity.

Empathy has been described as a vicarious response to another person's situation, particularly an emotional response (Aronfreed, 1968; Mehrabian & Epstein, 1972). Vicarious responses include the emotions that are evoked as a result of considering the conditions surrounding other people. Aronfreed (1968) also included the emotions evoked in response to observing the other person's affective reactions. In essence, people experience emotions not only in response to the thoughts they generate about a situation, but also in response to observations of other people's emotional reactions. To some degree, this conceptualization represents social contagion in that people's emotions are affected by the emotions of those around them. This is exemplified in Mehrabian and Epstein's (1972) original empathy tendency questionnaire, which included such items as, "The people around me have a great influence on my moods," and "I become nervous if other people around me seem to be nervous" (p. 528). Vicarious empathic emotional responses do not seem to be reactions to the consideration of the other person's predispositions, but rather are more visceral and autonomic reactions to stimuli. Thus, empathy that is vicarious is only affective and not cognitive. Nonetheless, vicarious empathic responses provide another foundation for social decentering when decenterers become cognizant of their own emotional reactions. For example, realizing you are feeling nervous because the person you are observing is acting nervous or is in a situation in which you would be nervous can help you appreciate and adapt to the other person's affective state.

Batson (2009) identified eight ways in which empathy has been defined, two of those involved this projective or imaginative use of self. He cited a number of different terms for describing empathy, including the original definition of empathy from 1909, role-taking, cognitive empathy, projective empathy, simulation, perspective-taking, decentering, and imagine-self perspective. While a myriad of terms have been used, they share a common denominator – a process whereby people imagine their thoughts and feelings as if they were in someone else's situation. This perspective is reflected further in the following discussion in which projection is viewed as a natural process that contributes to empathy:

> It seems the most natural thing in the world to attempt to put oneself – emotional or mentally – in the place of another person, to try to imagine what the other is feeling or thinking. Not only do we often intentionally attempt to imagine what may be in another person's mind, we also impute knowledge and feelings to people without being conscious of doing so. (Nickerson, Butler, & Carlin, 2009, p. 52)

In Nickerson et al.'s description, the process of use of self can involve attributing our own thoughts and feelings on another without our awareness of doing so. Nickerson et al. further observed that "the results of many experiments [...] support the general notion that people tend to use their own knowledge or their assumed knowledge – their model of their own knowledge – as a default indication of what other people are likely to know" (p. 52). Such observations regarding empathy suggest a prominent role of the use of self as a method of social decentering.

In developing a perception-action model of empathy which proposes that in perceiving another's state, perceivers activate their own representations of that state, Preston and de Waal (2002) contended that "there is no empathy that is *not* projection, since you always use your own representations to understand the state of another" (p. 15). While their model focuses primarily on empathy as an emotional process that occurs across species, often as a contagious response to distress, it confirms the use of projection as a method by which individuals engage in other-orientation.

In discussing the development of role-taking in children, Higgins (1981) distinguishes situational role-taking from individual role-taking in a manner similar to how social decentering distinguishes use of self from use of specific-other. Rather than considering how a role is affected by the person who occupies it (use of specific-other), situational role-taking involves asking what your own response would be if you were in the other person's situation or circumstance (use of self): "What would I do, think, feel, see, etc. if I were in that situation?" (p. 127). Together, these two types of role-taking were used as the basis for a proposal of how Max, a virtual human, might accomplish emotional understanding of humans and thus add to Max's believability in human-computer interactions (Boukricha, 2008).

Factors Affecting the Quality of Use of Self

The accuracy and quality of the use of self method of social decentering is affected by several factors. For example, the more a decenterer and target share similar experiences, the more effective the use of self should be. However, the actual impact of shared experience is mediated by the degree to which the decenterer has an adequate grasp of the situation. In a study of the impact of similar experiences, new mothers were videotaped discussing new motherhood. The experience of those who viewed the videos (new first-time mothers, those expecting, or those who have never been pregnant) corresponded to their levels of understanding and concern for new mothers (Hodges, Kiel, Kramer, Veach, & Villanueva, 2010). Afterwards, viewers wrote anonymous letters to the videotaped mothers. Letters from writers who were also new mothers were perceived by the videotaped new mothers as more understanding than messages from the never-pregnant writers. But experience had no effect on the viewers' ability to accurately guess the thoughts of the taped new mothers (empathic accuracy) during various points in the videotaped interview. Hodges et al. concluded that projection proved to be an effective strategy when new mother viewers projected their experiences onto the taped new mother primarily because of the general similarity of their experiences. So the use of self can be effective when there is some relevant homogeneity between two people and their situations.

The accuracy of use of self is also affected by the degree to which individuals recognize which information about themselves is typical and which is atypical. Karniol (1990) argued that we develop a self-as-distinct view of ourselves that includes (a) atypical information that emphasizes our uniqueness in comparison to other people, and (b) typical information that recognizes our commonalities with other people. In addition, Karniol recognized that we can even use the atypical information about ourselves to make predictions about another person when we believe that the other person is also being atypical within the given context. Our sense of atypicality is based on our developing a cogent sense of what is typical according to our cognitive development and experiences. As Karniol puts it, "To realize any specific experience is atypical, one must have a well-developed concept of what is typical" (p. 235). While even individuals who view themselves only as typical will be accurate when the target of their prediction is also typical, developing their atypical self-view will generally increase the accuracy of their predictions by reducing false consensus. Thus, delineating self-knowledge as typical or atypical, helps to identify additional sources of error. Specifically, error occurs when: (a) the social decenterer believes a given self-construct is typical when it is actually atypical, but applies it to the other person as if that person were typical, (b) the social decenterer misperceives an atypical other as typical and makes predictions based on the typical, and (c) the social decenterer sees the other as atypical when the other is actually typical. Ultimately, the quality of social decentering associated with the use of self method depends on the accuracy of their self-perception and conceptions of others.

Errors associated with atypical self-knowledge reflect a broader issue – an inaccurate, distorted, or biased self-concept. Use of self will likely produce inaccurate attributions about others when it is based on an inaccurate self-concept. Consequently, those with the most accurate sense of self are also more prepared to accurately use the self as a foundation for social decentering (within the inherent limits of this process).

Developmentally, we progress from being unable to differentiate ourselves from others, to a sense of our distinct self, a sense of specific others, and a sense of generalized others. Early in childhood, we do not recognize that others are different from us and thus do not develop a self-as-distinct view (Karniol, 1990). Piaget's and Vygotsky's work on cognitive development and Flavell's (1975) work on role-taking identify processes by which humans move from egocentric beings to decentered beings – from self-oriented to other-oriented. Barnett (1984) described children's social cognitive development as progressing from

> [...] (1) an egocentric view of their social world, to (2) understanding that other individuals may have contrasting perceptions, thoughts, and feelings, to (3) consideration of one's own and another's point of view in a separate and successive manner, and (4) consideration of a number of different perspectives in a coordinated, balanced, and simultaneous manner. (pp. 45)

Developmentally then, the use of self appears is the initial method by which we view others. We evolve cognitively to the point of being able to consider the world from other people's vantage points; however, these views are likely to be biased by our tendencies to confuse our own views as those of others.

The primary and most obvious limitation of the use of self method in considering other people's dispositions is that social decenterers might fail to recognize differences between themselves and their targets. Cheek (2014) expressed concern that the self-other overlap resulting from including similar others into their self-concept and heightening a sense of similarity. Cheek argued that this overlap leads to a failure to recognize differences in perspective. Such an overlap of believed similarity can actually undermine the enactment of social decentering because people believe they already understand their partners. In such situations, decenterers might falsely project inaccurate information that leads to ineffective strategies or inappropriate responses. In addition, Van Boven and Loewenstein (2005) observed that people's use of self is biased because people "project their current perceptions, preferences, and behaviors onto their predictions of what their reactions would be in a different situation" (p. 46). But how conscious of these differences does a person need to be in order to effectively decenter; surprisingly, not very conscious at all. Many times, individuals interact with people who are similar to them – friends, spouses, classmates, even coworkers. In these instances, this inherent similarity makes the use of self a viable method for processing information. The challenge in this process, then, is "to distinguish individuals for whom one's own mind can reasonably serve as a proxy from those for whom it cannot" (Mitchell, 2009, p. 1314).

The more homogeneous a person's social network, the greater the likelihood that use of self is an effective method for social decentering. Of course, no two people are alike, and sometimes even small differences can produce incorrect decentering. How well would the use of self serve a graduating 21-year-old major in electrical engineering in analyzing a graduating 21-year-old English major's disposition toward graduation and job searching? While the two students have similarities, the differences between their majors might be significant enough to undermine the use of self.

Individuals may also fail to employ use of self when the method could be effective for understanding other people's thoughts and feelings. For example, a heterosexual man decides not to use his own experience breaking up with his girlfriend as a basis for understanding his homosexual friend's recent breakup with his boyfriend. The heterosexual man assumes his friend's sexual orientation creates significantly different responses toward the breakup than his own, when indeed, their responses might actually be similar. Thus, decenterers might perceive differences to be relevant when they are not or inflate the impact of the differences. Interestingly, voicing such a perspective can have a negative impact on the target because it reveals the decenterer's focus on differences rather than similarities. For example, a woman could be insulted by a male coworker telling her that he can't understand her because she's a woman. Besides treating irrelevant differences as relevant, individuals might perceive or impose differences that aren't there and thus dismiss the option of applying use of self.

Other factors affecting the accuracy of the use of self method revolve around self-concept. A biased or distorted self-concept will produce biased and distorted analyses of other people. A person's self-concept is subject to self-serving bias, positivity bias, negativity bias, and better-than-average effect. For example, a self-serving bias, particularly actor-observer bias, leads individuals who are late for meetings to attribute their tardiness to external factors (circumstance) rather than to a fault in their character (internal cause). Individual's use of self in analyzing a target in such a situation, then, would also result in their attributing the target's tardiness to external factors. But research on fundamental attribution error and correspondence bias has shown that observers of other people being late are likely to attribute the tardiness to the people themselves (internal cause) rather than to external causes (circumstances). The discrepancy between these two conflicting propositions probably stems from the fact that when people make fundamental attribution errors, they are not engaging in use of self information processing. Studies in which participants were prompted to perspective take, or to compare others to themselves instead of comparing themselves to others, resulted in greater attribution to internal causes, reducing the impact of fundamental attribution error (Eiser, Pahl, & Prins, 2001; Moskowitz, 2005; Pahl, Eiser, & White, 2009). This research does not specifically tap into the use of self, but tends to involve the use of specific-other and use of generalized-other.

A study designed to evoke use of self might include such instructions as, "Think first about the reasons you might be late for a meeting and then list the reasons you think the other person was probably late." Such evocation of use of self creates an intriguing conundrum because, while it might reduce the fundamental attribution error, it might also prompt the imposition of self-serving biases onto the perception of others. As a result, individuals might fail to recognize harmful situations. For example, in applying use of self, people who see themselves as more honest and trustworthy than they really are (positivity bias), project those same qualities onto others, thus opening themselves to being taken advantage of – perhaps this is the foundation of naiveté. Of course, people who see themselves in a negative light while applying use of self, might be apt to project those negative qualities onto other people.

When individuals are asked to compare themselves to their conception of the average person, they evaluate themselves more positively across a spectrum of qualities, reflecting a better-than-average perceptual bias. Paradoxically, then, when individuals experiencing such an effect apply use of self social decentering, they should produce an image of the target person as also better-than-average. But one research project found that when individuals were directed to compare themselves to a specific individual, even just the picture of a stranger, the better-than-average effect was significantly reduced (Alicke, Klotz, Breitenbecher, Yurak, & Vredenburg, 1995). The researchers claimed that when people compare themselves to specific others, they engage in individuation, producing real distinctions that are not biased towards a self-perspective of being better. Within the social decentering context then, the very act of applying use of self with regard to a specific target appears to elicit a more objective comparison of the self with others and thus reduce or eliminate the impact of the better-than-average effect.

People vary in the complexity and clarity of their self-concepts which directly affects the effectiveness of their use of self. People with self-complexity have a self-concept composed of social roles, relationships, physical features, activities, and goals (Linville, 1985). In essence, self-complex individuals view themselves from a complex personal construct perspective. People whose self-concepts are composed of fewer self-constructs than other people are limited to explaining their own behaviors in simpler terms, which narrows their use of self social decentering. While contending with measurement issues, Zorn, McKinney, and Moran (1993) found a strong overlap between the constructs that individuals used to describe other people and descriptions of themselves. People's construct repertoires have two impacts on social decentering. First, the more complex their repertoire, the more the use of self method of social decentering will result in their complex attributions of others. Second, the repertoire's level of cognitive complexity (the complexity of the constructs individuals use to differentiate among people) affects the depth of their use of specific-other analysis which I discuss in the next section.

Self-concept clarity is the "extent to which the contents of an individual's self-concept (e.g., perceived personal constructs) are clearly and confidently defined, internally consistent, and temporally stable" (Campbell et al., 1996, p. 141). The effectiveness of use of self would be impacted by the clarity, consistency, and confidence in one's self-concept. Lower self-concept clarity, along with lower complexity, reduces the ability to use of self social decentering to generate valid insights, while higher clarity and complexity would enhance it. Self-concept clarity is often studied in terms of its relationship to mental health, particularly, depression (see review by Rafaeli & Hiller, 2010). Use of self provides a method for understanding and adapting to others which can be negatively impacted by lower clarity and complexity. As such, a lack of use of self might potentially undermine the successful management of interpersonal relationships – relationships that could be factors in positive mental health and reduced depression. Self-concept clarity and complexity are needed for effective use of self social decentering because, as Mitchell (2009) observes about mentalizing about others through self-projection, an individual must be able to "generate rich and accurate representations of one's own hypothetical mental states" (p. 1314).

1.2.3.2 Use of Specific-Other

In our interactions with other people, we are constantly learning new things about them. As mentioned, we create schemas for each person into which we place the information we learn, though not all information is retained. Some schemas are fairly shallow, perhaps only including the person's name (unless you're like me and forget those at times), where they're from, and their occupation. The more frequently we interact with someone, the more established our schema becomes. These schemas act as the base for the use of specific-other analysis. When we develop intimate relationships with complex schemas, we develop relationship-specific-social decentering which is discussed in the next chapter. Besides drawing on schemas to analyze a particular person, we can apply a schema we have established for one friend to understand another person who seems similar. While discussing interactions with strangers, Rusbult and Van Lange (2003) wrote that "individuals hold distinct and chronically accessible mental representations of 'significant others' and frequently use these representations as templates for interaction with unfamiliar partner" (p. 365). Rusbult and Van Lange observed that if new partners display traits found in that significant other, people will respond in a manner similar to how they would to the significant other. In this way, the schemas we create for specific others serves as a foundation for understanding and predicting new partners. The more people we know, the more schemas we create, which provides a broader base on which to draw in our use of specific-other analysis of new people. Such breadth provides for better matches between the preexisting schemas and other people.

In applying the use of specific-other method, individuals draw from their observations and knowledge about a specific person with whom they have interacted in order to analyze, interpret, and predict that person's dispositions within a given situation. As with the other two methods of social decentering, the use of specific-other involves the individual's attempts to observe, recall, or imagine the experiences, perspectives, thoughts, feelings, and other dispositions of a person they know within the context of a previous, current, or anticipated situation. Individuals can draw either on their experience-based knowledge of this person or they can generate imagination-based knowledge about that person. The most fundamental form the use of specific-other method involves observing a person in a given situation and recalling how that person previously responded in a similar situation. For example, when anyone is late to a meeting, the manager always makes a point of making an offhand remark about that person's tardiness; thus, people who arrive late for a meeting come to expect some critical remark from the manager. Such an application of the use of specific-other represents a fairly cursory application of social decentering. Nonetheless, it does involve considering the disposition of another specific person in a given situation. Considering the large number of people we encounter, most of the schemas that we create through this process are fairly incomplete, which means we lack specific information about a specific other and have to rely more heavily on extrapolating from what we know to what we imagine.

In its most advanced form, the other end of the use of specific-other method involves expanding beyond the basic learned data to generate new information in the form of personal theories and imagination-based information. For example, a college student, Jill, finds out that the mother of her close friend, Jackie, has died. Jill knows that Jackie has had a strained relationship with her mother and has not spoken to her mother in several weeks. In anticipating Jackie's disposition, Jill draws from what she knows about Jackie as she imagines her reaction to the situation. Jill's application of the use of specific-other method of social decentering leads her to believe that Jackie will be very hurt, angry, and probably guilty about the feelings she has harbored toward her mother. In this example, Jill uses both experience-based and imagination-based information to analyze Jackie's thoughts and feelings and develop a theory of what her reaction will be. Although Jill does not have a specific instance that she can simply recall and apply to predict Jackie's disposition, she instead uses her imagination. Unlike with the use of self method, for which Jill might have imagined how she would feel if her mom had died and used that as her basis for social decentering, Jill imaginatively transports Jackie into the new situation and considers the impact of this situation on Jackie. This example of Jill and Jackie reflects a number of factors that influence the use of specific-other: the amount of knowledge that Jill has about Jackie, the relevance of that knowledge, Jill's ability to analyze and apply that knowledge, Jill's ability to use what is known to effectively imagine what is not, Jill's sensitivity to the situation, the degree to which Jill has created personal theories about Jackie, and Jill's own propensity to even engage in social decentering.

We derive knowledge about other people primarily from their self-disclosures and from our personal observations of these people and secondarily, individuals might gain information from third parties. Thomas and Fletcher (1997) discussed empathy as a process that can be either data driven or theory driven; this distinction also applies to the use of specific-other social-decentering. As a process that involves recalling and applying information obtained through disclosures and observations of other people, social decentering is data driven. Predicting a manager's offhand remarks to those who are late to meetings is a data-driven process. But understanding why the manager makes these comments is a theory driven process. In this theory driven process, individuals develop personal theories relevant to the specific people they know. These theories represent cognitively processed and derived expectations. Jill employed use of specific-other method of social decentering to develop such a theory to predict Jackie's response to her mother's death. From the theory based perspective, the use of specific-other builds on theories that are developed and applied to known individuals while the use of generalized-others method (as discussed in the next section) draws on people's general personal theories of human behavior (implicit personality theories). The level of sophistication and complexity of these personal theories is affected by the information available to build such theories as well as by the cognitive and imaginative skills of the person who is generating them.

Self-disclosure is a rich source of information to draw on when applying the use of specific-other method of social decentering. The amount of personal information that has been disclosed by the target and that is available to the decenterer generally depends on the level of interpersonal intimacy that exists in their relationship. Exceptions to this principle include post-intimate relationships in which a decenterer still retains the information that the target disclosed and therapeutic relationships in which self-disclosure is primarily unilateral. Obviously, the more information that is available, the greater the potential is for complex and insightful social-decentering. William Ickes (2003) and his colleagues have found that empathic accuracy (accurately reading another person's mind at a given moment in time) increases over time as knowledge is acquired. Specifically, they found that empathic accuracy between acquaintances and friends increased rapidly for the first six months of their relationship and after that it increased only gradually. For married couples, empathic accuracy peaks in the first and second year of marriage and then declines (Ickes, 2003). These patterns parallel the pattern of self-disclosure that typically occurs in the early stages of relational development. Similarly, the use of specific-other method of social decentering should increase in both its application and effectiveness as personal information is disclosed and relationships become more intimate. But a number of factors might intervene to diminish this correlated relationship.

Self-disclosing involves a conscious decision to share information with another person in order to seek support, fulfill a duty or desire to educate the other person, convey attraction, or escalate the relationship (Greene, Derlega, & Mathews, 2006). Typically, as a relationship escalates, so does the breadth and depth of self-disclosure depending on such factors as the reciprocity of liking and associated rewards and costs. And as self-disclosure increases, so does the potential for developing and effectively applying the use of specific-other method of social decentering. This increase in the use of specific-other in social decentering can further enhance relational development. But it can also result in the de-escalation or termination of the relationship if the resulting analysis predicts a dissatisfying relational outcome. For example, while developing a romantic relationship, Betsy discloses to Jim her strong Christian commitment. Rather than disclose his atheistic beliefs, feeling that Betsy would regard him with disdain if she knew, Jim ends the relationship. Social decentering plays a critical role in helping Jim make a prediction about the viability of the romantic relationship. Whether Jim is correct or not depends on how complete his knowledge of Betsy is and the quality of his social decentering.

The quantity and quality of the information gained through self-disclosure directly influences the use of specific-other in social decentering. Acquiring a large amount of personal information through self-disclosure requires time; thus, the most effective applications of use of specific-other in socially decentering are limited to more developed relationships. Given the breadth of personal information that a person could self-disclose (Altman & Taylor, 1973), some aspects about a person might be fully shared while other aspects remain hidden. Missing vital information can strongly undermine the accuracy and effectiveness of use of specific-other in social decentering. People's level of information sharing is affected by their openness and trust. Even with sufficient time to disclose, people might intentionally withhold information in order to protect or enhance their self-image, maintain privacy, sustain autonomy, or because of expected non-responsiveness to the disclosure (Afifi & Guerrero, 2000). Withheld information creates gaps that can result in incomplete or inaccurate social decentering analysis. Individuals avoid topics in an attempt to manage how they are perceived (Afifi & Guerrero, 2000), in particular, they try to avoid being perceived in a negative or undesirable light. Thus, subsequent applications of social decentering that are grounded in these manipulated images are inherently distorted and inaccurate. Indeed, individuals might purposely withhold information in order to limit another person's ability to socially decenter. Knowing that sharing certain information about themselves allows other people to better understand, predict, and even control or manipulate them might lead individuals to refrain from self-disclosure or provide deceptive information. Such a strategy is akin to athletic teams holding closed practices to prevent opponents from better understanding and predicting their plays.

On the other hand, individuals might make a concerted effort to provide information in order to enhance their partners' understanding of them. Part of their self-disclosure process involves a conscious decision to let another person better understand them – to share more intimate information that provides greater insights into who they are. In sharing such information, individuals expect their partners to incorporate that information into subsequent decentering and adaptation. Failure to utilize such shared information is likely to have a negative impact on the relationship (this process reflects relationship-specific social decentering discussed in Chapter 2).

Self-disclosure provides the database from which the use of specific-other method of decentering can operate. However, just because someone self-discloses does not insure that the partner has heard or retains the disclosed information; skill in interpersonal listening is a prerequisite for the use of this method of social decentering. Listeners can fail in attending to, recognizing the importance of, storing, or recalling the disclosed information. Besides the need for effective listening skills, specific-other social decentering requires significant information processing skills.

Self-disclosure is as a transactional process, and as such, listeners' responses have a strong impact on whether their partners continue to self-disclose (Greene, Derlega, & Mathews, 2006). Indeed, Reis and Shaver's (1988) model of intimacy focuses not on self-disclosure as a major factor leading to intimacy, but on the interpretation that the discloser places on the listener's response. Social decentering can help a listener provide a rich response to another person's disclosures, thus enhancing intimacy by confirming that the discloser is understood, validated, and cared for. In this way, a reciprocal relationship exists between self-disclosing and social decentering in that self-disclosure increases the effectiveness of the use of specific-other method of social decentering, and effective social decentering in turn, increases self-disclosure.

We also acquire information about others through our personal observations or perceptions of them. These observations, along with our partners' self-disclosures, lead us to form impressions and schemata. In reviewing strategies for acquiring information about others, Berger and Bradac (1982) classified three strategies, passive (observation), active (gaining information from others), and interactive (information acquired in conversation with the target). The passive strategy provides the most information when we have the opportunities to observe a person in a variety of situations and engaging in a variety of activities (Beger & Bradac, 1982). Just watching a person sitting at the library reading does not provide a broad spectrum of information. Glancing at a person in the library by happenstance may result in acquiring limited information because our intention to seek information is minimal. On the other hand, strategically spying on that person may result in acquiring considerable information because of our strong desire to learn as much as we can. Our level of intention is another factor that affects our ability to socially decenter. We are also more likely to retain passive information that we acquire if our level of attention is high. Thus, some passive observations of specific others can be fruitful in creating an information base on which to socially decenter.

As the library example demonstrates, gaining information about an individual through personal observations does not require a personal relationship with the individual or even awareness by the individual of being observed; it can be done surreptitiously from a distance (though such behavior can cross the line into stalking). Personal observations provide a foundation of information about specific others that can be used in social decentering. For example, coaches can scout an opposing basketball team without having a relationship with the members of that team. By observing (watching games from the stands or reviewing game films), they can acquire a great deal of information that allows them to develop a game plan. This process is essentially social decentering – knowing what to expect from each opposing player, being able to predict their actions, and develop a counterplan. Such scouting occurs in many human interactions from sports to interpersonal relationships. Sometimes the scouting involves talking with other people who can share their knowledge (an active strategy). A new employee, for example, might seek insights about the manager by talking to other employees, thus enhancing the new employee's ability to take into consideration the manager's disposition.

Self-disclosure and personal observations serve as the foundation for a multitude of other socio-psychological processes, as well as for research on person perception and impression formation. Rather than reviewing this extensive body of literature, I will make only a couple of observations – those that seem most relevant to social decentering. Individuals form social judgments, schemas, constructs, impressions, and expectancies as a way of organizing information about specific partners in specific relationships. Such formulations involve the use of self for comparison and insight, the use of stereotypes and categories, and the use of prototypes, roles, and expectations as a way of understanding other people. Thus, besides simply collecting and storing partner information, individuals analyze and compare that information to preexisting references as a way of clarifying, simplifying, and classifying people. All of these processes affect the ability of individuals to socially decenter and to one degree or another, reflect the three methods of social decentering – use of self (as in the comparison of self-schemata to the perception of others), use of specific-other (impressions and constructs), and use of generalized-others (prototypes and stereotyping).

In sum, the use of specific-other method of social decentering relies on information derived from observation, obtained from partners' self-disclosures, and generated from person-specific theories all within the context of various social information processes.

Factors Affecting the Quality of Use of Specific-Other

The accuracy and effectiveness of the use of specific-other method of social decentering are diminished by biases and errors in perception, impression formation, attributions, and general social-information processing. For example, a fundamental attribution error occurs from our overestimation of the impact of a person's dispositions on that person's behaviors relative to the explanations we generate for our own behaviors. When we apply the specific-other method of social decentering, fundamental attribution error might inherently lead us to inadequately assessing the impact of the situation on that person. Sillars (1985) identified several factors that interfere with married couples' understanding (shared perceptions) of each other, including selective recall and recall that is biased by preexisting schemata. Indeed, the expectations created in intimate relationships can interfere with the acquisition of new information. Sillars (1985) wrote, "Rarely will conversation with a very familiar person lead to completely novel insights that are independent of prior expectations" (p. 293).

On the other hand, social decentering could possibly offset many of these biases and errors. According to fundamental attribution error, if a friend is late to pick you up, you are likely to attribute the tardiness to a character flaw rather than circumstance. But if you engage in effective social decentering, you would be inclined to consider contextual and circumstantial explanations. For example, engaging in the use of self method of social decentering to understand your friend's tardiness should lead you to generate an explanation for why you might be late sometime, and apply that same explanation to your friend, thus offsetting the fundamental attribution error. And in applying the use of specific-other decentering, you use information that you have gathered about your friend to arrive at a more objective analysis of the possible reasons for your friend's late arrival. Inherent in this effective application of social decentering is sensitivity, awareness, and knowledge of external circumstances. Recognizing that there is bad weather, the power is out, and stoplights are not functioning, leads to a different attribution for a friend's tardiness.

Besides fundamental attribution error, mis explanations can be caused by weak perceptual and cognitive skills. You are more likely to attribute your friend's lateness to a character flaw when you fail to recognize the impact of the weather on your friend's travels. Thus, another factor that negatively affects the use of specific-other method of social decentering (and the other methods as well) is the inability or failure to consider the situation and context. Considering the context involves consciously recognizing and collecting information about the context, and then integrating this contextual information with the information about the target. Social decentering then, involves integrating and analyzing information about the person and the specific situation. While considering the context involves similar perceptual process as considering the person, attention can be focused on one to the detriment of the other. In addition, decenterers must also recognize when they are deficient in their understanding of the context and, when necessary, adopt strategies for gaining additional information. Fortunately, when discussing personal troubles, people often describe the circumstances in detail allowing listeners to better understand the context. For example, a woman discussing her romantic breakup to a friend is likely to disclose details about the relationship and her romantic partner (the context) while describing the actual breakup interaction. The degree to which the friend recognizes and incorporates this contextual information into the use of specific-other affects the friend's level of analysis and understanding.

Finally, the accuracy of the use of specific-other method of social decentering is affected by the acquisition, retention, and management of the specific information that the decenterer has about the other person. Limited knowledge of a person limits the completeness and complexity of this method of decentering. Such a limitation can occur because the decenterer has failed to adequately collect necessary information or the other person has intentionally avoided disclosing personal information. In addition, decenterers might forget what they have learned about others or fail to recall it when needed. As with the context, decenterers need to recognize when they are missing information about a person that may be vital in order to socially decenter adequately. But there are times when gaining such information is impractical or even unnecessary since imagination-based information can fill in for missing information.

In summary, the factors that undermine the effectiveness of the use of specific-other method of social decentering fall into three categories: information-processing errors, contextual errors, and information limitations.

1.2.3.3 Use of Generalized-Other

The use of generalized-other method of social decentering draws on the recalled or imagined experiences, perspectives, thoughts, feelings, attitudes, and other predispositions that are associated with a general population or a specific group or classification of people (for example, students and nonstudents, men and women, youth and elderly) who are relevant to a given previous, current, or anticipated situation. While similar to previous notions of the concept of generalized other, as applied to social decentering, generalized-other serves as the foundation for the third method of social decentering analysis that a person might employ when considering another person's predispositions to a given situation.

Mead (1934) used the term *generalized other* to refer to the social groups or communities in which a person existed and which contributed to the development of the self. Berlo (1960), in applying this term to empathy, used it more narrowly to refer to an individual's generalizations about the roles that people enact: "The generalized other is an abstract role that is taken, the synthesis of what an individual learns of what is general or common to the individual roles of all other people in his group" (p. 127). Berlo saw the generalized other as a foundation for self-concept, providing us with a set of expectations about how we should behave in a given situation. In essence, we develop a sense of how people in general behave when playing a particular role and use that to guide our own behavior. When decentering, we can use those same general expectations about people's role-playing to evaluate and analyze a given person's dispositions.

Cronbach (1955) examined the methodological problems of measuring the accuracy of social perception (empathy or social sensitivity) based on predictions made about another person's responses to a self-measure. Despite the methodological problems, he identified one factor that contributed to the prediction process that he called "stereotype accuracy" which he defined as a person's "accuracy in predicting the generalized other" (p. 157). Myers and Hodges (2009) noted that Cronbach's stereotype accuracy has primarily been viewed only in terms of trait accuracy and that another type of stereotype accuracy exists that encompasses generalizations about thoughts and feelings. They observed that "people often use generalizations and representations when trying to understand another person" (p. 287).

In contrast to Mead's (1934) conceptualization of the generalized other as the group to which the perceiver belongs, Bronfenbrenner, Harding and Gallwey (1968) conceived of the generalized other as any large group or class of people about whom an individual holds some attitudes or judgments. As such, individuals develop sensitivity to many different generalized others. Bronfenbrenner et al. contended that there are different types of these sensitivities: sensitivity to generalized others, sensitivity to face-to-face groups (one's in which the perceiver is a member), and sensitivity to a particular other (interpersonal sensitivity). The theory of social decentering also rests on a multidimensional conceptualization of social perceptions, albeit using a somewhat different model than Bronfenbrenner et al. originally presented.

While use of generalized-other would seem to run counter to empathic accuracy (as defined and measured by Ickes, Stinson, Bissonnette, & Garcia, 1990), Myers and Hodges (2009) point out that while people might fail at the moment-to-moment measure of accurate inferences about their partners, people still seem to muddle through with successful interactions and relationships. Among the reasons why, they identify people's dependence upon both differentiating information and stereotyping for making inferences about others. They argue that most moment-to-moment empathic inaccuracies are never perceived by the target during an interaction. In essence, the level of inaccuracy in Ickes research tends to be more reflective of a research method than actual interactions. Applying a general understanding of another person based on accurate stereotypes probably provides a better tool for managing quickly evolving interpersonal interactions than being constantly attuned to each moment-to-moment change in a partner's thoughts and feelings.

The use of generalized-other method of social decentering might be viewed more clearly as incorporating two social perception processes. The first involves developing personal theories of general human behavior, or social-centered theories – the type of process that is reflected in implicit personality theory. The second involves developing group-centered theories, whereby individuals recognize the presence of a quality or qualities distinctive to a particular group or that distinguish one group from another. The group distinctions are accompanied by a set of specific impressions and expectations associated with each identified group. In essence, group-centered theories represent stereotyping. But both social perception processes reflect the same underlying process that Hastorf, Schneider, and Polefka (1970) noted: "Implicit personality theories are, in the final analysis, stereotypes we hold about other people" (p. 46). In essence, personal theories and group-centered theories both involve thinking in stereotypes.

Implicit Personality Theory and Stereotyping Applied to the Use of Generalized-Other

Ashmore (1981) defined implicit personality theory as "a hypothesized cognitive structure, often held nonconsciously, that comprises the attributes of personality that an individual believes others to possess and the set of expected relations (i.e., inferential relations) between these attributes" (pp. 40). In Rosenberg and Sedlak's (1972) seminal article, they write that implicit personality theory is reflected in the general propositions people make about themselves and other people. Implicit personality theories can apply to both the use of specific-other and the use of generalized-other methods of social decentering, because such theories can be generated to specifically fit a single individual, categories of people, or humankind in general. Typically, an implicit personality theory involves a process of associating a given trait or quality with other traits within some organizational framework. Thus, in developing implicit personality theory, individuals attribute a given trait to a particular person, resulting in their attributing a set of other related traits to that person.

Many of the research studies surrounding implicit personality theory focus on identifying the trait structure or trait matrix that people use in conceptualizing others (Schneider, 1973). These trait structures operate as a set of interwoven constructs or categories so that attributing a given trait to a person activates a number of inter-related constructs. Thinking of someone as extroverted triggers the application of other related qualities such as being friendly or caring. In this manner, an implicit structure can be discerned that remains primarily unconscious yet shapes and guides individuals' reactions and analyses of others. The nature of such trait structures is not critical to understanding the role that implicit personality theory plays in the use of general-other method of social decentering. What is important is understanding that individuals draw on standing trait structures to analyze others.

The implicit personality theory's focus on traits has led to a failure to adequately recognize the larger scope that the theory covers. Ashmore (1981) pointed out that people's cognitions about others that constitute their implicit personality theories also include social categories, feelings, and expected behaviors. *Social categories* are the means by which people classify those who they perceive as similar (Ashmore, 1981). People attach their particular personality theories to these social categories which provide the structure for a variety of traits, feelings, and expectations. The number and complexity of people's categories have a direct impact on how well they can engage in the use of generalized-other method of social decentering. Those with more extensive and observationally grounded categories and structures have a stronger foundation from which to make inferences about a specific other person.

The process is referred to as implicit because it theoretically occurs without individuals' awareness. More pointedly, scholars believe that as individuals are unaware of their own structuring of traits, any application of such a structure occurs unconsciously. While they may apply such structures unconsciously, they still might consciously consider and develop their own personal theories about others. Such personal theories are sometimes discussed in terms of being "stories" or "narratives" that people create (Fiske, 1993). As such, people blend together motives, traits, observations, and attributions to make as coherent a narrative as possible. This merger may even include disparate motives or attributions in order to achieve "constraint satisfaction" – that is, "a 'fit' among various elements in a system" (Reeder & Trafimow, 2005, p. 118). This fit is achieved by identifying a motive that explains a variety of actions, even those that are contradictory (Reeder & Trafimow, 2005). The pieces of people's implicit personality theories then are put together in a way that allows the various motives, traits, and observations to make the most sense.

One general dichotomy of implicit theories identifies people as having "entity theories" and "incremental theories" (Dweck, 1996; Dweck, Chiu, & Hong, 1995). People with entity theories tend to develop theories of other people based on the assumption that people have fixed attributes, whereas those with incremental theories see attributes as more malleable and dynamic. The application of one theory over the other affects people's motivation, interpretation, and reactions to others. Implicit entity theories provide people with a parsimonious and ready understanding of other people, whereas implicit incremental theories provide people with greater flexibility and constructive problem solving (Dweck, 1996). Those with a more rigid perspective on other people (entity theorists) are more likely to be prone to social stereotyping (Levy, Stoessner, & Dweck, 1998). Dweck and her colleagues' research primarily contrasts the types of attributions made by people identified as either entity theorists or incremental theorists. But other research shows that people appear to be able to develop and apply both entity and incremental theories and that these two theories can be thought of as occurring across a continuum (Poon & Koehler, 2006). And this research shows that activation of a given theory seems to follow the general principles governing the activation and acquisition of social knowledge such as priming.

The type of implicit theory that people use (entity or incremental) in applying the use of generalized-other method of social decentering affects the manner in which they process and analyze others and possibly the accuracy and effectiveness of their conclusions. Although entity theorists appear less likely to recognize the impact of the context, incremental theorists seem less inclined to apply generalities (Dweck, Chiu, & Hong, 1995) and therefore be more limited in their ability to engage in the use of generalized-other method. Seeing people's traits as malleable may undermine the ability to generate and apply general theories of human behavior and thus the use of generalized-others. On the other hand, a lack of information about an individual might act as a catalyst to employ the use of the generalized-other method of social decentering and to develop implicit entity theories.

The accuracy of implicit theories depends on such factors as the amount of experience interacting with other people, the diversity of those experiences, and feedback about the accuracy of observations and theories (Colvin & Bundick, 2001; Funder, 1999). People are unlikely to develop a repertoire of accurate implicit theories if their interactions are limited to homogeneous groups and if they receive little, if any, feedback about the accuracy of their theories. As Funder (1999) observed, "A person sitting alone in his or her room or otherwise avoiding interactions with others is denying himself or herself the chance to obtain the experience that could develop interpersonal knowledge" (p. 140). Colvin and Bundick (2001) argued that experience and feedback provide a foundation for being able to connect behavioral cues to personality and thus increase individuals' abilities to adapt and develop successful interpersonal relationships. Thus, people who have greater and more diverse interaction experiences and receive feedback to correct and improve their implicit theories should be stronger and more accurate in their use of generalized-other in social decentering.

Ames (2005) has criticized social psychologists for failing to recognize that stereotypes are a source of mind reading and mental-state inferences. Stereotyping is another tool that is incorporated into social decentering through the use of generalized-others. Stereotypes, role constructs, and schemata attached to groups all reflect the principle that people organize information in an efficient and economical manner. Being able to categorize groups of people and readily access relevant information helps people to make sense of and interact with the social world. Stangor (2005) noted that "stereotypes allow the individual to understand, predict, control, and 'master' their social worlds" (p. 280). Unfortunately, stereotyping is often considered synonymous with prejudice. Much of the research and theory on stereotyping views stereotyping as inherently "bad" and such research is plagued with conceptual and methodological shortcomings (Ashmore & Del Boca, 1981; Jussim, Cain, Crawford, Harber, & Cohen, 2009). Stereotyping, as incorporated into the theory of social decentering, is neither inherently negative nor inaccurate, but rather is part of the social cognitive process by which social information is managed. As a global and neutral social-information process, stereotyping is quite simply "a set of beliefs about the personal attributes of a group of people" (Ashmore & Del Boca, 1981, p. 16). This conceptualization of stereotyping corresponds with that of social decentering. Information from stereotyping is another source that individuals draw on in analyzing other people's dispositions, particularly when the decenterers have little in-depth information.

The two primary forms of stereotypes are *cultural* – those shared by a given group and learned through enculturation within that group, and *personal* – those developed by individuals based on their own beliefs about a given group (Ashmore & Del Boca, 1981; Jussim et al., 2009). These two forms of stereotypes emerge from different processes. Cultural stereotypes are conveyed within a cultural group and applied almost mindlessly. Such stereotypes might be prejudicial in nature, but they are also subject to change as individuals interact directly with members of the stereotyped group. Personal stereotypes are developed by individuals as they interact with their world, acquiring information about others and creating their own social classification schemes. Personal stereotypes are constructs that are associated with a given category created by the perceiver. People may draw on both forms of stereotyping within the context of social decentering. While cultural stereotypes inherently provide all members of a given culture with the same foundation from which to apply the use of generalized-other method of social decentering, those with a complex set of personal stereotypes can develop more sophisticated analyses of other's dispositions by which to achieve their goals.

Jussim et al. (2009) argued that much of stereotyping is accurate and thus useful for making judgments when information is limited to group membership. By adopting a more reasonable standard for judging accuracy (not having to be 100% perfect), Jussim et al. found from their review of previous research that stereotyping was moderately to highly accurate (the majority of correlations ranging from 0.40 to 0.60). But sometimes our stereotypes are highly inaccurate. What contributes to our adoption of inaccurate stereotypes is unclear, but certainly prejudice and hatred can cause us to create and sustain distorted stereotypes. On the other hand, the accuracy of our stereotypes is likely to be enhanced by our exposure to and interaction with members of any specific group, as predicted by Allport's contact hypothesis. In turn, the effectiveness of the use of generalized-other method of social decentering is likely to increase throughout our lifetime if, over time, our interactions with a variety of groups and people continue to expand.

Jussim et al. (2009) categorized the type of information individuals used in judging others including stereotyping based on having useful information that distinguishes between groups but not having information that distinguishes among individuals. In this instance, Jussim et al. challenge the notion that stereotyping "biases" judgments, preferring to characterize the effect as "influencing" or "informing" judgments. They conclude that

> [s]uch effects mean that people are appropriately using their knowledge about groups to reach as informed a judgment as possible under difficult and information-poor circumstances. If their knowledge is reasonably accurate, relying on the stereotype will usually increase, rather than decrease the accuracy of those judgments. (p. 215)

Jussim et al. argued that in the absence of any information about an individual except the group that the individual is a member of, applying information about that group is likely to be more accurate than a random guess. In other words, individuals can make rational inferences based on any information they have about another person. If you know that Jim is a senior in college, you can make several conclusions about Jim based on his educational status. Will they all be correct? No, but there is a chance that many will be. Knowing Jim is a senior in college is more informative than not knowing this piece of information, however, the informational value of this knowledge lies in the inferences that you can draw from Jim's educational status. Similarly, in applying the use of generalized-other method of social decentering, individuals use stereotypes as an information source for analyzing the dispositions of other people about whom they know little or nothing. Thus, according to Jussim et al.'s conclusions about stereotyping, the resulting social decentering analysis can be expected to be fairly accurate.

Jussim et al. (2009) observed that a number of meta-analyses demonstrate that individuals actually don't engage in that much stereotyping and are much more likely to rely on individuating information. This finding suggests that the use of generalized-other method of social decentering is not applied as frequently as are methods that rely on individuating information – the use of specific-other. The use of individuating information might not always be the appropriate or more accurate option. Some evidence indicates that we actually underutilize the information stored in categories and stereotypes, opting instead to focus on person-specific information, even though the general information might prove more applicable and accurate (Funder, 1995). In our interactions with a specific person, information from the immediate interaction becomes more salient and stereotyped information falls into the background (Funder, 1995). Given this evidence, we appear more apt to apply the use of generalized-other approach when analyzing others from afar than in face-to-face encounters – characters in a story, movie, or TV show, or people that we read about, hear about, or observe in the news.

Emotions can also be viewed from the perspective of stereotyping and stereotypic accuracy. Gnepp (1989) wrote about how in inferring a person's feelings in a given situation, children might generalize "across all people to determine what feelings people in general would have in response to those circumstances" (p. 157). For children, such generalizations are based on limited information, but the quality of such stereotyped emotional inferences likely improves with age and experience. Thus, a typical question to ask while engaging in the use of generalized-other method of social decentering focused on understanding another person's feelings is, "How do most people feel in that situation?"

Use of Generalized-Other: Development of Personal Theories

People create personal theories to explain and predict the dispositions of groups of people; and such personal theories inform the use of generalized-other method of social decentering. Inherent in personal theories is the use of categorization. People create and use categories in developing both implicit personality theories and stereotypes. They attach personal theories to categories, and their number of personal theories corresponds with the number and complexity of their categories.

Are personal theories effective tools to use in making sense of other people? Morris, Ames, and Knowles (2001) suggested applying "lay theories" to the same criteria used to typically evaluate scientific theories. First, theories have structure; specifically, theories identify qualities associated with some phenomenon and provide relationships between these qualities. In forming personal theories, people create a unifying theory for a given group consisting of a set of qualities and the relationships among those qualities that they can draw when employing the use of generalized-other method of social decentering to consider a given person's dispositions. Second, theories explain and predict (control) – two functions that motivate people to engage in social decentering. The quality of a theory depends on how well it fulfills either or both of these functions. Personal theories of generalized others seek to provide the most suitable explanation or allow for the most accurate prediction (and thus control their social world). If people's theories fail to fulfill such functions, they might seek to revise or develop alternative theories. But a phenomenon such as prejudice, indicates that at times people hold on to their personal theories even in the face of contradictory information. Third, theories can be empirically validated. This criterion has limited application to personal theories since people probably aren't concerned about validating most of the theories they develop (a person's level of confidence in their theories may reflect their sense of theory validity). For example, Greg might hold a personal theory about people from South America based on his exposure to the media without being particularly motivated to test its validity. Indeed, he might never even interact with someone from South America.

The final criterion of theory building that applies well to personal theories is that of scope or generalizability. Theories have greater value when their scope is broad and they have widespread applicability. Such theories reach the status of grand theories. In considering generalized others, implicit personality theory can be regarded as a grand theory with broad scope, whereas group-centered stereotypes have a much narrower application. Personal theories of general human behavior meet the need for efficiency of numbers (minimizing the number and depth of individual-centered theories) and offset an insufficiency of information about a particular individual. A need for efficiency suggests that people hold a finite number of stereotypes; that is, people can reasonably manage only a limited number of constructs and schemata. The creation of categories is fundamental to both stereotyping (Taylor, 1981) and implicit personality theory (Ashmore, 1981). The kinds of fundamental categories and the complexity of categorization can be constructed in a hypothetical taxonomy:

1. most basic category that all people are the same
2. global bipolar categories by which all people are divided (masculine and feminine)
3. categories spawned by blatant physical qualities differentiating groups (the big three being sex, race, and age, Macrae & Quadflieg, 2010).
4. categories reflecting differences in nonphysical qualities (for example, cultural background, socio-economic, education, attitudes, and beliefs)

5. idiosyncratic categories and role stereotypes (Taylor, 1981) generated within a certain context (for example, a manager who categorizes employees as either high or low maintenance, or a bus driver who categorizes passengers as cooperative or uncooperative).

Some categorizations are cultural stereotypes (that is, they are shared by given members of a culture) acquired through socialization. For example, the U.S. culture has stereotypes for men, women, Blacks, Whites, senior citizens, and teenagers. Idiosyncratic or individual categories are more unique to a given perceiver, but they are still linked to classifications found in a socially shared language. For example, a college English instructor might have a particular mind-set that she associates with female freshman engineering students. Implicit in such classification schemes is a comparative assessment. The English instructor might be distinguishing females from male engineering students, freshmen from seniors, or engineering from liberal arts students.

The use of generalized-other method of social decentering is affected by the manner in which individuals organize group-centered information and the types of stereotypes they develop. As individuals employ the use of generalized-other method of social decentering, their different levels of categories and stereotypes provide them with alternate perspectives on another person's dispositions. The level of stereotyping and categories that individuals draw on is affected by both the amount of effort required and the reliability and validity of any resulting analysis. The amount of effort is driven by the decenterer's motivation and the importance to the decenterer of a correct and thorough analysis. A viewer who is analyzing a TV character who differs racially from the viewer would probably exert minimal effort because a correct analysis would not be important. On the other hand, two unacquainted college freshmen of different races who are assigned to room together for the year will likely be very motivated to make an accurate analysis of each other early in their relationship. In the first example, the viewer would probably be content with a casual application of information from stereotypes and the use of generalized-other processing. In the second example, the roommates are more likely to move quickly to the use of specific-other method of social decentering.

Sources of Error in the Use of Generalized-Other

As with the other methods of social decentering, the quality of the use of generalized-other method is affected by numerous shortcomings associated with social information processing. The most prominent among these is creating inaccurate personal or implicit theories of others. The accuracy of such theories depends on our ability to objectively observe, process, structure, and apply meaningful information about others. Although, stereotypes can be accurate reflections of the average or typical attitudes and behaviors of a particular group, they can also be inaccurate or representative of only a small minority in a group. Stereotypes can be either learned through acculturation or personally developed. Those learned within the context of a given cultural group are likely to maintain imbedded prejudices and inaccuracies when mindlessly acquired. Personally developed stereotypes involve using our own observations to create stereotypes and are subject to a variety of perceptual flaws. One such flaw occurs when a stereotype is formed from a limited or biased sample of group members (Ottati & Lee, 1995). For example, a U.S. college student meets three Japanese exchange students on campus one semester and uses those interactions as the foundation for a stereotype about the Japanese. Japanese students attending a U.S. university might not be a representative sample of the Japanese people – the very fact that these students are pursuing an education in the U.S. makes them atypical. On the other hand, the U.S. college student might have a better foundation for future interactions with the Japanese based on that limited sample than she would have if she had never interacted with anyone from Japan. Among the challenges inherent in this example then, are the sample size (How many observations are needed to create a reliable stereotype?) and sampling technique (How representative are the observed samples of the larger population?).

Additional flaws in forming accurate stereotypes can come from a biased perception of the observed group while forming the stereotypic judgment, selective and biased recall of information, and overweighed pieces of information (Ottati & Lee, 1995). Accuracy in judging others might also be affected by variations in: judgment skills, ease of judging individuals, ease of judging certain traits, and the kinds and amount of information that actually yields accurate judgments (Funder, 1995). While all three methods of social decentering incorporate similar social information processes, the use of generalized-other method requires the additional ability to generalize about other people and create reliable categories.

People are challenged by the need for an efficient and streamlined social information process that favors keeping the number of categories to a minimum. On the other hand, a sufficient number of categories are needed to be able to usefully and meaningfully differentiate among groups of people. For example, you've just met an 18-year-old Iowa farm kid, John, whose pickup truck was stolen. Knowing how people in general react to their vehicle being stolen provides some basis for predicting and understanding John's dispositions. But if you have previously developed a category for Iowa teenage farm kids, you are likely to be more accurate and have a greater depth of understanding. Maintaining a large repertoire of categories is an unwieldy and probably unreasonable task; however, having a limited number of categories or failing to recognize differences between groups, limits the effectiveness of the use of generalized-other method of social decentering. In this stolen truck example, lacking information about John's age and background would force you to use more general categories, such as males and teenagers. But if you found out that John was from Iowa, you might apply the category of farm kid when John is actually from the city of Des Moines and has never set foot on a farm. Deciding which categories apply to a given individual and how much weight to give the relevant categories create other sources of error. Which categories, for instance, should you draw on when considering the dispositions of a 21-year-old Black female Notre Dame University student from Mississippi whose mother has just died? Each potential category contains information that changes the analysis, and some qualities are more pertinent than others in the given context. Failure to consider the most appropriate categories or stereotypes then may introduce error into the use of generalized-other in decentering.

Finally, people can simply mis-categorize others, placing them into groups in which they are not members. Employing the use of generalized-other method of social decentering based on this misplaced categorization will produce inaccurate analyses and inappropriate strategies. Misjudging a person's age, for instance, might lead to making attributions that are perhaps accurate for the given age group, but are not applicable to that particular person. Categories are often formed around the most obvious or salient features such as sex, race, and age because they allow for quick group classification. Sometimes such features can be misleading and result in mis-classification; for example, a Caucasian student at a U.S. college might be classified as a typical American college student when the student is actually from South Africa, Poland, or Peru. The ability to correct such errors depends on having the opportunities to collect further information, perhaps through direct interactions, as well as being open to re-classifying others.

1.2.3.4 Interaction of the Three Methods: Self, Specific-Other, Generalized-Other

Each of the three methods of social decentering can provide an effective analysis of other people's dispositions, and there are circumstances in which each method is more effective than the other two. But the strongest social decentering occurs when you apply all three methods. In discussing a model of how individuals develop coherent accounts of other people's behaviors, Read and Collins (1992) observe that "when a person accounts for an interaction, there are typically multiple knowledge structures active at the same time, and that often interpreting a sequence requires people to integrate these multiple sources of knowledge" (p. 128). In a similar manner, the three methods of social decentering act as multiple sources of knowledge which an individual can utilize to analyzing others. The combined three methods provide a 3D perspective that more fully creates an ephemeral other. Each method by itself, provides a two-dimensional perspective of the target person, but the three methods together add depth and correct for errors of perspective that are inherent in using a single method. The three methods act as a system in which each method affects the others. For example, in analyzing a particular target, you can compare the dispositions generated through the use of specific-other method of social decentering with the dispositions generated through the use of generalized-other method of social decentering (relevant stereotypes, implicit personality theories, or personal theories). This comparison highlights characteristics that are shared with and differ from the reference group providing additional insight into the target's character and dispositions. Such contrasting judgments are stimulated by information or observations about an individual that does not match those expected from an applied stereotype (Biernat, 2005). For example, if you know that most college seniors (generalized other) consume alcohol at some point during college, but that college senior Rachel (specific-other) has never done so, you have unique insight into Rachel. On the other hand, if you know that Rachel does drink alcoholic beverages, you become more confident in utilizing the use of generalized-other as a basis for attributing additional college senior attributes to Rachel.

The results of the three methods do not have to agree in order to provide a sound analysis of another person's dispositions. As with the example of Rachel, differences between the three methods provide valuable insights as long as you recognize those differences. Knowledge that you and a work colleague differ in reacting to stressful situations means that social decentering based on use of self and use of specific-other will lead to contrasting conclusions when considering your colleague's reaction to furloughs. In fact, some approaches assess empathy by discounting individuals' responses about themselves that match those of the target person because of assumed projection, using only the scores that differ between the individuals and the targets. While such approaches reflect the value of contrasting perspectives, they discount those dispositions that we share with others. Karniol's (2003) self-as-distinct model reflects the interaction of the three methods of social decentering. In Karniol's model, generic representations of prototypic others (generalized others) serve as the foundation for judging distinctiveness of both the self and well-known others (specific others). According to her model, we develop a sense of what qualities are distinct in ourselves and in well-known others. However, if we don't see the distinctions between generic representations of prototypic others from and ourselves or well-known others, then those general representations serve as the default for qualities about the self or well-known others. Thus, Karniol did not necessarily see the self as a source for making predictions about well-known others, but instead the self and well-known others are compared to the prototypic other. Doing so allows us to recognize similarities between ourselves and well-known others because of their shared distinctiveness from the prototypic other.

But some approaches do identify the self as a source for understanding others, depending on the quality and confidence individuals have in their use of self for decentering. This confidence can in turn, have a direct impact on their ability to apply the specific-other and generalized-other methods of social decentering. Research shows that the more confident individuals are in their ability to use constructs for self-evaluation, the more extensively and more definitively they are able to differentiate between others (Adams-Webber, 2002). In essence, individuals with more developed prototypes and constructs are better equipped and more confident to judge both themselves and others. For this reason, all three methods of social decentering relate to one another since they share a common set of prototypes and constructs to use in understanding and evaluating others.

Individuals' set of constructs affects the complexity of their social decentering. *Cognitive complexity* represents the breadth and depth of the constructs that individuals have available to them for differentiating between people and within themselves. As such, cognitive complexity is associated with individuals' perspective-taking abilities (Clark & Delia, 1977; Hale & Delia, 1976), because the more constructs that individuals can generate to describe people, the greater the foundation for understanding and explaining others' behaviors. Cognitive complexity affects all three methods of social decentering. Potentially, individuals who are cognitively complex might understand people who are not as cognitively complex better than those people understand themselves. But such a view is grounded, not in the role that complexity plays in employing the use of self to understand others, but in a general ability to think complexly both about the self and others. While this perspective applies more to the use of specific-other and generalized-other than to use of self, the underlying logic is similar.

The research and theory of role-taking provides another example of how the social decentering methods interact. Two types of role-taking are identified, situational and individual, which parallel the use of self and use of specific-other. Situational role-taking involves considering another person's situation from your own perspective, whereas individual role-taking involves recognizing that the other person is different and taking those differences into account when considering the other person's perspective. In both types, the role takers must recognize and appreciate the differences between their own and their target's situations, circumstances, and personal characteristics (Higgins, 1981). The strongest social decenterers, then, have the ability to recognize and incorporate both the use of self and use of specific-other methods of social decentering.

Batson, Early, and Salvarani (1997) compared the emotional responses of participants who imagined themselves in a given situation to that of participants who imagined another person in that situation. In their study, participants were instructed to either listen objectively, imagine how they themselves would feel in the situation, or imagine how the person in the situation felt. They then listened to a taped interview of a female student facing major distress. Both the imagine-self and the imagine-other participants had similar reports of empathy that were both stronger than the objective group, but the imagine-self participants reported feeling greater distress than did the other two groups, which were not significantly different from each other. In other words, by putting yourself into the situation, you experience stronger feelings of distress than you would by simply imagining how the other person feels. In asking participants to imagine another person, researchers were probably referring more to a generalized-other than a specific-other person since the scenario involved listening to an interview of a woman unknown to the participants. Thus, the participants had no specific historical knowledge of the target and relied instead on generalized knowledge. While this study focused on the emotions of empathy and distress, it does illustrate how an individual's emotional arousal might be more intense by applying the use of self rather than applying the use of generalized-other in social decentering. This study also illustrates how the different methods of social decentering inform one another. The distress evoked through the use of self is probably a more accurate reflection of what the other person was feeling than was the less intense response evoked by just imagining the other's feelings. In such cases, the most effective social decenterers use their self-analyses as the foundation for considering the other person's dispositions.

Vorauer (2013) described how imagine-other rather than imagine-self can produce negative effects on individuals when their targets are in a position to evaluate their perspective-taking efforts. In essence, knowing the targets will judge how well we understand them (imagine-other) creates more concerns than judging how well I've imagined myself in their situation. Vorauer contended that evaluation was inherent in face-to-face interactions and that individuals' preoccupation with being evaluated undermines their perspective-taking. This implies that individuals would be inclined not to engage in perspective-taking during a conversation. But as discussed earlier, the time needed for considering other's dispositions is limited during conversations. Vorauer argued that the positive effects from perspective-taking occur the most when there is little evaluation and ambiguity about response options. The decision to apply use of self or use of specific-other in social decentering appears to have possible shortcomings. Concern for evaluation might be one reason people elect not to display adaptive behaviors that might reflect insensitivity and errors in their understanding. The most likely application of social decentering might be in analysis done prior to encounters or subsequent to them where immediate evaluation is minimized.

Ames (2004) conducted a series of studies that relate to the use of self and the use of generalized-other. He manipulated various qualities associated with a target that were either similar or dissimilar to the participant and informed participants that the target was a member of one of three stereotyped college groups. His analyses found that similarity lead to the use of more projection (use of self) and less stereotyping (generalized other). In his study, he defined projection as the degree to which participants' self-ratings predicted their ratings of the targets. *Stereotyping* was the degree to which participants' ratings of the targets matched some predetermined group values. Of course, either form of evaluation could lead to accurate or inaccurate judgments. Indeed, the more similarities that exist between a perceiver and a target, the greater the accuracy of the use of self analyses. From a social decentering perspective, this study suggests that when decentering, individuals will increase their use of self and decrease their use of generalized-other as they perceive more similarity between themselves and the target (assuming individuals are adept at using both). But they might adopt the use of self that is actually based on an inaccurate perception of similarity, in which case the use of generalized-other might have been the more effective method.

When the three methods produce competing perspectives, decenterers are faced with a dilemma as to which analysis to accept. The three methods can actually interfere with each other and diminish the quality of all the methods. For example, role-tak-ing research with children suggests that children must learn to control the impact of the highly accessible and salient information on self when considering another person's perspective (Higgins, 1981). A tendency to be egocentric in applying the use of self method of social decentering can undermine the use of the other two methods. Dunning and Hayes (1996) found participants to be egocentric in their social judg-ments about others, most frequently using themselves as the source of comparison, followed by the use of acquaintances, population norms, and then people similar to the target. Epley and Caruso (2009) observed that using the most immediate and easily accessible information provided by an individual's own perspective and expe-riences (use of self method of social decentering) undermines efforts to engage in considering another person's perspective (use of specific-other).

1.3 Social Decentering Theory and Model: Part 1 Summary and Part 2 Preview

Social decentering is defined as a multidimensional social cognitive process that involves taking into account another person's feelings, thoughts, perspectives, and other dispositions in a given situation. Working from that conceptualization, the first steps in this theory and model are presented in this chapter. Specifically, the activation step reflects the factors that contribute to initiating people's efforts to socially decenter. Activation is spurred by both internal triggers that arise from a given person's own cog-nitive processing and by external triggers that stimulate social decentering. The next step involves input or information that is drawn from experiences and observations as well as from imagination. The third step discussed in this chapter is about the three methods used to analyze the information: use of self, use of specific-other, and use of generalized-other. When applying use of self, individuals use their own related expe-riences in a given situation or imagine their reactions to a given situation, and use the resulting analysis to decenter with others. Use of specific-other is the propensity to think about specific people the decenterer knows and apply that knowledge, observations, or imaginings to understanding the other. Finally, just as we have implicit personality theories that are applied to categories of people, the use of generalized-others involves utilizing our general understanding of people or groups of people as the foundation for analyzing a given person in a given situation.

The next chapter provides the final two components in the social decentering process: internal cognitive and affective responses and then, potentially, external responses in the form of strategy and actions. The external responses are not really part of the social decentering process, but instead reflect ways in which people might act upon the results of their social decentering. Thus, after considering a friend's dis-positions upon having his or her romantic relationship come to an end, an individual has lots of options for how to act, options which can be analyzed through social decentering, but which are dependent upon additional interpersonal skills.

1.4 References

Adams-Webber, J. R. (2002). Prototypicality of self and differentiating among others in terms of personal constructs. *Journal of Constructivist Psychology, 16*, 341–347.

Afifi, W.A., & Guerrero, L. K. (2000). Motivations underlying topic avoidance in close relationships. In S. Petronio (Ed.), *Balancing the secrets of private disclosures* (pp. 165–180). Mahwah, NJ: Erlbaum.

Alicke, M. D., Klotz, M. L., Breitenbecher, D. L., Yurak, T. J., & Vredenburg, D. S. (1995). Personal contact, individuation, and the better-than-average effect. *Journal of Personality and Social Psychology, 68*, 804–825.

Altman, I., & Taylor, D. A. (1973). *Social penetration: The development of interpersonal relationships*. New York, NY: Holt, Rinehart, and Winston.

Ames, D. R. (2004). Inside the mind reader's tool kit: Projection and stereotyping in mental state inference. *Journal of personality and social psychology, 87*, 340–353.

Ames, D. R. (2005). Everyday solutions to the problem of other minds: Which tools are used when? In B. F. Malle & S. D. Hodges (Eds.), *Other minds: How humans bridge the divide between self and others* (pp. 158–173). New York, NY: Guilford Press.

Aronfreed, J. (1968). *Conduct and conscience: The socialization of internalized control over behavior*. New York, NY: Academic Press.

Ashmore, R. D. (1981). Sex stereotypes and implicit personality theory. In D. L. Hamilton (Ed.), *Cognitive processes in stereotyping and intergroup behavior* (pp. 37–82). Hillsdale, NJ: Erlbaum.

Ashmore, R. D., & Del Boca, F. K. (1981). Conceptual approaches to stereotypes and stereotyping. In D. L. Hamilton (Ed.), *Cognitive processes in stereotyping and intergroup behavior* (pp. 1–36). Hillsdale, NJ: Erlbaum.

Barnett, M. A. (1984). Perspective-taking and empathy in the child's prosocial behavior. In H. E. Sypher & J. L. Applegate (Eds.), *Communication in children and adults* (pp. 43–62). Thousand Oaks, CA: Sage.

Batson, C. D. (2009). Two forms of perspective-taking: Imaging how another feels and imagining how you would feel. In K. D. Markman, W. M. P. Klein, & J. A. Suhr (Eds.), *Handbook of imagination and mental simulation* (267–280). New York, NY: Psychology Press.

Batson, C. D., Early, S., & Salvarani, G. (1997). Perspective-taking: Imaging how another feels versus imagining how you would feel. *Personality and Social Psychology Bulletin, 23*, 751–758.

Beebe, S. A., Beebe, S. J. & Redmond, M. V. (2017). *Interpersonal communication: Relating to others*. 8th ed. Boston, MA: Pearson.

Beer, J. S., & Ochsner, K. N. (2006). *Social cognition: A multi level analysis*. Brain Research, 1079, 98–105.

Berger, C. R. (2002). Goals and Knowledge Structures in Social Interaction. In M. L. Knapp & J. A. Daly (Eds.), *Handbook of interpersonal communication*, 3rd ed. (pp. 181–214). Thousand Oaks, CA: Sage.

Berger, C. R., & Bradac, J. J. (1982). *Language and social knowledge: Uncertainty in interpersonal relations*. Baltimore, MD: Edward Arnold.

Berlo, D. K. (1960). *The process of communication*. New York, NY: Holt, Rinehart & Winston.

Biernat, M. (2005). *Standards and expectations*. New York, NY: Routledge.

Bloom, P. (2017). Empathy, schmempathy: Response to Zaki. *Trends in Cognitive Sciences, 21*, 60–61.

Boukricha, H. (2008). A first approach for simulating affective theory of mind through mimicry and role-taking. Paper from The Third International Conference on Cognitive Science, Moscow, Russia.

Bronfenbrenner, U., Harding, J., & Gallwey, M. (1968). The measurement of skill in social perception. In D. C. McClelland et al. (Eds.), *Talent and society: New perspectives in the identification of talent* (pp. 29–111). Princeton, NJ: D. Van Nostrand.

Burgoon, J. (1978). A communication model of personal space violations: Explication and an initial test. *Human Communication Research, 4*, 129–142.

Byrne, R. M. J. (2005). *The rational imagination.* Cambridge, MA: MIT Press.

Campbell, J. D., Trapnell, P. D., Heine, S. J., Katz, I. M., Lavallee, L. F., & Lehman, D. R. (1996). Self-concept clarity: Measurement, personality correlates, and cultural boundaries. *Journal of Personality and Social Psychology, 70*, 141–156.

Carpenter, J. M., Green, M. C., & Vacharkulksemsuk, T. (2016). Beyond perspective-taking: Mind-reading motivation. *Motivation and Emotion, 40*, 358–374.

Cheek, N. D. (2015). Taking perspective the next time around. Commentary on: "Perceived perspective-taking: When others walk in our shoes." *Frontiers in Psychology, 6.* Retrieved from: https://doi.org/10.3389/fpsyg.2015.00434.

Clark, R. A., & Delia, J. G. (1977). Cognitive complexity, social perspective-taking, and functional persuasive skills in second- to ninth-grade children. *Human Communication Research, 3*, 128–134.

Colvin, C. R., & Bundick, M. J. (2001). In search of the good judge of personality: Some methodological and theoretical concerns. In J. A. Hall and F. J. Bernieri (Eds.), *Interpersonal sensitivity: Theory and measurement* (pp. 47–66). Mahwah, NJ: Erlbaum.

Cronbach, L. J. (1955). Processes affecting scores on "Understanding of others" and "Assumed similarity." *Psychological Bulletin, 52*, 177–193.

Cuff, B. M. P., Brown, S. J., Taylor, L., & Howat, D. J. (2016). Empathy: A review of the concept. *Emotion Review, 8*, 144–153.

Davis, M. H. (2005). A "constituent" approach to the study of perspective-taking: What are the fundamental elements? In B. F. Malle & S. D. Hodges (Eds.), *Other minds: How humans bridge the divide between self and others* (pp. 44–55). New York, NY: Guilford Press.

Deutsch, F., & Madle, R. A. (1975). Empathy: Historic and current conceptualizations, measurement, and a cognitive theoretical perspective. *Human Development, 18*, 267–287.

Devine, P. G., Hamilton, D. L., & Ostrom, T. M. (eds.) (1994). *Social cognition: Impact on social psychology.* San Diego, CA: Academic Press.

Dickson, W. P. (1982). Two decades of referential communication research: A review and meta-analysis. In C. J. Brainerd & M. Pressly (Eds.), *Verbal processes in children* (pp. 1–34). New York, NY: Springer-Verlag.

Dunning, D. (2001). On the motives underlying social cognition. In A. Tesser & N. Schwarz (Eds.), *Blackwell handbook of social psychology: Intraindividual processes* (pp. 348–374). Malden, MA: Blackwell.

Dunning, D., & Hayes, A. F. (1996). Evidence for egocentric comparison in social judgment. *Journal of Personality and Social Psychology, 71*, 213–229.

Dweck, C. S. (1996). Implicit theories as organizers of goals and behavior. In P. M. Gollwitzer & J. A. Bargh (Eds.), *The psychology of action* (pp. 69–90). New York, NY: Guilford.

Dweck, C. S., Chiu, C., & Hong, Y. (1995). Implicit theories and their role in judgments and reactions: A world from two perspectives. *Psychological Inquiry, 6*, 267–285.

Dymond, R. (1945). A preliminary investigation of the relationships of insight and empathy. *Journal of Consulting Psychology, 12*, 228–233.

Eiser, J. R., Pahl, S., & Prins, Y. R. A. (2001). Optimism, pessimism, and the direction of self-other comparisons. *Journal of Experimental Social Psychology, 37*, 77–84.

Epley, N., & Caruso, E. M. (2009). Perspective-taking: Misstepping into other's shoes. In K. D. Markman, W. M. P. Klein, & J. A. Suhr (Eds.), *Handbook of imagination and mental simulation* (pp. 295–309). New York, NY: Psychology Press.

Fiedler, F. (1968). Personality and situational determinants of leadership effectiveness. In D. Cartwright & A. Zander (Eds.), *Group dynamics: Research and theory*, 3rd ed. (pp. 362–380). New York, NY: Harper and Row.

Fisher, W. (1984). Narration as a human communication paradigm: The case of public moral argument. *Communication Monographs, 51*, 1–22.

Fiske, S. T. (1993). Social cognition and social perception. *Annual Review of Psychology, 44*, 155–194.

Ford, T. E., & Kruglanski, A. W. (1995). Effects of epistemic motivations on the use of accessible constructs in social judgment. *Personality and Social Psychology Bulletin, 21*, 950–962.

Förster, J., & Lieberman, N. (2007). Knowledge activation. In A. W. Kruglanski & E. T. Higgins (Eds.), *Social psychology: Handbook of basic principles*, 2nd ed. (pp. 201–231). New York, NY: Guilford Press.

Försterling, F. (2001). *Attribution: An introduction to theories, research and applications.* Philadelphia, PA: Taylor and Francis.

Frantz, C. M., & Janoff-Bulman, R. (2000). Considering both sides: The limits of perspective-taking. *Basic and Applied Social Psychology, 1*, 31–42.

Funder, D. C. (1995). Stereotypes, base rates, and the fundamental attribution mistake: A content-based approach to judgmental accuracy. In Y. T. Lee, L. J. Jussim, & C. R. McCauley (Eds.), *Stereotype accuracy: Toward appreciating group differences* (pp. 141–156). Washingon, DC: American Psychological Association.

Funder, D. C. (1999). *Personality judgment: A realistic approach to person perception.* San Diego, CA: Academic Press.

Gaut, B. (2003). Creativity and imagination. In B. Gaut & P. Livingston (Eds.), *The creation of art: New essays in philosophical aesthetics* (pp. 148–173). New York, NY: Cambridge University Press.

Gehlbach, H. (2004). A new perspective on perspective-taking: A multidimensional approach to conceptualizing an aptitude. *Educational Psychology Review, 16*, 207–234.

Gerace, A., Day, A., Casey, S., & Mohr, P. (2013). An exploratory investigation of the process of perspective-taking in interpersonal situations. *Journal of Relationships Research, 4*, 1–12.

Gnepp, J. (1989) Children's use of personal information to understand other people's feelings. In Saarni, C. & Harris, P. L. (Eds.), *Children's understanding of emotion* (pp. 151–180). New York, NY: Cambridge University Press.

Graham, T., & Ickes, W. (1997). When women's intuition isn't greater than men's. In W. Ickes (Ed.), *Empathic accuracy* (pp. 117–143). New York, NY: Guilford Press.

Greene, K., Derlega, V. J., & Mathews, A. (2006). Self-disclosure in personal relationships. In A. L. Vangelisti & D. Perlman (Eds.), *The Cambridge handbook of personal relationships* (pp. 409–428). New York, NY: Cambridge University Press.

Gudykunst, W. B., & Hall, B. J. (1994). Strategies for effective communication and adaptation in intergroup contexts. In J. A. Daly & J. M. Wiemann (Eds.), *Strategic interpersonal communication* (pp. 225–272). Hillsdale, NJ: Erlbaum.

Hale, C. L., & Delia, J. G. (1976). Cognitive complexity and social perspective-taking. *Communication Monographs, 43*, 195–203.

Harvey, J. H., & Omarzu, J. (1999). *Minding the close relationship: A theory of relationship enhancement.* New York, NY: Cambridge University Press.

Hastorf, A. H., Schneider, D. J., & Polefka, J. (1970). *Person perception.* Reading, MA: Addison-Wesley.

Heider, F. (1958). *The psychology of interpersonal relations.* New York, NY: Wiley.

Higgins, E. T. (1981). Role-taking and social judgment: Alternative developmental perspectives and processes. In J. H. Flavell and L. Ross (Eds.), *Social cognitive development: Frontiers and possible futures* (pp. 119–153). New York, NY: Cambridge University Press.

Hodges, S. D., Kiel, J. K., Kramer, A. D. I., Veach, D., & Villanueva, B. R. (2010). Giving birth to empathy: The effects of similar experience on empathic accuracy, empathic concern, and perceived empathy. *Personality and Social Psychology Bulletin, 36*, 398–409.

Hojat, M. (2016). *Empathy in health professions education and patient care*. New York, NY: Springer.

Honeycutt, J. M., Zagaki, K. S., & Edwards, R. (1990). Imagined interaction and interpersonal communication. *Communication Reports, 3*, 1–8.

Howard, J. A., & Renfrow, D. G. (2003). Social cognition. In J. Delamater (Ed.), *Handbook of social psychology* (pp. 259–282). New York, NY: Plenum.

Ickes, W. J. (2003). *Everyday mind reading: Understanding what other people think and feel*. Amherst, NY: Prometheus Books.

Ickes, W., Gesn, P. R., & Graham, T. (2000). Gender differences in empathic accuracy: Differential ability or differential motivation?, *Personal Relationships, 7*, 95–109.

Ickes, W., Stinson, L., Bissonnette, V., & Garcia, S. (1990). Naturalistic social cognition: Empathic accuracy in mixed-sex dyads. *Journal of Personality and Social Psychology, 59*, 730–742.

Jussim, L., Cain, T. R., Crawford, J. T., Harber, K., & Cohen, F. (2009). The unbearable accuracy of stereotypes. In T. D. Nelson (Ed.), *Handbook of prejudice, stereotyping, and discrimination* (pp. 199–228). New York, NY: Psychology Press.

Kahneman, D., & Miller, D. T. (1986). Norm theory: Comparing reality to its alternatives. *Psychological Review, 93*, 136–153.

Karniol, R. (1990). Reading people's minds: A transformation rule model for predicting others' thoughts and feelings. In M. P. Zanna (Ed.), *Advances in experimental social psychology*, Vol. 23 (pp. 211–248). San Diego, CA: Harcourt Brace.

Karniol, R. (2003). Egocentrism versus protcentrism: The status of self in social prediction. *Psychological review, 110*, 564–580.

Keysar, B. (2007). Communication and miscommunication: The role of egocentric processes. *Intercultural Pragmatics, 7*, 71–84.

Keysar, B., Barr, D. J., & Horton, W. S. (1998). The egocentric basis of language use: Insights from a processing approach. *Current Directions in Psychological Science, 7*, 46–50.

Krauss, R. M., & Fussell, S. R. (1996). Social psychological models of interpersonal communication. In E. T. Higgins, & A. W. Kruglanski (Eds.), *Social psychology: Handbook of basic principles* (pp. 655–701). New York, NY: Guilford Press.

Langer, E. J. (1978). Rethinking the role of thought in social interaction. In J. H. Harvey, W. J. Ickes, & R. F. Kidd (Eds.), *New directions in attribution research: Volume 2* (pp. 35–58). Hillsdale, NJ: Erlbaum.

Levy, S. R., Stroessner, S. J., & Dweck, C. S. (1998). Stereotype formation and endorsement: The role of implicit theories. *Journal of Personality and Social Psychology, 74*, 1421–1436.

Lin, S., Keysar, B., & Epley, N. (2010). Reflexively mindblind: Using theory of mind to interpret behavior requires effortful attention. *Journal of Experimental Social Psychology, 46*, 551–556.

Long, E. C. J. (1994). Maintaining a stable marriage: Perspective-taking as a predictor or a propensity to divorce. *Journal of Divorce & Remarriage, 21*, 121–138.

Macrae, C. N., & Quadflieg, S. (2010). Perceiving people. In S. Fiske, D. T. Gilbert, & G. Lindzey (Eds.), *Handbook of social psychology*, 5th ed. (pp. 428–463). New York, NY: McGraw-Hill.

Martin, L. L., & Achee, J. W. (1992). Beyond accessibility: The role of processing objectives in judgment. In L. L. Martin & A. Tesser (Eds.), *The construction of social judgments* (pp. 195–216). Hillside, NJ: Erlbaum.

Mead, G. H. (1932). Mind, self, and society. Chicago, IL: University of Chicago Press.

Mehrabian, A., & Epstein, N. (1972). A measure of emotional empathy. *Journal of Personality, 40*, 525–543.

Meneses, R. W., & Larkin, M. (2017). The experience of empathy: Intuitive, sympathetic, and intellectual aspects of social understanding. *Journal of Humanistic Psychology, 57*, 2–32.

Miller, D. T., Turnball, W., & McFarland, C. (1990). Counterfactual thinking and social perception: Thinking about what might have been. In M. P. Zanna (Ed.), *Advances in experimental social psychology*, Vol. 23 (pp. 305–332). New York, NY: Academic Press.

Mischel, W., & Shoda, Y. (2010). The situated person. In B. Mesquita, L. F. Barrett, & E. R. Smith (Eds.), *The mind in context* (pp. 149–173). New York, NY: Guildford Press.

Mitchell, J. P. (2009). Inferences about mental states. *Philosophical Transactions of the Royal Society B, 364*, 1309–1316.

Morris, M. W., Ames, D. R., & Knowles, E. D. (1998). What we theorize when we theorize that we theorize: Examining the "Implicit Theory" construct from a cross-disciplinary perspective. In G. B. Moskowitz (Ed.), *Cognitive social psychology: The Princeton symposium on the legacy and future of social cognition* (pp. 143–162). Mahwah, NJ: Erlbaum.

Moskowitz, G. B. (2005). *Social cognition: Understanding self and others*. New York, NY: Guilford Press.

Murray, S. L., Holmes, J. G., Bellavia, G., Griffin, D. W., & Dolderman, D. (2002). Kindred spirits? The benefits of egocentrism in close relationships. *Journal of Personality and Social Psychology, 82*, 563–581.

Myers, M. W., & Hodges, S. D. (2009). Making it up and making do: Simulation, imagination, and empathic accuracy. In K. D. Markman, W. M. P. Klein, & J. A. Suhr (Eds.), *Handbook of imagination and mental simulation* (pp. 281–294). New York, NY: Psychology Press.

Neuberg, S. L. (1989). The goal of forming accurate impressions during social interactions: Attenuating the impact of negative expectancies. *Journal Personality and Social Psychology, 56*, 374–386.

Nickerson, R. S., Butler, S. F., & Carlin, M. (2009). Empathy and knowledge projection. In J. Decety & W. Ickes (Eds.), *The social neuroscience of empathy* (pp. 43–56). Cambridge, MA: MIT Press.

Ottati, V. & Lee, Y. (1995). Accuracy: A neglected component of stereotype research. In Y. Lee, L. J. Jussim, & C. R. McCauley (Eds.), *Stereotype accuracy: Toward appreciating group differences* (pp. 29–59). Washington, DC: American Psychological Association.

Pahl, S., Eiser, J. R., & White, M. P. (2009). Boundaries of self-positivity: The effect of comparison focus in self-friend comparisons. *The Journal of Social Psychology, 149*, 413–424.

Park, H. S., & Raile, A. N. W. (2010). Perspective-taking and communication satisfaction in coworker dyads. *Journal of Business Psychology, 25*, 569–581.

Piaget, J., & Inhelder, B. (1969). *The psychology of the child*. New York, NY: Basic Books.

Ponn, C. S. K., & Koehler, D. J. (2006). Lay personality knowledge and dispositionist thinking: A knowledge-activation framework. *Journal of Experimental Social Psychology, 42*, 177–191.

Preston, S. D., & de Waal, F. B. M. (2002). Empathy: Its ultimate and proximate bases. *Behavioral and Brain Sciences, 25*, 1–71.

Rafaeli, E., & Hiller, A. (2010). Self-complexity: A source of resilience? In J. W. Reich, A. J. Zautra, & J. S. Hall (Eds.), *Handbook of adult resilience* (pp. 171–192). New York, NY: Guildford.

Read, S. J., & Collins, N. L. (1992). Accounting for relationships: A knowledge structure approach. In J. H. Harvey, T. L. Orbuch, & A. L. Weber (Eds.), *Attributions, accounts, and close relationships* (pp. 116–143). New York, NY: Springer-Verlag.

Redmond, M. V. (1989). The functions of empathy (decentering) in human relations. *Human Relations, 42*, 593–605.

Redmond, M. V. (1995). A multidimensional theory and measure of social decentering. *Journal of Research in Personality, 29*, 35–58.

Redmond, M. V. (2005). Interpersonal content adaptation in everyday interactions. Paper presented at the annual meeting of the National Communication Association, Boston, MA.

Redmond, M. V. (2006). Relationship-specific social decentering: Tapping partner specific empathy and partner specific perspective-taking. Paper presented at the annual meeting of the National Communication Association, San Antonio, Texas.

Reeder, G. D. (2009). Mindreading and dispositional inference: MIM revised and extended. *Psychological Inquiry, 20*, 73–83.

Reeder, G. D. & Trafimow, D. (2005). Attributing motives to other people. In B. F. Malle & S. D. Hodges (Eds.), *Other minds: How humans bridge the divide between self and others* (pp. 106–123). New York, NY: Guilford Press.

Reis, H. T., & Shaver, P. (1988). Intimacy as an interpersonal process. In S. Duck (Ed.), *Handbook of personal relationships* (pp. 367–390). New York: John Wiley & Sons.

Roese, N. J., & Sherman, J. W. (2007). Expectancy. In A. W. Kruglanski & E. T. Higgins (Eds.), *Social psychology: Handbook of basic principles*, 2nd ed. (pp. 91–115). New York, NY: Guilford Press.

Rosenberg, S., & Sedlak, A. (1972). Structural representations of implicit personality theory. In L. Berkowitz (Ed.), *Advances in experimental social psychology*, Vol. 6 (pp. 235–298). New York, NY: Academic Press.

Rusbult, C. E., & Van Lange, P. A. M. (2003). Interdependence, interaction, and relationships. *Annual Review of Psychology, 54*, 351–357.

Sakellaropoulo, M., & Baldwin, M. W. (2006). Interpersonal cognition and the relational self: Paving the empirical road for dialogical science. *International Journal for Dialogical Science, 1*, 47–66.

Schank, R. C., & Abelson, R. P. (1977). *Scripts, plans, goals and understanding: An inquiry into human knowledge structures*. Hillsdale, NJ: L. Erlbaum Associates.

Schneider, D. J. (1973). Implicit personality theory: A review. *Psychological Bulletin, 79*, 294–309.

Schwarz, N. (1998). Warmer and more social: Recent developments in cognitive social psychology. *Annual Review of Sociology, 24*, 239–264.

Sillars, A. L. (1985). Interpersonal perception in relationships. In W. Ickes (Ed.), *Compatible and incompatible relationships* (pp. 277–305). New York, NY: Springer-Verlag.

Sillars, A. L., Roberts, L. J., Leonard, K. E., & Dun, T. (2000). Cognition during marital conflict: The relationship of thought and talk. *Journal of Social and Personal Relationships, 17*, 479–502.

Sillars, A. L., & Scott, M. D. (1983). Interpersonal perception between intimates: An integrative review. *Human Communication Research, 10*, 153–176.

Simpson, J. A., Ickes, W., & Blackstone, T. (1995). When the head protects the heart: Empathic accuracy in dating relationships. *Journal of Personality and Social Psychology, 69*, 629–641.

Stangor, C. (2005). Content and application inaccuracy in social stereotyping. In Y. T. Lee, L. J. Jussim, & C. R. McCauley (Eds.), *Stereotype accuracy: Toward appreciating group differences* (pp. 275–292). Washingon, DC: American Psychological Association.

Stotland, E., Mathews, K. E., Sherman, S. E., Hansson, R. O., & Richardson, B. Z. (1978). *Empathy, fantasy and helping*. Thousand Oaks, CA: Sage.

Talbert, B. (2017). Overthinking and other minds: The analysis paralysis. *Social Epistemology, 31*, 545–556.

Tamir, D. I., & Mitchell, J. P. (2013). Anchoring and adjustment during social inferences. *Journal of Experimental Psychology: General, 142*, 151–162.

Taylor, S. E. (1981). A categorization approach to stereotyping. In D. L. Hamilton (Ed.), *Cognitive processes in stereotyping and intergroup behavior* (pp. 83–114). Hillsdale, NJ: Erlbaum.

Thomas, G., & Fletcher, G. J. O. (1997). Empathic accuracy in close relationships. In W. Ickes (Ed.), *Empathic accuracy* (pp. 194–217). New York, NY: Guilford Press.

Thomas, G., Fletcher, G. J. O., & Lange, C. (1997). On-line accuracy empathic accuracy in marital interaction. *Journal of Personality and Social Psychology, 72*, 839–850.

Thompson, E. P., Roman, R. J., Moskowitz, G. B., Chaiken, S., & Bargh, J. A. (1994). Accuracy motivation attenuates covert priming: The systematic reprocessing of social information. *Journal of Personality and Social Psychology, 66*, 474–490.

Van Boven, L., & Loewenstein, G. (2005). Cross-situational projection. In M. D. Alicke, D. A. Dunning, & J. I. Krueger (Eds.), *The self in social judgement* (pp. 43–66). New York, NY: Psychology Press.

Vorauer, J. (2013). The case for and against perspective-taking. In M. P. Zanna & J. M. Olson (Eds.), *Advances in experimentalsSocial psychology*, Vol. 48 (pp. 59–115). New York, NY: Academic Press.

Waldron, V. R. (1997). Toward a theory of interactive conversational planning. In J. O. Greene (Ed.), *Message production: Advances in communication theory* (pp. 151–170). Mahwah, NJ: Erlbaum.

Wyer, R. S. Jr. (2006). Three models of information processing: An evaluation and conceptual integration. *Psychological Inquiry, 17*, 185–255.

Wyer, R. S. Jr., & Guenfeld, D. H. (1995) Information processing in interpersonal communication. In D. E. Hewes (Ed.), *The cognitive bases of interpersonal communication* (pp. 7–50). Hillsdale, NJ: Erlbaum.

Zaki, J. (2014). Empathy: A motivated account. *Psychological Bulletin, 140*, 1608–1647.

Zaki, J. (2017). Moving beyond stereotypes of empathy. *Trends in Cognitive Sciences, 21*, 59–60.

Zaki, J., & Cikara, M. (2015). Addressing empathic failures. *Current Directions in Psychological Science, 26*, 471–176.

Zorn, T. E., McKinney, M. S., & Moran, M. M. (1993). Structure of interpersonal construct systems: One system or many? *International Journal of Personal Construct Psychology, 6*, 139–166.

2 Theory and Measurement of Social Decentering Part 2: Internal Responses, External Responses, the Multi-Dimensional Scale, and Relationship-Specific Social Decentering

Chapter 1 provides a definition of social decentering as well as a discussion of the first three steps in the social decentering process: activation, input, and analysis. This chapter continues laying out my theoretical model of social decentering with a discussion of outcomes, specifically internal cognitive and affective responses. Potential external responses (strategies and actions) are also presented as products of the social decentering process. Next, this chapter presents a discussion of the development of the multidimensional measure of social decentering.

Research using the Social Decentering Scale revealed a need to supplement the overall theory to include recognition of people's ability to successfully understand and adapt to intimate partners despite weaker social decentering skills. This recognition led to supplementing the social decentering theory by identifying relationship-specific social decentering (RSSD) as a particular form of social decentering that occurs within the context of specific relationships. The rationale for this addition is discussed as well as the development of a measure to assess RSSD.

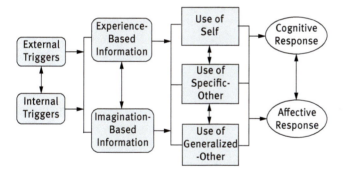

Figure 2.1: Outcomes: Internal responses.

2.1 Outcomes: Internal Responses

One of the most fundamental questions surrounding the concept of empathy is whether it is an affective or cognitive process. Empathy has been treated as either just affective or both affective and cognitive. One approach even uses specific labels to distinguish each – affective empathy and cognitive empathy. While perspective-taking has been

https://doi.org/10.1515/9783110515664-003

identified as a primary cognitive activity, some scholars have also used the phrase affective perspective-taking, recognizing it as a process that is distinct from cognitive perspective-taking. Inherent in this semantic confusion is the fact that humans react both cognitively and affectively to their worlds and that both responses must be included in any global concept of other-centeredness (see Figure 2.1).

The outcomes of social decentering represent the conclusions and reactions that emerge from the process of considering another person's dispositions – it is the product of the analysis, a product that has both cognitive and affective dimensions. But it is misleading to think of human cognition as an assembly line that ends with a final product because while processing information, individuals constantly produce responses that in turn become part of the analysis. Thought is not linear but is dialectical. As individuals analyze, assemble, disassemble, and reassemble information, they react both cognitively and affectively. In simplest terms, individuals respond to both their ongoing analyses and their completed analyses. Ongoing-analysis responses are the thoughts that then serve as a foundation for additional ongoing responses (thoughts and reactions) that continue to loop upon themselves until some end-point or completed-analysis response is reached. This process can involve emotions leading to other emotions, cognitions leading to other cognitions, cognitions leading to emotions, and emotions leading to cognitions (each of these pairs can be further extended any number of times). Thus, people's emotional response to recalling their own experiences in the target's situation can stimulate cognitive analysis and then a further emotional response.

Cognitive and affective responses share a reciprocal relationship: Our thoughts spur our emotions and our emotions spur our thoughts, including thinking about our emotions. The nature of the relationship between cognition and affect, like the nature of emotions in general, remains unsettled. Some have argued that emotions always involve some degree of cognition (Ortony, Clore, & Collins, 1988). Much of the research on emotion within cognitive and social psychology has primarily focused on how emotions affect cognitive processes such as information processing, judgment, impression formation, and stereotyping (for a review see Schwarz & Clore, 2007). Indeed, the relationship between emotional response and cognition comes with a caveat: Emotions can distort cognition (Berkowitz, Jaffe, Jo, & Troccoli, 2000; Clore & Huntsinger, 2007). For example, people in a happy mood process information differently than those in a bad mood (Bless, 2000). The emotional reactions that result from social decentering are likely to interfere with our objective-cognitive analysis and response. As Schwarz (1998) observed, " Feelings may influence judgments either directly, by serving as a source of information, or indirectly, by influencing what comes to mind" (p. 245).

Wyer and Srull (1989) presented a general model of social information processing that identifies a variety of units, such as "executor," "comprehender," "encoder/organizer," and "inference maker." They identify these units as stages in the cognitive process; for example, "inference maker" encompasses the same cognitive activities that contribute to the completed-analysis response of social decentering. The final unit of their model, "response selector," represents the final stage of social decentering, strategy, and actions. Suffice it to say, considerable research and theory has been directed toward mapping the manner in which humans process information and to capture the processes underlying emotion. I will not review that research here, but will instead focus on what is most germane to the theory of social decentering.

2.1.1 Cognitive Response

Cognitive responses consist of the thoughts, interpretations, expectations, judgments, inferences, decisions, and understanding that occur while considering another person's dispositions in a given situation. These responses build upon our observations, knowledge, and analysis of ourselves, people we know, the person we are considering, and people in general. Chapter 1 began with an example where a husband considers telling his wife about the woman that flirted with him but concludes that she might be jealous. His conclusion represents a cognitive response produced through social decentering. In addition, he made a decision on his external response (not to say anything) based on the results of the social decentering process.

One cognitive response might be to reevaluate or reassess the previous input and analysis that occurred while decentering. Having reached some conclusion about another person's dispositions, people might stop to consider how valid and legitimate their analysis has been. People seek to determine their level of confidence in their deductions. In doing so they might decide that their conclusions are based on inadequate information or insufficient analysis. For example, an older teacher considers adding a new assignment in the middle of the semester and reflects on how as a student she personally enjoyed unexpected changes and challenges (use of self). But she might be concerned that today's students won't enjoy the challenge of an additional assignment, so she seeks additional information from some students that she knows. This process of evaluation is almost concurrent with the process of analysis as tentative insights are developed and then assessed. The two processes can occur repeatedly as people strive to reach some point of acceptable confidence in their conclusions. Before reaching outcomes, social decentering involves developing a theory that fits the information and analysis; the subsequent cognitive responses include developing hypotheses and testing them against what is known or deduced. These hypotheses, which are either supported or rejected, serve as the basis for strategic planning (if any external response is even warranted). Rejected hypotheses necessitate amending the original theory – returning to the input and analysis stages of social decentering.

The most general conclusion reached as a cognitive response is understanding. The collection of information and the manner in which we organize and process that information represents our understanding of another person. Our understanding of another person allows us to identify why our partners have acted the way they did, to predict how they will act in the future, and to better develop strategies on how to behave towards them (Finkenauer & Righetti, 2011).

2.1.2 Affective Response

While theories and research on human emotion are extensive, no general theory of emotion has gained universal acceptance. Rather than reviewing the various perspectives, I will present a more general discussion that focuses on how emotions emerge from and affect the social decentering process. I define *affective responses* as the feelings and emotions individuals experience as the result of social decentering. In considering another person's situation, individuals may rekindle their own previous emotional responses. In applying the use of self method of social decentering, individuals may recall or even re-experience emotional memories. Those rekindled feelings might then serve as the basis for their further cognitive analysis and reflection. We have memories of feelings; we can remember feeling depressed, in love, fearful, or joyful. Such memories have both cognitive and affective elements. When we learn or infer another person's affective state, we use our memory of feelings. Through social decentering, you can infer the affective state of a friend who tells you she has fallen in love which can lead to reflecting on what it means to be in love and perhaps experiencing that emotion again yourself to some degree. But our emotional response to a situation might not be the same as that of our target. For example, parents might experience more nervousness than their children do when watching the children in a school pageant. Any emotional reaction that decenterers experience might lead to a cognitive analysis in which they reflect on whether the target is likely to be feeling the same emotions as they are. An important product of effective social decentering then is for decenterers to recognize that their own emotional reactions are similar to or different from their targets'. Batson (2009) cautioned that the feelings evoked through "imagine-self" may distract from and actually inhibit imagining other's emotional response.

Emotions may also be aroused in direct response to the cognitive analysis. After analyzing another person's perspective, individuals might experience emotional responses to their own thoughts. As a husband thinks about how his wife will react to his failure to get her an anniversary gift, he concludes that she will be disappointed and hurt which leads him to feel guilty. Such feelings of guilt are "social emotions" (Leary, 2000), that is emotional responses within the social context (e.g., guilt, jealousy, loneliness, or shame). One consequence of social decentering is likely to be social emotions – "emotions that are aroused by real, imagined, anticipated, or remembered encounters with other people" (Leary, 2000, p. 331). The cognitive analysis also might arouse emotions because of cognitive appraisal. Cognitive appraisal theory posits that emotions arise in response to "evaluative judgments about what is happening" (Lazarus, Kanner, & Folkman, 1980, p. 194). If the outcome of the social decentering process involves developing and evaluating adaptive strategies, then it evokes cognitive appraisal. This appraisal involves determining the impact and any associated benefit or harm that the other person might experience from a situation. Those determinations result in emotional responses – hope, joy, fear, anxiety. The type and degree of emotional arousal that decenterers experience are tied to the way in which they see themselves responding to the situation. As such, placing yourself in someone else's situation means considering how that situation affects the other person and then potentially experiencing the emotions that the other person is feeling. This consequence, experiencing the emotions that another person is experiencing, reflects the conceptualization of empathy as a vicarious response.

Within the theory of social decentering, empathy is a subcategory and is defined more narrowly than it is typically defined in the literature. Specifically, *empathy* is defined as that phenomenon in which people experience emotional responses that are concordant with their target's emotional responses. One scholar who has defined empathy in this manner sees it as "an affective response that stems from the apprehension or comprehension of another's emotional state or condition, and that is identical or very similar to what the other person is feeling or would be expected to feel" (Eisenberg, 2000, p. 677). The degree of concordance varies, and total concordance is rare. To have empathy in this sense at least, people's emotional responses need to be fairly similar to those of their target. For example, if you empathize with a friend who was in financial ruin but just won the lottery, you would experience a feeling of great relief, concordant with your friend's feeling. But the nature of your feelings of relief is unlikely to be exactly the same. How similar must such feelings be in order to truly be considered empathy? Empathy is best conceptualized as occurring in degrees along a continuum with the similarity between the emotional responses ranging from slight to complete.

An important quality of empathy as an emotional response is vicariousness. A truly empathic response occurs as the result of considering or becoming the ephemeral other, not as a direct result of the situation itself nor as a result of emotional contagion or mirroring. Finding out a parent has died might produce similar emotional responses from two siblings, but their emotional responses would not be considered being empathic. Empathy would occur when a good friend of one of the sibling experiences similar feelings by putting herself in that sibling's shoes. In other words, some level of cognitive processing must also take place that takes into account the other person. Eisenberg and Strayer (1987) argued that empathy involves the empathizers differentiating between themselves and others–they experience and distinguish their own emotional states from that of their targets. Thus, individuals recognize their own feelings while they experience the feelings of the other person.

Cognitive processing distinguishes empathy from emotional contagion or mirroring. In emotional contagion, a person engages in the same emotion as another person in response to the other person's behavior without social cognitive processing. For example, a person screams in fear, so the person next to her screams as well without any understanding why (without social cognitive processing). This contagion effect occurs across species, and there is neurological evidence of neuron mirrors that are fired in reaction to such emotional situations. After such automatic emotional reactions, however, people might reflect on the other person's emotional reaction, prompting social decentering, which then might lead to empathy or other emotional responses.

Most of the emotional reactions evoked in individuals from social decentering are likely to be discordant with the target's actual feelings. Discordant responses are not empathy, but they are still legitimate products of social decentering. Any type of emotion can be evoked through social decentering. Affective social decentering responses run the gamut of positive and negative human emotions – love, joy, happiness, anticipation, jealousy, fear, distrust, anger, disappointment. One discordant emotion that is often linked to being other-oriented is sympathy. Sympathy is a unique emotional reaction because it occurs as the direct result of social decentering. To feel sorry for another person's situation requires some consideration of the other person's situation – social decentering. As Eisenberg and Strayer (1987) put it, *sympathy* means "'feeling for' someone, and refers to feelings of sorrow, or feeling sorry for another" (p. 6). Chismar (1988) extended the notion of sympathy to include positive regard, a sense of concern, and even support and compassion. Eisenberg (2000) later added that sympathy is felt toward those who are distressed or needy. But it is possible to feel sorry for someone who is experiencing positive emotions. For example, a friend who wins the lottery is probably feeling ecstatic, but through social decentering, you feel sympathy because you know that he will be pestered by people wanting him to share his newfound wealth and that he doesn't know how to say "No." People sometimes want other people to feel sympathy for their plights. Perhaps feeling distressed or needy, they seek understanding and support. Underlying their desire for sympathy are their implicit expectations that the other person (expectations more likely held for a friend than a stranger) will appreciate their situation (socially decenter), feel sorry for their situation, and perhaps hopefully even provide comfort and support.

Providing a framework for identifying the various affective responses that can be created through social decentering, Ortony, Clore, and Collins (1988) explored possible emotional responses to other people, which they called "fortunes-of-others emotions." Under their framework, a given situation is classified as either desirable or undesirable to the other person. The observer can be either pleased or displeased by the other person's circumstance, thus producing four conditions: pleased – desirable, displeased – undesirable, pleased – undesirable, and displeased – desirable. These conditions create four respective categories of emotional responses: happy-for and sorry-for (good-will emotions), and gloating and resentment (ill-will emotions). Inherent in this model is the observer's evaluation of a situation being desirable or undesirable to the other person. Through social decentering, then, we can assess the desirability of a given situation from the other person's perspective. That assessment arouses the emotions associated with one of the four response categories. Thus, if we are displeased about something unpleasant happening to someone, we feel sorry for that person. But if we are pleased about something unpleasant is happening to another person, we are likely to gloat.

By engaging in social decentering, individuals are likely to experience emotional reactions that are different from those they would experience otherwise. In coming home from work to an elegant dinner that her husband has worked hard to prepare, the wife who does not socially decenter (i.e., takes a more egocentric perspective) might experience only the emotion of relief that she doesn't have to worry about fixing dinner. Thus, her husband might feel taken for granted and unappreciated. But if the wife engages in social decentering, she might experience greater feelings of love toward her husband because she understands the effort and loving care he put into making dinner. Thus, her husband is likely to feel that his wife understood, appreciated, and confirmed his effort and love. The impact on the husband in both cases will likely affect his subsequent behavior toward his wife (e.g., he may treat his egocentric wife coldly and never again make another elegant meal for her). A goal of social decentering is to produce affective responses that lead to effective interactions and relationships; that is, by taking into consideration another person's dispositions, the decenterer increases the likelihood of having emotional responses that are appropriate to the situation and facilitate successful interactions. Through social decentering, a person knows not to display inappropriate emotional responses (e.g., laughing at another person's troubling situation) because of the likely impact such a display would have on the other person. People may have their feelings hurt if they perceive their partner's emotional response is inappropriate, believing that their partner should be sensitive and understanding, that is, to socially decenter. Again, people have an expectation about their partners' ability and even responsibility to socially decenter. This expectation is a key element of a more specific form of social decentering, relationship-specific social decentering, discussed later in this chapter.

As with cognitive responses, individuals might reevaluate the input and analysis that led to the emotions they are experiencing in order to determine the accuracy, reliability, and appropriateness of those emotional responses. The person experiencing sympathy for his lottery winning friend might decide to refocus on the emotions his friend is experiencing, resulting in a more empathic response of joy and celebration. But emotions are not often easy to control or manage, and decenterers may express (at least nonverbally) their initial emotions to the other person. Feeling sympathy for the lottery winner might result in the decenterer initially displaying constrained or negative affective nonverbal behaviors that cause the lottery-winning friend to question his support. Such reevaluation of emotional responses represents another way in which affective and cognitive responses interact as individuals turn their thoughts toward their feelings.

2.2 External Responses: Strategies and Actions

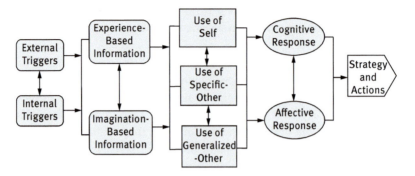

Figure 2.2: Strategies and actions: External responses.

Conceptually, the development of strategies and actions is not an actual stage within social decentering, but a separate activity that occurs subsequent to social decentering (see Figure 2.2). Often times the definition of empathy includes production of some empathic behavior (Hojat, 2016) but others argue that empathy should be viewed as a motive to behave rather than an inherent direct external response (Cuff, Brown, Taylor, & Howat, 2016). But as social decentering is conceptualized, individuals can stop the process at the internal response stage. They can reach an understanding of another person's situation without displaying an external reaction, such as a change in their behavior. In trying to explain the failure to find a correlation between self-ratings of perspective-taking and other's ratings of the target's perspective-taking, Park and Raile (2010) discuss two steps to perspective-taking: understanding the other's perspective and demonstrating that understanding to the other. They note a person's self-rating includes perspective-taking that stops after step one, but observer ratings focus on the behaviors and infer the cognitive process. Thus, people might engage in social decentering, as in perspective-taking and attribution, simply for the goal of understanding the other. Sometimes people appear as though they have not engaged in social decentering because they display no specific adaptive behaviors. For example, a socially decentering parent still scolds his child for eating a cookie right before dinner, even though he understands the child's urge for a cookie. The conclusions that people generate through social decentering provide the foundation for their decisions to act. Social decentering provides three functions relative to developing strategies and actions:

1. Determining the need to act and/or develop a strategy.
2. Providing a foundation for developing strategies.
3. Serving as a tool for assessing each potential strategy.

Social decentering helps us in meeting our personal goals by determining if we need to take any kind of action. In using social decentering as a sense-making activity, you reach a point where your need to act becomes apparent. You observe a woman sitting on a park bench crying, what do you do? You might impulsively express concern or offer help. Or you might stop to consider the cause of the woman's tears (social decentering) and whether you even need to act. When it becomes apparent that you need to do something for the crying woman, to take action, that need to act leads to developing a plan – a strategy. Strategies represent options from which we choose as a way of adapting, addressing problems, and ultimately accomplishing our personal goals.

But people often do not engage in social decentering and therefore don't act when they might otherwise have done so. They might intentionally shy away from social decentering because they are concerned about how they might feel or that they will be required to act. Requests for charitable contributions often begin by trying to activate an other-oriented perspective (to empathize or socially decenter) toward those in need that will in turn spur a donation. Batson (2009) suggested that the likelihood of an altruistic response depends on whether people employ an "imagine-other" or "imagine-self" perspective. Those adopting an imagine-other perspective feel empathy for the target and are likely to engage in altruistic behaviors. Those adopting an imagine-self perspective might be altruistic, but they might also feel personal distress causing them to design behaviors to relieve this tension between altruism and their personal distress (e.g., changing the TV channel to avoid the ad) – that is, to repress their other-orientation.

Social decentering's focus on another person's dispositions and the specific nuances of the situation provides a foundation for developing plans, strategies, and actions. Berger (1988) described the relationships between plans, actions, and goals:

> A plan specifies the actions that are necessary for the attainment of a goal or several goals. Plans vary in their levels of abstraction. Highly abstract plans can spawn more detailed ones. Plans can contain alternative paths for goal attainment from which the social actor can choose (p. 96).

Berger (1997a) viewed the planning process as moving from an abstract plan to concrete actions. Social decentering helps individuals move plans from the abstract to the concrete. The thoughts and feelings generated by social decentering provide the informational bases for developing strategies and plans. The most basic plan requires only the recollection and implementation of a previous strategy that has worked in a given situation with a given person (a canned plan). A wife travels for work with her male boss and understands that her husband feels jealous and insecure. During a prior trip she allayed his fears by talking to him online via Skype right before going to sleep each night. Recognizing that he probably still feels insecure, she uses the same strategy during her current trip. One weakness in repeatedly employing the same strategy is the potential to skip social decentering and apply the strategy out of habit. Such rote application of a strategy fails to make adaptations for changes that might have occurred. For example, the husband of the traveling wife no longer feels insecure, but he becomes concerned by his wife's continued efforts to assure him of her fidelity.

In Berger's (1997a) plan-based theory of strategic communication, people are motivated to formulate specific plans and courses of action when they lack any applicable canned plan. Berger further theorized that the stronger the desire to plan and the more complex the information, the more complex the plan. By generating insight into others and their situations, social decentering provides information that be used in social planning. As people come to understand the thoughts and feelings of others, they can develop and organize strategies around that understanding. Because the information and analysis generated through social decentering vary in complexity, the complexity of the strategies varies accordingly: the greater the complexity of the social decentering, the greater the complexity of the potential strategy. Part of that complexity arises from anticipating a partner's conversational moves which leads to greater success in achieving social goals (Berger, 2008). And anticipating a partner's moves means engaging in social decentering.

Berger (1997b) identified uncertainty as another factor that affects the development and complexity of plans. He proposed that "as uncertainty concerning the message target's linguistic/knowledge status, goals/plans, or affective state increases, planning should become increasingly data driven or bottom up" (p. 227). In essence, the less that individuals know about the other person, the more they need information to develop plans, which may motivate them to engage in social decentering. But individuals who specifically take into account their partner's goals (i.e., who are other-oriented) are generally more effective as well (Berger, 2008).

In discussing the activation stage of social decentering, I suggested that people can be motivated to socially decenter in order to analyze potential strategies. As they develop these possible strategies, people can use social decentering as a tool for assessing each strategy's impact and effectiveness. People apply the process of social decentering to each alternative strategy to predict its likely outcome and the probability of achieving their goals. The strongest decenterers should be the most effective at assessing the outcomes of various strategies and selecting the best. But just because people know the best strategy to implement doesn't mean the strategy will be successful. For example, a person might lack the skills or resources needed to implement the strategy. At the beginning of this chapter, social decentering was defined in terms of considering another person a given situation. Each potential strategy then can represent a variation in adapting to that given situation. But people are able to analyze potential strategies only if they are able to generate alternative situations or strategies – to plan. People might have an ability to socially decenter but little ability to generate alternative strategies.

People may possess *canned plans*, frequently used plans that have become part of their repertoire and can be plugged into given situations. They may implement such a plan without much deliberation or use of social decentering, or they may implement the plan after evaluating it to see if it applies to the situation. If a canned plan is the only strategy that they are considering, the best that social decentering can do is to help them decide whether to accept or reject that strategy. Thus, social decentering can reduce the likelihood of failure by ruling out unsuitable canned plans without necessarily increasing the likelihood of success since there are no alternative plans to consider. For example, a person applied the same canned plan ten times, but it only fit five of the situations resulting in five failed attempts. Suppose social decentering confirmed the appropriateness of the canned plan in four of the five situations, and correctly alerted the person four out of five times when the canned plan would not work. Applying social decentering then, resulted in the person acting appropriately four times (compared to five without social decentering), inappropriately two times (compared to five without social decentering), and withholding any action in four situations (compared to none without social decentering). However, recognizing the four cases in which the canned plan won't work may motivate the person to search for alternatives and thus improve on the five out of ten success rate.

2.2.1 Factors Limiting External Responses

Although social decentering does not always lead to a plan or any display of an external response, some approaches to other-centeredness center around external displays. For example, empathy and perspective-taking are often identified with specific behaviors, particularly in terms of counseling (see, for example, Carkhuff, 1969). While people's behaviors might directly reflect their use of social decentering, the absence of observable behaviors does not necessarily reflect their failure to engage in other-centeredness. Here are some factors that might contribute to the lack of an apparent or external response:

1. **Lack of ability.** Individuals might lack the ability to engage in the requisite behavior. Through social decentering, individuals can identify a specific strategy that may be an effective response, but they might lack the particular skills required to enact that strategy. In discussing plan-based strategic communication, Berger (1997a) noted that "knowledge structures are a necessary but not a sufficient condition for the production of effective social action. Various performance skills also determine the ultimate effectiveness of social action" (p. 7).

   For example, individuals who are extremely uncomfortable with acts of affection might be unable to provide a hug to a friend who is distraught about the death of a parent, even though they know it would help the friend.

2. **Lack of self-control.** Individuals might lack the ability to refrain from making an inappropriate response. Although through social decentering, individuals might know what the appropriate emotional response should be, they might still respond inappropriately. People might still laugh when they find other people's misfortunes amusing, even though they know that such a response will upset the other person. Lacking self-control, people blurt things out that they wish they had not (put their foot in their mouth), knowing that what they've said will

make the situation worse or evoke an unintended response from the other person. Claiming you have socially decentered and still acting inappropriately might be viewed by the target as an even worse offense.

3. **Lack of motivation.** Individuals might lack the personal motivation to enact a response or adapt, particularly when they regard the given relationship as unimportant or undesirable. They may be motivated enough to engage in social decentering but not enough to alter their behavior. An employee who understands the challenges a boss is facing in his divorce might choose not to provide comfort or support because she does not like him.

4. **Self-interest.** Individuals are less likely to enact or adapt a response if they regard their own personal goals and needs as more important than those of the other person. After considering another person's disposition, individuals might decide that the most effective response to the other person requires forfeiting or altering their own goals. Thus, they might decide not to accommodate the other person. For example, a husband understands his wife's feelings about going out for dinner on their anniversary, but doing so means not watching his favorite team play in the Super Bowl. His decision to stay home to watch the game makes it look like he has not socially decentered. A social decenterer must also weigh outside goals against the goals of the target when deciding on a response. Thus, despite understanding an employee's dispositions surrounding a personal crisis at home, a manager might decide to fire the employee because the employee is jeopardizing the company by his mistakes at work. In doing so, the manager is placing the organization's goals and her own managerial responsibilities above adapting to the employee's needs.

5. **Lack of confidence/self-efficacy.** Individuals might lack confidence or self-efficacy in their social decentering ability, thereby undermining their confidence in applying the strategies they develop. Sometimes, as people try to decide which course of action will work best with another person, they second-guess themselves. Individuals need to be confident in the information they have and in their analysis in order to develop an effective strategy; lacking such confidence, they are less likely to engage in any adaptive behavior. Those without self-efficacy believe they are incapable of enacting the strategy.

6. **Asynchronicity.** Individuals' social decentering ability might be asynchronous with their enacted behavior and thus the connection between the two is not apparent. Much of our social decentering occurs in response to two types of situations: an impending situation or a prior one. In the first situation, social decentering is part of planning; the strategies developed are for use at a later time. People think about how they might gain something from another person and, through analyzing the other person's dispositions, select a strategy to implement later. For example, in planning the best approach to ask your boss for a day off, you develop a strategy that involves waiting until Monday morning when the boss is usually in a good mood. In the second situation, social decentering

is used to reach an understanding of prior events; therefore, it does not typically call for any specific response. One value of such reflective social decentering is that the resulting conclusions and inferences become part of the information base on which to anticipate and analyze subsequent situations. But this post-mortem application, people might analyze why a situation turned out poorly and through social decentering, develop a way to repair the problem or regain lost goals; for example, deciding to apologize to your co-worker for something you said the day before.

7. **Noninteractive context.** Finally, individuals might engage in social decentering for situations in which external responses are not necessary. Watching the news about a family who has lost their home to a fire may trigger reflection on the family's experience but does not require specific adaptive behavior. Social decentering can be applied to people we observe in situations on TV, in a movie, in a novel, or whom we hear about from friends. In the narrowest sense of empathy, as a concordant emotional reaction to another person's situation, people may experience the same emotions as a character or observed person without conveying that to the target.

When individuals' affective and cognitive responses are followed by their decision to strategize or act, the breadth and depth of that external response depend on the thoroughness of the analysis and the quality of information that they gleaned. Cursory processing produces narrow and shallow affective and cognitive responses. But cursory processing, which minimizes resource expenditure, might still produce strategies that are sufficient to meet the decenterer's goals. When such cursory-based strategies do not produce the desired results, people might reengage in social decentering, seeking additional information and conducting a more intensive analysis depending upon their assessment of the deficiency. They might recycle through this process several times, depending on their social decentering skills, their ability to gain information, and their ability to develop and implement strategic responses (see Figure 2.3). Unfortunately, people sometimes engage repeatedly in the same failed strategy without recognizing the deficiency and the need to revise their approach. For example, a man with weak social decentering skills uses the same failed affinity-seeking strategy with each new woman he meets. His continued failures stem from not reexamining his strategy from the woman's perspective.

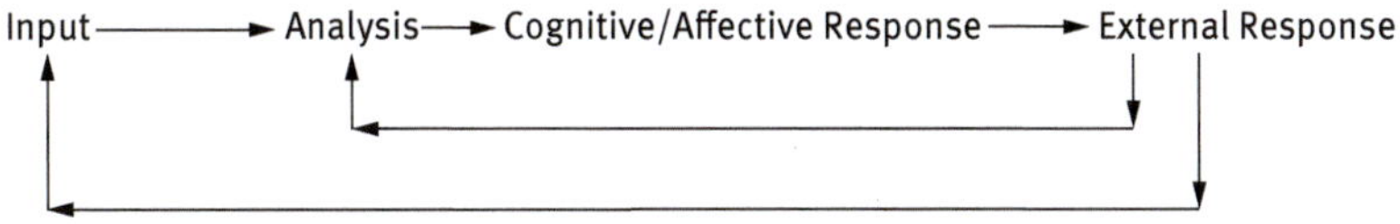

Input ⟶ Analysis ⟶ Cognitive/Affective Response ⟶ External Response

Figure 2.3: External response recycling.

2.3 A Multidimensional Measure of Social Decentering[1]

Conceptually, social decentering is multidimensional, having three primary dimensions: the input, the analysis, and the response. Within each primary dimension are additional subdivisions: Input is divided into experience-based information and imagination-based information; analysis is divided into use of self, specific-other, and generalized-other; and response is divided into cognitive and affective. The multidimensional conceptualization of social decentering led to the decision that the measure should also be multidimensional. The items that constitute the scale are direct extensions of each of the dimensions of social decentering. Such a multidimensional measure differs significantly from that of a popular measure of empathy, Davis's Interpersonal Reactivity Index (IRI).

Davis (1980, 1983) developed the IRI by pooling items from pre-existing measures of empathy as well as creating original items. He then subjected more than 50 items to a factor analysis that produced four significant factors, and he refined the relevant items to produce the final index. In labeling the four factors, he treated each factor as a subscale of empathy: fantasy scale, perspective-taking scale, empathic concern scale, and personal distress scale. An extensive amount of research has been conducted using the IRI as a measure of empathy with the analysis being based primarily on the subscales. But this research often only finds significant results on the perspective-taking and empathic concern subscales. Although Davis (1983) argued that his validation studies show that the four subscales are each tapping similar but different dimensions of empathy. The subscales are rarely combined as a single measure of empathy, which would seem to indicate that rather than measuring four dimensions, they are actually measuring four interdependent but different phenomena. The incorrect use of combining the scales as a measure of empathy led one researcher to publish a reprisal to other researchers about misusing the scale since some subscales are actually negatively related to each other (D' Orazio, 2004). Indeed, the perspective-taking subscale clearly focuses on the cognitive response, whereas the empathic concern and personal-distress subscales assess the affective response. One inherent problem with the IRI is it uses existing measures of empathy (e.g., Stotland's Fantasy–Empathy Scale) to define and operationalize empathy, so any errors or inaccuracies within those conceptualizations are embedded in the subscales. Another problem is that although the subscales measure some type of response, an examination of the items raises questions about whether those subscales are indeed assessing other-oriented or empathic responses. For example, the empathic concern subscale consists of such items as "I would describe myself as a pretty soft-hearted person,"

---

1 Portions of this section reprinted from *Journal of Research in Personality*, 29, Mark V. Redmond, A multidimensional theory and measure of social decentering, pp. 35–58. Copyright (1995), with permission from Elsevier.

"I often have tender, concerned feelings for people less fortunate than me," and "I am often quite touched by things that I see happen." Although such items do assess an individual's own emotional disposition, they do not particularly require taking into consideration the other person's dispositions. In using the scales to analyze romantic relationships, even Davis only used three of the four subscales as a measure of empathy, omitting the fantasy subscale (Davis and Oathout, 1987).

The variety of conceptual definitions of empathy has resulted in a corresponding variety of assessment measures (Bayne & Hays, 2017). Despite the variety of measures of empathy, role taking, and perspective-taking, few of them assess the social cognitive processes or abilities involved in making sense of other's behaviors. Social cognition research related to domains such as attribution and implicit personality theory has tended to be fairly state oriented, depending on the manipulation of inputs and an examination of outputs rather than on examining the processing abilities themselves. One reason for this failure to examine processing abilities might be the inherent problem of developing a multidimensional measure that reflects the process nature of social cognition. Many years ago, Taylor and Fiske (1981) suggested resolving this problem by developing middle-range methodologies for middle-range theories that set the levels and scope of a process model. The levels and scope of social decentering theory and its corresponding measure fit Taylor and Fiske's call for middle-range theories and methodologies.

2.3.1 Item Development and Reliability

The multidimensionality of social decentering is best operationalized by using a multivariate method such as the facet approach (Bell, 1986; Borg, 1979; Dancer, 1985). Facet theory, first introduced by Louis Gottman in 1954, combines a theoretical perspective with a statistical procedure (Canter, 1982). The facet approach provides a prespecified multivariate theoretical model that is subsequently tested (Canter, 1982). Comparing facet theory with its use of smallest space analysis to factor analysis, Maslovaty, Marshall, and Alkin (2001) noted the advantage of the facet approach in connecting theory and analysis. The use of smallest space analysis provides the flexibility of examining facets, partitioning items based on the theory, and analyzing more components or dimensions of the theory than does factor analysis.

Facets represent any set of mutually exclusive categories (Canter, 1985). According to Brown (1985) "facets are proposed by the investigator and are comprised of elements which define the different values that logically and completely describe all of the variations within any facet" (p. 22). The relationships among these sets of categories (facets) are specified in a mapping sentence. Drawing one element of each facet out from the mapping sentence creates a unique facet combination called a "structuple." Thus, a number of structuples (facet combinations) can be derived from any given mapping sentence by combining the various elements of each facet. Facet design sets the limits of the questions and the responses that are tested (Borg & Lingoes, 1987). Questionnaire items can then be generated for each of the facet combinations, thus providing a strong link between the originating theory and its corresponding measure. As a result, each questionnaire item contains more than one dimension.

The facet approach, then, prescribes the nature of the items and relations to be tested between the three dimensions of social decentering, and this nature is reflected in the construction of a mapping sentence:

When a person (X) considers another person's response (Y) to a given situation (Z), that person (X) might

draw upon (A)	(a1 experience-based) (a2 imagination-based)	information
applied to or derived from the use of (B)	(b1 self) (b2 specific-other) (b3 generalized-other)	analysis
producing a (C)	(c1 cognitive) (c2 affective)	response.

The three facets (A, B, C) in the 7 mapping sentence produce 12 unique structuples (facet combinations). Each structuple varies in its associated elements (two for facets A and C and three for facet B), thus producing a 2 × 2 × 3 factorial of 12 possible iterations. For example, one structuple reads: "When a person (X) considers another person's response (Y) to a given situation (Z), that person (X) might draw upon (a1) experience-based information applied to or derived from the (b1) use of self analysis, producing a (c1) cognitive response." This structuple is reflected in the following item that was developed for the instrument: "Sometimes I can understand what others are thinking by recalling the thoughts I have had when I experienced a similar situation." In this item, "recalling the thoughts" represents drawing on experience-based information, "I have had when I experienced a similar situation" represents use of self analysis, and finally, "Sometimes I can understand" represents a cognitive response. In the instrument, three such items were developed for each of the 12 structuples to create a 36-item measure.

Information concerning structuples and the social decentering theory was presented to three colleagues who then evaluated an initial pool of 75 items for each item's fit to one of the twelve structuples. Thirty items were dropped and others refined. Further testing of the remaining 45 items in two pilot studies led to further revisions, deletions, and additions of items in order to establish three reliable items for each structuple.

The multidimensional nature of each scale item means that items can be combined according to their shared elements to produce subscales. Seven subscales were created based on their association with the three facets and their elements: (a1) experience-based subscale, (a2) imagination-based subscale, (b1) use of self subscale, (b2) use of specific-other subscale, (b3) use of generalized-other subscale, (c1) cognitive response subscale, and (c2) affective response subscale. The two elements for the information facet mean that half of the 36 items reflect one element (experience-based), and the other half the other element (imagination-based), thus producing two 18 item subscales, one for each of the two elements. Similarly, two 18 items subscales emerge for responses – cognitive and affective. The analysis facet with its three elements results in 12 of the 36 items reflecting each of its elements; that is, the use of self consists of 12 items, use of specific-other consists another of the 12 items, and use of generalized-other consists of the remaining 12 items.

The validity and reliability tests for the Social Decentering Scale and its subscales were conducted between 1988 and 1990 using the final 36-item instrument – the Social Decentering Scale (see Appendix A). During this time the measure was administered to university students in various communication courses. A total of 587 surveys were completed: 256 males (44%), 315 females (54%), and 16 not reported (<3%). The average age of the participants was 22.26 years.[2] Participants responded to the items on a five-point scale, ranging from strongly agree to strongly disagree. The responses to all relevant items were totaled to create a score for each subscale. The total of all 36 items represents the respondent's overall score on the Social Decentering Scale with possible scores between a low of 36 to a high of 180 with the midpoint being 108. The means, standard deviations, and reliabilities for the overall instrument and each of the facet subscales are presented in Table 2.1 for the composite data collected between 1988 and 1990 (Redmond, 1995).

Between 1992 and 2010, I have collected data in six additional studies using the Social Decentering Scale. I combined and analyzed the responses to the Social Decentering Scale from these studies to obtain further evidence of the reliability of the scale and subscales. This analysis provides additional support for the strength of the scale (see Table 2.1).

One difference between the two samples is the average age of the respondents. The average age in the more recent sample is 26.1 years, whereas the average age of the participants in the 1988–1990 sample was 22.3 years. Part of the reason for the older average in the more recent sample is that the sample includes 101 married couples

---

2 Of the 587 participants, 267 were given a copy of the instrument with an incorrect item, resulting in four items for the first structuple and only two items for the third. I then removed the incorrect item and the affected structuples from analyses, however the remaining 35 items were used to calculate an adjusted overall social decentering score. The remaining 320 participants completed the corrected 36-item instrument (though four incomplete forms were discarded resulting in an N = 316). To maximize the power of some of the analyses (i.e., reliability and the ALSCAL analysis), I used the combined results from both sets of participants for the unaffected subscales. I examined the absence of the 36th item and found that it had a negligible impact on differences in the means and reliabilities between the 35-item and 36-item forms.

Table 2.1: Means, standard deviations, and alpha coefficients.

	1988–1990 Data (N = 316)			1992–2010 Data (N = 1,081)		
	Mean	**SD**	**α**	**Mean**	**SD**	**α**
Overall Social Decentering Scale (36 items)	122.32	16.62	0.91	124.53	16.48	0.91
Experience-based Subscale (18 items)	61.68	8.79	0.84	62.69	8.66	0.82
Imagination-Based Subscale (18 items)	60.59	8.76	0.82	61.84	8.71	0.83
Use of Self Subscale (12 items)	40.39	6.69	0.84	41.06	6.89	0.82
Use of Specific-Other Subscale (12 items)	44.62	6.37	0.80	44.84	6.34	0.79
Use of Generalized-Other Subscale (12 items)	37.26	6.28	0.76	38.63	6.30	0.76
Cognitive Response Subscale (18 items)	63.70	8.71	0.84	64.46	8.53	0.82
Affective Response Subscale (18 items)	58.62	9.95	0.88	60.07	9.76	0.85

(mostly nonstudents) with an average age of 47.1 years. Without those 202 respondents, the average age from the remaining recent five studies is 21.1 years. The more recent sample has a combined 1,081 participants: 483 males (44.7%), 590 females (54.6%), and 8 not reported (>1%). The populations represented in the 1988–1990 and 1992–2010 samples differ in both the age and nature of the participants (the more recent studies include dating couples, married couples, and students drawn from upper-level communication courses). For this reason, differences in means cannot be analyzed for examining possible longitudinal changes in the social decentering of college students. But the coefficients of reliability are unaffected by such variations in the samples and have remained consistent attesting to the strength of the measure.

Female respondents scored significantly higher than male respondents on the overall Social Decentering Scale in both the 1988–1990 sample (female mean = 129.9; male mean = 119; t = 8.71, df = 562, $p < 0.001$) and the 1992–2010 sample (female mean = 128.7; male mean = 119.64; t = 9.26, df = 1071, $p < 0.001$) and on all of the subscales. Such a sex difference is consistent with the research on empathy (Mehrabian & Epstein, 1972) and perspective-taking (Davis, 1980).

To examine test–retest reliability, I administered the Social Decentering Scale to students in an upper-level communication course and then readministered it 14 weeks later. The form used in this study contained the incorrect item that resulted in a 35-item Social Decentering Scale. Nonetheless, the test–retest produced a significant correlation of r = 0.84 (N = 25, $p < 0.001$). The subscale test–retest correlation coefficients ranged from 0.71 to 0.86.

2.3.2 Facet Analysis

I used the ALSCAL multidimensional scaling package of SPSS-X to analyze the facets and structuples (facet combinations) of the Social Decentering Scale. I combined the three items associated with each structuple to form measures of the 12 structuples. I then analyzed the 12 structuples for their fit in creating three unique planes in a three-dimensional model, each associated with a facet. The ALSCAL analysis was based on a treatment of the correlations among the subscales as conditional ordinal data using a Euclidean distance model. Kruskal's stress was 0.07 (R squared = 0.96). This stress value is considerably better than the 0.15 that Norton (1980) suggested for a good solution to nonmetric multidimensional scaling. The three dimension coordinates produced by ALSCAL using the 1988–1990 data show the relative location of the 12 facet combinations that are reported in Table 2.2.

Table 2.2: Coordinates for three-dimensional model of social decentering subscales.

Structuple	Dimension 1	Dimension 2	Dimension 3
ESC (Experience-Self-Cognitive)	0.1548	0.2215	−1.0408
ESA (Experience-Self-Affective)	1.2346	−0.6694	−0.4033
ISC (Imagination-Self-Cognitive)	−0.5106	−0.8357	−1.3520
ISA (Imagination-Self-Affective)	0.7234	−0.4497	−0.5026
EOC (Experience-Other-Cognitive)	−0.7222	1.0520	0.0368
EOA (Experience-Other-Affective)	1.7597	0.6412	0.5034
IOC (Imagination-Other-Cognitive)	0.0061	1.3912	−1.0383
IOA (Imagination-Other-Cognitive)	1.0290	1.0387	1.1597
EGC (Experience-General-Cognitive)	−2.5017	0.1799	0.5996
EGA (Experience-General-Affective)	0.7489	−0.7855	0.6641
IGC (Imagination-General-Cognitive)	−2.3742	−0.3541	0.3087
IGA (Imagination-General-Cognitive)	0.4522	−1.4002	0.7946

The ALSCAL program generated a series of two-dimensional graphs, plotting each of the combinations of dimensions (i.e., 1 with 2, 1 with 3, and 2 with 3), so I used SAS-GRAPH because it generated three-dimensional representations that present a clearer view of the relationships between the facets than can be provided by two dimensional plots. Figure 2.4 represents a plot in three-dimensional space of each of the twelve facet combinations. This plot creates a three-dimensional model in which the distances between each of the 12 facet combinations indicate their relationship to each other. Connecting those facet combination points that make up each of the three methods of social decentering (use of self, use of specific-other, and use of generalized-other) produces the three planes that define the spatial boundaries of each method. None of these planes overlap, which suggests that the instrument items assess different portions of the conceptual field of social decentering.

I also differentiated the items based on the cognitive – affective facet. Doing so created an axial division, with all the cognitive subscales on one side of the axis and all the affective subscales on the other. My imagination – experience facet did not emerge as clearly even though the imagination-based information items are clearly differentiated. In the three-dimensional model, the dimension 3 values (see Table 2.1) for the imagination facets tend to be further from the center than the experience facets with the most notable exceptions being the high value for ESC and low value for FGC. The values for this dimension approximate the pattern of concentric circles labeled a "circumplex" by facet theorists. An examination of the imagination items in the instrument provides one possible explanation for the failure to find a stronger differentiation for this facet. The items frequently asked respondents to assess their "experiences" at fantasizing or imagining, perhaps producing responses which confound imagination-based items with experience-based ones. Similarly, items tapping experience might depend on a certain level of imagination; for instance, one item asks about the respondents' tendency to take into consideration the situation, culture, and ethnic background in their efforts to understand another's behavior. Although this item is intended to assess the degree to which respondents draw on similar experiences, some imagination-based processing is probably required by respondents to consider such intercultural elements.

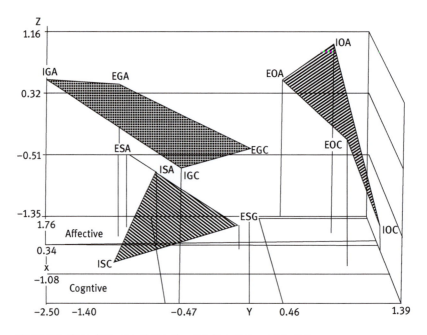

Figure 2.4: Three dimensional plot of social decentering subscales.

2.3.3 Convergent Validity: Measures of Similar Phenomenon

The Social Decentering Scale should correlate with Mehrabian and Epstein's (1972) Measure of Emotional Empathy, a widely used self-report of affective empathy.

The correlation should be moderate since the Social Decentering Scale assesses more than the affective response that the Mehrabian and Epstein instrument taps. This also means the emotional empathy scale should have a stronger correlation with the affective subscale of the Social Decentering Scale than the cognitive subscale. Nonetheless, a significant but weaker relation still might be expected with the cognitive subscale because the emotional empathy measure has previously been found to indicate perspective-taking (Eisenberg & Miller, 1987). Table 2.3 lists correlations between the Social Decentering Scale and several other scales. As Table 2.3 indicates, there is a moderate but significant correlation between the Measure of Emotional Empathy and the Social Decentering Scale. As predicted, the emotional empathy measure correlates more strongly with the affective subscale of the social decentering instrument than with the cognitive subscale (see Table 2.3).

Because role-taking represents the cognitive qualities reflected in social decentering, a moderate relation should also be found between the Social Decentering Scale and a measure of role-taking. Kelley, Phelps, and Simpson (cited in Chmielewski & Wolf, 1979) developed a multidimensional scale to measure three elements of role-taking: role projection, identification of thoughts and moods, and role flexibility. Chmielewski and Wolf examined this measure of role-taking and found supportive reliability for the overall instrument. But through factor analysis, they identified a different set of items and subscales than originally proposed. Thus, given the uncertainty of the subscales, I used only the overall scale in this convergent validation assessment. As predicted, this assessment found moderate but significant correlations between the Social Decentering Scale and the Role-Taking Ability Scale (see Table 2.3).

To provide a direct comparison to another multidimensional measure of other-centeredness, I correlated the Social Decentering Scale and its subscales with a multidimensional empathy scale, Davis's (1980, 1983) Interpersonal Reactivity Index (IRI) and its four scales: fantasy, perspective-taking, empathic concern, and personal distress. Correlations were predicted between the Social Decentering Scale and the first three of Davis's scales because both scales assess the process whereby we take on another's perspective. However, only moderate correlations were expected because the Social Decentering Scale is broader in its conceptualization and Davis's scale is more emotionally oriented. Davis's fourth scale, personal distress, was designed to measure feelings of anxiety and uneasiness in interpersonal settings and this only minimally overlaps with the broader affective subscale of social decentering, so a weak relationship was expected. The results comparing the social decentering scales and IRI scales are presented in Table 2.3. One of the strongest distinctions that occurred was the difference in the correlations between the affective subscales and the personal distress scale ($r = 0.34$, $p < 0.05$), and the cognitive subscale and the personal distress scale ($r = 0.05$, not significant). This distinction demonstrates the discriminative strength of the affective and cognitive subscales of the Social Decentering Scale.

Table 2.3: Correlations of social decentering scale with other scales.

	Social Decentering Scale	Experience-Based	Imagination-Based	Use of Self	Use of Specific-Other	Use of Generalized-Other	Cognitive	Affective
Emotional Empathy Scale (N = 117)	0.64	0.42	0.55	0.65	0.64	0.40	0.42	0.74
Role-Taking Ability Scale (N = 64)	0.43	0.37	0.44	0.48	0.32	0.32	0.40	0.38
Interpersonal Reactivity Index (N = 107)								
Fantasy	0.59	0.54	0.58	0.59	0.52	0.44	0.49	0.58
Perspective-taking	0.50	0.44	0.51	0.47	0.38	0.46	0.57	0.37
Empathic Concern	0.66	0.67	0.58	0.59	0.55	0.59	0.49	0.70
Personal Distress	0.23	0.26	0.17	0.25	0.25	0.09 (ns)	0.05 (ns)	0.34
Communication Competence (N = 68)	0.28	0.20	0.34	0.25	0.39	0.17 (ns)	0.34	0.19 (ns)
Conversational Sensitivity (N = 64)	0.54	0.48	0.53	0.58	0.36	0.45	0.52	0.45
Interpersonal Orientation (N = 114)	0.67	0.68	0.55	0.66	0.55	0.49	0.50	0.66
Personal Report of Communication Apprehension-24 (N = 68)	0.11 (ns)	0.06 (ns)	0.16 (ns)	0.07 (ns)	0.17 (ns)	0.07 (ns)	0.17 (ns)	0.19 (ns)

Note: ns = not significant at $p < .05$

In one study by Davis (1983), the fantasy, empathic concern, and personal distress scales significantly related to a measure of emotionality whereas the perspective-taking scale did not. The three emotionally oriented scales should correlate more strongly with the affective subscale than with the cognitive subscale, and the reverse should be true for Davis's perspective-taking scale. The results shown in Table 2.3 confirm these differences. Davis's fantasy scale should relate more strongly to the imagination-based subscale than to the other social decentering subscales, but the results did not support that expectation. The fantasy scale related only slightly more to the imagination-based subscale than it did to the experience-based subscale. Although the personal distress scale was considerably weaker in its correlation with the imagination-based subscale than the other three IRI scales were, there was little difference between the correlations of the imagination-based subscale with the other three IRI scales. An examination of the items making up the relevant IRI scales provides some insight into why the differences were not greater. Davis's fantasy scale appears to assess respondents' ability to imagine the feelings and actions of fictitious characters in movies, books and plays, whereas the imagination-based subscale was designed to tap respondents' abilities to imagine the feelings and thoughts of themselves, specific others and generalized others in a variety of situations.

2.3.4 Construct Validity: Measures of Related Constructs

Wiemann and Backlund (1980) identify empathy as the most predominant dimension of communication competence, referring to empathy as both a cognitive and affective phenomenon. In this most general sense, empathy is similar to social decentering; therefore, social decentering should be expected to contribute to communication competence. A significant relation should be found between the Social Decentering Scale and measures of communication competence such as the one developed by Wiemann (1975, 1977). But I actually expected the relation between Wiemann's instrument and the Social Decentering Scale to be small but significant because Wiemann's scale includes a number of items designed to assess the additional dimensions of interaction management and social relaxation that are not directly related to social decentering. Wiemann's measure focuses more on the cognitive and behavioral manifestations of communication competence in dyadic situations than on affect, so it was expected to be more related to the cognitive and use of specific-other subscales of the social decentering instrument than to their subscale counterparts. As Table 2.3 shows, the findings uphold these expectations.

Conversational sensitivity, a term coined by Daly, Vangelisti, and Daughton (1987), refers to a person's ability to attend to and interpret a conversation. Several of the skills that contribute to conversational sensitivity also contribute to social decentering: ability to detect deeper and multiple meanings, capacity to remember what was said, being able to come up with alternatives suited for a given situation, and an ability to imagine conversations. Conversational sensitivity is a prerequisite for effective social decentering because such sensitivity is associated with attending to and interpreting information used in social decentering. I expected and found strong relationships between conversational sensitivity, social decentering, and all of the social decentering subscales (see Table 2.3). Swap and Rubin's (1983) measure of interpersonal orientation, the product of research on bargaining and negotiation, was designed to assess how strongly a person has an interest in, reacts to, and takes personally another's behavior. Social decentering requires that a person make sense of another and as such should – and was found to – relate moderately to interpersonal orientation (see Table 2.3).

2.3.5 Predictive Validity

I conducted three specific predictive validity studies. In the first study, toward the end of a semester, five instructors of a basic speech communication course read a two-page description of the multidimensional theory of social decentering. They were then asked to assess (on a scale of 1–100) the level of social decentering that each of their students possessed. Students in one class of each of these instructors completed the social decentering instrument during the last week of the term ($N = 92$). If social decentering affects individuals' behaviors as hypothesized, then instructors should be able to observe some variations in the levels of social decentering displayed by their students during the semester. Instructor ratings should therefore produce a significant correlation with students' scores. Overall, instructor ratings did significantly correlate with student self-ratings ($r = 0.29$) although individual instructor correlations varied from a low of $r = -0.05$ to a high of $r = 0.45$ ($p < 0.05$, $N = 15$).

In the second study, students ($N = 30$) in an upper-level communication course completed the social decentering instrument. Several weeks later they were assigned the task of writing a paper about how they would react cognitively and affectively to a given hypothetical situation. The students were asked to write how they would feel, what they would think, how their best friend would feel, what that friend would think, and finally how people of their age and sex would feel and what they would think if confronted with the same situation. The participants' papers were expected to reflect how well they used the various methods of social decentering, and their ability to produce affective and cognitive responses. Evaluations of the amount of social decentering reflected in their papers should correlate with their scores on the social decentering instrument. But the assigned paper did not lend itself well into differentiating between using experience-based information or using imagination-based information, with examples of the former being limited to student references to their own behaviors and the recollection of other people's behaviors in similar situations.

Two communication faculty members were trained as coders. After carefully reading a discussion on the theory of social decentering, they were given a sample student paper to read and evaluate on the seven subscales and on the student's overall ability to decenter. We discussed their ratings and then they evaluated a second sample paper. After discussing that paper, the coders proceeded to independently evaluate all thirty student papers. The interjudge correlation across the 30 papers for the combined evaluations on the seven subscales was $r = 0.65$ and $r = 0.67$ for the overall social decentering item. The two coders' ratings were combined to produce ratings for each paper that was then compared to the students' actual scores on the social decentering instrument. This comparison resulted in a correlation of $r = 0.47$ between the coders' overall rating of social decentering and the students' social decentering scores, and a correlation of $r = 0.51$ between the combined total of the coders' seven subscale ratings and the students' social decentering scores. The correlations between the coders' and students' scores for each of the seven subscales are as follows: experience-based information, $r = 0.19$ (ns); imagination-based information, $r = 0.35$ (ns); use of self, $r = 0.47$; use of specific-other, $r = 0.42$; use of generalized-other, $r = 0.40$; cognitive response, $r = 0.14$ (ns); and affective response, $r = 0.56$.

The third predictive validity study was based on the premise that individuals who score high on one of the three processing subscales of the social decentering instrument (use of self, use of specific-other, and use of generalized-other) should be able to correspondingly make more discriminations between: (1) themselves and others, (2) their best friend and others, and (3) between some specific category of people and others in general. I developed three forms, one to tap each processing subscale in a procedure similar to Crockett's Role Construct Questionnaire. The forms asked the participants to write down qualities that distinguished: (1) themselves from most other people, (2) one of their best friends from other friends they have, and (3) a white American 80-year-old male from other people in general. Students in an upper level communication course first completed the social decentering instrument ($N = 43$; $M =14$; $F = 29$), and then two weeks later they completed the first two distinguishing forms. They were given five minutes to complete each form. They completed the form for distinguishing the general-other (white, 80-year-old male) a week later to minimize testing effects.

A trained coder and I independently counted the number of unique qualities generated by each participant for each form. The interrater correlation for each form was as follows: self, $r = 0.98$; best friend, $r = 0.97$; 80-year old male, $r = 0.82$. I combined the counts from both of us to form a score for the qualities associated with the self, best friend, and the 80-year-old male. I also combined all three of those scores to get the total number of qualities generated by each participant; overall interrater correlation for this combined total was 0.97. A comparison of the number of qualities identified by students with their scores on the corresponding social decentering subscales is shown in Table 2.4. The results provide some support for the predictive validity of

Table 2.4: Results of Predictive Validity Study 3.

Number of Qualities for:	Social Decentering Subscale	Correlation
1) Themselves from most other people	Use of Self	0.21 ($N = 42$)
2) One of their best friends from other friends	Use of Specific-Other	0.28* ($N = 42$)
3) White American 80-year-old male from other people in general.	Use of Generalized-Other	0.37* ($N = 32$)

* = significant at $p < .05$.

the social decentering with small but significant relationships found for the use of specific-other and use of generalized-other. While the correlation for use of self is positive, the failure to find significance suggests that students generate qualities that distinguish them from other people regardless of their social decentering abilities. This finding also suggests that the use of self might be the most accessible process for people to use when considering another person's dispositions.

2.3.6 Discriminant Validity

Theoretically, communication apprehension should not be related to social decentering. That is, a person's level of oral communication anxiety should not be related to that person's ability to process social information. But, communication apprehension is an appropriate concept to relate to social decentering because both have some impact on communication behavior, albeit for different reasons and with different impacts. McCroskey and Beatty's (1986) Personal Report of Communication Apprehension-24 (PRCA-24) is designed to assess a person's overall oral apprehension as well as a person's apprehension in four communication contexts (group, meeting, dyadic, and public). No significant relation was expected between the social decentering instrument and the PRCA-24, and as expected, the Social Decentering Scale was not found to correlate significantly with the overall PRCA-24 (see Table 2.3).

2.3.7 Validity Summary

As predicted, this multidimensional measure of social decentering related to measures of empathy, role-taking, communication competence, conversational sensitivity, and interpersonal orientation. Strong internal consistency was found for the overall instrument (alpha = 0.91). Each of the seven subscales had moderate to strong reliability. I conducted three studies that provide evidence of the predictive validity of the instrument.

Discriminate validity was partially established by comparing social decentering to communication apprehension. Despite inherent weaknesses and uncertainties, self-report instruments do provide a starting point for investigating a phenomenon. Such instruments allow researchers to classify people according to the quality being assessed (e.g., empathic or interpersonally sensitive), and then the researchers can begin to systematically examine the relations between that quality and other variables.

The social decentering instrument provides a basis for assessing individual differences in social decentering. Those variations can be explored in social behavior, attribution, communication, responses to various communication contexts, and social cognition in general. Social decentering can be examined for its impact in interpersonal relationships, decision making, learning, conflict management, and persuasion. But such an examination has been hampered by the failure to recognize the presence of a multidimensional process and then to develop an instrument that was not unidimensionally bound. Results of my own studies in some of these areas are presented in the later chapters.

The multidimensional Social Decentering Scale that I have presented here overcomes many of the deficiencies associated with previous instruments and should prove valuable in examining social interaction. The items directly correspond to the theoretical model of social decentering, and each dimension of the model is assessed by several items. By being multidimensional then, each of the various combinations of interactions between the three dimensions of input, analysis, and response are equally weighted in the measure.

2.4 Relationship-Specific Social Decentering (RSSD)

Some people are better than others at social decentering and the related skills of being empathic and perspective-taking. We might expect people who possess such other-oriented skills as these to be better able to effectively communicate and manage relationships and therefore would be more successful in their intimate relationships. But research results have failed to consistently demonstrate this effect. For example, several studies have found little to no relationship between such skills and marital satisfaction (Elliott, 1982; Sillars, Pike, Jones, & Murphy, 1984; Wachs & Cordova, 2007; Wastell, 1991). My own studies have failed to find a significant relationship between social decentering and satisfaction in intimate relationships. The failure to find the expected impact of other-oriented processes in intimate relationship is an indication of a more complex process happening in those relationships. These results led me to develop the following premise: in developing intimate relationships, people who lack general social-decentering skills can gain sufficient personal information about their partner to enable them to socially decenter with that particular partner. In other words, they develop a specific type of social decentering that is tailored to their intimate partner – relationship-specific social decentering (RSSD). As partners move toward intimacy and engage in self-disclosure, each partner provides a significant amount of information which creates the expectation that the other partner will retain and adapt to that information accordingly. As a result, a failure to develop social decentering with an intimate partner and adapt behavior accordingly is likely to produce negative responses from the partner and decrease the partner's relational satisfaction.

The effects expected from socially decentering, empathizing, or perspective-taking with a particular partner should be even more likely with the use of RSSD. For example, the ability to be other centered has been identified as an element of communication and interpersonal competence (Allen & Brown, 1976; Rubin, Martin, Bruning, & Powers 1993; Spitzberg & Cupach 1984; Wiemann & Backlund, 1980); as such, RSSD can also be expected to contribute to interpersonal competence, at least within a given relationship. Individuals who can adopt an other-oriented perspective are considered more capable of effectively managing their relationships (Redmond, 1989) and attaining their interpersonal goals (Lakey & Canary, 2002). In similar fashion, RSSD should enhance people's ability to manage specific close relationships and attain their interpersonal goals, albeit in selected relationships.

Research examining the impact of empathy or social decentering on interpersonal relationships has produced mixed results perhaps due to different conceptualizations and measurements of the concept. In a study of married couples, Wastell (1991) measured empathy according to each partner's perception of the spouse (for example, "My partner senses or realizes what I'm feeling." According to Wastall's measurement, empathy did not predict reported marital happiness. In another study of married couples, Thomas, Fletcher, and Lange (1997) adapted Ickes, Stinson, Bissonnette, and Garcia's (1990) method of measuring empathic accuracy. Thomas et al. measured empathic accuracy by having couples view a tape of themselves discussing a problem. After initially identifying their own thoughts, the spouses reviewed the tape and at specified points identified their own thoughts and those of their spouse. Empathic accuracy was then calculated on the basis of one spouse's ability to predict the thoughts identified by the other at those specified times. As measured, empathic accuracy was unrelated to relational satisfaction. And in a longitudinal study of newlyweds, Kilpatrick, Bissonnette, and Rusbult (2002) found that empathic accuracy declined during the first three years of marriage and was related to dyadic adjustment only at six months but not at 18 months or 30 months.

Arriaga and Rusbult (1998) studied undergraduate romantic partners responses to an imagined accommodative dilemma attributed to their partner and found that the respondents' general perspective-taking appreciably related neither to their accommodative behaviors nor to their level of commitment to their partner. And in a study I conducted (Redmond, 2002), I found that social decentering related to persuasive impact in less intimate relationships, but not in intimate ones. In another study (Redmond, 2002), I examined how similar partners were in their social decentering scores. Pairs of relational partners reported on their level of closeness and completed the Social Decentering Scale. Surprisingly, those partners in the closest relationship (the vast majority apparently romantic in nature) had the greatest amount of difference in social decentering scores while those in the least intimate relationships (casual friend and friends) had the most similarity of scores. The results suggest that for intimate relationships, partners form a complementary relationship where one partner's strength in social decentering complements the other partner's deficiency, while friends maintain relationships where they have similar social decentering abilities – a symmetrical relationship. One possibility for these findings is that in intimate relationships, when one partner makes adaptations as the result of social decentering, the other partner does not need to adapt. But another explanation might be that partners form a relationship-specific form of social decentering, which serves as a basis for both partners to consider and adapt to each other in spite of their differences in general social decentering.

2.4.1 Foundations of RSSD

The ability to engage in social decentering, empathy, or perspective-taking is a general social cognitive trait that varies among individuals and provides a foundation for individuals to adapt to various interpersonal interactions. But some of the underlying processes involved in adopting an other-oriented perspective might reflect a state or situational condition (a quality bound by external conditions and in response to a specific circumstance) that depend on gaining information about a particular person, as in intimate relationships. The acquaintanceship effect in which empathic accuracy increases as the level of involvement and information-exchange increases (Colvin, Vogt, & Ickes, 1997; Stinson & Ickes, 1992), provides evidence of this state-like condition. And Ickes's (1993) perspective that empathic accuracy requires a moment-by-moment awareness of another person's internal state infers it. Thomas and Fletcher (1997) described empathic accuracy as the outcome of a process of cognitive and affective perspective-taking and empathy. In this way, empathic accuracy appears to be a relationship-specific form of being other centered. But empathic accuracy has been found between strangers, indicating that it is not solely a state or relationship specific. One reason for this finding might be that the measure of empathic accuracy does not differentiate exclusively between a general ability to predict the thoughts of a person and the ability to predict the thoughts of a particular partner. Cast (2004) has speculated that there are two types of role-taking accuracy, one occurs at the global level and is highly stable while the other is relationship specific and more changeable.

In their study on perspective-taking, Arriaga and Rusbult (1998) differentiated between general perspective-taking and partner perspective-taking. They operationalized both of these concepts using three perspective subscale items from Davis's (1980, 1983) IRI which they adapted in creating three items for general perspective (e. g., "Before criticizing someone, I try to imagine how I would feel if I were in their place") and for three items to assess partner perspective-taking (e. g., "When I am upset or irritated at my partner, I try to imagine how I would feel if I were in his or her shoes."). But that adaptation produced items more akin to the use of self method of social decentering than adapting to the specific relational partner's perspective. In the example just provided regarding being upset or irritated, the focus is on the respondents' own feelings if they were in their partners' situation and not their perception of their partners' actual feelings. Partner-specific assessment then should determine the degree to which individuals understand their particular partners' perspective or feelings.

Long (1990) found that "no perspective-taking measures had been developed to assess perspective-taking within the context of a relationship" (p. 93), so he developed two scales: the Self Dyadic Perspective-Taking Scale (SDPT), which assesses how adequately one person perceives another person's cognitive orientation or perspective, and the Other Dyadic Perspective-Taking Scale (ODPT), which assesses how individuals rate their partner's perspective-taking skills. Long drew items for these scales from several other instruments, leaving out those items that assessed components of empathy as an emotional response and instead selecting items that assessed cognitive and intellectual understanding. As with Arriaga and Rusbult's (1998) measure, some of the SDPT items focused on the individual's own reactions (use of self) in their partner's situation. Despite Long's assertion that his scales did not address empathy, some items included statements that seem to assess emotional responses (e. g., "Before criticizing my partners, I try to imagine how I would feel in his/her place.") The strongest factor of the SDPT consists of items that focus on the *attempt* to understand and not on whether understanding is actually accomplished. In applying his dyadic measures to married couples, Long (1993) found that the general perspective-taking of females in high-adjustment relationships (M =18.88) was not significantly different from that of females in low-adjustment relationships (M =18.43); however, the general perspective-taking of males in high-adjustment relationships was significantly higher than that of males in low-adjustment relationships (M =17.14 vs. 15.15). But even though the means for women were not significantly different from each other, both were higher than that of the males in high-adjustment relationships. As found elsewhere, women generally score higher than men on measures of other-orientation, so it is not surprising that their scores were not linked to marital adjustment. Long did find, however, that both males and females in high-adjustment relationships had significantly higher dyadic (partner-specific) perspective-taking scores than both males and females in the low-adjustment relationships. That is, husbands and wives in high-adjustment relationships reported greater understanding of their spouses' point of view than did husbands and wives in low-adjustment relationships. Since no cause and effect can be claimed, it is unclear whether low adjustment leads to a lack of understanding one another, or if a lack of understanding of one another leads to low adjustment.

Thomas, Fletcher, and Lange (1997) sought to explain why they had not found a relationship between empathic accuracy and the availability of marital partners' behavioral cues. They speculated that partners might hold complex, local, relationship-specific lay theories about each other. As such, they contended that married partners' insights about their spouse relied on detailed knowledge of the spouse's personality, beliefs, feelings, or concerns surrounding a given issue. In addition, they suggested that "behaviors that mean nothing to an outside observer, such as a raised eyebrow or a vein throbbing in the forehead, may be pregnant with meaning to the partner because they are interpreted in light of local, relationship-specific lay theories and knowledge that are inaccessible to the observer" (p. 848).

An example of how relationship-specific orientation affects adaptation to a partner is found in a study on chronic insecurity by Lemay and Dudley (2011). They studied how people responded to romantic partners who were perceived as chronically insecure and found a variety of behaviors that reflect a partner-specific orientation:

> Vigilant perceivers appeared especially adept at detecting daily fluctuations in targets' feelings of insecurity, and they had especially good memories of targets' recent feelings of insecurity. These findings suggest that perceivers' vigilance tunes their cognitive systems to enhance processing of cues relevant to targets' insecurity. (p. 697)

Lemay and Dudley found that vigilant partners exaggerated affection toward their partners when they perceived a crisis, as well as after the crisis, when they remembered the insecurity that their partner experienced the day before. That is, the belief that their partner was chronically insecure led vigilant partners to use exaggerated affection as a strategy to avoid triggering insecurity or to dispel the threat.

2.4.2 A Theory of RSSD

The overarching principle embodied in this addition to the original social decentering theory is that regardless of general social-decentering ability, a person's understanding and ability to adapt to a specific partner generally increases as that relationship moves toward greater intimacy. In other words, people with weaker social-decentering skills are, nonetheless, able to socially decenter within the context of their specific intimate relationships. The resulting understanding serves as a framework for adaptation to a partner as well as creating an expectation in the partner for adaptation by the decenter. Finkenauer and Righetti (2011) see understanding one's partner and responsiveness as essential to close relationships. They contend that people "want to know and understand other's motivations and intentions, because it helps them explain others' behavior in the past, present and future" (p. 317). They note that people want their partners to be responsive by demonstrating that understanding. RSSD is the product of that understanding and the foundation for responsiveness.

Self-disclosure is one of the primary means by which partners gain information about each other and develop RSSD. Altman and Taylor (1973) see relational development as a process by which the move toward intimacy is connected to the breadth and depth of self-disclosure. The disclosure of more information and more intimate information leads to the development of more complex and complete RSSD. But RSSD doesn't derive just from self-disclosures, Colvin et al. (1997) describe the process for creating knowledge structures of partners that explains another manner in which RSSD develops. Colvin et al. wrote that partners "(1) experience common situations and events, (2) observe each other's behavior across these various situations and events, and (3) discuss the thoughts and feelings that occurred to each of them before, during, and after these events took place" (p. 189). The resulting knowledge structures are another element that contributes to RSSD. Implicit in these steps however is the need for a variety of other skills such as the ability to accurately perceive others and the necessary communication skills to discuss thoughts and feelings related to what was observed. The lack of such skills undermines the development of accurate knowledge structures and therefore undermines the development of RSSD. Thomas and Fletcher (2003) incorporated Ickes' empathic accuracy method as their measure of mindreading between dating couples, friends, and strangers. The higher accuracy found between dating couples was attributed to the fact that while the couple, friends, and strangers, each saw the same behavioral data while watching a video replay of an earlier discussion by the dating couple, dating couples were able to draw from "unique and detailed local relationship theories forged over a history of intimate interactions with their dating partner" (p. 1090). RSSD is essentially the combination of these local relationship theories that develop as couples moved toward intimacy.

Intimacy is often defined by the level of knowledge that people have of their partners; to reach the highest levels of intimacy in their relationship, partners must acquire an extensive amount of knowledge about each other. In formulating their intimacy process model, Reis and Shaver (1988) identified having an understanding of your partner as a quality necessary for intimacy, defining *understanding* as "A's belief that B accurately perceives A's needs, constructs, feelings, self-definition, and life predicaments" (p. 380). Such an understanding is the foundation on which RSSD develops in intimate relationships. But just because individuals have extensive knowledge about their partner does not automatically mean that their relationship is intimate; for example, couples in counseling and divorced couples have high-information, low-intimacy relationships.

Rowan, Compton, and Rust (1995) sought to explain the lack of a significant correlation between women's marital satisfaction and empathy scores in their study of married couples. They speculated that the reason for this lack of correlation was because married women might reach a ceiling whereby further increases in their empathy fail to produce corresponding increases in their satisfaction. Therefore, rather than expecting a linear correlation between intimacy and the development or accuracy of RSSD, there is probably an upper threshold at which an increase in knowledge does not create a corresponding increase in RSSD.

Strong social decenterers should more readily develop RSSD and thus move more readily toward intimacy than would weaker social decenterers. That assumption is supported by Arriaga and Rusbult's (1998) finding of a significant correlation ($r = 0.58$, $p < 0.01$) between their measures of general perspective-taking and partner-specific perspective-taking. But because of the interdependent nature of relationships, the rate of a couple's relationship escalation is probably tied to whichever partner is slower in acquiring RSSD. Thus, in a relationship composed of a strong and weak social decenterer, their progress toward intimacy is moderated by the rate by which the weaker social decenterer acquires information and adapts his or her behaviors to the partner. Thus, RSSD needs to be considered as both an individual quality and a quality of the dyad.

The development of mutual RSSD might be a prerequisite to reaching the highest levels of intimacy in a relationship. Finkenauer and Righetti (2011) indicated that feeling understood by a responsive partner showed that the other partner was committed to the relationship, supportive of the other's needs, and provided validation and acceptance of core elements of the other. As couples get to know each other, partners expect each other to adapt their behaviors to what they have learned – inherently expecting their partner to develop and apply RSSD. In essence then, the escalation of a relationship should directly correlate with the partners' increased RSSD abilities. Once a relationship reaches intimacy, we generally expect continued adaptation by our partners. Failure to demonstrate increasing partner-specific adaptation as the relationship escalates is likely to inhibit movement toward intimacy, increase a partner's relational dissatisfaction, and possibly evoke de-escalation and even termination of the relationship. But some individuals might accept their partner's lack of adaptation if, for example, the individuals have low self-esteem, are highly dependent, or have little need for confirmation from that partner. In addition, couples can develop scripts, rituals, or patterns of behavior that they use to more efficiently negotiate their daily interactions. While they might use RSSD to develop their scripts, once established, they no longer need to decenter each time they interact. If the script or routine is positive, its continued use will probably be effective and help maintain the relationship. But if the routine is negative, its continued use will likely have a debilitating effect; for example, the creation of demand-withdraw patterns in response to complaints or conflicts in relationships.

Other-centered processes have been linked to the performance of positive relational behaviors (Cast, 2004), providing additional support for the linking of RSSD with relational satisfaction. Adaptation confirms the value of another person. People's willingness to adapt to their partners conveys support and commitment to their partners. This claim is supported by studies finding that the presence of empathy or perspective-taking is associated with the enactment of positive relational behaviors. For example, Franzoi, Davis, and Young (1985) found that in the heterosexual couples they surveyed, the more that men used male perspective-taking, the more the couple reported using give and take to handle conflict; however, the women's use of perspective-taking was not significantly related. Kilpatrick et al. (2002) found that self-reports of accommodation related to empathic accuracy in married couples, with empathically accurate wives more likely to accommodate to their husbands than were husbands to accommodate to their wives. But in a study of role-taking in married couples, Cast (2004) found that wives reported greater role-taking accuracy than did their husbands but were less likely to behave supportively. Arriaga and Rusbult (1998) reported that partner perspective-taking correlated with reports of positive emotional reactions, relationship enhancing attributions, and constructive preferences. On the other hand, Thomas, Fletcher, and Lange (1997) did not find a significant correlation between married couples' empathic accuracy and positive verbal behaviors, self-reports of satisfaction (either for the self or spouse), or depression. Are individuals who lack other-oriented skills doomed to a life of unsatisfactory and failed intimate relationships? While possessing such skills might increase people's overall effectiveness and efficiency in managing their relationships, their ability to develop RSSD provides one way that they can have relational success even if they lack general interpersonal skills.

The development of RSSD signals a growing intimacy in a relationship. By acquiring, retaining, and using information to adapt to their partners, people convey their relational involvement and commitment; conversely, people who fail to retain and use information from their partners convey a lack of relational involvement and commitment. That is, when people engage in adaptive behavior that reflects an understanding of their partners, people convey their willingness to exert effort and incur a cost for their partner's benefit, thus signaling that they feel the relationship is important. We generally do not put ourselves out for people we do not care about, and we realize that we can increase the effectiveness of our efforts the more we understand our partners and engage in RSSD. But the impact that adaptation has on our partners depends on whether our partners see these behaviors as relevant and helpful (Reis & Shaver, 1988).

2.4.3 Caveats of RSSD

So far this discussion of RSSD has probably created the impression that all individuals develop this skill as their relationships move toward intimacy. But that is an overgeneralization, and there are several factors that limit or prevent RSSD's development. As with general social decentering, RSSD depends on several factors: being motivated to develop RSSD; being motivated to apply RSSD; acquiring sufficient information (through observation, partner self-disclosure, asking questions, and effectively listening); retaining and utilizing the information; recognizing the nuances of a given situation that call for its use; and willingness of the partner to self-disclose.

Developing RSSD takes time and effort; therefore, the decision to develop it depends on the perceived costs and benefits associated with doing so. For this reason, the level of effort people put into developing RSSD correlates with the level of intimacy and commitment to their partner. Individuals are less likely to work on developing RSSD when they perceive their relationships as having little value or lacking the potential for value. But RSSD might occur even when there isn't intimacy if the relationship is perceived as having value or if the benefits of developing RSSD outweigh the costs. For example, employees might be motivated to develop RSSD with their manager as a tactic for successfully managing the manager. Such a situation creates an intriguing interpersonal circumstance in which decenterers need to gain more information about a target with whom they may not have a particular strong or positive relationship.

Even if they have established RSSD, people might not be motivated to apply it if, as with general social decentering, they do not want to invest the required time and effort. One reason people probably employ scripts and routines rather than constantly decentering and adapting is because such routines are easier and save time. As with general social decentering, RSSD may be activated when scripts or routines fail, and a person wants to understand why. The advantage of RSSD over social decentering is that with RSSD, people have more in-depth information about their partners to draw from, which should result in more accurate and successful adaptation, assuming that they have the necessary motivation and skills to enact whatever strategies they develop. Individuals' lack of motivation to engage in RSSD can have negative effects on their relationships and might reflect their acquiescence to its de-escalation or termination.

Developing a base for RSSD requires pre-requisite skills in listening, observing, analyzing, retaining, recalling, and analyzing information. Weaknesses in any of these areas undermine the completeness and effectiveness of RSSD. For example, people who do not listen well and have not acquired specific information about their partners will not be able to effectively develop RSSD.

In addition to managing information about their partner, individuals need to manage information about the given situation – to recognize the impact of a given situation on their specific partner. Failure to do so can occur because they lack information about the situation, fail to consider the nuances of the situation, or fail to connect the situation to their knowledge about their partner. Responding to a close friend who has been fired is difficult without knowing the reasons behind the firing. While it is possible to provide general comfort and support, the response might be quite different if the reason for the firing was that the friend stole money. At a social gathering of coworkers and their spouses, after someone shares a funny story about getting stranded at an airport, a wife suggests that her husband should tell the story about how he once got stuck on an elevator for three hours. He declines and later expresses his dismay over her suggestion because he felt the story was embarrassing and would have make him look bad to his cow-orkers and boss. The wife had failed to recognize that even though it was a social situation, her husband was still concerned about his work image. Connecting information about a given partner to a given situation then, requires skill at syn-thesizing diverse information.

Since RSSD depends upon acquiring information from a partner, it can be under-mined by a partner who is reluctant to share personal information (Rosenblatt & Wieling, 2013). Limiting self-disclosure can be used as a strategy for preventing the escalation of a relationship (Beebe, Beebe, & Redmond, 2017), as when someone is uncertain about the relationship or because of commitment issues. Partners might withhold information that they worry will be viewed negatively, or that makes them vulnerable. Sometimes information is not shared or lies are told in order to prevent harming the relationship or the partner (Rosenblatt & Wieling, 2013). Besides limiting self-disclosures, people might choose to limit their partners from meeting or interacting with their family and friends, again restricting the ability to gain insight and understanding of the partner's values, beliefs, attitudes, and behaviors from these sources. For example, if the partner comes from a dysfunctional family, the opportunity to interact and observe that family can help in developing a sensitivity about how such factors affect the partner. Lower scores on a measure of RSSD might be the result of a partner withholding personal information rather than inadequate skills on the part of the decenterer.

People's ability to use RSSD is also limited by their egocentrism, self-absorption, and even narcissism. When people fail to recognize the concerns of others, they are inherently unable to employ other-oriented processes such as RSSD. Egocentrism has been studied primarily in terms of child development, and these studies have found that increases in people's concern for others correspond to getting older. Since much of the egocentrism research relates primarily to visual and spatial tasks, such a finding makes sense. But from a cognitive perspective, egocentrism is reflected in an individual's general inclination to think primarily of themselves (their values, perspectives, thoughts, and feelings) to the detriment of their being sensitive to the disposition of others. Murray, Holmes, Bellavia, Griffin, and Dolderman (2002) found that married individuals acted egocentrically toward their partners by projecting their values, day-to-day feelings, and traits onto their partner. Egocentrism was measured as the degree to which projections of self-qualities on the partner differed from those actually reported by the partner. They found that greater egocentrism was related to greater relational satisfaction and less conflict. In other words, egocentrism led to the perception of greater similarity with the partner, with such similarity perhaps influencing satisfaction. In both married and dating couples, Murray et al. also found that feeling understood increased satisfaction, which suggests that the perception of a partner's RSSD should also relate to greater relational satisfaction. In addition, simply perceiving similarity led participants to feel understood by their partners. The results of this study raise questions about the impact of the actual understanding one's partner on various relational outcomes. Thus, a measure of RSSD as an independently occurring phenomenon will be useful in studying the relationship of such variables as perceived understanding, actual understanding, egocentrism, relational satisfaction, and conflict.

2.4.4 Measurement of RSSD

The measure of RSSD is an extension of the measure of social decentering that I described earlier. The RSSD Scale is a modification of the subscale for assessing the use of specific-other in the social decentering measure. As such, the items are again multidimensional, each containing a reference to either experience- or imagination-based information, to the use of self, other, or generalized-other and finally to a cognitive or affective response. The 12 items from the use of specific-other subscale were modified as were the instructions for the RSSD Scale. While the use of specific-other subscale in the social decentering measure does ask respondents to "think about a close friend," the questions do not require them to think about the same specific-other person when responding to each question. In that way, a sample is taken of how they respond to specific others in general. For the RSSD Scale, the items and instructions ask the respondents to focus on one specific partner. For example, in a study examining escalating and de-escalating mixed-sex relationships, both partners were present while completing the RSSD Scale and instructed to complete the items in regard to the partner that was with them. In a study examining marital communication, the instructions and 12 items directed participants to respond relative to their spouse.

Since the use of specific-other subscale has some items directing respondents to think of a particular person, questions arise about whether the RSSD Scale will actually be discriminating and if the RSSD Scale assesses different cognitive processes than does the use of specific-other subscale as claimed. In the study of escalating mixed-sex relationships, the RSSD Scale and specific-other subscale had a moderate correlation of $r = 0.40$ ($p < .001$, $n = 172$). The RSSD Scale's correlation with the overall Social Decentering Scale was 0.46 ($p < .001$), which is also moderate but is considerably less than the specific-other scale's strong correlation with the overall decentering scale of 0.82 ($p < .001$). These moderate relationships that account for 16% and 21% of the shared variance between the RSSD Scale and the other two scales, respectively, seem reasonable given that all three scales share the same three dimensions and focus on taking into account other people's dispositions. But the fact that 84% of the variance in the RSSD Scale is not shared with the use of specific-other subscale provides support for RSSD being a discreet variable. Similar results were found with the married couple sample though the correlations were stronger between the RSSD Scale and use of specific-other subscale ($r = 0.56$, $p < .001$, $n = 202$) and between the RSSD Scale and the overall decentering measure ($r = 0.54$, $p < 0.001$). These are still considerably less than the correlation of 0.90 found between the overall measure and the use of specific-other subscale.

Reliability of the RSSD Scale was good, producing a Cronbach's alpha of 0.87 ($n = 172$) from the sample of escalating mixed-sex couples, and 0.79 ($n = 197$) for the married couples sample. I will present further detail on how this measure relates to additional concepts such as relational satisfaction, relational assessment, and intimacy in the chapters on interpersonal relationships and marital relationships.

2.5 A Preview of the Impact of Social Decentering on Social Interactions and Interpersonal Relationships

The remainder of this book details the impact of social decentering on all aspects of our lives, especially on our interpersonal relationships. Social decentering provides us with an invaluable understanding of those with whom we are closest and have the greatest amount of personal information. Our use of social decentering affects our development and maintenance of interpersonal relationships. Fortunately, weakness in social decentering does not prevent people from developing interpersonal relationships. Later in the book, I present evidence showing that social decentering can exist as a complementary relational skill in which one member is a high social decenterer and the other is a low one. High social decenterers are more likely to understand and adapt to their partners lack of social decentering. But even in these complementary relationships there are limits to partners' willingness to accommodate. Social decentering is simply another tool we can use to achieve and manage our social and personal goals but does not insure either happy or successful relationships.

The immediacy of interpersonal interactions limits the depth of social decentering, but does not negate its impact entirely. Individuals do adapt their immediate reactions to their partners. By socially decentering, speakers consider their listeners' knowledge and perspectives and adapt the examples and information that they provide. They might elect to withhold information because they predict that it will have a negative impact on their listeners. Failure to apply social decentering can have negative consequences as people make insensitive statements to their partners; statements the person "should have known better" not to say. Failure to adapt can result in hurt feelings, the deterioration or end the interaction, and even damage the relationship.

Social decentering applies to our relationships with family, friends, spouses, and coworkers. I discuss the impact of social decentering on manager-subordinate relationships in detail later, but suffice it to say, the impact can be both positive and negative. Although social decentering can help managers effectively adapt messages to employees and build positive working relationships, it can also undermine objective decision making when their decisions become focused on the welfare of a given employee over that of the organization.

Within a marriage, spousal social decentering interacts with a variety of other variables to affect marital satisfaction. In the most intimate relationships, people expect their partners to understand them and display that understanding through their sensitivity and appropriately adapted behavior. Failure to show such sensitivity is likely to erode relational satisfaction. Even those spouses with weak social decentering skills are expected to develop RSSD. Such RSSD develops because of the amount of disclosure and interaction that occurs within intimate relationships. Because intimate partners come to know each other extremely well, they develop certain expectations regarding that mutual knowledge. But just because spouses develop strong RSSD does not mean that their marriage will be successful or satisfying. Factors such as shared decision making, fidelity, equity, role fulfillment, and communication quality, all impact the quality of a marriage. The role in marriage of other-oriented phenomena, such as social decentering, is more complex than most people imagine.

Taking into consideration another person's dispositions through social decentering provides insight that we might not otherwise garner, helping us to accomplish our personal and social goals. Social decentering also makes us susceptible to feelings and thoughts we would not have otherwise experienced. We are vulnerable to manipulation by others who exploit our other-orientation. People might provide false information that undermines our ability to accurately analyze information about them thus leading to responses that favor the manipulators. In addition to false or incomplete information, a variety of perceptual and conceptual biases discussed in Chapter 1 also affect the accuracy of the process. Nonetheless, the ability to consider another person's thoughts, feelings, perspectives and other dispositions is a powerful cognitive tool that allows us to connect with other people on an almost magical level.

2.6 References

Allen, R. R., & Brown, K. I. (1976). *Developing communication competence in children*. Skokie, IL: National Textbook Company.

Altman, I., & Taylor, D. A. (1973). *Social penetration: The development of interpersonal relationships*. New York: Holt, Rinehart, & Winston.

Arriaga, X. B., & Rusbult, C. E. (1998). Standing in my partner's shoes: Partner perspective-taking and reactions to accommodative dilemmas. *Personality and Social Psychology Bulletin, 24*, 927–948.

Batson, C. D. (2009). These things called empathy: Eight related but distinct phenomena. In J. Decety & W. Ickes (Eds.), *The social neuroscience of empathy* (pp. 3–15). Cambridge, MA: MIT Press.

Bayne, H. B., & Hays, D. G. (2017). Examining conditions for empathy in counseling: An exploratory model. *Journal of Humanistic Counseling, 56*, 32–52.

Bell, R. A. (1986). The multivariate structure of communication avoidance. *Communication Monographs, 53*, 365–375.

Berger, C. R. (1988). Planning, affect, and social action generation. In R. L. Donohew, H. Sypher, & E. T. Higgins, (Eds.), *Communication social cognition and affect* (pp. 93–116). Hillsdale, NJ: Lawrence Erlbaum.

Berger, C. R. (1997a). *Planning strategic interaction: Attaining goals through communication action.* Mahwah, NJ: Erlbaum.

Berger, C. R. (1997b). Producing messages under uncertainty. In J. Greene (Ed.), *Message production: Advances in communication theory* (pp. 221–244). Mahwah, NJ: Lawrence Erlbaum.

Berger, C. R. (2008) Planning theory of communication in L. A. Baxter and D. O. Braithwaite (Eds.), *Engaging theories in interpersonal communication: Multiple perspectives* (pp. 89–102). Thousand Oaks, CA: Sage.

Berkowitz, L., Jaffee, S., Jo, E., & Troccoli, B. T. (2000). On the correction of feeling-induced judgmental biases. In J. P. Forgas (Ed.), *Feeling and thinking: The role of affect in social cognition* (pp. 131–153). New York: Cambridge University Press.

Bless, H. (2000). The interplay of affect and cognition. In J. P. Forgas (Ed.), *Feeling and thinking: The role of affect in social cognition* (pp. 201–222). New York: Cambridge University Press.

Borg, I. (1979). Some basic concepts of facet theory. In J. C. Lingoes & I. Borg (Eds.), *Geometric representations of relational data* (pp. 65–102). Ann Arbor: Mathesis.

Borg, I., & Lingoes, J. (1987). *Multidimensional similarity structure analysis.* New York: Springer-Verlag.

Brown, J. (1985). An introduction to the uses of facet theory. In Canter, D. (Ed.), *Facet theory: Approaches to social research* (pp. 17–57). New York: Springer-Verlag.

Canter, D. (1982). Facet approach to applied research. *Perceptual and Motor Skills, 55,* 143–154.

Canter, D. (1985). *Facet theory: Approaches to social research.* New York: Springer-Verlag

Cast, A. (2004). Role-taking and interaction. *Social Psychology Quarterly, 67,* 296–309.

Chmielewski, T. L., & Wolf, L. (1979). Assessing the reliability of a scale to measure role-taking ability. Paper presented at the annual convention of the Speech Communication Association, San Antonio, TX.

Clore, G. L., & Huntsinger, J. R. (2007). How emotions inform judgment and regulate thought. *Trends in Cognitive Science, 11,* 393–300.

Colvin, C. R., Vogt, D., & Ickes, W. J. (1997). Why do friends understand each other better than strangers do? In W. J. Ickes (Ed.), *Empathic accuracy* (pp. 169–193). New York: Guildford Press.

Cuff, B. M. P., Brown, S. J., Taylor, L., & Howat, D. J. (2016). Empathy: A review of the concept. *Emotion Review, 8,* 144–153.

D' Orazio, D. M. (2004). Letter to the editor. *Sexual Abuse: A Journal of Research and Treatment, 16,* 173–174.

Daly, J. A., Vangelisti, A. L., & Daughton, S. M. (1987). The nature and correlates of conversational sensitivity. *Human Communication Research, 14,* 167–202.

Dancer, L. S. (1985). On the multidimensional structure of self-esteem: Facet analysis of Rosenberg's Self-Esteem Scale. In D. Canter (Ed.), *Facet theory,* (pp. 223–236). New York: Springer-Verlag.

Davis, M. H. (1980). A multidimensional approach to individual differences in empathy. *JSAS Catalog of Selected Documents in Psychology, 10,* 85.

Davis, M. H. (1983). Measuring individual differences in empathy: Evidence for a multidimensional approach. *Journal of Personality and Social Psychology, 44,* 113–126.

Davis, M. H., & Kraus, L. A. (1991). Dispositional empathy and social relationships. In W. H. Jones & D. Perlman (Eds.), *Advances in personal relationships* (Vol. 3) (pp. 75–115). London: Jessica Kingsley.

Eisenberg, N. (2000). Empathy and sympathy. In M. Lewis & Haviland-Jones, J. M. (Eds.), *Handbook of emotions,* 2nd edn. (pp. 677–691). New York: Guilford.

Eisenberg, N., & Miller, P. A. (1987). The relation of empathy to prosocial and related behaviors. *Psychological Bulletin*, 101, 91–119.

Eisenberg, N., & Strayer, J. (1987). Critical issues in the study of empathy. In N. Eisenberg and J. Strayer (Eds.), *Empathy and its development* (pp. 1–13). New York: Cambridge University Press.

Finkenauer, C., & Righetti, F. (2011). Understanding in close relationships: An interpersonal approach. In W. Stroebe & M. Hewstone (Eds.) *European Review of Social Psychology*, Vol. 22, (pp. 316–363). New York: Psychology Press.

Franzoi, S. L., Davis, M. H., & Young, R. D. (1985). The effects of private self-consciousness and perspective-taking on satisfaction in close relationships. *Journal of Personality and Social Psychology*, 48, 1584–1594.

Hojat, M. (2016). *Empathy in health professions education and patient care*. New York: Springer.

Ickes, W. (1993). Empathic accuracy. *Journal of Personality*, 61, 587–610.

Ickes, W., Stinson, L., Bissonnette, V., & Garcia, S. (1990). Naturalistic social cognition: Empathic accuracy in mixed-sex dyads. *Journal of Personality and Social Psychology*, 59, 730–742.

Kilpatrick, S. D., Bissonnette, V. L., & Rusbult, C. E. (2002). Empathic accuracy and accommodative behavior among newly married couples. *Personal Relationships*, 9, 369–393.

Lakey, S. G., & Canary, D. J. (2002). Actor goal achievement and sensitivity to partner as critical factors in understanding interpersonal communication competence and conflict strategies. *Communication Monographs*, 69, 217–235.

Lazarus, R. S., Kanner, A. D., & Folkman, S. (1980). Emotions: A cognitive-phenomenological analysis. In R. Plutchik & H. Kellerman (Eds.), *Emotion: Theory, research, and experience*, Vol. 1. (pp. 189–218). New York: Academic Press.

Leary, M. R. (2000). Affect, cognition, and social emotions. In J. P. Forgas (ed.), *Feeling and thinking: The role of affect in social cognition* (pp. 331–356). New York: Cambridge University Press.

Lemay Jr., E. P., & Dudley, K. L. (2011). Caution: Fragile! Regulating the interpersonal insecurity of chronically insecure partners. *Journal of Personality and Social Psychology*, 100, 681–702.

Long, E. C. J. (1990). Measuring dyadic perspective-taking: Two scales for assessing perspective-taking in marriage and similar dyads. *Educational and Psychological Measurement*, 50, 91–103.

Long, E. C. J. (1993). Perspective-taking differences between high- and low-adjustment marriages: Implications for those in intervention. *The American Journal of Family Therapy*, 21, 248–259.

Maslovaty, N., Marshall, A. E., & Alkin, M. C. (2001). Teacher's perceptions structured through facet theory: Smallest space analysis versus factor analysis. *Educational and Psychological Measurement*, 61, 71–84.

McCroskey, J. C., & Beatty, M. J. (1986). Oral communication apprehension. In W. H. Jones, J. M Cheek & S. R. Briggs (Eds.), *Shyness: Perspectives on research and treatment* (pp. 279–293). New York: Plenum Press.

Mehrabian, A., & Epstein, N. (1972). A measure of emotional empathy. *Journal of Personality*, 40, 525–543.

Murray, S. L., Holmes, J. G., Bellavia, G., Griffin, D. W., & Dolderman, D. (2002). Kindred spirits? The benefits of egocentrism in close relationships. *Journal of Personality and Social Psychology*, 82, 563–581.

Norton, R. W. (1980). Nonmetric multidimensional scaling in communication research: Smallest space analysis. In P. R. Monge, & J. N. Cappella (Eds.), *Multivariate techniques in human communication research* (pp. 309–331). New York: Academic Press.

Ortony, A. Clore, G. L., & Collins, A. (1988). *The cognitive structure of emotions*. New York: Cambridge University Press.

Park, H. S., & Raile, A. N. W. (2010). Perspective-taking and communication satisfaction in coworker dyads. *Journal of Business Psychology, 25*, 569–581.

Redmond, M. V. (1989). The functions of empathy (decentering) in human relations. *Human Relations, 42*, 593–605.

Redmond, M. V. (1995). A multidimensional theory and measure of social decentering. *Journal of Research in Personality, 29*, 35–58.

Redmond, M. V. (2002). Social decentering, intimacy, and interpersonal influence. Paper presented at the annual meeting of the National Communication Association, New Orleans.

Reis, H. T., & Shaver, P. (1988). Intimacy as an interpersonal process. In S. Duck (Ed.) *Handbook of personal relationships* (pp. 367–390). New York: John Wiley & Sons.

Rosenblatt, P. C., & Wieling, E. (2013). *Knowing and not knowing in intimate relationships*. New York: Cambridge University Press.

Rowan, D. G., Compton, W. C., & Rust, J. O. (1995). Self-actualization and empathy as predictors of marital satisfaction. *Psychological Reports, 77*, 1011–1016.

Rubin, R. B., Martin, M. M., Bruning, S. S., & Powers, D. E. (1993). Test of a self-efficacy model of interpersonal communication competence. *Communication Quarterly, 41*, 210–220.

Schwarz, N., & Clore, G. L. (2007). Feelings and phenomenal experiences. In A. W. Kruglanski & E. T. Higgins (Eds.), *Social psychology: Handbook of basic principles*, 2nd edn. (pp. 385–407). New York: Guilford Press.

Spitzberg, B. H., & Cupach, W. R. (1984). *Interpersonal communication competence*. Beverly Hills: Sage.

Stinson, L., & Ickes, W. (1992). Empathic accuracy in the interactions of male friends versus male strangers. *Journal of Personality and Social Psychology, 62*, 787–797.

Taylor, S. E., & Fiske, S. T. (1981). Getting inside the head: Methodologies for process analysis in attribution and social cognition. In Harvey, J. J., Ickes, W., & Kidd, R. F. (Eds.), *New directions in attribution research*, Vol. 3 (pp. 459–524). Hillsdale, N.J.: Erlbaum.

Thomas, G., & Fletcher, G. J. O. (1997). Empathic accuracy in close relationships. In W. Ickes (Ed.), *Empathic accuracy*. (pp. 194–217). New York: Guilford Press.

Thomas, G., & Fletcher, G. J. O. (2003). Mind-reading accuracy in intimate relationships: Assessing the roles of the relationship, the target, and the judge. *Journal of Personality and Social Psychology, 85*, 1079–1094.

Thomas, G., Fletcher, G. J. O., & Lange, C. (1997). On-line empathic accuracy in marital interaction. *Journal of Personality and Social Psychology, 72*, 839–850.

Wastell, C. A. (1991). Empathy in marriage. *Australian Journal of Marriage and Family, 12*, 27–38.

Wiemann, J. M. (1975). An exploration of communicative competence in initial interactions. Unpublished doctoral dissertation, Purdue University.

Wiemann, J. M. (1977). Explication and test of a model of communicative competence. *Human Communication Research, 3*, 195–213.

Wiemann, J., & Backlund, P. M. (1980). Current theory and research in communication competence. *Review of Educational Research, 50*, 185–199.

Wyer, R. S. Jr., & Srull, T. K. (1989). *Memory and cognition in its social context*. Hillsdale, NJ: Erlbaum.

3 Social Decentering, Relationship-Specific Social Decentering (RSSD), and Interpersonal Relationships

One of the significant reasons for using social decentering presented in Chapter 1 was to achieve our social goals. Social decentering and relationship-specific social decentering (RSSD) are tools people use to manage their relationships and meet personal goals. The ability to socially decenter enhances individuals' abilities to select and adapt communication strategies that help them successfully attain their social goals, such as increased relational intimacy. Consider the most egocentric person you have known, someone lacking sensitivity to others – like Sheldon of Bing Bang Theory. Perhaps you have noticed that person has difficulty in forming and maintaining relationships. Sheldon's friendships exist primarily because his friends' social and relationship-specific decentering help them recognize his egocentrism and quirkiness, feel sympathy, evoke tolerance, and prompt accommodation which often serves as the basis for much of the show's humor. The response to Sheldon demonstrates that social decentering does not occur in a vacuum and that its application is moderated by a variety of personal and relational factors such as interpersonal needs, personality, attraction, similarity, partner familiarity, relational history, and social information processing skills.

This chapter focuses on how social decentering contributes to the development, maintenance, and termination of interpersonal relationships, particularly in adult relationships. Adults have reached a point of personal and relationship development that continues throughout their life. In an article published in *Human Relations* (Redmond, 1989), I identified several functions that empathy and social decentering play in interpersonal relationships. On a general level, social decentering adds to people's ability to understand others and to predict other people's behaviors or reactions. Those two general abilities then allow for the accomplishment of other goals such as an increased ability to persuade or gain compliance from others and the ability to make decisions about others (though a sympathetic response might lead to less objective decision making). Social decentering contributes to impression formation by increasing the accuracy of attributions through contextual awareness and mindfulness. People tend to form positive impressions of others who are empathic, and by association, those who socially decenter, often because those qualities are reflected in active listening and confirming responses. Communication reflecting empathy and social decentering validates and confirms other people's sense of self which contributes to the development and maintenance of relationships. Relationship building is often identified as a key element of counseling and therapeutic relationships and is another function of empathy and social decentering. The development of interpersonal relationships and social decentering, particularly RSSD, reflects an interdependent relationship. In new relationships, social decentering provides a foundation on which to adapt when little else is known

https://doi.org/10.1515/9783110515664-004

about the partner, but RSSD requires self-disclosure and extended observation of a partner which occurs in concert with relationship escalation. After reviewing research on empathic accuracy, Colvin, Vogt, and Ickes (1997) concluded that people's empathic accuracy with friends is based on "their accumulated observations of the targets' behavior-in-context across varied situations, and over an extended time frame" (p. 187). In a similar manner, RSSD develops by accumulating observations over time and across contexts. Early in relationship development, effective social decentering can lead to additional interactions between new acquaintances and thus more opportunities to observe. Those opportunities then lead to the escalation of the relationship to the point where partners interact in a greater variety of activities and contexts.

The final functions identified in my article dealt with the more emotional impact of empathy on relationships: providing comfort, conveying caring, and reflecting. These functions are often identified as qualities that define close relationships. Underlying these functions is an arousal of emotions in an observer who then provides comfort and support, and helps the other person understand his or her situation and feelings. The affective and cognitive processes that contribute to social decentering and RSSD allow people to not only share in the emotion of the other person, but also to adapt responses to the other person and achieve positive outcomes. For example, knowing an appropriate response to the news of the death of a friend's parent might prompt both sadness and a decision not to say anything but instead to just hug the friend. Decentering enhances our understanding of others and an appreciation of their situation. Sharing or reflecting that understanding to the other person often helps increase that person's understanding of her or his own situation. For these reasons, empathy and perspective-taking have long been elements associated with effective counseling. Social decentering informs the counselor's decision to provide feedback by enhancing their consideration and prediction of the client's reaction to what might be shared. In a like manner, social decentering helps us in evaluating what and when to provide feedback to others.

Surprisingly, not a lot of research has been done on the direct impact of empathy, perspective-taking, or social decentering on relationship development. Most studies are context specific, examining empathy and perspective-taking within the context of organizations, leadership, nursing, patient care, counseling, marriage, etc. The research that does examine interpersonal relationships tends to focus on observable behaviors such as empathic listening and does not explore the process that contributes to such listening behavior.

A general model of relationship development stages reflecting escalation toward intimacy and de-escalation from intimacy provides a useful template for discussing the role of social decentering and RSSD in interpersonal relationships. Part of this discussion draws from extant theory and research and part of the discussion presents the outcomes that can be expected from applying social and RSSD to interpersonal relationships development from a theoretical perspective.

A variety of relationship stage models have been generated, often reflecting a specific theoretic slant. For example, Altman and Taylor's (1973) social penetration theory identified four stages of relationship escalation (orientation, exploratory affective exchange, affective exchange, and stable exchange), which are built around changes in self-disclosure. Their model lists only one stage of de-escalation – depenetration. Mark Knapp (1984) developed a more communication-oriented stage model with five escalation stages and five de-escalation stages that has served as the structure for several research studies (see for example, Dunleavy & Booth-Butterfield, 2009; Welch & Rubin, 2002). I adapted Knapp's model to reflect additional aspects of relational development for use in an introductory interpersonal communication textbook (Beebe, Beebe, & Redmond, 2017). Like Knapp, my model has five escalation stages and five de-escalation stages, where each stage reflects variations in self-disclosure, communication, and the relationship. While the number of stages included in models often varies, the underlying principle is the same across models; that is, the relationships go through discernable changes as they move toward and away from intimacy. As such, the role and application of social decentering and the development and use of RSSD should correspond to movement from one stage to another. Movement often depends on assessing the current value of the relationship and the potential value of moving to the next stage. Social and RSSD aid this assessment by facilitating the appraisal of a partner's likely reaction to moving to another stage. Decentering also facilitates the development of strategies that can be used to move the relationship to the desired stage.

The following is a brief overview of the relationship development escalation and de-escalation stages (see Figure 3.1) discussed in Beebe, Beebe, and Redmond (2017). Following that overview, each stage is discussed in terms of the roles played by social decentering and RSSD. The first stage, pre-interaction awareness, occurs when a person acquires some information about another person but has not interacted with the other person in any meaningful way beyond a passing, "Hello". The information that is learned is usually from mutual acquaintances or from simply observing the other person in some context. The result of this stage is the development of an initial impression that affects subsequent interactions. This stage is skipped in the instances where two strangers meet for the first time and immediately begin interacting.

The second stage, acquaintance, involves two phases. The first phase is the introductory interaction that occurs the very first time two people meet. This phase is never repeated between the same two strangers unless they both forget that they've already met. The interaction is typically routine and is usually limited to sharing basic impersonal information. Conversants can extend the introduction phase as they move into the second phase of acquaintance – casual banter. In the casual banter phase, conversations expand to include additional topics with limited disclosure of personal information; although, that disclosure is more than occurs during the introductory phase. Subsequent meetings between first time conversants generally involve continued casual banter until they decide to and negotiate a move to the next stage – exploration.

STAGES OF RELATIONAL ESCALATION:

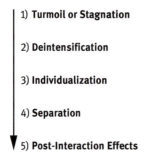

5) **Intimacy**

4) **Intensification**

3) **Exploration**

2) **Acquaintance (POV)**

    a. Introduction Phase: routine, initiation

    b. Casual Banter Phase: continued routine and impersonal interactions

1) **Pre-Interaction Awareness**

Increasing Intimacy

STAGES OF RELATIONSHIP DE-ESCALATION

1) **Turmoil or Stagnation**

2) **Deintensification**

3) **Individualization**

4) **Separation**

5) **Post-Interaction Effects**

Decreasing Intimacy

Figure 3.1: Relationship development stages.

The exploration stage reflects a decision to establish an ongoing, interpersonal relationship. Partners engage in more substantive self-disclosure, spend more time together, and consider each other to be friends. As mutual trust and enjoyment increases, partners escalate the relationship to the intensification stage. The intensification stage is characterized by personal self-disclosures, the creation of a sense of "we-ness," and labeling the relationship as best friends or, if romantic, as boyfriend/girlfriend. The final stage, intimacy, is marked by a strong sense of confirmation of each partner's value, intimate disclosure, and relationship commitment.

The number of stages toward intimacy that a relationship reaches affects how many de-escalation stages occur when relationships move toward termination. Relationships that reach the intimacy stage and de-escalate, generally experience all five of the de-escalation stages beginning with the turmoil or stagnation stage.

Sometimes the level of conflict and tension in an intimate relationship reaches a point that the relationship is no longer in the intimate stage. At other times, intimate partners might lose interest in each other and the relationship becomes less fulfilling leading to stagnation and lack of relational energy. Further deterioration in the relationship is reflected in the deintensification stage in which self-disclosure, affection, and interest in the partner decrease. While technically remaining in the relationship, during the individualization stage, partners spend more time independent of one another and thus less communication and disclosure. During the separation stage , partners either drift into or decide to go their separate ways, and they both regard the relationship as over. During this stage, there might still be interaction because of shared work or social networks, but those interactions mimic the casual banter phase. Finally, the post-interaction effects stage occurs in which separated individuals internalize the effects of their terminated relationship resulting in continued long-term effect on their sense of self and on other relationships.

3.1 Social Decentering, RSSD, and Relationship Development

Social decentering has general application to the management of any relationship, providing people with ways to understand and adapt to partners regardless of the level of intimacy. However, RSSD is inextricably linked to the development of interpersonal relationships. RSSD does not exist outside the confines of a specific relationship since it depends upon interactions with a specific other for development and application. RSSD plays a significant role in the maintenance of close relationships and in achieving relational satisfaction. Failure to develop or apply RSSD is likely to undermine the relationship. As partners develop a more and more intimate relationship, there is a growing expectation that the information they disclose to their partner will be appreciated, retained, and incorporated into their partner's communication and responses to them. Wright and Roloff (2015) found that after one partner in a romantic relationship did something that upset the other, the other became combative or gave the silent treatment if the partner failed to understand the other's feelings and needs without being told. In essence, the failure to effectively apply RSSD had a negative effect on the relationship. This principle of retention of information about the other and adaptation to that information is woven into the discussion of the relationship development stages and explored in the research on relationship development presented in Chapter 4.

In reading the brief descriptions of each of the relationship development stages you would probably have already identified instances where empathy, perspective-taking, and social decentering are likely to have an impact. But some applications might not be as obvious as others. The following sections examine the role that other-centeredness (and lack of other-centeredness) plays in moving relationships both toward and away from intimacy.

3.2 Relationship Escalation

3.2.1 Pre-Interaction Awareness Stage

We often form initial impressions and make attributions about people based on observation without direct interaction. Noticing someone running to catch a bus might lead you to infer that the person is late for work or school. Social decentering helps facilitate understanding others, even from a distance. Understanding others during the pre-interaction awareness stage illustrates the roles of the three analysis methods used in social decentering. Being other-centered during this stage draws heavily from use of self and use of generalized-others in making sense of what is observed. If you've run to the bus because you've been late for work or class, or have observed that behavior in others, those experiences provide a basis for interpreting the person's behavior running to the bus. Remember, however, that social decentering is not simply making attributions, but it is considering the situation from the other person's perspective. In this example, you might feel some relief that the person made it to the bus, or you might have reflected on the concern and relief the person must have felt after nearly missing the bus. Factors that affect our ability to socially decenter during the pre-interaction awareness phase include the amount of information we have about the target person, the degree to which we have parallel experiences, and observations of people you know or people in general who are related to the observed situation.

Social decentering should enhance people's ability to assess their compatibility with other people by providing an answer the following question, "To what degree would that other person be attracted to me or be likely to get along with me?" Social decentering allows people to consider the other person's perception of them. Accomplishing this assessment is dependent upon on how accurately and honestly people know themselves. Thus, if you thought you were a really funny person and had been observing a new co-worker who often laughed at other people's humorous comments, you might conclude that person would find you attractive. But, if you are not really funny, you'll probably be disappointed after interacting with the new person and finding the other person doesn't find you funny and thus, not attractive.

The depth of pre-interaction awareness depends upon the number and length of opportunities to observe or collect information about another person. Berger and Bradac (1982), in presenting their theory of uncertainty reduction, identified strategies for acquiring information about others, two of which are particularly applicable to this discussion: (1) passive strategies where another person is observed, and (2) active strategies of getting information from other sources, such as friends or the Internet. Berger and Bradac assert that being able to observe another person in a variety of social interactions and situation provides more substantive information than watching a person in non-social interactions, such as typing on their laptop. The more important the other person is to the observer, the more effort that will be made to gain information. The desire and effort to reduce uncertainty by gaining knowledge would increase the ability to effectively and accurately decenter.

Among the possible negative consequences of social decentering are errors in conclusions and adaptations due to faulty or incomplete information. Another consequence is that as interaction occurs the target might be disconcerted by the adaptive and predictive abilities of the social decenterer. In an episode of the old Andy Griffith TV show the Mayberry townsfolk get up in arms when a stranger comes to town and knows all about them. He's practically run out of town until it is explained that he knew all about everyone because he subscribed to and had been reading the local paper for a couple of years. He decided this was a town he would like to live in and that they would accept him. But he failed to predict how people would react to his having extensive knowledge of them. His comments, based on a low level of RSSD, caused alarm when talking to the townsfolk because he was referencing personal information that they had not disclosed to him.

The application of RSSD to pre-interaction awareness is limited not only because there isn't a relationship, but because there hasn't been the self-disclosure needed on which to build insights. Nonetheless, some degree of unique predictions of a specific person might be possible if there is sufficient information. For example, students in classes learn to predict which students will raise their hand to answer a question or make some joke during class. But that ability has little effect on the observed person. In ongoing interpersonal relationships, the other person is aware of their partner's adaptations because RSSD grows relative to the other person's willingness to self-disclose.

3.2.2 Acquaintance Stage: Introductory Phase and Casual Banter Phase

The acquaintance stage is quite similar to the pre-interaction awareness stage in terms of having limited information and forming impressions of others. But the acquaintance stage has the potential for learning more specific information from the partner, though such information is often limited by the scripted nature of the introductory phase. This phase usually involves sharing names, occupations/majors, hometowns, discussion of the situation at hand, the weather, or other general topics (Kellermann, 1991). Future interactions by way of casual banter are usually just extensions of the introductory phase, with subsequent interactions reflecting continued bantering about topics of mutual interest – sports, TV, music, classes, travel, and so on. Self-disclosure is limited in this stage to fairly impersonal information but provides a potentially stronger base for social decentering than the pre-interaction awareness stage. People's behaviors during the acquaintance interactions provide additional information about people's personality and character.

Since the introductory phase is the first interaction between two people, the immediacy of the conversation limits the ability to apply social decentering. As Bavelas and Coates (1992) noted, the nature of dialogue is such that participants quickly improvise responses to each other and that "there is no time to stop and think in conversation" (p. 304). Generally, social decentering requires time for processing; however, in situations that are particularly familiar or with people who seem to be familiar, a person might be able to apply conclusions previously developed through social decentering. Rusbult and Van Lange (2003) noted that in interactions with strangers "representations of partners with whom one has a history are easily evoked, activated, and applied to new partners" (p. 356).

Use of self would probably be the least used of the three forms of analysis during the introductory phase because it requires a bit more processing time to focus on the other person's dispositions and then consider one's own dispositions. Use of specific-other would occur to a limited degree when conversational partners appear similar to people already known. Social decenterers can utilize the knowledge and attributions associated with their specific-others who are most similar to their conversational partners, narrowing their specific-other choices as more information is gained during the interaction. Generalized-other will be relied on the most because it can be generated with the least amount of information and can thus be readily applied in introductory interactions. Rusbult and Van Lange (2003) described a process similar to the use of generalized-other, "Expectations are not particularly accurate in new relationships, as they must be based on probabilistic assumptions about how the average persons would react in a given situation" (p. 361). But those assumptions can be improved as you learn more information that allows you to apply information relevant to specific categories of people. Learning that your partner is from Hong Kong might evoke adaptation both in the topics you discuss and in your interpretation of your partner's behaviors.

In a study on accurate perceptions, college students interacted one-on-one with 3 to 12 other college students for 3 minutes each and after each interaction completed a personality assessment of their partner (Human & Biesanz, 2011). Those assessments were averaged to create a measure of the observers' general impression of others. Partners also completed personality assessments which were averaged to create a measure of normative accuracy. Well-adjusted participants perceived "new acquaintances on average as similar to the average person, reflecting an accurate understanding of what people generally tend to be like" (p. 356). But well-adjusted individuals assumed more similarity between themselves and their partners than there really was. Well-adjusted individuals were no better than the less-adjusted individuals in identifying unique partner characteristics. Three minutes greatly restricts how much information can be obtained from a partner, but the study does demonstrate the dependence on the use of generalized-other as a basis for understanding a new acquaintance.

An acquaintance relationship sustained in the banter phase gives people the opportunity to use social decentering to consider their partner's dispositions between one interaction and the next. The banter stage varies in terms of how much information the conversants self-disclose and the variety of social situations in which it occurs. Some acquaintanceships involve little more than saying "Hello" from time to time and thus little information is gained on which to expand the social decentering base. Other acquaintanceships can include continued discussion about previously shared information ("Your football team is really doing well") or expansion into new topics of discussion. The more information shared during the bantering phase, the more opportunity to fine tune the social decentering.

Social decentering, in and of itself, is a quality that might increase a person's attractiveness. Hogan (1969), Grief and Hogan (1973), and Redmond (1989) claimed that empathy is viewed as a positive personal attribute. If a person is perceived as trying to understand the target's thoughts and feelings, that could translate into affinity toward the social decenterer. The need to gain information on which to socially decenter might lead to increased question asking, attention to the partner, and other behaviors that increase the decenterer's attractiveness. Bodie, St. Cyr, Pence, Rold, and Honeycutt (2012) examined what behaviors people attribute to a competent listener and are likely to create a positive impression. Listeners who showed understanding through paraphrasing and seeking elaboration during initial interactions, positively affected the speaker's feelings of being understood, communication satisfaction, and attraction (Weger, Bell, Minai, & Robinson, 2014). Behaviors associated with social decentering and RSSD in initial interactions include showing interest, asking questions, and communicating understanding both explicitly and implicitly. Such behaviors should positively affect attraction and satisfaction with the social decenterers.

A colleague, Denise Vrchota, and I conducted a study on attraction in initial interactions that included social decentering, uncertainty reduction, and interaction competence (Redmond & Vrchota, 1994). For our study, 101 pairs of undergraduate male and female students who were strangers to each other engaged in getting acquainted conversations which began with interactions limited to 2, 4, 6, 8, and 10 minutes. After completing several measures, participants continued their conversations for another 6 minutes for total interaction times from 8 to 16 minutes and then completed a second set of measures. After both interactions, participants completed a seven-item measure of attraction incorporating three items from McCroskey and McCain's (1974) measure of social attraction and four additional items relevant to interactions between strangers such as "I would like to continue interacting with this person at this time." Reliability for the scale was $\alpha = 0.85$ after the initial interaction and $\alpha = 0.89$ after the extended interaction. After the extended interaction, participants completed the 36-item social decentering scale with reliability for this study of $\alpha = 0.90$.

No significant correlations were found between one partner's level of social decentering and the other partner's reported level of attraction after either the initial or extended interactions. This finding is not particularly surprising since social decentering's influence on a partner's attraction is limited by the routine and scripted nature of initial interactions and by the lack of time to reflect and adapt to the partner. The impact also might be affected by the similarity and difference between partners' levels of social decentering which were explored by examining pairs of high, low, and mixed level social decentering respondents. Females were divided into high and low groups relative to their mean; the same was done for males. This created four combinations of social decenterers: (1) both high in decentering; (2) both low; (3) the female high and male low; and (4) the male high and female low.

An analysis of variance of the attraction between partners across the four groups produced a significant difference after both the initial interaction [F (3,198) = 3.53, p = 0.016] and the extended interaction [F (3,198) = 2.97, p = 0.033]. Tukey's HSD post hoc analysis identified only two groups that were significantly different ($p < 0.05$) after the initial interaction: pairs of high social decenterers reported a higher level of attraction than pairs of low social decenters (see Table 3.1). Stronger social decenterers are likely to be sensitive to their partners' displays of social decentering and thus see similarity with their partner which in turn increases their attraction. After the chance for extended discussion, two other pairs emerged as significantly different: higher social decentering pairs reported stronger attraction than the pairs made up of high socially decentering men with low decentering women (see Table 3.2).

Table 3.1: Initial attraction means for and low social decentering pairs.

Table 3.2: Extended time attraction means high for high and low social decentering pairs.

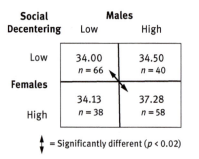

Social Decentering	Males Low	High
Low	34.00 $n = 66$	34.50 $n = 40$
Females		
High	34.13 $n = 38$	37.28 $n = 58$

↕ = Significantly different ($p < 0.02$)

Social Decentering	Males Low	High
Low	34.55 $n = 66$	33.95 $n = 40$
Females		
High	35.39 $n = 38$	37.69 $n = 58$

↕ = Significantly different ($p < 0.05$)

After the initial interactions, males reported greater attraction than the females; there was no significant difference in attraction levels after the extended interaction. In addition, the males' attraction was not significantly different between any of the four groups either after the initial or the extended interactions. Male attraction seemed unaffected by either the length of the interaction or the level of females' social decentering. Given that in general, women are higher in social decentering and empathy than men (78% of the women in this study scored higher in social decentering than the men's average), might led to men not being affected by variations in women's social decentering because they have a preconception of women as strong social decenterers and thus fail to notice the variations.

Analysis of the females' attraction across the four groups was not significantly different after the initial interaction but were significantly different after the extended interaction (F (3,97) = 2.88, p = 0.04). This result suggests that as the interaction progressed, females became more cognizant of the males' level of social decentering which then impacted their attraction. A Tukey HSD post hoc analysis found that higher socially decentering females paired with higher socially decentering males reported stronger attraction (M = 37.83, n = 29) than the lower socially decentering females paired with higher socially decentering males (M = 32.75, n = 20, p = 0.07). The lower level of attraction reported by lower socially decentering women partnered with higher socially decentering men parallels a finding reported in Chapter 6, where low social decentering wives reported the lowest level of satisfaction when paired with a high decentering husband. Interactions with strong social decentering men might negatively affect the self-esteem of lower social decentering women. Such women might see themselves failing to meet the social expectation that women should be empathic and understanding; thus, the women negatively react to the interaction and their partner. In addition, men who are strong at understanding and adapting to women might be viewed as manipulative by women who lack such skills.

The differences between men's and women's reactions to their partner's level of social decentering in the introductory phase of acquaintanceship might be an indication that the importance of understanding and adapting in cross-sex interactions is viewed differently by men and women. For example, in a study of 10th grade Australian student friendships, females were more likely to identify males who with higher empathy as friends but males selection of female friends was not related to female levels of empathy (Ciarrochi, Parker, Sahdra, Kashdan, Kiuru & Conigrave, 2016).

The results of our attraction study are likely to under-represent the role of social decentering in initial interactions. Given that this getting-acquainted interaction was done in a research setting inevitably influenced the participants' goals, decisions, and assessments. Without an expectation for further interactions with each other, the participants had no real need to gather or evaluate information about the other. Thus, their questionnaire responses were based on a cursory evaluation of their partners. Social decentering is likely to play a more important role than our study demonstrated when people are in interactions where there is the potential for developing ongoing relationships.

Further analysis in our study involved dividing the respondents into high and lower groups based on the three process subscales – self, specific-other, and generalized-other. The level of attraction was different between those who were higher in use of specific-other compared to those who were lower. Neither use of self or use of generalized-other produced any significant differences. While limited during short scripted initial interactions, immediately adapting to information learned about the partner by applying use of specific-other is more likely to be noticed by a partner.

In addition, the immediacy of the interaction reduces the time to reflect on one's own perspective or on people's perspectives in general. Less time is needed to adapt and respond to the new information about the partner in confirming similar interests or asking pertinent follow-up questions which can promote attraction. This finding is consistent with previous research on affinity seeking by Bell and Daly (1984) who found that engaging in other oriented behaviors such as confirming, listening, and supportiveness increases affinity.

One of the major goals of the acquaintance stage is to decide whether the relationship should remain at this stage or escalate to the exploration stage. This goal is accomplished by reducing uncertainty about the partner (increasing predictability) and assessing the predicted outcome value of future interactions or relationship escalation. Sunnafrank (1986) asserts in his predicted outcome value theory that in initial interactions participants try to determine the likelihood that continued or future interactions would be rewarding. Given that social decentering involves predicting partners' dispositions and behaviors, it can contribute to the ability to assess future outcomes. In the study on attraction reported above (Redmond & Vrchota, 1997), participants responded to a modified measure of uncertainty, Clatterbuck's CLUES7 (1979). The seven-item scale measures global uncertainty about another person. Respondents assess their confidence in predicting a partner's behaviors, emotions, values, attitudes, liking for them, and their empathy. In getting-acquainted interactions, participants are limited as to how much information they collect and thus how much uncertainty that can be reduced. And as already mentioned, without an expectation for continuing a relationship after the study, participants had less need to reduce uncertainty. Under normal circumstances, social decentering, particularly, use of generalized-other, will increase a person's ability to make predictions and reduce uncertainty.

In our study, social decentering significantly correlated with uncertainty reduction ($r = -0.20$, $p < 0.05$). Separately, both men's and women's level of social decentering correlated with their perception of reduced uncertainty ($r = -0.25$, $p < 0.05$; $r = -0.23$, $p < 0.05$, respectively). These findings suggest that those who are most active in seeking understanding and adapting to others are more confident in their predictions about people they have just met. That finding parallels Stinson and Ickes' (1992) research finding that conversational involvement between male strangers related to higher empathic accuracy. Social decentering should help people recognize their partners' uncertainty and thus lead them to self-disclose more in an effort to help reduce it which was supported by the findings. While not particularly strong, higher levels of one partner's social decentering was related to reduced uncertainty in the other ($r = -0.15$, $p < 0.05$), suggesting that those stronger in social decentering helped their partners feel more informed about them.

The lack of correlation between use of self and uncertainty reduction indicates that the immediacy of initial interactions apparently limits the application of this analysis.

Use of specific-other was related to a reduction of uncertainty ($r = -0.14$, $p < 0.05$). Respondents probably gained enough information about their partners to form some general impressions. They might also have been able to see similarity between the partner and other specific friends which provided a base for making predictions. A larger correlation ($r = -0.25$, $p < 0.001$) was found for the use of generalized-other and uncertainty reduction indicating that those with a stronger understanding of people in general possess the self-efficacy to predict the behaviors, values, and attitudes of a new acquaintance. Those strong in use of generalized-other are likely to have more person schemas and greater depth in those schemas, creating greater accuracy in categorizing new acquaintances. This was also made easier in this study because of the relative homogeneity of the college-student participants in the study. But use of generalized-other should be as strong or stronger when dealing with heterogeneous partners for individuals with experience interacting with diverse partners.

Social decentering should relate to a person's ability to manage initial interactions by not only reducing uncertainty but also by increasing their ability to adapt to other people. Douglas (1991) created the six-item Initial Interaction Competence Scale to measure people's self-assessment of their ability to manage initial interactions. The scale includes such items as "how often do you run out of things to talk about" and "how often do you say the 'right' things." For our study, we revised the items to apply to the assessment of how well a respondent felt they managed a particular initial interaction. Social decentering was found to relate ($r = 0.15$, $p = 0.03$) to participants' reports of how well they managed the getting-acquainted conversation. Management of cross-sexed interactions is likely to be perceived differently by men and women, so separate analyses were made of men's and women's responses. Women's social decentering positively related ($r = 0.23$, $p = 0.02$) to how well they felt they managed the interaction. No such relationship was found for men nor were any of the subscales related to men's initial interaction competence.

In a study examining how younger and older women's accurate affective and cognitive empathy might vary, Blanke, Rauers, and Riediger (2016) had partners in getting-acquainted conversations discuss a positive and negative event in their lives. Women's empathic accuracy regarding their partner's positive thoughts and feelings related to the women's communication satisfaction. Empathic accuracy was not related to the partner's communication satisfaction nor to accuracy regarding negative thoughts and feelings. The researchers indicated that the short interaction time reduced the display of understanding or empathy and thus participants' empathic accuracy did not have a chance to affect their partners. Empathizing with a partner's positive situation was thought to elevate positive feelings and satisfaction with the conversation but that does not happen when empathizing about a negative situation. An interesting implication of their study is that people might avoid or terminate interactions with acquaintances in which the application of social decentering results in experiencing negative thoughts and feelings. Or, rather than terminating the interaction, people might choose not to engage in social decentering. In initial interactions where partners express positive thoughts and feelings, social decentering can be used to better understand the other person's situation and thus increase the decenterers' own positive emotional experience and overall satisfaction.

Despite the limited information and scripted nature of initial interactions, Sunnafrank (1984) and Redmond and Vrchota (1997) found that individuals assessed the attractiveness of their partners as well as their own desire to continue the relationship. Being attracted to a partner and having a desire to continue the relationship provides motivation to develop RSSD. Such motivation is needed if people are to exert the energy needed to attend to and retain information about their partners. The decision to move the relationship to the exploration stage involves a decision to seek more information which inherently leads to RSSD.

3.2.3 Exploration Stage

The exploration stage reflects a decision by both partners to establish an ongoing, interpersonal relationship. Partners engage in more substantive self-disclosure, spend more time together, and consider each other a friend. As partners gain more trust and enjoyment with each other, they escalate the relationship to the intensification stage where the partners identify each other as close friends or best friends. And as partners experience greater variety in social activities and interactions, the more opportunities they have to observe and learn about each other (Berger & Bradac, 1982). The opportunity to see a partner among friends, family, and co-workers provides further information on which RSSD can be built and facilitates decisions about the relationship. Sometimes relationships are limited to only one context or situation such as interacting only at the workplace with co-workers or only in the classroom or hallway with classmates. Relationships limited to narrow, contextually bounded interactions means the subsequent relationship-specific understandings and expectations will also be limited. For example, you might be surprised to find a co-worker acting wildly at a club or bar in contrast to your workplace image of the co-worker as quiet and laid back.

The increased level of self-disclosure that occurs during this stage results in significant development of RSSD. Social decentering continues to be used and it serves as a yardstick by which information about the relational partner is evaluated. For example, knowledge and understanding of the partner is weighed against knowledge and understanding of one's self, other partners, and people in general, and your partner's emotionality is judged relative to the emotionality of you and others.

Brem (1989) observed that empathy and showing understanding required people to self-disclose to the target, essentially switching back and forth from empathizer and discloser to be effective in interpersonal encounters. Social decentering and RSSD provide a foundation on which to make decisions about the appropriateness of any given disclosure by taking into account the predicted reaction of the partner. I've previously written about self-disclosure as a dance where each partner reacts to the movements of the other (Beebe, Beebe, & Redmond, 2017). As such, social decentering helps people recognize the need to slow down or speed up their disclosing in response to their partner's self-disclosing behavior.

Developing RSSD is facilitated by two of the uncertainty reduction strategies identified by Berger and Bradac (1982): interrogation and self-disclosure. Interrogation involves asking questions to gain the desired information and clarify ambiguity. Berger and Bradac caution that the actual interaction can actually inhibit gaining information because we become too distracted in presenting our self. For example, we fail to remember the name of someone we've just met because we are focused on presenting ourselves. Self-disclosure as a strategy to solicit disclosures from our partners relies on the dyadic effect of reciprocating disclosures. So rather than asking if the other person likes jazz, you simply disclose that you like jazz with the expectation the other person will declare his or her like or dislike or indicate some other musical preference. Both strategies provide the information needed to develop RSSD. As the relationship escalates information continues to be acquired adding to the complexity and effectiveness of RSSD.

As mentioned in the Chapter 2, time spent together provides opportunities to share experiences, observe partners, and discuss thoughts and feelings regarding those experiences. In this way, a knowledge structure is created that serves as the foundation for RSSD. This structuring process is described by Lewis and Hodges (2012) in their discussion of the development of schemas and expectations:

> [...] as time goes by and we gather more and more information about a person, the mental schemas we construct become richer, providing a basis for more accurately inferring detailed thoughts that would be difficult, if not impossible, to read by simply observing the person's behavior in the immediate situation. (p. 76)

Stinson and Ickes' (1992) studies on empathic accuracy included a study focused on comparing the interactions of male friends and pairs of male strangers. Their study's results apply to both the acquaintance stage and the exploration stage. Despite finding few differences in the personalities of the pairs, sociability levels were correlated between friends but not between strangers, leading Stinson and Ickes to conclude that friends see things in the same way, have greater rapport, and thus greater empathic accuracy. After correcting for issues of interdependence and guessing, friends were found to have greater content accuracy than strangers "derived from knowledge structures activated by the specific content of their interaction, rather than from lucky guesses or from general stereotypes about their interaction partners" (Stinson & Ickes, 1992, p. 793). They also concluded that the information used for accurate empathy was based on prior knowledge, not just knowledge obtained in the interaction. The results corroborate the claim that individuals in the exploration stage develop a basic level of RSSD and are less dependent upon the use of generalized-other social decentering. It should be noted that while the empathic accuracy level between friends was significant, it only accounted for about 14% of the variance in their scores. The level of empathic accuracy could be a reflection of a general weakness in males' empathic accuracy skills as well as a lower level of intimacy in their friendships.

Besides the expectation for increased understanding associated with relationship development, there is also an expectation for increased support and comfort. Egbert, Miraldi, and Murniadi (2014) found that behavioral intentions to interpersonally intervene with a friend exhibiting depression (based on a hypothetical scenario) positively related to participants' perspective-taking and emotional concern, but not to their reported communicative responsiveness (including ability to appropriately respond). These results indicate that a level of compassion and understanding occurs during the exploration stage, but there is a question of self-efficacy in actually helping a friend manage a stressful situation. The more participants felt emotional contagion (similar negative emotional response) with the depressed friend, the less they were inclined to intervene. In essence, the concern that one's own negative feelings will be evoked when dealing with a depressed friend undermines intervening. The depth and specificity of understanding associated with RSSD should lead to both increased self-efficacy in responding to the specific other, as well as an ability to manage the cognitive and affective responses, and better meet the needs of the other person.

Another study examining support among friends, assessed participants' supportive responses to a hypothetical situation where a friend was having alcohol problems (Trobst, Collins, & Embree, 1994). The results indicated that women with higher levels of dispositional empathy (operationalized with Davis' empathic concern and perspective-taking subscales) were more likely to be socially supportive of friends than were men. The researchers contended that dispositional empathy led to greater feelings of concern and therefore stronger inclinations to engage in helping behaviors. While females scored higher than males, males still indicated some support for their friends which was likely related to their level of dispositional empathy. The results of that study further support the contention that social decentering and RSSD increase the probability of providing support to friends. Such support is likely during the exploration stage but should be even stronger as the relationship escalates.

3.2.4 Intensification Stage

The intensification stage is marked by the establishment of a close relationship in which partners often label their relationship "best friend" or "boyfriend/girlfriend." Among the qualities associated with this stage are: greater dependence on each other for self-confirmation, more intimate self-disclosure, more time together, greater variety of shared activities, decreased personal physical distance, more physical contact, and personalized language (Beebe, Beebe, & Redmond, 2017). Many of these changes both enhance and reflect RSSD. Partners shared experiences serve as unique references that they incorporate into their conversations knowing that their partner will understand the reference. For example, a couple who previously ate a horrible meal at a place called *Tony's* might comment to each other, "Reminds me of *Tony's*" while dining at another bad restaurant with friends, but their friends would not understand their reference.

In reaching the intensification stage, partners are exposed to a significant amount of information about the other on which to form their RSSD. Such exposure does not automatically mean that an individual will develop RSSD. A number of factors can inhibit such development as discussed in Chapter 2. Nonetheless, as the relationship develops people increasingly expect their partners to develop and use RSSD. The development of RSSD increases the likelihood for stability in relationships that reach this stage. In their study on social networks, Kardos, Leidner, Pléh, Soltész, and Unoka (2017) found that participants' level of empathic concern and perspective-taking (using Davis' IRI scales) positively related to the number of people who made up their social support group (weekly contact and close relationship) but not to the level of closeness. Participants were asked to indicate how much they engaged in each type of dispositional empathy with each of their partners, a measure similar to RSSD. Participants reported more empathic concern and perspective-taking with their support group members than others in their social network. The researchers concluded that "people utilize their empathic abilities in a strategic pattern to maintain their closest social relationships" (p. 4). They concluded that "maintenance of these relationships requires, or at least benefits from, mutual emotional understanding and concern" (p. 4). Social decentering and, more specifically, RSSD allow partners to better understand and adapt to their partners during the intensification and intimacy stages.

Social decentering and the development of RSSD allow partners to convey an understanding of each other which has several positive impacts on the relationship. Being understood helps to confirm our sense of self and self-worth, positively influences the management of conflict, and allows individuals to feel greater autonomy (Hadden, Rodriguez, Knee, & Porter, 2015). Being understood by someone we care about makes us feel good and is one of the reasons we work hard at developing and maintaining close relationships. Relationship quality has been positively related to the feeling of being understood (Finkenauer & Righetti, 2011; Pollman & Finkenauer, 2009), as well as understanding whether a partner's attitudes are influenced more by a meta-attitudinal base of emotions or beliefs (Tan, See, & Agnew, 2015). Tan, Agnew, et al. (2015) found that the greater a participant's understanding of whether a partner's attitudes are dominated by emotions or beliefs, the stronger the partner's feelings of satisfaction, love, trust, and commitment. Social decentering and RSSD reflect processes by which we come to understand the foundations of our partners' attitudes and thus should provide similar positive relational impacts as found by Tan et al. – satisfaction, love, trust, and commitment. But the impact on relational partners often depends on partners recognizing that the other understands them, which in turn is usually dependent on the other engaging in observable actions and adaptations. Remember that people can engage in social decentering but choose not to or are unable to exhibit adaptive behaviors which might evoke responses like "You just don't understand me." Not feeling understood by partners increases the likelihood that the relationship will end. But social decentering and RSSD can help manage misunderstandings. College students described a misunderstanding (the relationships were primarily intimate) and completed several self-reports including perspective-taking in a study conducted by Edwards, Bybee, Frost, Harvey, and Navarro (2016). Levels of students' perspective-taking positively correlated with reports of fewer misunderstandings in the relationship, greater use of integrative strategies to address the misunderstanding, and greater communication satisfaction after the misunderstanding. Similarly, social decentering and RSSD can be expected to not only reduce the number of misunderstandings that occur but facilitate positive outcomes after misunderstandings.

While social decentering and RSSD can strengthen and help in maintaining interpersonal relationships, they can also be used in deciding to de-escalate or terminate relationships. As more and more information is learned about a partner, social decentering and RSSD allow people to better determine how well they can achieve their personal goals within a given relationship. A point is often reached where people's analyses lead them to recognize that they will be unable to achieve their goals within a given relationship and decide to de-escalate or terminate that relationship. For example, people sometimes reach a point in romantic relationships where, through decentering, they predict the relationship would be more satisfying as a friendship. Another example would be a person in a romantic relationship who wants to have children ending the relationship when decentering leads him or her to predict the partner would not be a good parent, or simply finds the partner's personal goals do not include children. Ultimately, social decentering and RSSD are not about being subservient or accommodating to any partner, but instead are tools that help individuals achieve their own personal goals. One of those goals might be a serious, long-term, committed relationship that represents reaching the final escalation stage – the intimacy stage.

3.2.5 Intimacy Stage

The intimacy stage represents the closest level of relationship that two people can attain sometimes reflected in romantic partners seeking formal public endorsement as a married couple. At this stage partners have engaged in extensive self-disclosure, sharing highly intimate information built on the development of trust. The extensive amount and depth of information that has gotten the relationship to the intimacy stage serves as the basis for well-developed RSSD. I define interpersonal intimacy as "the degree to which relational partners mutually confirm, value, and accept each other's sense of self" (Beebe, Beebe, Redmond, 2017, p. 244). Partners develop communication patterns specific to their relationship that include more expressions of oneness ("us" and "we"), more use of personal idioms and nicknames, increased conversation with future references, increased communication efficiency (fewer words are needed to convey ideas), and greater sensitivity to each other's nonverbal cues

(Knapp, 1984; Mongeau & Henningsen, 2015). Achieving intimacy means that both partners feel they can totally be themselves and still be accepted by the other. Both partners become more and more dependent on one other to confirm their sense of self and their self-worth. One of the ways that such confirmation occurs is through the application of RSSD. Partners expect each other to understand them, be sensitive, adaptive, comforting, and confirming. RSSD plays a significant role in our management of knowledge of specific others and provides the foundation for positively valued adaptive behavior. Displaying understanding of a partner promotes positive feelings, enhances trust, reduces conflict, and increases relationship quality (Finkenauer & Righetti, 2011). Perception of a partners' responsiveness increases the perceivers' efforts to maintain the relationship (Finkenauer & Righetti, 2011).

Clark and Lemay (2010) argue that responsiveness is the key to successful relationships. Responsiveness includes helping partners meet needs, endorsing a partner's goals, providing support to reach those goals, spending time together, celebrating a partner's accomplishments, affirming a partner's self-concept, restraint of negative comments, and providing appropriate constructive criticism (Clark & Lemay, 2010). Many of these forms of responsiveness require a strong understanding of the partner to facilitate selecting the most appropriate and effective response. RSSD is a key to effective responsiveness. RSSD helps people better understand their partner's needs and goals and develop appropriate responses in support of their partner. The benefits associated with responsiveness in an intimate relationship are facilitated by RSSD. Clark and Lemay (2010) discuss how a person might decide not to help a partner with a given task (tying a child's shoelace) and instead let the partner accomplish the goal that the partner can achieve by him or herself and thus increase the partner's self-confidence. Through RSSD a person knows the capabilities of the partner and can predict the partner's behavior and outcome. While responsiveness has the ultimate goal of supporting a partner's well-being, RSSD does not. If a person engages in a behavior that undermines a partner's goals that would not be responsive, but that person might still have engaged in RSSD before deciding to behave against the partner's interests. Clark and Lemay (2010) observe that responsiveness is relationship specific and as such the demands of being responsive limit its application to a few prioritized relationships. These constraints apply to RSSD as well, further confirming its similarity to responsiveness.

When people in intimate relationships do not feel that their partners are being responsive or do not feel understood by their partners, they are more likely to feel dissatisfied and undermine the relationship (Finkenauer & Righetti, 2011). Failure to apply and act upon RSSD in an effective manner is likely to create stress in the relationship and if sustained might bring about de-escalation or even dissolution. Finkenauer and Righetti (2011) see a chain reaction occurring where not feeling understood leads to keeping secrets and keeping secrets then leads to even greater lack of understanding as well as feelings of stress, loneliness, and isolation. Similarly, withholding information undermines the ability to effectively engage in RSSD leading to failures to understand and appropriately adapt, thus fostering further negative consequences.

In a study I conducted to determine the role of social decentering in interpersonal relationships, I collected social decentering scores from participants in relationships of varying levels of closeness and sex makeup (Redmond, 2002). As discussed in Chapter 2, those in the earlier stages of relationship development (casual friends, friends) had smaller differences in partners' social decentering scores than those in the most intimate relationship (my best friend/fiancée/lover/spouse) even with adjustments to the effect of sex differences in scoring. Social decentering appears to be more important in the early stages of development as partners look for similarity.

In the study, participants identified their relationship as acquaintance (0); casual friend (0); friend (17); close friend (17); one of my best friends (24); my best friend/fiancée/lover/spouse (42). Differences in the partners' social decentering were calculated and an analysis of variance indicated significant difference among the relationships [F (3,96) = 4.82, p = 0.004]. Post hoc analysis revealed that partners in the most intimate relationship had significantly greater differences in their social decentering scores than friends (see Figure 3.2).

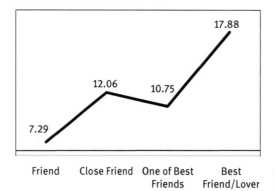

Friend	Close Friend	One of Best Friends	Best Friend/Lover

Figure 3.2: Differences in partners' social decentering by closeness.

As a trait, individuals' social decentering should remain fairly constant throughout the development of a relationship and thus the social decentering means should remain constant throughout changes in closeness. No significant differences in social decentering between the relationships were found. While the averages in each relationship were not different, that does not mean that each partner in the relationships had the same level of social decentering. Respondents were divided according to their social decentering scores into those above the mean labeled *high* and those below the mean labeled *low*. Women were divided according the mean for women, and men according to the mean for men which meant men were not classified relative to the intrinsically higher scoring women. For each of the four levels of closeness, partners were further classified on the basis of both partners being low social decenterers, both partners being high social decenterers, or partners being mixed, with one high social decenterer and one low social decenterer. Table 3.3 shows the relative percentages of pairs for each of these levels of closeness. Among friends,

Table 3.3: Percentages of respondents by social decentering pairing and closeness.

Social Decentering Pairing	Friends (n =17)	Close Friends (n = 17)	One of Best Friends (n = 24)	Best Friends/ Lover/Spouse (n = 42)
Both Low	47.1	23.5	25	14.3
One High/One Low	17.6	47.1	50	73.8
Both High	35.3	29.4	25	11.9

the majority are composed of partners where both partners were either high social decenterers or both partners were low social decenterers. That distribution changes dramatically in the remaining relationships. The number of mixed pairs in the relationships increases substantially between friend and close friend and another sizeable increase occurs as relationships move to the intimacy stage (best friend/lover/ spouse) with almost 74% of the partners engaged in complementary relationships with one partner a high social decenterer and the other partner as a low social decenterer. While not longitudinal, this study does represent samples from a fairly homogenous group and should be a reliable indication of the nature of the relationships at each level of closeness.

Given the claim that social decentering is unlikely to change much over the course of the relationships, the observed change in the combinations of social decenterers probably reflects the emergence of the combination (one high and one low) which best endures the move to intimacy. Friendships in the acquaintance and exploration stage appear to favor partners who share similar levels of social decentering, with only a few of those relationships continuing toward more intimacy. While fewer early friendships are composed of partners with complementary levels of social decentering (one high and one low), those relationships appear more likely to develop intimacy. Each level of closeness consists of relationships for which a particular balance of social decentering is best suited – symmetrical (both high or both low in social decentering) for low intimacy relationships and complementary (one high and one low) for intimate relationships. The impact of symmetry and complementarity was also found in the research on married couples reported in the Chapter 6. Among friends, similarity would seem to be a significant factor in the decision to establish and maintain a friendship. More intimate relationships appear to rely more on the ability of one partner to understand and accommodate the other. In addition, adaptation and accommodation by both partners becomes a key element in the maintenance of intimate relationships and is more dependent on the development and utilization of RSSD than social decentering.

No reports regarding changes in RSSD are available for this study because the RSSD scale was not yet developed. Indeed, the finding in this study that partners low in social decentering still developed satisfying intimate relationships was an indication to me that some other process was occurring that allowed for reciprocal adaptation – partners developing a relationship-specific form of social decentering. This was further explored in a study that examined RSSD across all the stages of escalation and de-escalation that is discussed in the next chapter.

Social decentering should allow people to more effectively influence others by adapting appropriate compliance gaining strategies. This was partially explored in the above study. Besides completing the measure of social decentering, the 50 pairs of respondents rated each other's ability to influence them on a four-item scale of interpersonal influence that included "This person is effective at arguing his or her point and swaying me to his or her position" and "This person isn't very effective at winning me over to his/her way" (reverse scored). No overall correlation was found between social decentering and interpersonal influence. But in less intimate relationships (casual friends, friends and close friends), one partner's social decentering significantly correlated with the level of interpersonal influence reported by the other partner ($r = 0.46$, $p < 0.01$, $n = 32$) as did each of the social decentering subscales (use of self, $r = 0.46$, $p < 0.01$; use of specific other, $r = 0.43$, $p < 0.05$; use of generalized other, $r = 0.35$, $p < 0.05$; affective response, $r = 0.50$, $p < 0.01$; and cognitive response, $r = 0.34$, $p < 0.10$). No significant correlations were found for the most intimate relationships (my best friend/lover/spouse, $n = 38$). These results indicate that in casual relationships social decentering is an effective foundation for developing interpersonal influencing strategies. But when the relationships reach intimacy, social decentering no longer serves as the basis for influencing strategies. While no data on RSSD were collected, the development of RSSD in intimate relationships probably supplants social decentering as the source for strategizing. As couples become intimate and develop roles and routines there is less use of compliance gaining. Additionally, as intimate couples become aware of each other's influencing strategies, they are more prepared to resist the other's influence (Miller & Boster, 1988), which explains the failure to find a relationship between influence and social decentering in intimate relationships.

3.3 Relationship De-Escalation

Dissolution of relationships typically follows one of three patterns: sudden death, fading away, or incrementalism (Beebe, Beebe, Redmond, 2017). The termination of a relationship can occur abruptly as the result of some major transgression such as cheating by a romantic partner (sudden death), can occur slowly without deliberation as communication decreases such as friends moving away after college (fading away), or can go through specific stages of de-escalation finally reaching a point where one or both partners moves to end the relationship (incrementalism). How disengagement progresses, depends on the level of intimacy and interdependence – the more intimate the relationship, the longer the de-escalation process. For example, during the exploration stage a partner might simply turn down an invitation to get together and thus end the relationship rather easily. But such an approach would not go over too well in a marriage. Our romantic relationships generally involve greater deliberation and formal commitment than in our friendships. As a result, de-escalation in romantic relationships tends to be more deliberative and more strategic in breaking the bonds of commitment. In considering de-escalating or reacting to a partner's efforts to de-escalate, individuals increase their cognitive efforts to analyze themselves, their partners, and the relationship (Duck, 2005; Fletcher, Fincham, Cramer, & Heron, 1987). Such cognitive efforts include the use of social decentering and RSSD to make sense out of the partner's dispositions and to make predictions about the partner and relationship. But as the relationship de-escalates, so does the motivation to gain knowledge and understanding of each other (Harvey & Omarzu, 1999). Harvey and Omarzu (1999) presented a theory of *minding* whereby partners reciprocally seek to know each other (RSSD) and make relationship enhancing attributions. They contend that the decrease and end of information sharing leads to an "eventual shutdown of the minding process and, we hypothesize, the relationship itself" (p. 43). While a decrease in information impacts the effectiveness of RSSD, it is the decrease in efforts to consider the dispositions of a partner and adapt accordingly which more likely contributes to the de-escalation of the relationship.

While the de-escalation stages apply to friendships, they are more pronounced in romantic relationships which have received most of the research focus. Even so, I found little research on empathy and perspective-taking related to the de-escalation and termination of intimate relationships. Baxter (1987) observed that the research that has been done on relationship termination focuses on a single event rather than the de-escalation process. Specifically, research on empathy and perspective-taking is often in the context of managing transgressions, seeking forgiveness, and managing conflict. This is not surprising since empathy is often linked to positive or altruistic outcomes rather than the more negatively oriented process of "dumping" a partner. Social decentering and RSSD are neither inherently positive nor negative, but instead allow people to evaluate the impact of alternative responses. Social decentering and RSSD are utilized during de-escalation to evaluate potential strategies. The strategy that is chosen usually reflects the disengager's level of concern for the partner's feelings and well-being.

Prior to deciding to abruptly end a relationship due to a transgression, people might apply social decentering and RSSD to analyze the partner's failure. Initial volatile responses to transgressions might be mitigated by such analysis. Emotional empathy for both men and women positively relates to forgiving others (Macaskill, Maltby & Day, 2002). While empathy is often found to correlate with forgiveness (Riek & Mania, 2012), these findings might be unduly influenced by how empathy is measured. For example, in one study only the perspective-taking subscale of Davis' empathy measure was found to positively relate to granting forgiveness (Hodgson & Wertheim, 2007). Perspective-taking allows partners to cognitively consider the offender's viewpoint and motivations which appears to then increase the likelihood of forgiving. Like perspective-taking, social decentering and RSSD provide fairly detached analyses of transgressions rather than the emotional response of sympathy or altruism produced by emotional empathy. The decentering process allows people to draw from their understanding of their partner in analyzing the transgression while weighing their own self-interests in developing their response.

The focus of the remaining de-escalation discussion is on the incremental de-escalation of relationships that is reflected in the stage model. While Altman and Taylor's (1973) model of relationship development presents depenetration as the reversal of social penetration, the reality is that as a relationship ends partners don't just erase all the information they learned about by their partners overnight. Similarly, RSSD doesn't just disappear once a relationship begins de-escalating or even when it is terminated. Sometimes, post-intimacy relationships are maintained with each partner continuing to use their RSSD to effectively adapt and respond to one another, though the motivation to apply generally diminishes over time.

RSSD can contribute to the decision to de-escalate or terminate nonviable relationships. As intimate knowledge continues to be gained, RSSD might lead to predicting negative personal and relational outcomes. For example, knowing that your intimate romantic partner has different religious beliefs might be of minor concern in the initial stages, but in considering marriage and a family, the partner's hardline religious views might lead to predicting significant issues in raising children and a decision to end the relationship. When people choose not to engage in RSSD, they might fail to recognize potential relational problems which might otherwise have been avoided.

Termination of relationships also vary in terms of whether the decision to end a relationship is *bilateral* with both partners sharing interest in ending the relationship or whether the decision is *unilateral* with only one partner choosing to end the relationship. The role of social decentering and RSSD differs in these two patterns. When both partners share in the decision to de-escalate they are likely to share more information about their thoughts and feelings which enhances their RSSD and understanding of each other's positions. In a unilateral breakup, the departing parties often engage in a sequence of strategies beginning with indirect strategies such as reducing their level of self-disclosure followed by direct strategies of expressing a desire to end the relationship (Baxter, 1987). Several factors contribute to the slow process of disengagement: disengagers are often motivated to protect the feelings and face of their partners; disengagers are also concerned with their own face, not wanting to be viewed negatively; and disengagers want to minimize the post-relationship repercussions (an ex-partner betraying confidences or turning a shared social network against the disengager). Social decentering and RSSD can contribute to developing and implementing strategies to manage these factors.

Social decentering and RSSD can also have a negative impact on the decenterers themselves. Social decentering and RSSD might predict negative or hostile reactions from the partner to a request to terminate the relationship. As a result, social decentering and RSSD would add further to the disengager's distress. One way of coping with that distress would be to delay efforts to directly terminate the relationship, increase one's resolve to tough it out, or increase efforts to subvert the relationship.

According to Miller and Parks (1982), disengagers enact compliance gaining strategies to persuade their partners to dissolve the relationship. The success of these compliance gaining strategies is improved by the level of understanding and accuracy of predictions about partners that people can make based on their RSSD. But as discussed earlier, the more intimate the relationship, the more possible a partner can use his or her understanding to counter the influence. Unilateral disengagers often work toward achieving an ideal termination wherein their partners grant permission or at least agree to end the relationship – changing the decision from unilateral to bilateral (Baxter, 1984b). The level of partner resistance to granting that permission or agreement tends to extend the disengagement process. The partner might propose alternatives to ending the relationship such as seeking counseling or repairing relational problems. Throughout this process, RSSD plays a critical role for disengagers in deciding what to say and how to behave relative to predicted responses from their partners. In some instances, the disengagers might discover that they are missing information needed to make such predictions. This uncertainty necessitates getting the partner to disclose additional information often by engaging in relationship talk (Baxter, 1987). To the degree that each stage of de-escalation involves interacting within new circumstances and within a redefined relationship, RSSD can prove to be ineffectual at times. A lack of ongoing relationship talk, might undermine a person's understanding of the partner's thoughts and feelings about the current status of the relationship. Such relationship uncertainty reduces the effective application of RSSD. For example, having little knowledge of how a partner has reacted to previous relationship break-ups (if any) makes it challenging to predict that partner's reaction to the current decision to separate. Social decentering can provide some understanding by utilizing one's own experience, knowledge of other close friends' break-up experiences, and understanding people's reactions in general, to the loss of a relationship. The effectiveness of social decentering depends on how well these referents parallel the current relationship and partner. In contrast to the absence of information, new information is gained simply by observing a partner's reactions and behaviors during de-escalation (Baxter, 1983). We might find that our partner is much more understanding, committed, caring, or accommodating then we expected. Unfortunately, we might also uncover more negative characteristics about our partner, such as an inclination toward hostility, violence, or threatening behavior that was not previously known. Acquiring such new information causes us to modify RSSD resulting in revisions of our strategies and behaviors.

Leslie Baxter (1984a) classified termination strategies as indirect (withdrawal, pseudo-de-escalation, and cost escalation) and direct (negative identity management, justification, de-escalation, and positive tone). The strategies vary in terms of the degree to which they attempt to protect the other's feelings and face. Social decentering and RSSD can help individuals select and implement a strategy designed for their specific relational circumstances. For example, positive tone involves directly stating a desire to end the relationship but affirming the positive qualities and value of the other person in an attempt to end the relationship on a positive note. Positive tone was seen as a strategy used by people who are strong perspective takers who see their partner needing help in adjusting to the relationship ending (Banks, Altendorf, Greene, & Cody, 1987). RSSD helps disengagers recognize the needs of a partner, and to develop and enact an effective positive tone strategy. Justification involves a clear desire to end the relationship along with an honest explanation of why. Strong RSSD skills help in assessing a partner's ability to handle a direct declaration and straightforward explanation and in developing a message that will best protect the partner's face. Remember though that decentering doesn't necessarily mean a person engages in behaviors that have a positive impact on their partners. People might choose withdrawal as the strategy to end their relationships because it requires less effort and protects their face even when RSSD predicts that their partner will be stressed by the uncertainty and suffer loss of esteem (Baxter, 1987).

3.3.1 Turmoil or Stagnation

The first stage toward de-escalation of an intimate relationship typically follows one of two patterns. The first, turmoil, reflects increased conflict, more fault finding, and less tolerance. The second, stagnation, involves one or both partners losing interest in the other and/or relational boredom. Relational boredom consists of seeing the relationship as lacking fun, lacking excitement, having no spark, and/or partners just being sick and tired of each other (Harasymchuk & Fehr, 2012). These two patterns occur both in friendship and romantic relationships. Regardless of the pattern, a significant drop in the use of social decentering and RSSD is likely as one partner's interest in the other partner declines and as they become more self-oriented.

Many factors contribute to waning interest in a partner and those factors affect the engagement in and depth of social decentering and RSSD. For example, a partner talks with food in her mouth which had not been an issue because her partner's RSSD leads to tolerance through understanding that the partner was raised in a household devoid of dinner etiquette. But in the turmoil/stagnation stage, the partner no longer applies RSSD to achieve that understanding and instead of tolerance, criticizes the behavior. Such increasing intolerance adds to the turmoil and de-escalation of the relationship.

RSSD can be particularly destructive during conflict when an individual decides to abandon self-censorship and civility. The accumulated knowledge about a partner means that RSSD can be used in a particularly negative and hurtful manner to generate messages and actions that specifically target the known weaknesses of the other. Messages perceived as intentionally hurtful tend to further damage relationships that are already fragile (McLaren & Solomon, 2014).

Just as ongoing conflict can be an indication of trouble, so can the lack of conflict (Levinger, 1983). Avoiding conflict means couples are either censoring their responses to their partners, avoiding discussing issues of difference, and/or minimally disclosing their thoughts and feelings. The longer the stagnation lasts, the less and less a partner is aware of his/her partner's current dispositions and the more out-of-date and ineffective their RSSD – essentially the couples just grow apart.

RSSD peaks during the intimacy stage with partners reaching a fairly complete and profound understanding of each other. As a result, partners are better positioned to make long-range forecasts about each other. In some instances, those forecasts might present a less than satisfying future for the relationship – one that is not going to meet personal needs and goals. As a result, RSSD can be both a cause of stagnation and the product of stagnation. Because there is not the same level or type of commitment, friends are more likely to engage in fading away as a strategy to de-escalate stagnating relationships than are romantic couples. Romantic couples can be expected to endure stagnation longer than most friendships.

3.3.2 Deintensification

At the point of deintensification, partners have pulled further away from each other "decreasing their interactions; increasing their physical, emotional, and psychological distance; and decreasing their dependence on the other for self-confirmation" (Beebe, Beebe, Redmond, 2017, pp. 253–254). Knapp and Vangelisti (2005) call this stage circumscribing, since communication is constricted and information exchange decreases in quality and quantity as well as breadth and depth. The continuing decline of self-disclosures further undermines effective RSSD. Knapp and Vangelisti also see an increase in the number of topics that are touchy and potential conflict triggers. Partners become more sensitive to what is said, and new rules are introduced about what is out-of-bounds. Such changes in the communication rules necessitate incorporating those rules into a person's RSSD. Unfortunately, motivation to incorporate such information tends to fade during de-escalation and failure to do so is likely to contribute to hostility, anger, conflict, and further relationship deterioration. Imagine the impact of a women saying, "I don't want you to keep comparing us to how my mother and father fought" and the next day her romantic partner says, "You're acting just like your parents did before they got divorced." The failure to either incorporate the new rule into RSSD or the decision to intentionally violate that rule is likely to exacerbate the situation.

People can use social decentering to compare their thoughts and feelings, as well as their partner's thoughts and feelings, to other people they know and to people in general. Considering what other people would do or feel at this stage of de-escalation can provide comfort when it parallels their own feelings and actions. Consideration of what other friends have felt and done when faced with the de-escalation of close relationships might also provide strategies to consider in managing deintensification.

During deintensification or at some other point during de-escalation, partners are likely to engage in a relationship dissolution talk in which they review the relationship history, compare their behaviors to social relationship norms, entertain proposals for increasing satisfaction, evaluate the costs and benefits of the relationship, and experience and express feelings of guilt or anger (Duck, 2005). During such discussions, some expectations derived from RSSD are affirmed while others are contradicted as new information is learned about a partner. For example, Felix sees his close friend and messy roommate, Oscar, as melodramatic. Felix announces that he is going to move to his own place. And just as Felix predicted, Oscar moans and groans that "All is lost!" and "My life is falling apart." In anticipation of this, Felix already had prepared a strategy to address Oscar's concerns. But such anticipation cannot always be done, as relationships de-escalate, couples are less likely to be open and thus RSSD becomes more and more unreliable. For example, one partner might not discover that his or her partner's antagonism was the result of jealousy about the excessive amount of time the partner spent at work because the partner had not shared those feelings.

3.3.3 Individualization

During the individualization stage, partners tend to operate mostly independent of each other, spending time in their own social networks and engaging in activities without the other partner. Nonetheless, they still consider themselves in a relationship with each other. They might still be married, refer to the relationship as boyfriend/girlfriend or best friends but they do not actually consider themselves to be in such relationships. They are like a couple quietly sitting together at an airport waiting for their flight to separation. Generally, there is little conflict because there is minimal interaction with both keeping a distance from each other. The interactions they do have are primarily impersonal and task oriented.

At this point partners have probably accepted the impending end of the relationship and might seek to end the relationship amicably, which RSSD can help to accomplish. Sometimes partners in intimate relationships might agree to continue the relationship as a post-intimacy relationship (post-romantic relationship). Previous research has found that the ability of one's partner to continue to provide resources contributes to the continuation of post-intimacy relationships (Busboom, Collins, Givertz, & Levin, 2002). Rather than continuing to the separation stage, partners in a post-intimacy relationship might move back to the exploration stage of escalation. Partners seek to maintain the relationship as friends, enjoying the resources that such a relationship provides. Gaining knowledge about a partner's desire to maintain a less intimate relationship is added to an RSSD mindset of respecting the other's individualism while still showing concern for the other's welfare. RSSD again becomes a tool for maintaining a positive relationship, albeit, at a less intimate level.

Hess (2002) had college students provide accounts of how they controlled the amount and nature of interactions they had with people they disliked. Three categories of strategies were identified: avoidance, disengagement, and cognitive dissociation.

Such strategies reflect the types of behaviors and thoughts likely to occur during individualization. Avoidance includes preventing and/or limiting interactions. Disengagement involves hiding information about self and interacting less personally. Cognitive dissociation reflects a change in the way a person thinks about the partner through mentally disregarding messages, entertaining derogatory thoughts, and envisioning separation and being detached. One outcome of these strategies is undermining a partner's ability to enhance or apply his or her RSSD on the other. Avoiding interactions takes away the opportunities for a partner to display any understanding or adaptation to the other. Disengagement prevents the acquisition of information about the partner's current dispositional state rendering previous RSSD out-of-date. And cognitive dissociation might lead to less time spent thinking about the partner and thus less engagement in RSSD.

Steve Duck's (1982, 2005) model of relationship dissolution focuses on the role of the social network including the process of letting other people know that the couple's relationship is over. Because partners are individually spending more time with friends and family, it becomes apparent to others that the relationship is in trouble or over. As a result, individuals begin to "focus on accounting, attribution, and the creation of psychologically palatable stories about one's own and the partner's role in the relationship decline" (Duck, 2005, p. 212). People provide accounts to others of what and why the relationship is de-escalating; then after the break-up, they develop and provide post-dissolution accounts (Duck, 1982). In constructing these accounts, social decentering and RSSD come into play, not for dealing with the partner, but for adapting their stories to the people with whom they discuss the break-up. For example, developing a story about why you and your boyfriend or girlfriend broke up that you expect will be most palatable to your parents. Duck (2005) labels the process after the breakup as *grave-dressing* where people create simple, face-saving accounts:

> Topics in grave-dressing are likely to be plausible stories about the betrayal of self by Partner, or else depict the difficulties of two honest folk working together on a relationship that requires more work than it is worth. In such cases, different audiences are addressed in different ways, with relevant narrative being specifically crafted for them. (p. 212)

These stories continue to be refined as part of the social process after the partners have separated. Social decentering through the use of generalized-other allows people to create stories they believe will be acceptable to the public. These stories are also likely to be shared at some point during the development of a new relationship.

3.3.4 Separation

In the separation stage, individuals usually move toward eliminating further interactions or at least restricting interactions to specific contexts – such as the classroom or workplace. Separation might involve one partner moving out of a shared living space, dividing property and resources, and even dividing members of their shared social network. When the disengagement is amicable, RSSD can facilitate these divisions by helping partners reach an understanding of what and who is important to the other, strengthening their openness to accommodation. When the disengagement is hostile, RSSD can be used to undermine the division when people know which things are most important to their partners and for that reason choose to make things more difficult by resisting their partner's claims. Once the partners actually part company and are no longer interacting, decentering is obviously no longer needed to understand or predict the partner's dispositions.

Separation does not necessarily mean that there are no longer any interactions. Sometimes couples separate romantically but maintain friendships in which case decentering continues to contribute to the management of the friendship. Other times, couples either eliminate or diminish their interactions only to resurrect the relationship later. This rekindling occurs both for romantic and non-romantic relationships such as friends who reconnect after not interacting for several years. Reasons for continuing or restarting relationships that had been romantic include the existence of strong commitment, returning to friendship, social network support, the partner as a source of resources, and satisfaction with those resources (Busboom et al., 2002; Tan, Agnes, VanderDrift, & Harvey, 2015).

The process of maintaining or re-kindling a relationship after separation is facilitated by partners' having a preexisting understanding of each other through RSSD, assuming the RSSD was relatively accurate and effectively used previously in adapting to the partner. A lack of or failure to apply RSSD before might well be one of the reasons the relationship ended. Depending on how much time passes before reconnecting, RSSD provides a quick foundation for understanding and adapting to the partner at a level that is beyond that found in acquaintanceships. In some instances, significant changes might have occurred in each partner which necessitates significant RSSD revision. In reconnecting, comparison of new observations of partners with predictions based on the original RSSD can lead to an appreciation of the positive changes made by the partners and updating of the original RSSD. For example, if the original RSSD included a partner's disposition to be possessive but the current observation was of a more confident and self-sufficient partner, the partner could be perceived as more attractive. In this way, RSSD plays a significant role on whether relationship escalation reoccurs by highlighting the new, improved attributes of the partner or lack thereof.

Many times, we run into people with whom we formerly had very close relationships. Those interactions are often awkward since we have intimate knowledge of each other, yet our interaction occurs on a level more akin to casual banter with an acquaintance. In such interactions, our use of RSSD for adaptation generally focuses on selecting the topics we predict the other person feels comfortable discussing in the current context. Such topics might include asking how the other person's family members are doing, finding out what the other person is doing, or reminiscing about old times. Over time RSSD becomes less applicable as information fades from memory and little new information about the partner is acquired. Adaptation to the other becomes more dependent on the application of use of generalized-others social decentering skills by the interactants.

3.3.5 Post-Interaction Effects

In the model of relational development used in this chapter, the post-interaction effects stage was created to acknowledge that even when partners are no longer interacting, the experience of the relationship has a lasting effect on the individuals. Our reactions to and behavior in new relationships are affected by our past relational experiences. Each relationship becomes part of who we are and influences future perceptions and interactions. During this stage, depending on the depth and importance of the relationship, people engage in a relationship post-mortem in which they try to understand what happened in the relationship and learn from that experience (Duck, 1982). For Duck (2005) this stage offers "the chance to review and adjust psychological beliefs about Self, Others, and Relationships that might hold up better in the future" (p. 212). When reviewing non-marital breakups, Ann Weber (1998) wrote "So much of our cognitive work of the breakup process is focused on obsession, attribution, and explanation of what happened that it seems clear we must establish some sense of meaning in order to grieve and move on" (p. 297).

Our relational experiences and the insights gained through retrospection and the post-mortem contribute to the continued development of all three forms of social decentering analysis. Every one of our relationships potentially adds to our self-knowledge – our likes and dislikes, the level of our need for confirmation, inclusion, independence, support, control, and so on. This knowledge becomes part of our use of self form of social decentering used to analyze the dispositions of others. If we felt depressed after the breakup of a long-term intimate romantic relationship, that experience becomes one option for understanding and adapting to a friend who recently experienced a similar breakup. The partners in terminated relationships become part of our use of specific-others' repertoire. When we meet someone new who reminds us of that former partner, we are likely to use knowledge of our ex to make predictions about the new person. We will also discover differences between the new partner and the old that help us form alternative predictions. Finally, each former relationship becomes part of the collective about how people in general think and feel that is the foundation of the use of generalized-other. Each new relational experience increases the depth and applicability of the use of generalized-other. On one hand, the more relational experience someone has, the greater potential for developing strong social decentering. On the other hand, the inability to sustain relationships might reflect a failure in interpersonal competence including an inability to learn from those relationships or develop RSSD. The question this leads to is: Who is more likely to develop a long-lasting romantic relationship, the person who has had 20 romantic relationships over 10 years or the person who has had 2 romantic partners of 10 years? One answer is, whoever learned the most from their experiences.

People with strong RSSD are likely to have more productive relationship postmortems than those with weak RSSD. When relationship disengagement is due to differences in partners' goals or incompatibilities, those with strong RSSD who have been honest with themselves will likely have noticed those differences and anticipated the end of the relationship. Their post-dissolution rumination will primarily involve confirming their earlier recognition of differences. They still might consider what they might have done differently to bridge the differences and sustain the relationship at some level of intimacy. Those weak in RSSD are more likely to be baffled by the end of their relationships because of their limited understanding of their partners' needs and dispositions. We are also likely to be mystified about what happened in a relationship that ended earlier than we anticipated if we did not have the opportunity to develop RSSD. We are perplexed when a person we've dated a couple of times no longer returns our calls; our uncertainty is high, and we have little personal information about the partner on which to form a more than a general conclusion. We will probably utilize social decentering to provide possible explanations, particularly the use of generalized-other.

Throughout the relationship escalation and de-escalation stages, the role of social decentering and development and application of RSSD play a variety of roles. The changes in RSSD and application of decentering associated with changes in stages are one reason that makes researching the role of other oriented cognitive process so challenging – it is not consistent throughout relationship development. The preceding discussion of the stages provides a model of the fluctuating relationships between other oriented processes such as social decentering and RSSD and relational stages. The next chapter presents a study I conducted that examines some of those relationships within the context of escalation and de-escalation stages.

3.4 References

Altman, I., & Taylor, D. A. (1973). *Social penetration: The development of interpersonal relationships.* New York: Holt, Rinehart & Winston.

Banks, S. P., Altendorf, D. M., Greene, J. O., & Cody, M. J. (1987). An examination of relationship disengagement: Perceptions, breakup strategies and outcomes. *Western Journal of Speech Communication, 51*, 19–41.

Bavelas, J. B., & Coates, L. (1992). How do we account for the mindfulness of face-to-face dialogue? *Communication Monographs, 59*, 301–305.

Baxter, L. A. (1983). Relationship disengagement: An examination of the reversal hypothesis. *Western Journal of Speech Communication, 47*, 85–98.

Baxter, L. A. (1984a). Accomplishing relationship disengagement. In S. Duck & D. Perlman (Eds.), *Understanding personal relationships: An interdisciplinary approach*, (pp. 243–265). Beverly Hills, CA: Sage.

Baxter, L. A. (1984b). Trajectories of relationship disengagement. *Journal of Social and Personal Relationships, 1*, 29–48.

Baxter, L. A. (1987). Self-disclosure and relationship disengagement. In V. J. Derlega & J. H. Berg (Eds.), *Self-disclosure: Theory, research, and therapy* (pp. 155–174). New York: Plenum Press.

Beebe, S. A., Beebe, S. J., & Redmond, M. V. (2017). *Interpersonal communication: Relating to others* (8th edn.). Boston, MA: Pearson.

Bell, R. A., & Daly, J. A. (1984). The affinity seeking function of communication. *Communication Monographs, 51*, 91–115.

Berger, C. R., & Bradac, J. J. (1982). *Language and social knowledge: Uncertainty and -interpersonal relations.* Baltimore, MD: Edward Arnold

Blanke, E. S., Rauers, A., & Riediger, M. (2016). Does being empathic pay off? Associations between performance-based measures of empathy and social adjustment in younger and older women. *Emotion, 16*, 671–683.

Bodie, G. D., St. Cyr, K., Pence, M., Rold, M., & Honeycutt, J. (2012). Listening competence in initial interactions I: Distinguishing between what listening is and what listeners do. *International Journal of Listening, 26*, 1–28, doi:10.1080/10904018.2012.639645

Brems, C. (1989). Dimensionality of empathy and its correlates. *The Journal of Psychology, 123*, 329–337. doi:10.1080/00223980.1989.10542989

Busboom, A. L., Collins, D. M., Givertz, M. D., & Levin, L. A. (2002). Can we still be friends? Resources and barriers to friendship quality after romantic dissolution. *Personal Relationships, 9*, 215–223.

Ciarrochi, J., Parker, P.D., Sahdra, B. K., Kashdan, T. B., Kiuru, N., & Conigrave, J. (2016). When empathy matters: The role of sex and empathy in close friendships. *Journal of Personality, 85*, 494–504. doi:10.1111/jopy.12255.

Clark, M.S., & Lemay, E. P. (2010). Close relationships. In S. T. Fiske, D. T. Gilbert, & G. Lindzey (Eds.), *Handbook of social psychology* (5th edn., Vol. 2, pp. 898–940). Hoboken, NJ: John Wiley & Sons.

Clatterbuck, G.W. (1979). Attributional confidence and uncertainty in initial interaction. *Human Communication Research, 5*,147–157.

Colvin, C. R., Vogt, D., & Ickes, W. (1997). Why do friends understand each other better than strangers do? In W. Ickes (Ed.), *Empathic accuracy* (pp. 169–194). New York: Guilford Press.

Douglas, W. (1991). Expectations about initial interaction: An examination of the effects of global uncertainty. *Human Communication Research, 17*, 355–384.

Duck, S. (1982). A topography of relationship -disengagement and dissolution. In S. W. Duck (Ed.) *Personal-relationships 4: Dissolving personal relationships* (pp. 1–29). London: Academic Press.

Duck, S. (2005). How do you tell someone you're letting go? *The Psychologist, 18*, 210–213.

Dunleavy, K. N., & Booth-Butterfield, M. (2009). Idiomatic communication in the stages of coming together and falling apart. *Communication Quarterly, 57*, 416–432.

Edwards, R., Bybee, B. T., Frost, J., K., Harvey, A. J., & Navarro, M. (2016). That's not what I meant: How misunderstanding is related to channel and perspective-taking. *Journal of Language and Social Psychology, 36*, 188–210.

Egbert, N., Miraldi, L. B., & Murniadi, K. (2014). Friends don't let friends suffer from depression: How threat, efficacy, knowledge, and empathy relate to college students'; intentions to intervene on behalf of a depressed friend. *Journal of Health Communication, 19*, 460–477. doi:10.1080/10810730.2013.821554

Finkenauer, C., & Righetti, F. (2011). Understanding in close relationships: An interpersonal approach. In W. Stroebe & M. Hewstone (Eds.), *European review of social psychology* (Vol. 22, pp. 316–363). New York: Psychology Press.

Fletcher, G. J. O., Fincham, F. D., Cramer, L., & Heron, N. (1987). The role of attributions in the development of dating relationships. *Journal of Personality and Social Psychology, 53*, 481–489.

Grief, E. B., & Hogan, R. (1973). The theory and measurement of empathy. *Journal of Counseling Psychology, 20*, 280–284.

Hadden, B. W., Rodriguez, L. M., Knee, C. R., & Porter, B. (2015). Relationship autonomy and support provision in romantic relationships. *Motivation and Emotion*, *39*, 359–373.

Harasymchuk, C., & Fehr, B. (2012). A prototype analysis of relational boredom. *Journal of Social and Personal Relationships*, *30*, 627–646.

Harvey J. H., & Omarzu, J. (1999). *Minding the close relationship: A theory of relationship enhancement*. New York: Cambridge University Press.

Hess, J. A. (2002). Distance regulation in personal relationships: The development of a conceptual model and a test of representational validity. *Journal of Social and Personal Relationships*, *19*, 663–682.

Hodgson, L. K., & Wertheim, E. H. (2007). Does good emotion management aid forgiving? Multiple dimensions of empathy, emotion management and forgiveness of self and others. *Journal of Social and Personal Relationships, 24*, 931–949.

Hogan, R. (1969). Development of an empathy scale. *Journal of Consulting and Clinical Psychology, 33*, 307–318.

Human, L., J. & Biesanz, J. C. (2011). Through the looking glass clearly: Accuracy and assumed similarity in well-adjusted individuals' first impressions. *Journal of Personality and Social Psychology, 100*, 349–364.

Kardos, P., Leidner, B., Pléh, C., Soltész, P., & Unoka, Z. (2017). Empathic people have more friends: Empathic abilities predict social network size and position in social network predicts empathic efforts. *Social Networks, 50*, 1–5.

Kellermann, K. (1991). The conversation MOP II: Progression through scenes in discourse. *Human Communication Research*, *17*, 385–414.

Knapp, M. L. (1984). *Interpersonal communication and human relationships*. Boston: Allyn & Bacon.

Knapp, M. L., & Vangelisti, A. L. (2005). *Interpersonal communication and human relationships* (5th edn). Boston: Allyn & Bacon.

Levinger. G. (1983). Development and change. In H. H. Kelley (Ed.) *Close relationships* (pp. 315–359). New York: W. H. Freeman.

Lewis. K. L., & Hodges, S. D. (2012). Empathy is not always as personal as you may think: The use of stereotypes in empathic accuracy. In J. Decety (Ed.), *Empathy* (pp. 73–84). Cambridge, MA: The MIT Press.

Macaskill, A., Maltby, J., & Day, L. (2002). Forgiveness of self and others and emotional empathy, *The Journal of Social Psychology*, *142*, 663–665, doi:10.1080/00224540209603925

McCroskey, J. C., & McCain, T. A. (1974). The measurement of interpersonal attraction. *Speech Monographs*, *41*, 261–266.

McLaren, R. M., & Solomon, D. H. (2014). Contextualizing experiences of hurt within close relationships. *Communication Quarterly*, *62*, 323–341.

Miller, G. R., & Boster, F. (1988). Persuasion in personal relationships. In S. W. Duck (Ed.), *A handbook of personal relationships* (pp. 275–288). New York: Wiley.

Miller, G. R., & Parks, M. R. (1982). Communication in dissolving relationships. In S. Duck (Ed.), *Personal relationships 4: Dissolving personal relationships* (pp. 127–154). New York: Academic Press.

Mongeau, P. A., & Henningsenm M. L. M. (2015). Stage theories of relationship development: Charting the course of interpersonal communication. In D. O. Braithwaite & P. Schrodt (Eds.), *Engaging theories in interpersonal communication* (2nd edn.) (pp. 389–402). Los Angeles, CA: Sage.

Pollman, M. H., & Finkenauer, C. (2009). Understanding is more important than knowledge. *Personality and Social Psychology Bulletin*, *35*, 1512–1527.

Redmond, M. V. (1989). The functions of empathy (decentering) in human relations. *Human Relations, 42*, 593–606.

Redmond, M. V. (2002). Social decentering, intimacy, and interpersonal influence. Paper presented at the annual meeting of the National Communication Association, New Orleans.

Redmond, M. V., & Vrchota, D. A. (1994). The effects of varying lengths of initial interaction on attraction and uncertainty reduction. Paper presented at the 1994 annual SCA meeting, New Orleans.

Riek, B.M., & Mania, E.W. (2012). The antecedents and consequences of interpersonal forgiveness: A meta-analytic review. *Personal Relationships*, *19*, 304–325.

Rusbult, C. E., & Van Lange, P. A. M. (2003). Interdependence, interaction, and relationships. *Annual Review of Psychology*, *54*, 351–375.

Stinson, L., & Ickes, W. (1992). Empathic accuracy in the interactions of male friends versus male strangers. *Journal of Personality and Social Psychology*, *62*, 787–797.

Sunnafrank, M. (1984). A communication based perspective on attitude similarity and interpersonal attraction in early acquaintance. *Communications Monographs*, *51*, 372–380.

Sunnafrank, M. (1986). Predicted outcome value during initial interactions: A reformulation of uncertainty reduction theory. *Human Communication Theory*, *13*, 3–33.

Tan, K., Agnew, C. R., VanderDrift, L. E., & Harvey, S. M. (2015) Committed to us: Predicting relationship closeness following nonmarital romantic relationship breakup. *Journal of Social and Personal Relationships*, *32*, 456–471.

Tan, K., See, Y. H. M., & Agnew, C. R. (2015). Partner's understanding of affective-cognitive meta-bases predicts relationship quality. *Personal Relationships*, *22*, 524–535.

Trobst, K. K., Collins, R. L., & Embree, J. M. (1994). The role of emotion in social support of provision: Gender, empathy and expressions of distress. *Journal of Social and Personal Relationships*, *11*, 45–62.

Weber, A. (1998). Loving, leaving, and letting go: Coping with nonmarital breakups. In B. H. Spitzberg and W. R. Cupach (Eds.), *The dark side of close relationships* (pp. 267–306). Mahwah, NJ: Erlbaum Associates.

Weger Jr., H., Castle Bell, G., Minei, E. M., & Robinson, M. C. (2014) The relative effectiveness of active listening in initial interactions. *International Journal of Listening*, *28*, 13–31. doi:10.1080/10904018.2013.813234

Welch, S. A., & Rubin, R. B. (2002). Development of relationship stage measures, *Communication Quarterly*, *50*, 24–40. doi:10.1080/01463370209385644

Wright, C. N., &. Roloff, M. E. (2015). You should just know why I'm upset: expectancy violation theory and the influence of mind reading expectations (MRE) on responses to relational problems, *Communication Research Reports*, *32*, 10–19. doi:10.1080/08824096.2014.989969

4 A Study of Social Decentering, Relationship-Specific Social Decentering (RSSD), and the Escalation and De-escalation of Relationships

A number of relationships between social decentering, relationship-specific social decentering (RSSD), relationship escalation, and relationship de-escalation were advanced in Chapter 3. In this chapter, two studies are presented that were conducted to examine some of those relationships. The first study focused on escalating relationships and the second study focused on de-escalating or terminated relationships. Both studies follow a similar design using cross-sex partners as participants. Partners came to the study center at the same time and then individually completed questionnaires about themselves and their relationship. Both studies are discussed concurrently to facilitate comparisons between them.

College students were recruited from various classes to participate and received extra credit for their participation. They were instructed to bring someone of the opposite sex who they knew and who would be willing to participate. For the escalation study, students were told that a variety of cross-sex relationships were being examined and they were free to bring a cross-sex friend or a romantic partner. For the de-escalation study, volunteers were instructed to identify a cross-sex partner with whom they once had a close relationship, but which had since de-escalated, deteriorated, or ended. They were to invite that partner to also participate in the study. Partners in the de-escalation study had the option of not attending at the same time, so long as the first partner communicated a matching code to their partner. For the de-escalation study, volunteers from classes received extra credit for participating while their partners received a gift certificate from Dairy Queen.

In both studies, each relationship partner sat on opposite sides of the study room to ensure confidentiality and independent responses. They received a packet of materials with a brief description of the purpose of the study, an assurance of confidentiality, and a statement that completion of the forms indicated their agreement to participate.

4.1 Participants

Escalation Study: There were 172 participants (86 couples) who initially completed the questionnaire. Participants were provided with a list of seven relationship labels that were described as indicating increasing levels of closeness ranging from acquaintance to spouse and asked to indicate the current level of closeness of their relationship. Another question asked for the highest level of closeness the relationship had ever reached. Given the focus on stable or escalating relationships, pairs where one

https://doi.org/10.1515/9783110515664-005

partner indicated a drop of two or more relationship levels or where both partners indicated a drop of one or more relationship levels were excluded from further analysis. The final analysis involved 132 participants. Their age ranged from 18 to 36 with a mean of 20.9 (*SD* = 2.28). Sixty participants perceived the relationship to be romantic and 72 did not. The length of knowing each other ranged from one week to 20 years with the average being 2.95 years (*SD* = 4.13 years).

De-escalation Study: One hundred and ninety-eight participants (99 pairs) took part in the de-escalation study. Pairs of participants were dropped from further analysis if one of them failed to complete sections of the questionnaire or if they did not indicate a decline of at least one point (on a 21-point scale) of intimacy. This resulted in the responses of 56 pairs (112 participants) being used in the analyses. The average age was 20.13 with a range from 18 to 26. Thirty-three indicated that the relationship had not been romantic (one other was left blank but paired with a nonromantic respondent) and 77 indicated that it had been romantic (with one respondent selecting both options). The average length of knowing each other was 2.2 years (*SD* = 1.85 years) and ranged from one month to 10 years. Participants completed two copies of all the measures except social decentering. After providing demographic information, participants completed a section of the questionnaire labeled *The Current State of the Relationship* with questions appropriately worded in the present tense. The second section they completed was labeled *Questions About the Closest Period of the Relationship* with the questions phrased in the past tense.

4.2 Measures

Reliabilities are based on the combined responses of the escalation respondents and de-escalation respondents' responses for the current state of relationship. Participants in the de-escalation study completed all but the social decentering scale twice; once relative to their current relationship status and once relative to the closest period of their relationship.

Social Decentering. Social decentering was assessed with the 36-item Social Decentering Scale discussed in Chapter 2 (see Appendix A) using five-point Likert response scales. Previous reported reliability was α = 0.91 and in the current study was 0.89 (*n* = 244).

Relationship-Specific Social Decentering. The 12-item Relationship-Specific Social Decentering Scale described in Chapter 2 (see Appendix B) was used to assess participants' level of understanding their specific partner's dispositions. Respondents were asked to assess the degree to which each item applied to their specific partner using a five-point Likert scale. Reliability for the scale was α = 0.89 (*n* = 244).

Relationship Intimacy/Closeness. Relationship intimacy was assessed by combining the results of three measures of intimacy. The first was Lemieux and Hale's (1999) measure of relational intimacy which consists of six items with a seven-point Likert scale that taps elements of relational intimacy with questions such as "There is nothing I can't tell my partner" and "I feel close to my partner most of the time." Reliability for this measure was $\alpha = 0.92$ ($n = 244$). The second measure had respondents select the term which best described the level of closeness in their relationship from a list of labels described in the instructions as representing "equal increments of increasing levels of closeness": (1) Acquaintance, (2) Casual Friend, (3) Friend, (4) Close Friend, (5) One of My Best Friends, (6) My Best Friend/Fiancee/Lover, and (7) Spouse (a special form of friend). The third measure of intimacy was Aron, Aron, and Smollan's (1992) Inclusion of Other in the Self Scale (IOC). The IOC is intended to determine how much a person's self includes another person by selecting from a set of circles labeled self and other that overlap, increasing from just touching to being almost concentric. Participants selected the image that best reflected the closeness of their relationship from among the seven pairs of overlapping circles.

The average score from the measure of Relational Intimacy was combined with the relationship labels measure and measure of IOC to create an overall intimacy scale. Combining the three measures provides a strong and comprehensive measure of intimacy. Since each of the three measures was based on a seven-point scale, they equally impact the final scale. The reliability of the three measures as a single scale was $\alpha = 0.90$ ($n = 244$). The average intimacy score on the 7- to 21-point scale was 12.62 ($SD = 4.15$).

Stages. The responses from participants in escalating relationships and the previous peak responses of de-escalating participants were used to create four groups of increasing levels of intimacy that were then treated as the four escalation stages (see Table 4.1). The current level of intimacy from the de-escalation relationships was used for sorting the relationships into four de-escalation stages. The same ranges of intimacy used to create the four escalation stages were used to create a reverse ordering for the four de-escalation stages [highest (5) to lowest (8)]. Distributions associated with each stage are presented in Table 4.1.

Table 4.1: Intimacy and frequency distributions across the relational stages.

Stage	Intimacy Range	Escalation N =	De-escalation at Peak N =	Stage	De-escalation Currently N =
1 – Acquaintance	7– 9.5	13	10	8 – Separation	52
2 – Exploration	9.6–12.38	32	24	7 – Individualization	25
3 – Intensification	12.39–16.35	34	45	6 – De-intensification	27
4 – Intimate	16.36–21	53	32	5 – Stagnation/Turmoil	8

Relationship Satisfaction. To measure relationship satisfaction, I used the three-item scale with a six-point response set developed by Rusbult (1983). The first item asks how happy the respondent is in the relationship, the second asks how the respondent was attracted to the partner, and the third asks how satisfied the respondent is in the relationship. While Rusbult reported 12 different reliabilities because of the longitudinal nature of her study, subsequent use has reported a Cronbach's alpha of 0.86 for this instrument (Roloff & Ifert, 1998). In the current study, Cronbach's alpha was 0.58 (n = 243) which is marginally acceptable. The attraction item might not have been as valid a measure for respondents in friendships compared to those in romantic relationships, but the three items collectively still provide an adequate measure of satisfaction.

Relational Assessment. Changes in people's assessment of their relationship are expected to occur as relationships escalate and de-escalate. Hendrick (1988) developed the Relationship Assessment Scale (RAS) using items from her earlier marital scale with a reported reliability of α = 0.86. Relationship assessment was operationalized as a cumulative response on a five-point scale to seven items measuring satisfaction, problems, expectations, and needs. The items reflect a general measure of relational satisfaction that taps into a broader range of perceptions than does Rusbult's measure. In the current study, reliability was α = 0.80 (n = 241).

A certain level of error might be expected in the participants' recall in de-escalating relationships concerning the relationship during its peak, but there was no significant difference in the RSSD scores at Stage 4 (intimacy) between those in the escalating relationships and those recalled in the de-escalating relationships. The RSSD mean for participants in the escalating relationships currently at Stage 4 was 51.19 (SD = 4.7, n = 53) and the RSSD mean for participants in the de-escalating relationships who previously reached Stage 4 was 51.88 (SD = 5.2, n = 32). These results suggest that de-escalating participants were able to accurately recall their level of RSSD when the relationship was closest and provides confidence in the accuracy of their other peak period responses. One caveat is that responses from both escalating and de-escalating might reflect a shared social desirability bias and not their actual experience. But if that were the case, social desirability would predict high scores across all the stages, which did not occur.

4.3 Results

4.3.1 Intimacy/Stages and RSSD/Social Decentering

Given that social decentering is regarded as a trait quality, no significant changes were expected relative to changes in intimacy and none were found. On the other hand, RSSD positively correlated as expected with feelings of intimacy/closeness in the combined sample of escalating and de-escalating relationships (r = 0.76, p < 0.001, n = 244). For participants in escalating relationships, RSSD significantly related to intimacy (r = 0.70, p < 0.001, n = 132). RSSD scores and intimacy/closeness scores were also significantly related among those in de-escalating relationships in both the current state of the relationship (r = 0.68, p < 0.001, n = 112) and the peak state (r = 0.70 (p < 0.001, n = 122). For de-escalating relationships, the correlation actually reflects a decline in the level of intimacy/closeness associated with a decline in RSSD.

As has been found in the past, females had significantly higher social decentering scores (M = 133.66, n = 122) than males (M = 122.97, n = 122; t = 5.81, df = 242, p < 0.001) based on the combined escalation and de-escalation samples, as well as in separate analyses of the escalating and deescalating samples. Females were also statistically higher in RSSD (M = 46.96) than males (M = 44.48) (t = 2.56, df = 242, p = 0.01) based on the combined escalation and peak-stages' de-escalation responses. No significant difference in RSSD was found between females and males in the current de-escalating relationships. While women show a stronger ability and tendency to understand and adapt to their partners when the relationship is escalating and intimate, once the relationship begins deteriorating they appear to decrease their efforts at understanding and adapting to their partners to the same degree or perhaps, even more so than the males.

Though social decentering did not correlate with intimacy, it did significantly correlate with RSSD in the escalating relationships (r = 0.52, p < 0.001, n = 132) and in the peak stages of the de-escalating relationships (r = 0.28, p < 0.005, n = 112), but not in their current stages of de-escalating (r = 0.09, p = 0.373, n = 112). Participants who were stronger in social decentering were also more likely to be stronger in RSSD. Correlations do not measure cause and effect, but we can deduce that people who are strong in social decentering would be more adept at developing RSSD. The correlation between social decentering and RSSD was significantly stronger among those in the escalating relationships than for those in the escalating relationships during their peak stages (z = –2.31, p = 0.02). The failure to develop strong RSSD is likely to have contributed to the de-escalation of those relationships. Given that social decentering contributes to the development of RSSD, why did social decentering contribute to the escalating relationships but not to the escalating stages of the relationships that de-escalated? Even though social decentering means of both the escalating and de-escalating samples were not significantly different for any of the escalation stages, other factors occur during escalation that reduce the impact of social decentering on the development of RSSD. Such factors include attraction, relational satisfaction, commitment, the motivation to develop RSSD, and the prospect of other potential relationships.

A further examination of the connection between RSSD and the four escalation stages and the four de-escalation stages was done using analysis of variance (ANOVA). Changes in RSSD during the four escalation stages were analyzed using the scores from the escalation participants combined with scores from the de-escalation participants at their peak level (essentially their escalation scores). RSSD was found to significantly differ among the four escalation stages RSSD [$F(3, 240)$ = 61.49, p < 0.001] with each stage significantly different (p < 0.05) from the others based on Tukey post hoc analysis (see Figure 4.1).

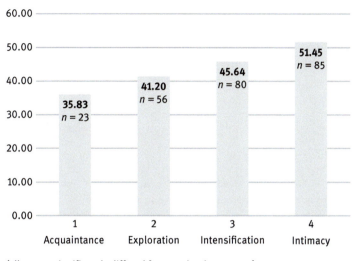

(all means significantly differed from each other, p < .05).

Figure 4.1: RSSD by escalation stages.

The above analysis included both romantic and nonromantic relationships which are not equally represented in the sample. In the escalating relationship sample, 45.5% identified their relationship as romantic, and the 54.5% who identified it as nonromantic chose one of the friendship labels to describe their relationship. In the deescalating relationship sample, 68.8% of the participants identified the relationship as having been romantic and 29.5% as nonromantic friendships. The process of terminating romantic relationships tends to be more deliberative and salient than terminating friendships which might explain the higher proportion of romantic relationships in the de-escalating sample than in the escalating sample. Figures 4.2 and 4.3 show separate analyses based on the combined escalating and de-escalating samples of those in nonromantic relationships and those in romantic relationships. Both ANOVAs showed significant ($p < 0.001$) differences between the stages. In the nonromantic relationships, RSSD in stage 1 was significantly lower than in the other three stages while RSSD in stage 4 was significantly higher than the other three. RSSD averages in stages 2 and 3 were not significantly different. In the romantic relationships RSSD significantly differed between the three stages with each successive stage significantly stronger than the ones before. Not surprisingly, none of the relationships which fell into the acquaintance stage were viewed as a romantic relationship by the respondents.

Since stage 1 had no romantic relationships to compare to nonromantic relationships, the comparison was based only on stages 2, 3, and 4. Participants in romantic relationships had significantly ($p < 0.01$) higher RSSD scores overall than the nonromantic participants ($m = 48.27$, $n = 137$; $m = 44.28$, $n = 82$, respectively). Romantic relationships were also higher than nonromantic relationships on intimacy, relationship satisfaction, and relational assessment, but not social decentering. Those differences are likely

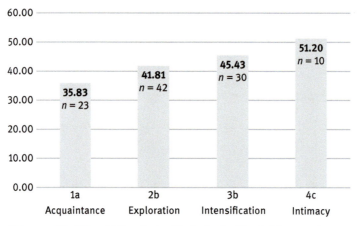

(Columns with different letters (a, b, c) indicate significant differences in means, $p < 0.05$)

Figure 4.2: RSSD by escalation stages – nonromantic.

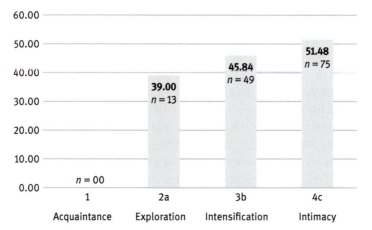

(Columns with different letters (a, b, c) indicate significant differences in means, $p < 0.05$)

Figure 4.3: RSSD by escalation stages – romantic.

the result of a larger proportion of romantic relationships reaching intensification and intimacy than the nonromantic relationships. Many cross-sex friendships do not reach the intimacy stage because partners limit their disclosure of intimate information which also inhibits the development of RSSD. But those nonromantic relationships that reached stage 4 intimacy had a similar level of RSSD ($m = 51.2$) to the RSSD in stage 4 romantic relationships ($m = 51.48$). Overall RSSD increased as relationships moved toward intimacy regardless of whether they were romantic or friends, but male–female friends were less likely to reach the intimacy stage than romantic partners.

An analysis of changes during de-escalation was conducted using the current RSSD scores from the de-escalation respondents. A significant difference was found among

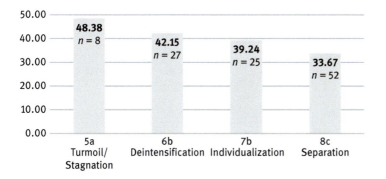

(Columns with different letters (a, b, c) indicate significant differences in means, $p < 0.05$)

Figure 4.4: RSSD by de-escalation stages.

the four de-escalation stages [F (3, 108) = 22.32, $p < 0.001$]. The level of RSSD in stages 5 and 8 significantly differed from all other stages ($p < 0.05$) but RSSD was not significantly different between stages 6 and 7 ($p = 0.29$) (see Figure 4.4).

Figures 4.1 and 4.4 graphically reflect the escalation and de-escalation of RSSD that accompanies changes in the stages of relationship development. As the relationship escalates, more intimate and more personal information is shared resulting in increased RSSD. In addition, as attraction and desire to escalate the relationship increase, there is more motivation to understand the partner and utilize that information. But the reason for a decline in RSSD during de-escalation isn't an erosion of partner knowledge, but instead, a decreased effort to consider and apply that knowledge. Besides items designed to assess the degree of perceived partner knowledge in the measure of RSSD, there are items that ask about the level of effort being exerted to obtain and apply that knowledge and the effect of that knowledge on the perceiver. For example, RSSD includes items such as "I try to understand how my partner thinks [...]," "I feel the pain my partner feels [...]," "I pay attention to the things I learn about my partner [...]," "My emotional state sometimes seems determined by my partner's emotional state [...]." In de-escalating relationships, participants' responses to such items capture decreased motivation to adapt and decreased impact, resulting in an overall decline in RSSD. Further decline in RSSD occurs over time as changes in a partner cause personal information to be outdated, less complete, and less accurate.

Each successive stage of de-escalation in the study includes participants whose relationship peaked at different stages of escalation; for example, of the 52 participants at Stage 8 – Separation, only 8 were participants who reached the intimacy stage, 17 who reached the intensification stage, 17 peaked at exploration, and 10 never made it past the acquaintance stage. Thus, the average RSSD for the separation stage doesn't provide a complete picture of how much the RSSD actually fell for those

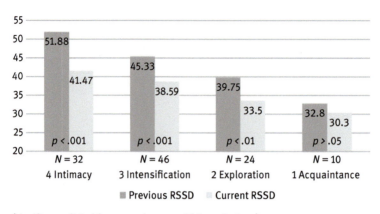

(significance listed for mean changes within each stage)

Figure 4.5: RSSD Mean changes based on the most intimate stage reached in de-escalating relationships.

who reached the higher levels of intimacy. To examine this, the RSSD scores from their peak stage were compared to their current RSSD scores. Significant decrease in RSSD scores occurred for those who peaked at the intimacy stage, the intensification, stage, and the exploration stage, but not the acquaintance stage (see Figure 4.5). The decreased RSSD among the more intimate relationships is tempered by different degrees of decreased intimacy among the participants. Of the 32 participants who reached the intimacy stage, 8 de-escalated to separation, 8 to individualization, 8 to deintensification, and 8 were still in the intimacy stage but their intimacy scores had declined.

One assumption might be made that the length of the relationship determined the level of RSSD. A comparison of the relationships sorted by their peak stage found no significant difference among the stages in how long participants reported knowing each other. Though not statistically significant, the length did decline from an average of 28.5 weeks for those that reached the intimacy stage to 21.8 weeks among acquaintances. A regression analysis predicting RSSD at the peak stage based on intimacy, length of knowing each other, and length of romantic involvement produced a significant multiple R of 0.65 ($r^2 = 0.43$) but intimacy was the only factor that contributed to predicting RSSD with a significant beta of 0.68. Rather than how much time participants spent together, personal factors that lead to developing intimate relationships appear to be more significant in the development of their RSSD. Such personal factors as attraction, trust, and self-disclosure apparently influence the development of intimacy and RSSD more than the amount of time partners spend together. Though it takes time to develop trust and to disclose information, couples vary in the length of time needed to fully disclose; some might spend a weekend of intense disclosing while others might take years to reach the same point.

The pattern of decline in RSSD indicates that partners don't simply shut off their RSSD but instead choose to ease off as their level of dissatisfaction with the relationship increases. Indeed, the RSSD level in the first stage of de-escalation (turmoil/stagnation) was not significantly different than the level of RSSD in the intimate stage of escalation indicating that while moving toward de-escalation, partners continued to use RSSD to understand and adapt to their partner. As discussed in Chapter 3, RSSD is a tool that can actually make the process of de-escalating easier as partners consider options for ending the relationship relative to their ability to predict the other partner's responses.

4.3.2 Relationship Satisfaction and Relational Assessment

Only responses from those in the escalation study were used in analyzing the relationship between social decentering and relationship satisfaction and relational assessment in escalating relationships. Including the responses from the de-escalation participants' peak period were not used to reduce the possibility of distorting results since there was no social decentering score from their peak stage. Therefore, a separate analysis examined de-escalation participants' current social decentering and their current relationship satisfaction and assessment.

No significant correlations were found between social decentering and relationship satisfaction or relational assessment (RAS) in the escalating relationships. Social decentering scores of males did not relate to either their own or their partners' satisfaction or assessment. Females' social decentering did not relate to their own or their partners' relationship satisfaction. Females' social decentering was positively related to their relational assessment ($r = 0.29$, $p = 0.017$, $n = 66$) but not with their partners' assessment. Overall, social decentering in these on-going relationships had little statistical connection to participants' levels of satisfaction or relational assessment. One reason for this is that the development of RSSD reduces the need for and application of general social decentering skills. Nonetheless, social decentering remains a tool for navigating relationships. Both social decentering and relational assessment involve the use of social information processing and require introspection skills which would contribute to their significant correlation. For women, consideration of another person's dispositions through social decentering relates to some of the qualities assessed by RAS – sensitivity to relational problems, awareness of their own expectations, and awareness of needs.

Not surprisingly, no significant relationships were found in the de-escalating study between participants' social decentering scores and their relationship satisfaction or relational assessments nor with their partners' relationship satisfaction or assessment. Though social decentering can provide people with the ability to better understand and adapt to their partners, partners' motivation and desire to engage in decentering is likely to decrease as their relationship de-escalates. But as discussed earlier, social decentering can be used to help make sense out of what is happening rather than being used to adapt to the partner.

RSSD was expected to significantly contribute to relational satisfaction and positive relational assessment. RSSD scores from the escalation and peak stage de-escalation respondents, significantly related to their feelings of relationship satisfaction ($r = 0.51$, $p < 0.001$, $n = 244$) and positive relational assessment ($r = 0.46$, $p < 0.001$). Separate correlations using only participants in escalating relationships were similarly significant, as were those using only peak stage de-escalating respondents. Analysis based on the scores from the current state of de-escalating relationships produced similar significant ($p < 0.001$, $n = 112$) correlations between RSSD and relationship satisfaction ($r = 0.36$) and relational assessment ($r = 0.49$). When de-escalating, participants who understand their partner (higher RSSD) appear to feel more satisfied and positive about their relationship, perhaps because they are able to continue to manage their needs and expectations and more effectively manage the problems and conflicts.

While it might appear that maintaining RSSD during de-escalation helps mitigate feelings of relational dissatisfaction and distress, the results of analyzing each stage separately produced a different conclusion. Separate analysis of each of the four escalating stages using data only from the escalating study indicated no significant relationship between RSSD and relationship satisfaction or relational assessment in any of the first three stages. Only in stage 4 – intimacy, did RSSD significantly relate to relationship satisfaction ($r = 0.33$, $p < 0.02$, $n = 53$) and relational assessment ($r = 0.38$, $p < 0.01$). The data from the peak stages of the de-escalating study produced similar results with significant correlations only in stage 4 – intimacy, between RSSD and satisfaction ($r = 0.27$, $p < 0.02$, $n = 32$) and assessment ($r = 0.37$, $p < 0.01$).

Among the four de-escalating stages, RSSD related significantly to relationship satisfaction and relational assessment only for couples in the stage 7 – individualization ($r = 0.42$, p < 0.05, $n = 25$; and $r = 0.44$, $p < 0.05$, respectively). The reason RSSD was important in stage 7 might be linked to the participants' future goals and expectations for the relationship. Of the 25 respondents in stage 7, 16 indicated the relationship was previously romantic but 14 of those no longer considered it romantic as this time. Those 14 respondents and the 9 who never defined the relationship as romantic are more likely to try to either maintain the relationship as friends (essentially, stage 2-exploration) or are preparing to move toward stage 8 – separation. In either case, RSSD allows those participants to better understand what their partner was thinking and feeling, which would help them come to terms with the current state of the relationship, and thus positively affect their relationship satisfaction and relational assessment.

The following analysis sought to determine the degree to which one partner's RSSD might have affected the other partner's satisfaction and assessment scores. A separate analysis of the data from the escalating and de-escalating studies found no significant correlations between partners' scores based on the de-escalating data either from their peak intimacy stages or current de-escalation stages. But analysis based on the responses from the escalating study did identify significant relationships and are reported here. RSSD for males in the escalating study significantly correlated with their partner's relationship satisfaction ($r = 0.30$, $p = 0.01$, $n = 66$) and relationship assessment ($r = 0.24$, $p = 0.51$). Females' RSSD significantly correlated with their partner's relationship satisfaction ($r = 0.41$, $p = 0.001$) and relational assessment ($r = 0.38$, $p = 0.002$). The correlation coefficients suggest that the impact of women's RSSD on the men was greater than the impact of men's RSSD on the women. These results emphasize the important role that developing RSSD plays during the escalation of a relationship. Another recurring theme is that men appear to be more affected by the women's display of understanding and adaptation than women are by men's. However, both partners' relationship satisfaction and positive assessment of the relationship appear linked to their partner engaging in RSSD.

The systematic decline found in partners' RSSD in de-escalating relationships (see Figure 4.4) did not correlate with changes in the level of their partner's relational satisfaction. One reason might be that despite having significant understanding of partners at the intimacy stage, partners no longer chose to utilize that understanding in ways that positively affected their partner. Another possibility is that even when RSSD is being applied by one partner, it is insufficient to offset the collection of factors contributing to the other partner's increasing relational dissatisfaction. This possibility is supported by the contrast in the stepwise decreases in relationship satisfaction and relational assessment compared to the decreases that occurred in RSSD. As relationships moved from stage 5 (turmoil/stagnation) to stage 6 (deintensification), satisfaction in de-escalating relationships dropped by 15% from 4.96 to 4.06, compared to a drop of only 6% in RSSD. Though the mean for stage 5 – satisfaction, was based on only eight respondents, a drop to 4.96 from the peak satisfaction mean of 5.28 ($n = 32$) in the stage 4 – intimacy (a 5.3% decline), seems like a valid level of decline. In stage 5, participants begin questioning their relationships and their satisfaction begins to slowly decline. The 5.3% drop in satisfaction from stage 4 to stage 5 foreshadowed the more dramatic drop that occurred as relationships moved to stage 6 (de-intensification). The rate of decline of satisfaction slows down between stages 6 and 7 falling by only 2.5% (4.06 to 3.91), but during that time respondents appear to engage in significantly less RSSD as their scores dropped by 10.6%. The final drop between stages 7 and 8 was fairly similar for both satisfaction (7.2%, 3.91 to 3.48) and RSSD (6.7%). Changes in relational assessment were similar to the changes in relational satisfaction with a 10.6% drop between stage 5 ($m = 4.02$, $n = 8$) and stage 6 ($m = 3.49$, $n = 27$). While RSSD remains relatively strong between stages 5 and 6, satisfaction and positive relational assessment take significant drops indicating that a major shift in partners' feelings about the relationship – de-escalation, has begun in earnest. The understanding provided by RSSD appears insufficient to offset the substantial change in feelings and negative assessment of the relationship that occurs in moving from stage 5 to stage 6 which might be the impetus for reducing RSSD efforts after stage 6.

As relationships de-escalate and people experience emotional turmoil, conflict, and feel increased concern for their own welfare, they are likely to reduce their use of RSSD as a tool for supporting their partner's welfare. Conflict has been found to cause empathy to be replaced with antipathy where individuals might take pleasure in the other's suffering (Zaki & Cikara, 2015). As a result, it is likely that one partner's strength in RSSD is less likely to relate to their partner's level of relationship satisfaction. As discussed earlier, during de-escalation people might use RSSD to develop strategies that hurt or push their partner away, thus reducing instead of increasing a partner's relationship satisfaction. The results suggest that this occurs most prominently as relationships move toward deintensification. Despite this, when partners are inclined to do so, RSSD can be used to mitigate a partner's hurt feelings and support the partner as they transition out of their relationship.

The results of the escalation and de-escalation studies were discussed in terms of how relationships move from one stage to another and the changes associated with that movement. Though the de-escalation study did assess the relationship at two different points, the two studies did not assess changes in a couple's relationship development from one stage to another as would a longitudinal study. The assumption made in these studies was that since the respondents were fairly homogenous, the changes found between each stage would be relatively good indices of the changes found with a longitudinal study. Nonetheless, more insights could be obtained by the tracking changes in social decentering, RSSD, relational satisfaction, and relational assessment having couples complete the various measures throughout the course of their relationships.

Though sexual orientation was not specifically examined in this study, the impact of social decentering and RSSD on relationship development is not expected to differ significantly between same-sex and cross-sex romantic relationships. There is little reason to believe that individuals in romantic same-sex relationships would be any less likely to utilize social decentering and RSSD to manage their relationships than heterosexual couples.

Finally, the three studies I conducted, that were discussed in this chapter and Chapter 3, used only male–female interactants. The findings of these studies regarding social decentering and RSSD's role in the relationship development might not readily apply to same-sex non-romantic relationships. In general, the development of intimate relationships whether romantic or non-romantic or same-sex or cross-sex should involve the same shift from early use of social decentering to the development and predominant use of RSSD. Differences in openness to self-disclosure, feelings of trust, and level of commitment between same-sex male and same-sex female friendships, are likely to result in differences in the development and application of RSSD. For example, females tend to have higher levels of social decentering, empathy, and RSSD and a greater desire for intimate same-sex friendships (Fehr, 2004); thus, they are likely to be more negatively affected than men by a same-sex partner who does not share those qualities and desires. Both men and women see self-disclosure, emotional support, loyalty, and trust as contributing to intimacy and these qualities contribute to and are enhanced by social decentering and RSSD.

But women see these qualities as more likely to produce intimacy and satisfaction than men (Fehr, 2004). As a result, women are likely to feel less satisfaction with partners who fail to develop and apply RSSD as their same-sex friendships move toward intimacy than are men.

4.4 Summary and Conclusions

The role of social decentering and RSSD in interpersonal relationships was examined in this chapter by focusing on how other-centered processes are integrated into to the escalation and de-escalation of interpersonal relationships. Specifically, social decentering and RSSD were discussed in terms of their roles in each of the five stages of escalating to intimacy (Pre-Interaction Awareness, Acquaintance, Exploration, Intensification, and Intimacy) and the five stages of de-escalating from intimacy (Turmoil or Stagnation, Deintensification, Individualization, Separation, and Post-Interaction Effects). This approach highlights the proposition that the application of other-oriented processes is not statically applied to relationships but instead evolves and adapts to changes that accompany relationship escalation and de-escalation. General forms of other-orientation, such as social decentering, play a strong role in the early stages of relationships by providing a base for understanding and adapting to acquaintances and as a factor in the development of attraction. Social decentering becomes less significant as relationships escalate and RSSD develops. Movement toward intimacy is accompanied by increased mutual self-disclosure and an expectation that our partners will retain and adapt (RSSD) to what they learn about us. Our relational expectations are tied to how we define our relationships, and those definitions are linked to expectations associated with each stage in the relationship. If we perceive and define our relationship as limited to the acquaintance stage, then we have little expectation that we or our partners will develop RSSD and instead rely on understandings and predictions generated through social decentering. But when the relationship reaches the intimacy stage, we have a strong expectation that our partner will have developed and will apply RSSD. Failure to meet that expectation can contribute to relational de-escalation.

The importance of motivation to apply other-centered processes is particularly visible during the de-escalation of relationships. What we know about our partner and our RSSD is not erased or immediately disabled just because the relationship is de-escalating. What changes is our motivation to use RSSD. As relational satisfaction and attraction decrease, there is less motivation to expend the energy needed to engage in RSSD. Less RSSD means less adaptation to the partner which further contributes to a partner's feelings of relational dissatisfaction.

The primary application of general other-oriented trait processes such as social-decentering and global empathy is in nonintimate relationships and interactions. As relationships develop toward intimacy, participants have the opportunity to develop RSSD or apply more dispositional empathy. While many of the participants in the studies presented in this chapter developed fairly high levels of RSSD relative to the level of intimacy, not everyone did. In some instances, large differences in partners' RSSD might have prevented their relationships from reaching the intimacy stage, in other instances, relationships might have reached intimacy but the failure of a partner to understand and adapt (lack of RSSD) contributed to the eventual de-escalation. In sustained intimate relationships with large differences in RSSD, the partner with higher RSSD is likely to experience less satisfaction and more stress than their partner.

Interpersonal relationships are systemically connected to social decentering and RSSD – each affects the other. Social decentering and RSSD are tools that people can apply in the initiation, development, and termination of their interpersonal relationships. Social decentering and RSSD develop because of our interpersonal relationship experiences and social cognition. The application of social decentering and RSSD is dictated by the nature of the relationship, the relational partners, and the circumstances. Not only are social decentering and RSSD important skills that individuals develop and apply to accomplish their personal goals, they are also important to their partners who expect the information they share to be used as a foundation for support, personal confirmation, and affirmation.

4.5 References

Aron, A., Aron, E. N., & Smollan, D. (1992). Inclusion of Other in the Self Scale and the structure of interpersonal closeness. *Journal of Personality and Social Psychology, 63*, 596–612.

Fehr, B. (2004). A prototype model of intimacy interactions in same-sex friendships. In D. J. Mahek and A. Aron (Eds.), *Handbook of closeness and intimacy* (pp. 9–26). Mahwah, NJ: Erlbaum.

Hendrick, S. S. (1988). A generic measure of relationship satisfaction. *Journal of Marriage and the Family, 50*, 93–98.

Lemieux, R., & Hale, J. L. (1999). Intimacy, passion, and commitment in young romantic relationships: Successfully measuring the triangular theory of love. *Psychological Reports, 85*, 497–503.

Roloff, M. E., & Ifert, D. (1998). Antecedents and consequences of explicit agreements to declare a topic taboo in dating relationships. *Personal Relationships, 5*, 191–205.

Rusbult, C. E. (1983). Longitudinal test of the investment model: The development (and deterioration) of satisfaction and commitment in heterosexual involvements. *Journal of Personality and Social Psychology, 45*, 101–117.

Zaki, J., & Cikara, M. (2015). Addressing empathic failures. *Current Directions in Psychological Science, 26*, 471–476.

5 Social Decentering and Relationship-Specific Social Decentering (RSSD) in Marital Relationships

Marital relationships provide a valuable landscape for examining the nature of inter-personal relationships and communication. A marriage represents the most intimate and one of the most significant relationships that people form. It encapsulates a full range of interpersonal communication processes, including relationship initiation, self-disclosure, interpersonal conflict, relational maintenance, and relational termi-nation and its responsibilities extend beyond those of other relationships to include parenting, managing money, and household maintenance. Nonetheless, studying married couples provides a valuable insight into the workings of all interpersonal relationships. And a study of long-term marriages allows us to examine how interper-sonal processes change over time. For these reasons, this chapter takes an in-depth look at social decentering and relationship-specific social decentering (RSSD) within marriage. In this chapter, I review previous theory and research as I build a model of the role of social decentering and RSSD in marriage. Studies on romantic relationships often draw on samples that include those who are dating, cohabitating, or married, so the findings don't always reflect effects that are unique to marriage. My discussion of relationships in Chapter 3 includes the findings from many of those studies, so they are minimally discussed in this chapter.

Theory and research on marriage have often worked on the proposition that understanding one's spouse, empathy, and empathic communication contribute to marital satisfaction. But the research has produced mixed support for that prop-osition and generally tends not to support it. The failure to find a definite linear relationship between empathic communication and marital satisfaction demon-strates the complexity of marital relationships (Sillars, Pike, Jones, & Murphy, 1984), and the failure is particularly disappointing to communication scholars who argue the importance of communication in human interactions. But this failure does not indicate that empathy and communication are unimportant tools for managing relationships. That is, these skills might be used to effectively manage interactions rather than necessarily to create satisfaction. If anything, such skills might enhance the ability to successfully dissolve a relationship rather than main-tain it. Underlying spouses' decisions to apply these skills are a myriad of factors, such as commitment, self-esteem, the presence of children, sexual satisfaction, sex and gender roles, equity, religious convictions, and interdependency. Any of these factors might mitigate the impact of social decentering and communication on marital satisfaction.

https://doi.org/10.1515/9783110515664-006

5.1 Previous Research on Empathy and Perspective-Taking in Marriage

Studies associating marital satisfaction with empathy conducted in the 1950s and 1960s produced contradictory results; some of which can be attributed to the impact of assuming similarity in predicting a spouse's response (Cronbach, 1955, 1960). Later studies using various measures have had little more success in finding such a relationship. Elliott (1982) measured marital empathy as the average of couples' responses to 40 scenarios in terms of such qualities as reciprocal role-playing and role-playing to conform to spouses' desires. She too found no significant relationship between marital empathy and satisfaction as measured with the Locke and Wallace's Marital Adjustment Test and Bienvenu's Marital Communication Inventory. In a study of 44 married couples, Wastell (1991) found no significant correlation between empathy, as measured with items from Barrett–Lennard's Relationship Inventory, and marital happiness, as measured by Spanier's Dyadic Adjustment Scale (DAS). And Wachs and Cordova (2007), who studied 33 married couples, found no significant correlation between marital satisfaction as measured with Spanier's DAS and empathy as measured with the perspective-taking and emotional concern subscales of Davis's (1983) Interpersonal Reactivity Index (IRI).

A study on marital satisfaction by Rowan, Compton, and Rust (1995) combined the perspective-taking and emotional-concern subscales of Davis's IRI as a measure of "total empathy." They found no significant relationships between these scales and marital satisfaction for wives. But the perspective-taking scale did show a significant correlation ($r = 0.49$, $p < 0.05$) with marital satisfaction for husbands. One interpretation of these results is that emotional empathy (via the Davis measure) is not a factor for either spouse's marital satisfaction, but that husbands' marital satisfaction is related to their ability to cognitively take their wives' perspectives. But rather than being causal, the relationship might be spurious because the qualities that the perspective-taking scale assessed by (e.g., "belief there are two sides to every question" and "before criticizing somebody, I try to imagine how I would feel") relate to qualities that reflect satisfaction in a relationship (being less dogmatic and less critical).

Franzoi, Davis, and Young (1985) had students in an introductory psychology course complete several questionnaires, including the Davis's perspective-taking subscale and a modified version of Locke's Marital Adjustment Test. While not exclusively focused on married couples (23% were married or engaged), this study again failed to find direct significant correlation between the two measures. The researchers subsequently performed a regression analysis that controlled variables such as length of the relationship, self-disclosure, and self-consciousness. They found that male and female perspective-taking significantly contributed to a prediction of male satisfaction, but only female perspective-taking contributed to predictions of female satisfaction. These results indicate a sex-based difference in effects where men are affected by women's perspective-taking, but women are not affected by men's perspective-taking. This difference might be a result of factors such as sex role expectations, variations across romantic relationships, or measurement issues.

While not specifically about empathy or perspective-taking, Pollmann and Finkenauer's (2009) study on the impact of knowledge and understanding on marital adjustment has direct implications of the processes of being other orientated. In their study of 199 newlywed couples, they found that (a) spouses' reported understanding of their partners related to their own marital adjustment, (b) feeling understood by one's partner related to marital adjustment, (c) partners' reported level of understanding of their spouses related to spouses' adjustment only in shorter-term relationships, and (d) specific knowledge of one's partner did not relate to adjustment. The researchers offered several explanations as to why such knowledge did not affect adjustment but failed to recognize what might be the most obvious: Increased knowledge is not inherently positive or beneficial. Information can be either positively or negatively valenced, so some information will invariably produce negative reactions. For example, in their study, couples completed a questionnaire on their own and their partner's "Big-5" personality traits; among those traits was neuroticism. Over the course of a marriage, increasing knowledge of a partner's neuroticism could understandably affect marital adjustment.

In another study of newlyweds, Sillars, Roberts, Leonard, and Dun (2000) videotaped couples as they discussed an unresolved disagreement. Participants individually watched a replay of the interaction, and every 20 seconds, they were prompted to state what they were feeling and thinking. The researchers coded and assessed these responses in order to capture the participants' thoughts and feelings while engaged in conflict. Although this process provided many insights into how these men and women viewed their conflict discussions, the researchers "found few examples of complex perspective-taking during interaction" (p. 496). A problem underlying social-decentering's use during interactions is that it takes time and thus is less likely to be reflected in adaptive behaviors. This problem is reflected in Sillars et al.'s (2000) observations about engaging in marital conflict:

> Participation in live interaction does not afford the opportunity for searching reflection because of the involving nature of communication and the need to integrate multiple items of information, reconcile conflicting goals, and respond in real time (Waldron & Cegala, 1992). In addition, the often stressful and disorderly nature of marital conflict may further limit the capacity and inclination for complex thought. (p. 496)

Sillars et al.'s finding is in keeping with Fiske's (1993) description of individuals as cognitive misers who limit how much they allow themselves to process in a given interaction as it occurs (Chapter 1). In addition, individuals' tendency to rely on scripts is likely to limit their social decentering. Furthermore, on-going discussions of unresolved conflicts are subject to becoming so patterned (e.g., falling into routines such as demand – withdraw) that neither partner attempts to take the other's perspective.

But when the issue is important to both partners and the need to act on the issue is more immediate, they should be more motivated to socially decenter.

The need to socially decenter explains the findings of a study of first-time parents with 3- to 12-months-old babies (Rosen, Mooney, & Muise, 2016). Using a measure of dyadic empathy based on Davis's IRI developed by Péloquin and Lafontaine (2010), the researchers found a small but significant correlation between mothers' and fathers' dyadic empathy scores ($r = 0.18$, $p < 0.01$). But even though the fathers' dyadic empathy strongly correlated with the mothers' report of marital adjustment ($r = 0.75$, $p < 0.001$), the mothers' empathy did not significantly correlate with the fathers' adjustment ($r = 0.09$). This result suggests mothers feel comforted and supported when fathers display understanding and adaptive behaviors, but that fathers might have less need to feel such understanding (i.e., social decentering) from their partners. Rosen et al. also found that both self and partner dyadic empathy positively correlated with sexual satisfaction of the self and partner, which suggests that understanding a partner improves individuals' ability to appropriately adapt to their partners and thus more successfully meet their partners' and their own sexual needs.

Rosen et al.'s study suggests that partners are influenced by each other's level of empathy, although that was not the case in Wastell's (1991) study where spouses rated their perceptions of partners' empathy on an adapted version of Barrett–Lennard's Relationship Inventory that included items such as "He/she usually senses or realizes what I'm feeling." Wastell found that perception of a partner's empathy did not significantly relate to reported marital happiness. Perhaps, weak perceptual skills limited partners' ability to accurately perceive empathic behaviors, or partners might associate different behaviors with empathy. If identifying partners' empathic behaviors is difficult, then identifying partners' thoughts at any given moment is likely to prove even more difficult as several studies examining empathic accuracy in married couples have shown.

Another study that illustrates the challenges of assessing perceived empathy and perspective-taking was conducted by Kellas, Willer, and Trees (2013). They sought to identify behaviors displayed by husbands and wives that communicated perspective-taking. Couples were videotaped while sharing a story related to a stressful experience in their relationship. The partners independently reviewed the video of the storytelling and every minute rated their partners' communicated perspective-taking and listed what behaviors influenced their assessment. Rather than relating to good listening, supportive responses, or synchronized interaction, the level of communicated perspective-taking related primarily to what they didn't do. Husbands saw wives as communicating less perspective-taking the more their wives displayed negative tone, disagreement, or interfered in their storytelling (constrained). For wives, husbands level of inattentiveness, irrelevant contributions, constraining their storytelling, or disagreement related to lower ratings of the husbands' perspective-taking. Unfortunately, the operationalization of perceived perspective-taking involved rating the degree to which partners felt understood/misunderstood, ignored/acknowledged, and disconfirmed/confirmed their perspectives. Inherent in these three ratings are some of the behaviors that were explicitly identified; for example, disagreement was observed and disconfirmed rated. While the spouses might have perceived the behaviors they reported, they might not truly reflect that their partners had engaged in perspective-taking.

5.2 Empathic Accuracy and Marriage

As discussed in Chapter 1, empathic accuracy focuses on the ability to make accurate inferences about what another person is thinking at any given moment during a specific interaction. When such inferences are made based on intimate knowledge that spouses are expected to have about their partners, they are similar to those made from RSSD. Research on empathic accuracy and relevant conceptual development has primarily rested on videotaping an interaction between partners. This interaction is often stimulated by the researcher toward a particular goal, such as managing an ongoing conflict or issue. The interaction is replayed to the partners individually, and they indicate their thoughts and feelings either at designated points (e.g., every two minutes) or as they freely recall them. The tape is replayed for the other partner, and at each of the identified points on the tape, that partner is asked to predict what the other partner was thinking and/or feeling. The predictions are compared to the partner's self-report, and the resulting agreements are used as a measure of accuracy. Thomas, Fletcher, and Lange (1997) incorporated such a measure to assess empathic accuracy and found that the ability to predict the other's immediate responses was unrelated to relational satisfaction.

While empathic accuracy might be expected to continue to improve as couples spend more time together and thus learn how to read each other's behaviors and minds more effectively, research results have found otherwise. In a longitudinal study of newlyweds' display of empathic accuracy during videotaped conflicts, empathic accuracy was found to relate to accommodation, commitment, and dyadic adjustment when assessed after the first year of marriage. But no such relationships were found after the second year (Bissonnette, Rusbult, & Kilpatrick, 2002). The researchers provided two possible explanations. First, the warm-up process prior to the videotaping might have activated different skills and motives from year one to year two. This explanation suggests some inherent problems in the assessment procedure for empathic accuracy. Second, couples might become more automatic in their responses as time passes, thus reducing their motivation to engage in empathic accuracy. Since this study depended on a directed effort to engage in empathic accuracy within a laboratory-induced conflict interaction, it leaves open the question of how couples behave in their spontaneous day-to-day interactions. Do they daily engage in empathic accuracy of their own volition? Perhaps the findings after the second year of marriage reflect a more realistic sampling of couples' everyday interactions. In addition, what happens after more than 2 years?

Kilpatrick, Bissonette, and Rusbult (2002) later hypothesized that empathic accuracy declines over time in marriage, arguing that the newness in the early years requires more monitoring of the partner's thoughts and feelings and that over time recognizable patterns and habits develop so that such monitoring is less needed. Their argument emphasizes the degree to which empathic accuracy is tied to perceptual sensitivity rather than accumulated knowledge and understanding. It also reinforces the prospect that the motivation to decenter is likely to decline over time, regardless of the level of knowledge and understanding spouses have.

Thomas et al. (1997) also found less empathic accuracy in couples who had been married longer, suggesting that "as marriages develop over many years, couples become less motivated in resolving disputes, their relationship theories become ossified, and they are more likely to assume that they know what their partners are thinking" (p. 847). They proposed a U-shaped pattern of empathic accuracy across the length of marriage:

> It seems likely that, in fact, there is a curvilinear association between relationship length and empathic accuracy, with empathic accuracy increasing during the process of acquaintanceship, peaking during the early years of marriage, and then declining during the mature stage of the marital life cycle. (pp. 847–848)

They also found no correlation for empathic accuracy with either relational satisfaction or verbal positivity.

Another study of empathic accuracy had partners' (56% of the sample were married) identify positive and negative emotions after discussing two emotional incidents (Cohen, Schulz, Weiss, & Waldinger, 2012). They found that the men's relationship satisfaction was significantly related to their ability to accurately identify their partner's positive emotions but not to their partner's satisfaction. Women's empathic accuracy of positive emotions, however, was not significantly related to either partner's satisfaction. Both men's and women's empathic accuracy in reading negative emotions significantly related to their partner's satisfaction. While women's empathic accuracy of negative emotions related to their own satisfaction, the same was not true for men. And while both women's and men's perceptions of their partners' efforts to understand them significantly related to their relationship satisfaction, the correlation was higher among women. Women's perception of their partners' effort to understand them was more important to their relational satisfaction than their partners' empathic accuracy in reading negative emotions. This finding implies that the impact of social decentering and RSSD on spouses' marital satisfaction might depend on their ability to perceive the efforts of their partners to understand and adapt. Thus, social decentering and RSSD are unlikely to strongly correlate with marital satisfaction because effective decentering can occur without any significant display of observable adaptive behaviors.

5.3 The Measurement of Other-Orientation in Marriage

How empathy and perspective-taking have been operationalized is one factor that can create confusing, inconsistent, and weak results in studies of married couples. As discussed in Chapter 2, a number of scales have been developed to measure empathy and perspective-taking, but their application to the study of married couples has been limited. Davis's (1983) IRI is probably the most widely used measure of empathy because it is intended to measure both cognitive and affective responses. But the four subscales – perspective-taking, fantasy, empathic concern, and personal distress – represent a fairly narrow conceptualization of empathy. Perspective-taking represents adopting the others' cognitive point of view, fantasy deals with imagining the feelings of fictional characters, empathic concern represents sympathy (focusing on one's own emotional reaction of another person's situation) rather than empathy, and personal distress represents feelings of anxiety or tension that reduce self-esteem and interpersonal functioning.

In contrast, social decentering incorporates a broad definition of empathy that includes any similar emotional response shared by both the empathizer and target, such as joy, interest, fear, anticipation, shame, or anger, not just distress or anxiety. In analyzing studies on marriage and other-orientation, we must examine what is actually measured. Studies often use or adapt only the IRI subscales of perspective-taking and empathic concern to measure perspective-taking or empathy and sometimes combine the results of those two scales as a measure of empathy. When studies fail to find significant results after employing Davis's IRI subscales to measure empathy, they often search for an alternative theoretical explanation rather than questioning the measure's validity. For example, Bakker and Demerouti (2009) found evidence of the crossover process in which spouses' feelings of engagement in their job related to their partners' own feeling of job engagement. They hypothesized that empathy and perspective-taking moderated this crossover process. But emotional empathy measured with the empathic concern subscale of the IRI did not moderate crossover of engagement, and "only perspective-taking moderated the crossover of work engagement effect, and showed that work engagement was most likely to cross over when men were characterized by the spontaneous tendency to adopt the psychological perspective of their partner" (p. 230). They speculated that perhaps empathic concern was limited to a crossover effect associated with strain rather than positive experiences. They make this claim, despite pointing out that empathic concern should relate to warmth, compassion, and concern for others – all qualities that should be associated with positive experiences as well. Unfortunately, their reliance on IRI might mean they didn't really measure the emotional empathy skills of the spouses or their impact on engagement crossover.

The failure to find a relationship between marital satisfaction and empathy as measured by two of Davis's subscales led Rowan, Compton, and Rust (1995) to speculate that since women are higher on the empathy scores than men are, perhaps increases in women's empathy have no impact beyond a certain threshold. But that seems unlikely because all women do not have the same capabilities in managing their interactions. Again, the failure to find an expected finding led researchers to reconsider their conceptual model rather than considering the validity of the empathy measure.

Long's (1990) Self and Other Dyadic Perspective Scales have been employed in studies of romantic relationships with samples that include both married and unmarried participants. But the unique impact of marriage on the dynamics of perspective-taking is often not included in the analyses. Among studies on perspective-taking and empathy are those that examine how these skills are affected by counseling sessions, classes, or training geared toward becoming more other-centered. Typically, these studies seek to demonstrate improvement in a number of skills including empathy. For example, one 4-week treatment program for expectant parents focusing on mindfulness combined three of Davis's IRI subscales as a measure of general empathy and used Long's two scales on perspective-taking as measures of self and partner empathy (Gambrel & Piercy, 2015). For women, all three measures had small but significant increases, while no changes were found in men's general empathy, self-empathy, or partner-empathy. Inherent in that study was the recurrent problem of how empathy and perspective-taking are defined and measured. For example, both the authors and Long (1990) consider perspective-taking as a dimension of empathy without clearly identifying perspective-taking's role. When people have emotional reactions to their thoughts about others, is that empathy or perspective-taking? Is that considered the same process as thinking about another person's feelings? Is there a difference in thinking about another person's feelings and another person's thoughts and is one perspective-taking and the other empathy?

Péloquin and Lafontaine (2010) addressed some of the weaknesses in Davis's IRI by modifying the perspective-taking and empathic concern subscales to more clearly distinguish between cognitive and affective responses. The result is their Interpersonal Reactivity Index for Couples, which changes the focus of the IRI from a global measure to a measure that is relationship specific (referred to as dyadic empathy). Their effort parallels that represented in the more global measure of social decentering and the partner measure of RSSD. Péloquin and Lafontaine continue Davis's emphasis on empathy as concern rather than a shared emotional reaction, using items such as "I often have tender, concerned feelings for my partner when he/she is less fortunate than me." Other items seem quite tangential to the notion of emotional empathy (e.g., "In my relationship with my partner, I would describe myself as a pretty soft-hearted person"). So far only a few studies have incorporated this variation in Davis's scales.

5.4 Theoretical Relationship between Social Decentering, RSSD, and Marital Satisfaction

In what ways might the skill of taking into consideration a spouse's feelings, attitudes, thoughts, and general dispositions affect marriage? The impact of empathy and perspective-taking on marriage has been examined in a few studies and produced some confusing, contradictory, and inconclusive results. As discussed in the first two chapters, social decentering theory is offered as a more theoretically cohesive and encompassing theory of other-orientation than can be found associated with theories of empathy, perspective-taking, role-taking, or theory of mind. While these other approaches provide the foundation for some of expectations regarding social decentering and marriage, the ensuing discussion and research study aim to go beyond that foundation.

By far the most common dependent variable examined in studies of empathy and perspective-taking in marriage is marital or relational satisfaction or adjustment. In general, researchers argue and hypothesize that being empathic or engaging in perspective-taking has a positive effect on marital satisfaction. On the basis of that proposition, social decentering and RSSD also should be expected to positively affect martial satisfaction. The study reported in Chapter 6 examined the impact that one spouse's social decentering and RSSD had on the other spouse's level of marital satisfaction. In addition, the relationship between a spouse's social decentering and RSSD was examined in terms of how it related to his or her own level of marital satisfaction.

Generally, studies on the impact of other-orientation assume that other-centered behaviors are the cause and that satisfaction is the effect. Given the number of factors that affect people's efforts to engage in other-centered behaviors, the level of satisfaction could be the cause and social-decentering and RSSD could be the effects. Peoples' happiness in marriage leads them to be more open and to be concerned with understanding their spouses, thus increasing the motivation and ability to decenter, while unhappiness not only restricts information flow but also impairs the ability to decenter. Even with information in hand, dissatisfaction could result in the use of decentering to provoke negative outcomes. Burleson and Denton (1997) discussed the importance of taking into consideration the intent and motives of the spouses when looking at the role communication played in distressed and nondistressed marriages. In interpreting some of their results, they posited that husbands in nondistressed marriages produced messages intended to have a positive effect, thus increasing how much they were liked by their wives, while in distressed marriages, husbands used those same skills to produce messages with the intention of hurting or upsetting their wives. Accordingly, the level of spouses' satisfaction will likely impact whether they use social decentering and RSSD to produce positive or negative messages.

Another issue that underlies the relationship between satisfaction and social decentering is whether both partners need to be strong in social decentering and RSSD to create happiness for both? While that seems intuitively true, perhaps only one spouse needs to effectively understand his or her partner and to adapt to and/or accommodate his or her partner. If so, do gender roles dictate who should accommodate to whom? Do gender roles affect the impact of a husband's or wife's social decentering in different ways? For example, having a high socially decentering husband and low decentering wife might be considered a reverse in gender roles and perhaps create dissatisfaction in both partners.

The theoretic framework of social decentering suggests a nonlinear relationship with marital satisfaction, in contrast to the assumption of previous scholarship on empathy and perspective-taking. Just because one spouse keenly understands the other, it doesn't mean that understanding inherently leads to greater satisfaction. Knowing why a spouse has acted cold and indifferent doesn't mean the perceiver has to be happy about it. We often understand people we don't like; indeed the more information that is acquired about a person, the greater the likelihood we'll find something to dislike, which might even lead to termination of the relationship. Understanding others is neither intrinsically positive nor negative. What understanding should do is improve people's ability to achieve their own interpersonal goals whether that is sustaining a marriage or terminating it.

Acitelli, Kenny, and Weiner (2001) studied the impact of stereotypes on couples' similarity in marital ideals and their ability to identify each other's ideals. Their study used a sample of unmarried couples living together over 6 months (average 3.3 years) and couples who had been married less than 25 years (average 11.3). They found that while couples ratings of marital ideals were not different, their perception of each other's ideals was falling along traditional gender lines. Interestingly, they appear to apply a set of partner ideals drawn from the use of generalized-other social decentering, rather than applying RSSD to identify ideals specifically held by their partners. Such an application could be because of the ease by which pre-existing socially defined ideals can be accessed in comparison to the effort needed to identify partner-specific ideals. Acitelli et al. also found that understanding a partner's ideals when adjusted for stereotyping was unrelated to satisfaction. Acitelli et al. concluded that "understanding of a partner's values does not lead to enhanced relationship satisfaction" (p. 180). Since the results are correlational, the results would more accurately be described as meaning that either understanding doesn't lead to satisfaction or satisfaction doesn't lead to understanding. In terms of social decentering and RSSD, the implication is that a person could be strong or weak in decentering yet still have satisfying relationships. But satisfaction might have an impact on spouses' decentering – dissatisfaction might reduce efforts to socially decenter and understand partners. The results also mean that strength in social decentering and RSSD does not insure relational satisfaction. Spouses with strong understanding of their partners often remain in unsatisfactory relationships for a myriad of reasons. Remaining in relationships under such conditions creates a dysfunctional relationship where there is little satisfaction, but in which a person remains (often because of commitment or concern for children).

Theoretically RSSD develops as relationships become more and more intimate. But the majority of information spouses learn about each other occurs relatively early in the relationship and marriage. Thus, some upper level threshold probably exists at that point information acquisition is noticeably reduced. But just because relationships endure over time, it does not mean that partners continue to be open to or actively seek additional information about each other, nor motivated to utilize partner knowledge and continue efforts to adapt. A significant amount of research demonstrates that marital satisfaction follows a U-shaped curvilinear relationship with the length of the relationship (Kelley, 2012). This pattern of change in satisfaction change has been linked to corresponding changes in other marital factors such as a couple's parental roles (Kelly, 2012); thus, a similar pattern might be expected for RSSD. A reduction in satisfaction might mean less focus and concern on the partner and thus a decline in the application of RSSD with a resurgence in the later stages of the relationship. The reverse also might be true, such that a decline in RSSD negatively impacts marital satisfaction.

The discussion and analysis of social decentering's relationship to age applies to RSSD as well. If, as research suggests, people decline in their empathy and increase in egocentricism, then RSSD can be expected to decline with age, in spite of the availability of additional knowledge and understanding of one's partner. Spouses might also get to a point in time where some responses to each other are more routine and habitual than strategic and deliberative (Dainton & Aylor, 2002). Couples might be actively engaged in RSSD as the marriage begins producing successful patterns of adaptation and interaction, but over time those adaptations become scripted or routine, reducing the need and/or motivation to engage in further decentering.

Edgar Long's studies on perspective-taking incorporate measures that parallel those developed for social decentering and RSSD. He measures both general perspective-taking (akin to social decentering but without the emotional component) and dyadic perspective-taking that is perception of a person's spouse (akin to RSSD again without the emotional component). In Long (1994) and Long and Andrews' (1990) examinations of perspective-taking's impact on marriage, three measures of perspective-taking were employed. General perspective-taking was assessed with the perspective-taking subscale of Davis' IRI. The second measure, the Self Dyadic Perspective-Taking Scale, was previously developed by Long to assess respondents' specific understanding of their spouses. The third measure, the Other Dyadic Perspective-Taking Scale, also by Long, was intended to measure respondents' perception of the other spouse's dyadic perspective-taking. Unfortunately, the scales are not independent nor are they solely parallel forms of recontextualized items. All the seven items composing Davis' general scale are reworded and included on the Other Dyadic scale, and five are incorporated in the Self Dyadic scale. All 13 of the Self Dyadic scale items are rephrased and included in the Other Dyadic scale with another seven new items added. Thus, the scales represent some assessment of the same conceptualization of perspective-taking, but with some difference in operationalization. These factors confound and undermine the reliability and interpretability of the results. The following table lists the results of regression analyses for each scale as a percent of variance for marital adjustment scores (Spanier's DAS; Long & Andrews, 1990) and for the propensity for divorce as well as the bivariate correlation coefficients (Long, 1994).

	Husbands' Adjustment	Wives' Adjustment	Husbands' Propensity to Divorce	Wives' Propensity to Divorce
Spouse's general perspective-taking	8%	4%	3% (r = 0.01 ns)	5% (r = 0.07 ns)
Spouse's reported dyadic perspective-taking	8%	2%	7% (r = −0.34)	2% (r = −0.16)
Perception of spouse's dyadic perspective-taking	22%	50%	7% (r = −0.44)	26% (r = −0.54)

ns, not significant

Although statistically significant, only 2–8% of the variance in marital adjustment was related to either the respondent's or spouse's general or dyadic perspective-taking. The impact of perspective-taking on marital adjustment is small but that might reflect the problems of measurement discussed earlier. While a stronger relationship was found between adjustment and a respondent's perception of a spouse's perspective-taking, especially for women, the effect might be more a product of a perceptual halo effect than perspective-taking. More satisfied spouses might attribute more of the positive behaviors listed in the instrument to their partners then were actually occurring.

Long (1993) also analyzed the data from the above study by dividing respondents into two categories based on their marital adjustment scores: high (n = 259) and low (N = 43). For the wives, no significant difference was found in the general perspective-taking of those in high or low adjustment marriages, but those in the high adjustment marriages had significantly higher dyadic perspective-taking scores than those in the low adjustment marriages. Husbands in high adjustment marriages had significantly higher scores on both general and dyadic perspective-taking measures than those in the low adjustment marriages. Long contended the results indicated that husbands and wives had stronger understanding of their spouses in the higher adjusted groups. A similar pattern of results was found in the spouses' perceptions of their partners' dyadic perspective-taking with both husbands and wives in the high adjustment groups reporting higher other dyadic perspective-taking scores for their spouses than those in the low adjustment group. Ratings given by husbands and wives in the high adjustment group of their spouses' perspective-taking were fairly similar (52.3 and 50.6, respectively), while in the low adjustment group, husbands rated their spouses higher than the wives did (34.21 and 24.41, respectively).

Long (1993) hypothesized that similarity between the spouses' general perspective-taking would positively relate to adjustment as would similarity in dyadic perspective-taking. No significant correlations were found for general perspective-taking for either wives or husbands. For similarity in dyadic perspective-taking and adjustment, no significant correlation was found for wives and a significant but weak negative correlation (r = −0.19) was found for husbands. Husbands reacted negatively to having wives who understood them to the same degree they understood their wives. Given gender role expectations where women are stronger in empathy, perhaps having wives with the same level of dyadic perspective-taking is disappointing to the husbands. Aside from possible problems with methodology, the failure to find a relationship between the spouses' similar perspective-taking abilities and marital adjustment suggests that perhaps perspective-taking is a complementary skill (a strong perspective-taking partner compensates for a weak perspective-taking partner) or that understanding is not automatically connected with accommodating one's partner. Long's research demonstrates the complex nature of the relationships between social decentering, RSSD, marital satisfaction, and the sex of the spouse.

Another study that also sought to examine partner-specific perspective-taking was conducted by Arriaga and Rusbult (1998). In their 3-year longitudinal study of 53 married couples, they adapted Davis' perspective-taking scale to assess respondents' specific perspective-taking of their spouse (similar to the RSSD measure). Results of their examination of adaptive behaviors led them to conclude that taking on a spouse's perspective has "substantial adaptive value," specifically:

> When a partner enacts a potentially destructive behavior, individuals with greater self-reported tendencies toward partner perspective-taking indicate that they are substantially less likely to react destructively and more likely to react constructively. There was insufficient change over time to determine whether partner perspective-taking predicts change in inclinations to accommodate. (p. 934)

The participants in the study were recruited from a list of applicants for married licenses with the average length of marriage of 8 months; thus, the conclusions made by Arriaga and Rusbult might not be applicable to more long-term couples. Given that previous research shows marital satisfaction decreasing over the course of a marriage or following a U pattern of decreasing and then increasing after many years, a drop in adaptation after the newlywed period could be reasonably expected.

As with dyadic perspective-taking, a substantial part of RSSD depends upon how well people understand their partners. Gurung, Sarason, and Sarason (2001) referred to the ability to form a clear conception of a partner as significant-other-concept clarity. Drawing from Campbell, Trapnell, Heine, Katz, Lavallee, and Lehman's (1996) study of clarity as it applied to self-concept, Gurung et al. defined significant-other-concept clarity as the level of confidence and degree of consistence and overall stability in peoples' conception of their partners. They examined significant-other-concept clarity among 78 college undergraduate couples that included married, living together, and engaged couples. Respondents' levels of significant-other-concept clarity related to their own relationship satisfaction but not to that of their partners. In other words, the more confident you are that you have a clear conception of your partner, the more satisfied you feel about the relationship. This finding again reflects the impact of how an individual's certainty and perceived understanding of their partner affects his or her own feelings about the relationship but not the partner's. An inability to understand one's partner can be readily seen as undermining relationship satisfaction but probably just in those situations where a person is actively attempting to achieve such understanding. Finding that clarity did not positively affect the partner's satisfaction suggests other factors are undermining the impact. Perhaps couples fail to utilize significant-other-concept clarity when they interact and respond to each other, or perhaps the sense of clarity is a false perception, which then produces ill-adapted behaviors that fail to increase a partner's relational satisfaction. The results of this study suggest those people who feel more clarity about their RSSD will feel more relational satisfaction, but their partners won't. Partners might fail to recognize the others' level of RSSD or the RSSD might be inaccurate.

5.5 The Role of Social Decentering and RSSD in Marriage

The confusing and contradictory findings in the research examining the relationship between other-orientation processes and marital outcomes is probably due to the complex relationship between social decentering (empathy and perspective-taking) and marital relationships. Socially decentering and RSSD can be used by spouses to adapt to their partners and potentially enhance their partners' marital satisfaction, but a positive relationship between decentering and satisfaction is not as inviolate as is often assumed. Decentering can be employed to manipulate partners and develop self-serving strategies, potentially reducing partner satisfaction.

Given the intimate nature of marital relationships, spouses develop an expectation that their partner's should understand them or a belief that they do understand them. People expect their partner to develop and apply RSSD. Expecting that one spouse understands the other impacts the subsequent attitudes and behaviors of the spouse holding the expectation. In functional marriages, when spouses think their partners understand their positions, feelings, thoughts, etc., spouses should be stimulated to respond with positive and comforting communication to their partners. In a study of 77 couples who had been married for less than 3 years, Sanford (2005) found such positive communication behavior during couples' discussions of recent conflicts among those couples who held expectations for being understood by their partner and had expectations for less negative communication. Sanford concluded that "Given the ultimate importance of being understood by one's partner, couples may be particularly attentive to indicators regarding the extent to which such understanding is likely" (p. 263). Extrapolating that conclusion to social decentering – decreases in decentering and subsequent decreases in positive communication are likely to decrease marital satisfaction. But what leads to decreases in social decentering and RSSD over the course of marriage?

As discussed in Chapter 1, individuals must be motivated to engage in social decentering and a variety of factors can reduce or remove such motivation in marriage.

People with strong social decentering skills might consciously choose not to use them in understanding their partners or if they do decenter, choose not to act on it or adapt to it. This is one possible explanation for the failure to find strong support for a linear relationship between understanding/empathy and marital satisfaction or other positive marital communication behaviors. The decision not to decenter might be based on a variety of extenuating variables such as dissatisfaction, a loss of commitment, interest in pursuing other relationships, inequity, loss of interest, neutral or negative feelings, or establishment of routine interactions. But deciding to engage in social decentering doesn't insure positive outcomes for the partner – social decentering can be used to produce negative outcomes – to hurt or punish a partner. To find a positive relationship between social decentering and partner's relational satisfaction requires motivation to socially decenter and motivation to use it in positive ways.

Possessing strong general social decentering skills and strong RSSD skills means having a greater understanding of one's spouse. People with strong decentering should be adept at predicting their spouses' responses to various situations, events, and communication strategies. This ability to predict does not automatically imbue them with the ability to manipulate their partners for self-gain. For example, person (A) might understand that his or her partner (B) is uncomfortable being touched because of childhood abuse, but this does not increase A's ability to adapt to this condition in order meet his or her own needs for affection. Possessing such skill might actually exacerbate the situation because such sensitivity might necessitate (A) having to subordinate his or her needs to those of the spouse. Another person (X) who lacks such sensitivity might continue to get his or her needs met at the expense of the partner (Y). As a result, A and Y might be quite dissatisfied, while B is satisfied in the relationship because of the partner's adaptation, and X is satisfied by the partner's accommodation. The ability of people to understand their partners and elicit positive responses (positive marital adjustment) from their partners was demonstrated in two studies of married couples (Long, 1990; Long & Andrews, 1990). On the other hand, Sillars et al. (1984) found a negative correlation between individuals' level of understanding the salience of ten marital conflict topics to their partners and their own reported marital satisfaction. In evaluating the couples' conflict discussions, they observed that "more understanding spouses were responsive to their partner, but this did them little good" (p. 345). Furthermore, they observed that the more understanding spouses moderated their positive communication responses to their partners in anticipation of negative reactions from their partners, though that still failed to elicit positive responses. Their results suggest that being strongly understanding might not be as related to positive behaviors and therefore not as readily observable as generally predicted. The results also indicate that one partner might fail to observe the other partner's adaptive behaviors.

Given the results of studies that examine the change in empathy and perspective-taking over the course of marriage, social decentering and RSSD are similarly expected to decline over time. For example, newlyweds seem more cognizant of their spouses' attitudes and feelings than do longer married couples (Bissonette, Rusbult, & Kilpatrick, 1997). In the first 9 months of marriage, the amount of understanding reported by one spouse related to the adjustment of the other spouse, but this effect did not endure (Pollmann & Finkenauer, 2010). Pollmann and Finkenauer (2010) suggest that the uncertainty that exists in the early stages of marriage lead to increased effort to gain information about each other and that as time passes couples feel more confident about their understanding of each other while actual knowledge remains unchanged. Motivation to engage in cognitive work and perspective-taking decreases the longer a couple is married, perhaps because they feel they know what each other is thinking or the relationship becomes stagnant (Thomas et al., 1997).

Besides declining over time, motivation to socially decenter is likely to decline as dissatisfaction and marital distress increase as suggested in Long's (1993) study of low versus high adjusted couples particularly in terms of his dyadic perspective-taking measure (akin to RSSD). Burleson and Denton (1997) found that perceptual and predictive accuracy were associated with liking in nondistressed couples but were not related to liking in distressed couples. If people are dissatisfied or indifferent toward their partners in their marriages, they are unlikely to exert the effort needed to understand and adapt to their partner through decentering, particularly RSSD, unless they are motivated to either improve the relationship or terminate it. They might also choose to exert the effort to relationally specific decenter if they are motivated to undermine their spouses' goals or disconfirm and demean their spouses.

Unfortunately, research tends to focus on the impact of empathy/perspective-taking on marital satisfaction and not vice versa. In addition, much of the research depends upon correlations that don't assess cause and effect. Correlations can be interpreted to mean the level of marital satisfaction might be the cause of a given level of empathy/perspective-taking. This is particularly likely in the instance of RSSD where people's decentering is directly connected to a specific relationship. Conducting experimental studies where satisfaction with one's spouse is manipulated to determine the impact on empathy has obvious practical and ethical obstacles.

5.6 Social Decentering and RSSD as Complementary or Symmetrical?

To what degree are married couples similar or different in their general ability to take into account other people's dispositions (socially decenter)? As discussed earlier, people might form symmetrical relationships where they are attracted to those who have the same level of skill such as both being low in social decentering or both being high. On the other hand, the relationship could be complementary, where the skill possessed by one partner proves compatible with the lack of skill in the other partner.

One secondary finding from my study on social decentering and persuasion in interpersonal relationships, discussed in Chapter 3, was that social decentering scores were more similar among casual friends and friends than in the more intimate relationships (Redmond, 2002). Partners in the most intimate relationships (best friends, lovers, spouses) had significantly greater differences in their social decentering than partners in less intimate relationships. These results indicate that for casual friend and friend relationships participants experienced symmetrical social decentering relationships, while for the most intimate relationships participants experienced complementary social decentering relationships. Given that the study had few married participants and included nonromantic relationships, the degree to which similar symmetrical and complementary relationships might be expected across the life span of marriages is uncertain.

To my knowledge, no studies have been conducted that examine the impact of similarity and differences in empathy or perspective-taking levels across the life span of marriage. Many studies have examined similarity in empathy and perspective-taking in newlyweds and in the early years of marriage, but less attention has been given to similarities, differences, and changes over the life-span of marriage. Studies of longer married couples tend to focus on how empathy impacts some aspect of their relationship, such as comforting in times of illness or managing conflict. Despite the lack of studies on empathy/perspective-taking compatibility, complementarity and symmetry of other qualities and skills in longer-term married couples have been studied.

Shiota and Levenson (2007) examined how the similarity of the Big Five personality traits related to marital satisfaction among 40 year olds and 60 year olds over a 12-year period. Initial similarity was unrelated to satisfaction, but the more similarity at the beginning of the study, the more likely a negative decline in satisfaction over the next 12 years particularly for the 40 year olds. Shiota and Levenson observed that while similarity among young couples might help with intimacy, attachment, and equity, changes in life tasks might favor couples who have more complementary personalities (e.g., a partner who is laisse faire paired with a partner who is detail oriented). Another study on the impact of similarity on the Big Five personality among Swiss couples with an average length of relationship of 24.21 years also failed to find a significant impact; this time on life satisfaction (Furler, Gomez, & Grob, 2013).

Burleson and Denton (1992) examined the relationship of married couples' similarity in social information processing, perceptual accuracy, and communication effectiveness with marital satisfaction and liking. In their sample of 60 couples (a mean length of marriage of 6.8 years), they found similarly low-skilled couples were not significantly different than similarly high-skilled couples in satisfaction and liking. Similarity appeared to be more important than having the skills that were expected to enhance relationships and satisfaction. Further confusing the situation was the finding that "the husband's communication skills appeared to be less important predictors of his wife's marital satisfaction than her skills were of his satisfaction" (p. 987). Burleson and Denton speculated that individuals are most comfortable interacting with someone who has similar communication skill levels and that "achieving accurate and sensitive understandings through verbal communication" (p. 283) might not be that important to low-skilled individuals. The sex of who has those skills also appears to affect satisfaction. We might expect then little difference in the level of satisfaction in couples' where both partners are high in social decentering and/or RSSD and in couples where both partners are low. We might also expect that the wives level of decentering skills is more influential than the husband's.

In the premarriage and early marriage phase of relationships, similarity in social decentering levels is likely to create attraction and produce a symmetrical relationship, but similarity is likely to become less significant over time. Similarity in RSSD should be fairly high in the early years of marriage as couples as partners have exerted significant effort in getting to know each other. While that knowledge will remain over the course of the marriage, the degree to which spouses continue to exert the effort to continue to learn about each other is likely to be impacted by a variety of factors such as the birth of children and job demands.

5.7 A Model of Social Decentering and Marriage

The model presented here is built from and reflective of the previous discussion on marriage and empathy, perspective-taking social decentering, and RSSD. Two primary assumptions underlie this model:

1. The level of relational satisfaction of married couples impacts a variety of dynamics including the development and application of social decentering.
2. The degree to which a couple's social decentering is symmetrical (both spouses high or both spouses low) or complementary (one spouse high and one spouse low) affects and/or is affected by a variety of marital behaviors and outcomes including marital satisfaction and adjustment.

While the identified behaviors are distinguished by their relationship to satisfaction, the model is not intended to be interpreted as positing a cause–effect relationship. So, for example, satisfied social decentering couples might display mutual concern for each other's welfare, but is satisfaction the product of showing concern or is showing concern the product of being satisfied? The likely answer is both – satisfaction and showing concern probably have a systemic relationship with each promoting development of the other. Satisfaction is expected to have such a relationship with each of the behaviors and qualities identified in the model.

A Model of Social Decentering and Marital Satisfaction

Type I. Symmetrically Strong Couple: Both Husband and Wife Are Strong Social Decenterers

Satisfied Couple

> Strong mutual understanding.
>
> Strong use of confirming communication.
>
> Frequent use of information seeking behaviors.
>
> Display of active and mutual listening behaviors.
>
> Mutual concern for the other's welfare.

Dissatisfied Couple

> Little interaction.
>
> Minimal conflict.
>
> Few attempts to influence or persuade each other.
>
> Stagnant relationship.

Type II. Nontraditional Mixed Couple: Husband Is Strong Social Decenterer and Wife Is Weak Social Decenterer

Satisfied Couple

> Wife more satisfied than the husband.
>
> Husband engages in accommodating behavior toward wife.
>
> Wife appreciates husband's understanding.
>
> Husband harbors some resentment toward his wife and feels taken for granted at times.
>
> Relationship viewed as a gender role reversal from traditional marital relationship.

Dissatisfied Couple

> Both are dissatisfied but for different reasons.
>
> Wife's self concept, and thus satisfaction, is threatened by husband's decentering.
>
> Husband is frustrated by doing all of the accommodating and thus less satisfied.
>
> Husband infrequently accommodates his wife.
>
> Relationship discussions prove to be unfruitful – no change or improvements.
>
> Husband "chooses" not to socially decenter with his wife.
>
> Husband is more likely to initiate relational termination if he feels the situation is futile.

Type III. Traditional Mixed Couple: Wife Is Strong and Husband Is Weak Social Decenterer

Satisfied Couple

> Similar level of satisfaction for both the wife and husband.
>
> Husband plays a more traditional role.
>
> Wife accommodates toward the husband.
>
> Husband is dependent upon the wife to be a confidant and friend.
>
> Wife seeks and gains relational satisfaction in friendships outside the marriage.

Dissatisfied Couple

> Wife resents husband.
>
> Husband doesn't understand wife's discontent; sees things as okay and comfortable.

(continued)

(continued)

Wife wants changes in the husband and he is unwilling to alter his behavior.

Wife is more likely to initiate conflict.

Wife is likely to initiate relational termination if she feels her situation is futile.

Type IV. Symmetrically Weak: Both Husband and Wife Are Weak Social Decenterers

Satisfied Couple

Higher amounts of conflict but with little relational damage or long-term effects.

Fairly independent operating couple.

Each does their own thing and leaves the other spouse alone.

High role definition and expectation.

Dissatisfied Couple

High amounts of conflict leading to damaged relationship and likely termination.

Perception that the other spouse is blocking their goals and preventing their happiness.

Each are frustrated by the lack of accommodation by the other.

High degree of independence.

5.8 The Relationship between RSSD and Marriage

Unlike the trait nature of social decentering, the state nature of RSSD leads to some differences in its relationship to marriage. People do not enter into a relationship with a pre-existing level of RSSD but instead develop it as they get to know new partners. The growth of RSSD is in concert with the movement toward close, intimate relationships. As discussed in the last chapter, the more intimate the relationship, the higher the level of RSSD. Indeed, the level of intimacy, relational satisfaction, and RSSD can all be expected to reach a maximum point where little further increase occurs. On the other hand, if one partner does not reach the requisite higher level of RSSD, the relationship is likely to decrease in intimacy and if the couple is fortunate, dissolve altogether before reaching marriage. As relationships develop, partners expect each other to have greater understanding and thus greater RSSD. To the degree that RSSD is like empathic accuracy in depending upon the acquisition of partner information, then RSSD's role in marriage should parallel the patterns of development and use of empathic accuracy. Given the results reviewed earlier that showed empathic accuracy declining after the second year of marriage, RSSD can also be expected to decline from a peak achieved in the first years of marriage.

Combining the conceptualization of RSSD provided in Chapter 2 and discussion of empathy and perspective-taking provided in this chapter lead to the propositions listed below. Research suggests dramatic changes in marriage after the first year or two and as children are born, leading to change in the relational dynamics and decreased satisfaction. As the children get older, more independent, and move out of the house, couples have more time to devote to their relationships starting around 20 years or so into the marriage. Other significant changes occur as couples move toward retirement accompanied by more time together and increased relational awareness, somewhere after 30 or so years of marriage. The changes that occur during these three periods of marriage have an impact on RSSD and related behaviors.

In the first years of marriage:
1. Both spouses will be strong in RSSD (a symmetrical relationship).
2. Spouses will possess strong understanding of each other and of strong feelings of being understood by the partner.
3. Both spouses will display strong adaptation and accommodation to their partners.

As marriages progress (~3 to ~20 years):
4. Increasing individual responsibilities (work/family) negatively impact the time and effort spent refreshing and/or applying knowledge of the partner; thus RSSD will decline.
5. Since wives start with a higher level of RSSD, and to the degree they are more involved in childcare, their level of decline in RSSD will be relatively larger than their husbands.
6. Adaptation and accommodation to the partner will decrease.
7. Spouses will feel less understood and that increases the probability for conflict.

Later years of marriage (~21+):
8. RSSD will increase over the previous years of marriage.
9. To the degree that wives have been more involved in childcare, the reduction in responsibilities will have a greater positive effect on wives' RSSD than on the husbands.

Some of the above relationships were examined in a study on social decentering and RSSD that I conducted with 101 married couples. The study specifically focused on changes in social decentering and RSSD, comparisons between husbands and wives, and the impact on satisfaction, relational attitudes, and relational communication.

5.9 A Reflection Exercise to Promote Social Decentering

The following ten questions were developed as a way to operationalize each of the dimensions of social decentering to focus individual's thinking about a spouse's dispositions. The questions have been successfully utilized in teaching social decentering, having individuals share a personal emotional situation and then having a partner consider and answer each of the following questions. As they proceed, the target indicates the accuracy or inaccuracy of those responses. These questions should be useful for married couples who are interested in improving their sensitivity to and understanding of each other.

10 Questions to Answer that Facilitate Social Decentering

1. What factors or circumstances are affecting my spouse regarding this situation?
2. How can I determine if there are factors I don't know about or don't fully understand?
3. What do I know about my spouse that explains his or her behaviors and feelings?
4. What is going through my spouse's mind regarding this situation at this time?
5. What are my spouse's feelings about the situation at this time?
6. What other explanations could there be for my spouse's actions?
7. What would I think if I were in the same situation?
8. How would I feel if I were in the same situation?
9. What would other people think if they were in that situation?
10. What would other people feel if they were in that situation?

5.10 References

Acitelli, L. K., Kenny, D. A., & Weiner, D. (2001). The importance of similarity and understanding of partners' marital ideals to relationship satisfaction. *Personal Relationships, 8*, 167–185.

Arriaga, X. B., & Rusbult, C. E. (1998). Standing in my partner's shoes: Partner perspective-taking and reactions to accommodative dilemmas. *Personality and Social Psychology Bulletin, 24*, 927–948.

Bakker, A. B., & Demerouti, E. (2009). The crossover of work engagement between working couples. *Journal of Managerial Psychology, 24*, 220–236.

Bissonette, V. L., Rusbult, C. E., & Kilpatrick, S. D. (1997). Empathic accuracy and marital conflict resolution. In W. J. Ickes (Ed.), *Empathic accuracy* (pp. 251–281). New York, NY: Guilford Press.

Bissonette, V. L., Rusbult, C. E., & Kilpatrick, S. D. (2002). Empathic accuracy and accommodative behavior among newly married couples. *Personal Relationships, 9*, 369–393.

Burleson, B. R., & Denton, W. H. (1992). A new look at similarity and attraction in marriage: Similarities in social–cognitive and communication skills as predictors of attraction and satisfaction. *Communication Monographs, 59*, 268–287.

Campbell, J. D., Trapnell, P. D., Heine, S. J., Katz, J. M., Lavallee, L. F., & Lehman, D. R. (1996). Self-concept clarity: Measurement, personality correlates, and cultural boundaries. *Journal of Personality and Social Psychology, 7*, 141–156.

Cohen, S., Schulz, M. S., Weiss, E., & Waldinger, R. J. (2012). Eye of the beholder: The individual and dyadic contributions of empathic accuracy and perceived empathic effort to relationship satisfaction. *Journal of Family Psychology, 26*, 236–245.

Cronbach, L. (1955). Processes affecting scores on "understanding of others" and "assumed similarity." *Psychological Bulletin, 53*, 177–193.

Cronbach, L. (1960). *Essentials of psychological testing* (2nd ed.). New York: Harper & Row.

Dainton, M., & Aylor, B. (2002). Routine and strategic maintenance efforts: Behavioral patterns, variations associated with relational length, and the prediction of relational characteristics. *Communication Monographs, 69*, 52–66.

Davis, M. H. (1983). Measuring individual differences in empathy: Evidence for a multi dimensional approach. *Journal of Personality and Social Psychology, 44*, 113–126.

Elliott, M. W. (1982). Communication and empathy in marital adjustment. *Home Economics Research Journal, 11*, 77–88.

Fiske, S. T. (1993). Social cognition and social perception. *Annual Review of Psychology, 44*, 155–194.

Franzoi, S. L., Davis, M. H., & Young R. D. (1985). The effects of private self-consciousness and perspective-taking on satisfaction in close relationships. *Journal of Personality and Social Psychology, 48*, 1584–1594.

Furler, K., Gomez, V., & Grob, A. (2013). Personality similarity and life satisfaction in couples. *Journal of Research in Personality, 47*, 369–375. doi.org/10.1016/j.jrp.2013.03.002.

Gambrel, L. E., & Piercy, F. P. (2015). Mindfulness-based relationship education for couples expecting their first child-Part I: A randomized mixed-methods program evaluation. *Journal of Marital and Family Therapy, 41*, 5–24.

Gurung, R. A. R., Sarason, B. R., & Sarason, I. G. (2001). Predicting relationship quality and emotional reactions to stress from significant-other-concept clarity. *Personality and Social Psychology Bulletin, 27*, 1267–1276.

Kellas, J. K., Willer, E. K., & Trees, A. R. (2013). Communicated perspective-taking during stories of marital stress: Spouses' perceptions of one another's perspective-taking behaviors. *Southern Communication Journal, 78*, 326–351.

Kelley, D. L. (2012). *Marital communication*. Malden, MA: Polity Press.

Kilpatrick, S. D., Bissonette, V. L., & Rusbult, C. E. (2002). Empathic accuracy and accommodative behavior among newly married couples. *Personal Relationships, 9*, 369–393.

Long, E. C. J. (1990). Measuring dyadic perspective-taking: Two scales for assessing perspecti-ve-taking in marriage and similar dyads. *Educational and Psychological Measurement, 50*, 91–103.

Long, E. C. J. (1993). Perspective-taking differences between high- and low-adjustment marriages: Implications for those in intervention. *The American Journal of Family Therapy, 21*, 248–259.

Long, E. C. J. (1994). Maintaining a stable marriage. *Journal of Divorce & Remarriage, 21*, 121–138.

Long, E. C. J., & Andrews, D. W. (1990). Perspective-taking as a predictor of marital adjustment. *Journal of Personality and Social Psychology, 59*, 126–131.

Péloquin, K., & Lafontaine, M. (2010). Measuring empathy in couples: Validity and reliability of the interpersonal reactivity index for couples. *Journal of Personality Assessment, 92*, 146–157.

Pollmann M. M., & Finkenauer, C. (2009). Investigating the role of two types of understanding in relationship well-being: Understanding is more important than knowledge. *Personality and Social Psychology Bulletin, 35*, 1512–1527.

Redmond, M. V. (2002). "Social decentering, intimacy, and interpersonal influence." Presented at the annual meeting of the National Communication Association, New Orleans.

Rosen, N. O., Mooney, K., & Muise, A. (2016). Dyadic empathy predicts sexual and relationship well-being in couples transitioning to parenthood. *Journal of Sex & Marital Therapy*, DOI: 10.1080/0092623X.2016.1208698.

Rowan, D. G, Compton, W. C., & Rust, J. O. (1995). Self-actualization and empathy as predictors of marital satisfaction. *Psychological Reports, 77*, 1011–1016.

Sanford, K. (2005). Attributions and anger in early marriage: Wives are event-dependent and husbands are schematic. *Journal of Family Psychology, 19*, 180–188.

Shiota, M. N., & Levenson, R. W. (2007). Birds of a feather don't always fly farthest: Similarity in Big Five personality predicts more negative marital satisfaction trajectories in long-term marriages. *Psychology and Aging, 22*, 666–675.

Sillars, A. L., Pike, G. R., Jones, T. S., & Murphy, M. A. (1984). Communication and understanding in marriage. *Human Communication Research, 10*, 317–350.

Sillars, A., Roberts, L. J., Leonard, K. E., & Dun, T. (2000). Cognition during marital conflict: The relationship of thought and talk. *Journal of Social and Personal Relationships, 17*, 479–502.

Thomas, G., Fletcher, G. J. O., & Lange C. (1997). On-line empathic accuracy in marital interaction. *Journal of Personality and Social Psychology, 72*, 839–850.

Wachs, K., & Cordova, J. V. (2007). Mindful relating: Exploring mindfulness and emotion repertoires in intimate relationships. *Journal of Marital and Family Therapy, 33*, 464–481.

Wastell, C. A. (1991). Empathy in marriage. *Australian Journal of Marriage and Family, 12*, 27–38.

6 A Study of Social Decentering and Relationship-Specific Social Decentering (RSSD) within Marriage

This chapter reports the results of a study I conducted to investigate the roles of social decentering and relationship-specific social decentering (RSSD) in marriage. This study examines some of the observations and predictions discussed in Chapter 5. In addition, the study explored social decentering and RSSD in relationship to long-term changes in marriage, marital satisfaction, communication attitudes, and communication behaviors. One hundred and one married couples, primarily from the Midwest of the United States, completed an extensive set of questionnaires including self-reports of social decentering and RSSD, marital satisfaction, and other variables.

To identify and solicit the involvement of married couples in this study, I relied on students in a variety of courses at Iowa State University to contact married couples who they thought might participate in the study and give them a flyer describing it. At the bottom of the flyer was a tear sheet on which one of the spouses was asked to write name and contact information, the student's name who made contact, and whether the couple was willing to participate. Students gave couples willing to participate a self-stamped envelope that included two smaller envelopes, one addressed to wife and the other to husband. Students received extra credit for getting the tear sheet filled out regardless of whether the couple agreed to participate. If students chose not to contact any married couples, they were given an alternative extra-credit option. And for additional credit, students could also contact and distribute a second set of materials. I recruited most of the student volunteers right before spring break when many would be returning home and thus likely to enlist their family or hometown friends to complete the questionnaires.

6.1 The Couples

The instructions students provided to the married couples directed them to independently complete the questionnaire and to not discuss it until both spouses had completed it. Upon completing the questionnaire, each spouse was to place it in the separate envelope marked for that spouse, seal the envelope, and place it in the larger postpaid envelope that the spouses were to use for mailing it to me. A total of 101 married couples ($N = 202$) returned completed and usable questionnaires (additional incomplete questionnaires were excluded from the analysis). While a code number appeared on each questionnaire to allow matching of the responses, no other identifying information was required.

Respondents' ages ranged from 20 to 81 years, with an average age of 47 (SD = 13.52). The average length of marriage was 20.96 years (SD = 13.3), with a range from 6 months

https://doi.org/10.1515/9783110515664-007

to 58 years. The average number of children that the couples had was 1.86 with a mode of 2.0 (41.6%) and a range from no children to seven. Of the participants, 30 (14.6 %) indicated that they had been married before (16 males and 14 females). Responses to the racial identity item indicated that 183 participants were Caucasian, 7 Asian, 6 African American, 3 Hispanic, and 1 other (2 participants left the item blank). Table 6.1 lists the educational attainment of the respondents; Table 6.2 lists their religious affiliations.

Spouses were asked to indicate from a list of income ranges their total household income, which is listed in Table 6.3.

Table 6.1: Highest level of education.

(N = 202)	
High school degree	40 (19.8%)
Some college or a 2-year degree	48 (23.8%)
Four-year degree	74 (36.6%)
Advanced degree	36 (17.8%)
Left blank	4 (2.0%)

Table 6.2: Religious affiliation.

(N = 202)	
Protestant	72 (35.6%)
Catholic	69 (34.2%)
No religious affiliation	22 (10.9%)
Evangelical Christian	20 (9.9%)
Other	14 (6.9%)
Muslim	2 (1.0%)
Jewish	1 (0.5 %)
Left blank	2 (1.0%)

Table 6.3: Combined income.

(N = 101)	
Up to $25,000	9 (8.9%)
$25,001–$50,000	10 (9.9%)
$50,001–$75,000	20 (19.8%)
$75,001–$100,000	16 (15.8%)
$100,001–$125,000	11 (10.9%)
Over $125,000	29 (28.7%)
Missing	6 (5.9%)

6.2 The Measures

Social Decentering. Social decentering was measured using the 36-item Social Decentering Scale (see Appendix A) discussed in Chapter 2. Participants responded using a Likert scale indicating strong agreement or disagreement on a five-point scale. Using Cronbach's alpha to test reliability for the scale and seven subscales yielded the following coefficients: overall measure, $\alpha = 0.92$; experienced-base subscale, $\alpha = 0.82$; imagination-based subscale $\alpha = 0.88$; use of self, $\alpha = 0.85$; use of specific-other, $\alpha = 0.78$; use of generalized-other, $\alpha = 0.80$; cognitive, $\alpha = 0.87$; affective, $\alpha = 0.86$.

RSSD Scale. I modified the 12-item RSSD scale developed to assess social decentering within a given relationship with a given partner so that spouse was used to refer to the other person. The items asked about the ability to consider the spouse's dispositions, and each multidimensional item reflected the three components that constitute social decentering (see Appendix B). The RSSD scale had a reliability of $\alpha = 0.79$.

Marital Satisfaction. A number of scales measure the various manifestations of marital satisfaction that often include items that tap a variety of variables indirectly related to satisfaction, such as communication. Differences between scales accounts for part of the reason previous studies have produced inconsistent results when relating marital satisfaction to empathy and perspective-taking. Funk and Rogge (2007) used item response theory in examining 180 items from a variety of such scales to create a four-item scale, Couples Satisfaction Index-4), with a reported reliability of $\alpha = 0.94$. The Couples Satisfaction Index-4 had a reliability of $\alpha = 0.95$ in my study. I used this scale because it focuses directly on marital satisfaction and is "relatively free from contaminating communication variables by rigorously screening and eliminating communication items from the item pool" (p. 580). Items such as "In general, how satisfied are you with your relationship?" were evaluated on a six-point Likert scale ranging from not at all to completely.

Positive Relationship Discussion Scale. Spouses who have strong understanding of each other's dispositions should be at an advantage for having positive and productive relationship discussions. I developed the positive relationship discussion scale to measure the frequency with which couples engaged in discussions that produced positive outcomes. Spouses responded to a seven-point scale ranging from never (1) to always (7). The three items constituting the scale were as follows: (a) "Discussions of our relational issues produce positive changes," (b) "Open discussions of how we both feel about the relationship have led to its improvement," and (c) "We have improved our relationship through productive conversations" ($a = 0.90$).

Relational Attitude Scales. I developed three scales to measure spouses' attitudes toward their partners in order to examine the impact of decentering in spouses' attitudes toward their relationship: the resentment scale, concern for other scale, and spouse as best friend scale (see Table 6.4 for items and reliabilities). The three attitudes that these scales measure could affect spouses' motivation to socially decenter. Three additional scales were constructed from these scales but with the items worded to assess spouses' perceptions of their partner's attitudes, allowing comparison between one spouses' self-reported attitudes and the perception of those attitudes by the other spouse. Such comparisons help to determine the impact of both social and RSSD.

Resentment. Resentment occurs in response to conflicts, inequities, or unmet expectations and can undermine relationship satisfaction. We might expect that individuals who are strong decenterers would be more sensitive to their partner's feelings of resentment and thus be in a better position to allay those feelings. My measure of resentment used three items that tap these feelings by asking about bitterness over imbalances, lack of contentment, and resentment of underbenefit.

Concern for Other. Three items were used to assess spouses' concern for their partner. These items dealt with general concern for the partner's welfare and well-being.

Spouse as Confidant/Friend. Three items measured spouses' reliance on their partner to discuss problems, receive support, and be a friend.

Relational Communication Scales. To develop scales for measuring relational communication, I had initially intended to use the Communication Patterns Questionnaire (Christensen & Sullaway, 1984); however, that instrument mostly focuses on communication surrounding relationship problems and conflict. But the goal for this study was to assess a breadth of communication behaviors, especially those most likely to be associated with social decentering and RSSD. So, I drew from previous measures of marital communication, pretesting items concerning romantic relationships, revising the items and the instrument, and performing a factor analysis to select the strongest correlated items. Four scales emerged from this process: the supportive communication scale, negative communication scale, blaming behavior scale, and ignoring/failing to consider knowledge of partner scale (see Table 6.4).

Supportive Communication. The supportive communication scale focuses on positive communication behaviors that reflect supportive and confirming communication. The four items in this scale include asking questions that seek information about the other, showing interest, confirming the other's value, and being supportive.

Negative Communication. A variety of communication behaviors exist that can have a negative impact on one's partner. The negative communication scale consists of seven items that represent a breadth of negative communication behaviors: sending mixed messages, teasing at inappropriate times, pointing out the partner's mistakes, nagging, sending confusing messages, criticizing, and failing to adequately explain.

Blaming Behavior. The blaming behavior scale sought to determine the degree to which spouses admitted their blame or placed the blame on their spouse. The three items in this scale include admitting or refusing to admit blame, and blaming the spouse. Higher spouses' scores indicated shunning personal responsibility and instead blaming their partners.

Ignore/Fail to Consider Knowledge of Partner. One claim that has been made about social decentering and RSSD is that people can engage in decentering but choose not to act in a way that benefits the partner. People can ignore the conclusions they have reached in response to decentering or they can choose to not even engage in social decentering if they do not feel motivated to do so. To assess this directly, I developed three items that asked respondents the degree to which they ignored their understanding of their partner in favor of their own self-interests or simply did not take their partner into consideration. I dropped one item (i.e., "I can predict my husband's negative reactions to things I might do but I do them anyway") because it had a low inter-item correlation and its inclusion reduced the reliability of the scale.

Table 6.4: Relational scales.*

RELATIONAL ATTITUDE SCALES

Resentment/Discontent ($\alpha = 0.76$; perception of spouse's perspective $\alpha = 0.83$)
I feel bitterness toward the imbalances in our marriage.
I am not very content with how our relationship is right now.
Differences in what we each get out of the relationship have led to my feeling resentment.

Concern for Spouse's Welfare ($\alpha = 0.59$; perception of spouse's perspective $\alpha = 0.70$)
I have strong concern for the general welfare of my husband.
I have little concern for my husband's well-being.
I worry about my husband's general welfare.

Spouse as Confidant/Friend ($\alpha = 0.81$; perception of spouse's perspective $\alpha = 0.79$)
My husband is the person I turn to the most when I have problems.
I turn to other people more than my husband for support and friendship.
My husband is my best friend.

RELATIONAL COMMUNICATION SCALES

Supportive/Positive Communication ($\alpha = 0.78$; perception of spouse's behavior $\alpha = 0.86$)
I ask questions to find out more information about husband's concerns.
I display a genuine interest when my husband is talking.
I make statements that make my husband feel positive about himself; that make him feel valued.
I provide supportive comments when my husband expresses concerns, doubts, or fears.

Negative Communication ($\alpha = 0.76$; perception of spouse's behavior $\alpha = 0.80$)
I send mixed messages that are confusing.
I tease my husband at the wrong times.
I am quick to point out my husband's mistakes or failings.
I nag my husband.
I make statements that are confusing because they are not adapted to what my husband knows.

Table 6.4: (continued)

I criticize my husband's ideas.

I fail to adequately explain myself, which leads to misunderstandings.

Blaming Behaviors ($\alpha = 0.76$; perception of spouse's behavior $\alpha = 0.78$)

I admit when I am wrong.

I refuse to admit when I am wrong.

When something is wrong, I blame my husband.

Ignore/Fail to Consider Knowledge of Partner ($\alpha = 0.83$; perception of spouse's behavior $\alpha = 0.88$)

I ignore what I know about my husband and act for my own self-interests.

I fail to take into consideration my husband's thoughts and feelings.

I can predict my husband's negative reactions to things I might do but I do them anyway (this item dropped).

---

* For the scales asking for the perception of the spouse's perspectives and behaviors, I replaced self-references with reference to "husband" or "wife." Thus, "I admit when I am wrong" became "My husband admits when he is wrong" or "My wife admits when she is wrong." The titles for each scale are preceded with "Perception of Spouse's [...]"

6.3 Research Challenges Unique to Studies on Other-Orientation

Studies of other-orientation face two major research challenges relating to skewing of results caused by sex differences and the issue of how accurately partners can assess each other. Addressing these issues has an impact on both the conceptual basis of the other-orientation and the methods of analysis.

 Research Challenge 1: Social Decentering and Respondent's Sex. Classifying spouses into high and low scoring groups according their social decentering and RSSD scores can potentially bias results because males, according to recurring findings, tend to score lower than females do on measures of other-orientation (e.g., social decentering and empathy). This tendency means that the lower scoring group will have disproportionately more males than females, and the higher scoring group will have disproportionately more females than males. Thus, differences found between such high and low decentering groups are distorted by a difference between the sexes rather than difference in decentering ability. There are at least four ways to address this issue: (1) Ignore this issue when comparing husbands and wives since the impact of differences in scores should be consistent across couples; (2) report results separately for the husbands and wives; (3) standardize or adjust husbands' scores by adding the difference between the husbands' and wives' average score to each husband's score, which creates the same mean for both groups; and (4) consider the third of the husbands who scored the lowest relative to other husbands and the third of the wives who scored the lowest relative to other wives as the low decentering group, and the highest third of husbands and highest third of wives and treat them as the high decentering group; thus, the weakest husbands and wives will be compared to the strongest husbands and wives. The decision as to which option to apply and variations in those applications should be dictated by the question being addressed. For example, in comparing the complementarity or symmetry of spouses' social decentering, I compared husbands ranked in the top and bottom thirds with similarly ranked wives. With this method then, spouses who were both in the upper third of their sex group were considered a high decentering couple and spouses who were both in the lower third group of their sex group were considered a low-decentering couple.

For other analyses, I divided all respondents, regardless of sex, into two groups – high and low social decenterers and high RSSD and low RSSD. Labeling groups as high or low is not the same as labeling them as strong or weak. The bifurcation into high and low groups allows for relative evaluations against each other. The midpoint for the RSSD scale was 36, with only 6% of the wives and 7% of the husbands falling below that point, indicating that very few spouses were weak in RSSD. Thus, analysis is of how the strongest RSSD spouses compare to those who are simply less strong. The same interpretation applied to social decentering scores, though a larger number of husbands fell below the midpoint, indicating a larger number who could be considered weak. The midpoint for the social decentering scale was 108, with 11% of wives and 32% of the husbands falling below that point.

Research Challenge 2: Social Decentering and Accuracy of Other-Orientation Assessments. A conundrum exists with the overall method used in this study that undermines any study that asks individuals to provide insights into a partner's worldview. That is, the very skills under study, social decentering and more specifically, RSSD, affect the ability of spouses to provide accurate assessment of their spouse's dispositions. People who are strong in RSSD should be more accurate and reliable in reporting on their spouse's thoughts and feelings than should people who are weaker in RSSD. The responses from people low in RSSD are likely to be more affected by such factors as egocentrism/projection, social desirability, level of relational satisfaction, resentment, etc. A study of dating and married couples found that respondents acted with a degree of egocentrism, projecting "their own traits, values, and day-to-day feelings onto their partners, seeing similarities that were not evident to their partners" (Murray, Holmes, Bellavia, Griffin, & Dolderman, 2002, p. 576), which is similar to Cronbach's (1955) earlier findings. But RSSD involves sensitivity to differences between the perceiver and partner that should reduce the impact of such projection. This reduction in projection for those who are strong in RSSD should generate more differences between self-ratings and perceptions of spouses than would occur for those who are weaker in RSSD.

To test for this effect in this study, wives and husbands were divided, respectively, into three groups – high, middle, and low – based on their RSSD scores. I tested this effect relative to the scale with the most significant findings – supportive communication. I created a score for supportive communication difference by subtracting respondents' self-scores from their ratings of their spouses. I then conducted a t-test comparing the high and low RSSD respondents' supportive communication difference scores. As expected, those lower in RSSD saw significantly less difference ($M = 5.05$, $n = 80$) between themselves and their spouse [t (146) = -6.42, $p < 0.001$] than did the high RSSD respondents ($M = 5.97$, $n = 68$). Results were similar when comparing the responses of the husbands and the wives separately, that is, high RSSD husbands reported greater difference between themselves and their spouse ($M = 5.79$, $N = 34$) than did low RSSD husbands ($M = 4.71$, $n = 39$) [t (71) = -5.24, $p < 0.001$], and high RSSD wives reported greater difference between themselves and their spouse ($M = 6.15$, $N = 34$) than did low RSSD wives ($M = 5.37$, $n = 41$) [t (73) = -4.28, $p < 0.001$].

To further examine perceptual biases, the ratings for respondents' evaluations of their spouse can be compared to their spouse's self-report. This comparison teases out the effect of projection versus the degree to which they accurately perceive their spouse's ability to provide supportive communication. For those high in RSSD, no significant difference was found between their rating of the other spouse ($M = 5.72$, $n = 68$) and their spouse's self-rating ($M = 5.71$, $t = 0.14$, $p = 0.89$); in other words, high RSSD respondents accurately assessed their partner. For those low in RSSD, their perception of their spouse's supportive communication behaviors ($M = 4.94$, $n = 80$) was found to be significantly lower than their spouse's self-report of such behavior ($M = 5.30$, $t = 2.71$, $p = 0.008$), indicating a weaker ability to accurately assess their partner. These results suggest that a spouse's RSSD ability affects their ability to accurately assess their partner's supportive communication behavior, with those low in the ability being more likely to project their own behavior onto their spouse.

If having low RSSD skills indeed affects respondents' perception and evaluation of their spouse's behaviors and feelings, then the results of any comparison between high and low RSSD respondents have to be considered carefully. The results might not reveal differences that actually exist, or show differences that don't really exist. Thus, the results might exhibit the Type 1 classic error problem presenting a finding or difference that does not exist and the Type II classic error problem of rejecting a finding or difference that does exist. The reader should consider the relevant results of this study with this effect in mind.

6.4 Results

This section begins with an examination of social decentering as complementary or symmetric in married couples and how the length of marriage and age of the spouses relates to changes in decentering. Next the effect of length of marriage and age on changes in RSSD is analyzed, followed by analysis of the relationship between social decentering and RSSD. Results are presented regarding the effect of social decentering and RSSD on marital satisfaction, communication attitudes, communication behaviors, and positive relationship discussions.

6.4.1 Social Decentering

If married partners share similar levels of social decentering, the relationship is symmetrical, so the level of each spouse's social decentering should positively correlate. If one partner is stronger in social decentering than the other partner, the relationship is complementary, so the levels of each spouse's social decentering should negatively correlate. The overall correlation of wives' social decentering scores with those of their husband was $r = 0.21$ ($p = 0.036$, $n = 101$). While statistically significant, this is not a particularly strong correlation, but it does indicate some degree of symmetry in couples' social decentering. The unique nature of social decentering, however, suggests a more complex role within married couples. Overall, wives ($M = 127.2$) had significantly higher social decentering scores than their husbands did ($M = 115.5$, $t = -4.76$, $p < 0.001$). Such a difference makes it less likely to find a partner with the same level of social decentering. Scores relative to the midpoint of the scale (108) suggest an even greater distinction, with 32% of the husbands having scores below the midpoint compared to only 7% of the wives. Most of the social decentering subscales significantly correlated (albeit at a low level) between husbands and wives (see Table 6.5), but wives' scores were significantly higher than husbands' scores on all the subscales.

These subscale results suggest that spouses are more similar in their ability to recall and observe information about others (experience) than they are in their ability to imagine and extrapolate other people's dispositions (imagination). Spouse's similarity in their views on people they know (specific-other) and sensitivity to others who are different (generalized-others) might occur because the spouses have shared experiences relating to people and cultures. A spouse's use of self and use of imagination-based information in social decentering are likely to be less evident to the other spouse since they are intrapersonal communication processes and thus less of a factor to their attraction to each other and their subsequent relationship development.

Table 6.5: Correlations between husbands and wives on social decentering subscales.

Subscale	Correlation
Experience-based information	0.27**
Imagination-based information	0.10 ns
Use of self	0.13 ns
Use of specific-other	0.24*
Use of generalized-other	0.22*
Cognitive response	0.21*
Affective response	0.24*

($n = 101$, * $p < 0.05$, ** $p < 0.01$, ns, not significant)

One way to test for complementarity and symmetry between spouses is to divide both the husbands and the wives into groups representing high and low decenterers and examine the distributions. That is, husbands were evenly divided into two groups relative to other husbands: high social decenterers and low social decenterers. Wives were similarly divided into high and low groups relative to the other wives. Both spouse's groupings were plotted on a 2 × 2 grid consisting of the following four combinations: both wife and husband high decenterers ($n = 27$), both wife and husband low decenterers ($n = 26$), wife high and husband low decenterers ($n = 24$), and wife low and husband high decenterers ($n = 24$). The resulting number of couples in each of the four quadrants was fairly evenly distributed. Social decentering does not appear to be either overwhelmingly complementary or symmetrical among the couples in this sample. These combinations are explored further when I examine the impact of social decentering on marital satisfaction.

Since social decentering exists as a quality independent of the marriage, changes in people's social decentering should not be affected by changes in marriage. Thus, how long people are married should not affect their level of social decentering. But a person's age might relate to it. Looft (1972) argued that changes in social processing occur during the later years of a person's life cycle, resulting in increased egocentrism which would thus reduce social decentering. O'Brien, Konrath, Gruhn, and Hagen (2012) found an inverse-U-shaped relationship between age and Davis's measures of perspective-taking and empathic concern with the scores on the measures peaking at 50–60 years of age and then declining. Their findings support previous research and theory that the ability to form and use emotional representations increases until middle age and then declines. A similar trend was thus expected of social decentering and RSSD.

A large-sample study of men and women (ages 22 to over 92) that Schieman and Van Gundy (2000) conducted in Ontario examined a variety of factors affecting empathy as measured with items drawn from Davis' (1983) and Mehrabian and Epstein's (1972) scales. Although women in their study were significantly higher in self-reported empathy than were men, a regression analysis found that empathy declined for both men and women throughout their lifetimes, but that gap between men and women slowly narrowed. Applying this finding to married couples then, we might expect that while social decentering would decline for both husbands and wives with age, the difference between the husband and wife should decrease. Other factors might also influence changes in social decentering over the life span, such as decreases in social contact, "information-seeking, social comparison, identity strivings, and achievement motivations" (Carstensen, 1998, p. 345).

The current study found a small but significant negative correlation between age and social decentering ($r = -0.21$, $p = 0.002$, $N = 201$), indicating that social decentering decreased relative to the respondents' increasing age, a finding that concurs with that of Schieman and Van Gundy's (2000) empathy study.

A curvilinear analysis using a quadratic equation (best suited for evaluating an inverse U) revealed a significant but relatively small amount of variance in social decentering ($R^2 = 0.07$, $F (2, 199) = 6.96$, $p = 0.001$) was accounted for by age, which means that other factors besides age are significantly affecting variations in social decentering. To examine the relationship further, respondents were divided according to their age into the following groups: 20–29, 30–39, 40–49, 50–59, and 60+. An analysis of variance (ANOVA) found a significant difference between the five groups [F (4, 196) = 3.45, p = 0.10]. The resulting means for each group are displayed in Figure 6.1. Rather than reflecting an inverse U, the resulting means reflect a U-shaped curvilinear relationship between the groups with social decentering decreasing between those in their 20s to those in their 50s, but increasing after the age of 60.

An examination of the social decentering scores by age and sex revealed differences in how social decentering changes over time for husbands and wives. The scores for the husbands were significantly different between the age groups [F (4, 96) = 2.45, p = 0.01] and followed the inverted U pattern (see Figure 6.2). The wives' scores by age, however, were not significantly different [F (4, 95) = 1.25, p = 0.29]. While the average score for the 60+ group of wives reflects a large drop off from the younger wives (20–29 group), the small sample of six undermines the ability to generate significance (see Figure 6.3). Nonetheless, the rise in the 60+ husbands' social decentering scores

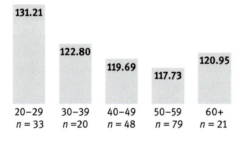

131.21	122.80	119.69	117.73	120.95
20–29	30–39	40–49	50–59	60+
n = 33	n =20	n = 48	n = 79	n = 21

Figure 6.1: Social decentering by 10–year age groups.

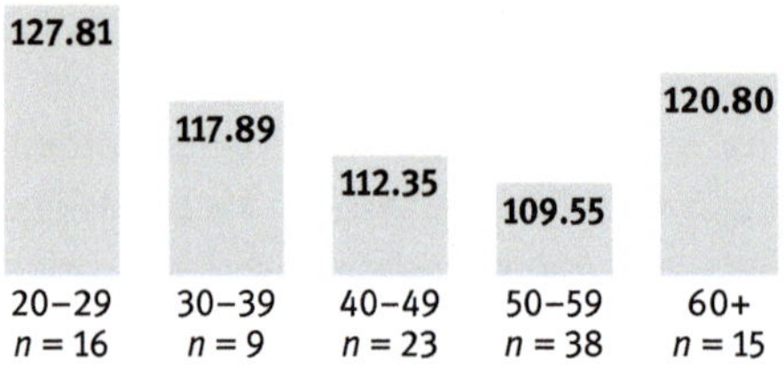

127.81	117.89	112.35	109.55	120.80
20–29	30–39	40–49	50–59	60+
n = 16	n = 9	n = 23	n = 38	n = 15

Figure 6.2: Husbands' social decentering by age.

134.41	126.82	126.44	125.32	121.33
20–29	30–39	40–49	50–59	60+
n = 17	n = 11	n = 25	n = 41	n = 6

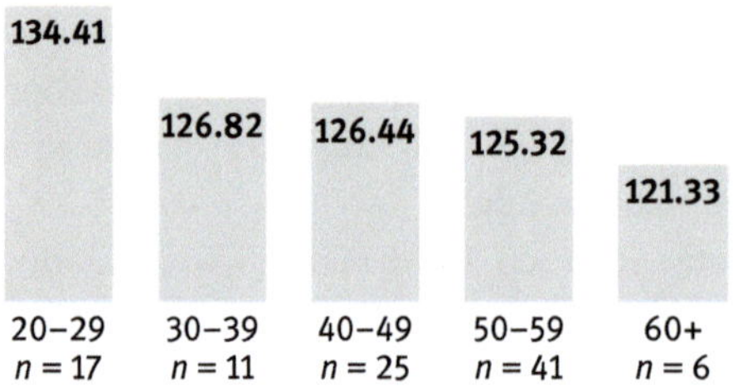

Figure 6.3: Wives' social decentering by age.

created the highest similarity between the husbands' and wives' scores. The difference between husbands and wives, however, did not follow a gradual pattern toward convergence throughout their lifetimes as suggested by Schieman and Van Gundy's (2000) empathy study. The rise in older husbands' social decentering might be the result of a life-style change due to retirement, in which spending more time with their wife requires them to adapt to new interaction routines, nonwork place relationships, and activities.

ANOVA between the age groups for all respondents revealed significant differences ($p < 0.05$) in the reported scores for all the social decentering subscales except affective response. Post hoc analysis using Tukey honest significant difference (HSD) revealed a general pattern of decline beginning with the scores of the youngest respondents. Since those declines were gradual over time, they often did not significantly differ until later in life. Scores for the experience-based information, use of specific-other, and generalized-other subscales were significantly different ($p < 0.05$) only between the first group (ages 20–29) and the fourth group (ages 50–59). Scores for imagination-based information and cognitive response subscales showed a quicker decline, resulting in significant differences between the first group (ages 20–29) and both the third (ages 40–49) and fourth groups (ages 50–59). Of all the subscales, scores for use of self declined the quickest, creating significant differences between the youngest respondents and the next three age groups, but not with the oldest group (ages 60 and over). The decline and resurgence in the use of self parallels typical increases and decreases in family and workplace demands over a lifespan. Demands of family and work might undermine people's inclination to consider their own experiences and feelings in a given situation. For example, in responding to their teenagers' disruptive behaviors, they opt not to reflect on their own history of similar behavior because the situation demands that they consider the situation from an adult parent's perspective.

Separate analyses of the husbands' and wives' scores found no significant differences between the wives' age groups on their subscale scores, but found significant differences between the husbands' age groups for all of their subscales including affect. Post hoc analysis revealed the same pattern of differences for all husband subscales, with the scores for the first age groups (20–29) being significantly higher ($p < 0.05$) than those for the fourth age group (50–59). Additionally, the only scores for any spouse that fell below the midpoint of 3.0 were for the husbands' use of self in the 50–59 age group ($M = 2.98$), and the husbands' affective response in the 40–49 ($M = 2.91$) and 50–59 age groups ($M = 2.93$). Even though a significant change was found only between the husbands' age groups, the correlations between the wives' age and each of the subscales were all greater than the corresponding correlations for the husbands, indicating a gradual and consistent decline in the wives' subscale scores.

Length of marriage was analyzed in a manner similar to that for age groups. Four groups were compared: 0–10 years ($n = 54$), 11–20 ($n = 16$), 21–30 ($n = 96$), and 31–40 ($n = 26$). The sample for couples married over 40 years was too small for analysis (only

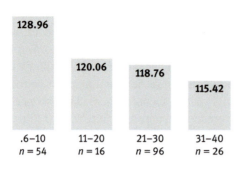

Figure 6.4: Social decentering by marriage length: 10–year increments.

five couples). Significant differences were found between these groups [$F(3, 188) = 4.84$, $p = 0.003$]. As reflected in Figure 6.4, couples married the shortest length of time were significantly stronger in social decentering than were those married 21 or more years (Tukey HSD, $p < 0.05$). Separate analyses for husbands and wives found significant differences between the length of marriage for husbands but not for wives [$F(3, 92) = 3.28$, $p = 0.024$] and [$F(3, 92) = 2.43$, $p = 0.071$], respectively. Post hoc Tukey analysis of the husbands' results found that social decentering scores were significantly lower ($p = 0.035$) for those married 20–30 years than for those married 0–10 years. But since this is not a longitudinal study, all the differences reported between groups might not be due to changes that occur over time in marriage. Instead, the results might reflect the greater inclination of higher ability social decenterers to divorce, which would cause a gradual decrease in average decentering scores over the course of marriage. Or the results might reflect cohort effects imbedded in changes in social and cultural experiences that have resulted in increased other centeredness over the last 40 years such that those getting married today are more other oriented. But the initial premise of decreasing social decentering in individuals over time seems most valid because the results parallel previous research that has found similar patterns of change.

Since the social decentering measure is made up of seven subscales, a similar pattern of decline would be expected of them as well. Indeed, as with age, the scores for all but the affective response subscale significantly differed among the couples, following a pattern of decline based on the length of marriage. Respondents married 6–10 years had significantly higher scores ($p < 0.05$) than did those married 21–30 and 31–40 years on the following subscales: experience-based information, imagination-based information, use of self, use of generalized-other, and cognitive response. For the use of specific-other, the more newly married couples scored significantly higher only than the longest married couples ($p < 0.01$). The overall average score for affective response ($M = 3.28$, df = 0.59, $N = 202$) was significantly lower ($t = -7.43$, $p < 0.000$) than that for cognitive response ($M = 3.48$, df = 0.49, $N = 202$), so perhaps the initially low score for affective response meant it was less likely to fall significantly further. Thus, the respondents' feelings in reaction to other people's situations (affective responses) appeared to remain fairly constant regardless of the length of their marriage, while their level of thinking about other people's situations declines.

The results of comparing the social decentering scores of husbands versus those of the wives according to length of marriage found wives' scores were significantly higher than the husbands' scores in the 0–10 year group (t = –2.15, df = 52, p = 0.036). No significant difference was found in the next group (11–20 years) because wives' social decentering scores dropped considerably after 10 years of marriage to more closely match those of the husbands (see Figures 6.5a and 6.5b). In the third group (21–30), wives' social decentering scores increased while those of the husbands continued to decrease, producing another significant difference (t = –4.11, df = 94, p < 0.000). Finally, differences between spouses for the longest married group (31–40) approached significance (p = 0.07). The overall pattern for the husbands then is a continual decline in social decentering and the related subscales, whereas the pattern for wives reflects a steep drop-off after the first 10 years of marriage and then just minor fluctuations for the remainder of the first 40 years of marriage.

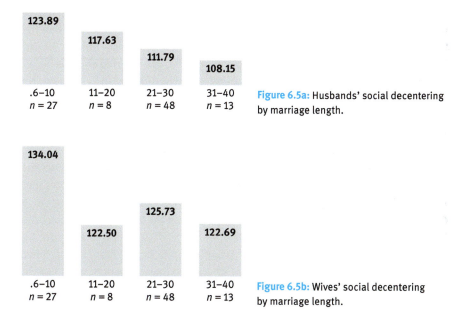

Figure 6.5a: Husbands' social decentering by marriage length.

Figure 6.5b: Wives' social decentering by marriage length.

Age and length of marriage are highly correlated (r = 0.84, p < 0.001, n = 201). But some people get married or remarried later in life; for example, this study included a wife and husband, both 52 years of age, who had been married for two years and another wife and husband in their 70s who had been married 14 years. While interaction effects between age and length of marriage are likely, a stepwise linear regression with social decentering entered as the dependent variable (adjusted r^2 = 0.04, p = 0.002) found that age was a significant negative predictor (β = –0.288, p = 0.002) but that length of marriage was not a significant predictor. Thus, age appears to be the more dominant factor related to decreasing social decentering – not how long individuals have been married.

Examining the results for age, length of marriage, and sex of the respondents leads to a general observation that, for the most part, social decentering is stronger among younger and more newly married couples and decreases as spouses age and remain married. The role of social decentering then appears to be more significant earlier on in a marriage, but as spouses' commitment to each other is established over time, their ability to understand other people's dispositions becomes less relevant to their marriage.

6.4.2 RSSD

Given that RSSD develops as relationships become more intimate, spouses should develop relatively strong RSSD. The RSSD scale ranges from 12 to 60, with a midpoint of 36. For this study, the overall average was 45.76 (N = 202, SD = 6.0), with the wives' average (47.02, n = 101, SD = 5.7) significantly higher (t = –3.08, p = 0.004) than that of the husbands (44.47, n = 101, SD = 6.0). All means were significantly higher than the midpoint (overall, t = 23.07, df = 201, p < 0.000; wives, t = 19.29, df = 100, p < 0.000; husbands, t = 14.15, df = 100, p < 0.000), indicating that these married couples developed strong RSSD. That is, they reported a strong understanding of their spouses. No significant correlation was found between the spouses' RSSD scores (r = 0.07, p = 0.48, n = 101), indicating that the changes in RSSD that took place over the course of their marriages differed for wives and husbands.

No significant correlation was found between RSSD and marriage length (r = –0.11, p = 0.14, N = 202), indicating that RSSD did not continue to linearly increase over the length of a marriage. No significant correlation was found between RSSD scores and marriage length for either the wives (r = –0.05, p = 0.60) or the husbands (r = –0.16, p = 0.12). A curvilinear analysis using a quadratic equation (to test for a U-shaped relationship) was significant [R^2 = 0.04, F (2, 199) = 3.96, p = 0.02], as was a test for an S-shaped distributions (cubic equation) [R^2 = 0.05, F (3, 199) = 3.28, p = 0.02]. Since the curvilinear change begins occurring after 20 years, a regression computed just for the first 20 years of marriage found a significant linear relationship between marriage length and RSSD [R^2 = 0.20, F (1, 33) = 8.30, p = 0.007]. A comparison of mean scores for those married under 3 years (M = 48.28, n = 32) and those married 20–24 years (M = 43.30, n = 32) found a significant drop in the level of RSSD (t = 3.68, df = 62, p < 0.000). A significant drop occurred for both the wives and husbands. These results support my earlier observation that although couples begin marriage with strong RSSD, it steadily declines over the next 20 years, with factors such as decreased motivation to decenter, development of scripted responses, and life changes (e.g., such as raising children) appearing to diminish RSSD.

An ANOVA for RSSD according to length of marriage (sorted by 10-year increments) indicated significant differences between the groups [F (3, 188) = 3.40, p = 0.02]. A Tukey post hoc analysis revealed a significant (p = 0.04) drop in spouses' reported

RSSD scores between the first 10 years and the second 10 years (see Figure 6.6). A comparison of the wives' RSSD scores to those of the husbands in each length-of-marriage group found no significant differences in their scores in the first (0–10) or second group (11–20). But a resurgence in the wives' RSSD scores in the third group (21–30) was not matched in the husbands' scores, thus producing a significant difference in their scores ($t = 2.58$, df = 94, $p < 0.011$). Wives' scores dipped again in the fourth group (31–40) and thus again did not significantly differ from those of the husbands. Separate analyses of the RSSD scores for husbands comparing each length-of-marriage group found no significant differences in the average RSSD scores between the groups (see Figure 6.7a). A similar analysis comparing the four length-of-marriage groups for wives found no significant differences in average RSSD scores (see Figure 6.7b).

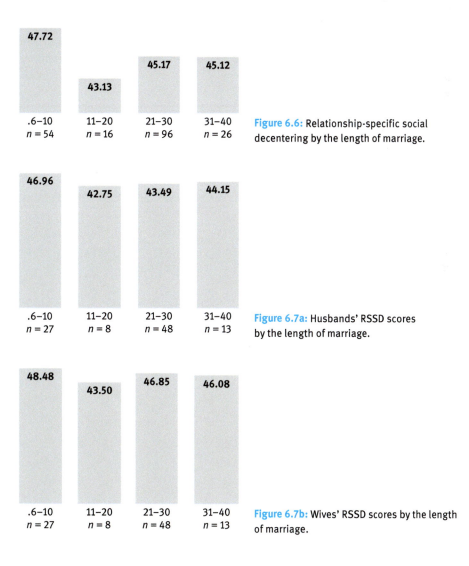

Figure 6.6: Relationship-specific social decentering by the length of marriage.

Figure 6.7a: Husbands' RSSD scores by the length of marriage.

Figure 6.7b: Wives' RSSD scores by the length of marriage.

Like social decentering, RSSD scores declined as the respondents' age increased [$r = -0.19$, $p = 0.006$, $N = 201$ (missing age on one spouse)]. Age was also analyzed using a curvilinear regression analysis, which found a significant U-shaped relationship (quadratic equation) between age and RSSD [$R^2 = 0.05$, $F (2, 198) = 5.34$, $p = 0.006$; see Figure 6.8]. A significant negative correlation was found between husbands' RSSD scores and their age ($r = -0.24$, $p = 0.016$, $n = 101$), indicating a tendency for RSSD to decline as husbands grew older. No significant correlation was found between wives' RSSD and their age ($r = -0.11$, $p = 0.27$, $n = 101$) (see Figures 6.9a and 6.9b). A curvilinear analysis of husbands' and wives' RSSD scores and age produced a significant U-shaped relationship for husbands [$R^2 = 0.08$, $F (2, 98) = 4.38$, $p = 0.015$] but not for wives.

Comparing the RSSD scores of the five age groups using ANOVA revealed a significant difference [$F (4, 196) = 2.90$, $p = 0.02$] between the groups, with a Tukey post hoc analysis indicating a significant ($p = 0.02$) drop in scores between those who were ages 20–29 years and those who were ages 50–59 years. Similar results were found

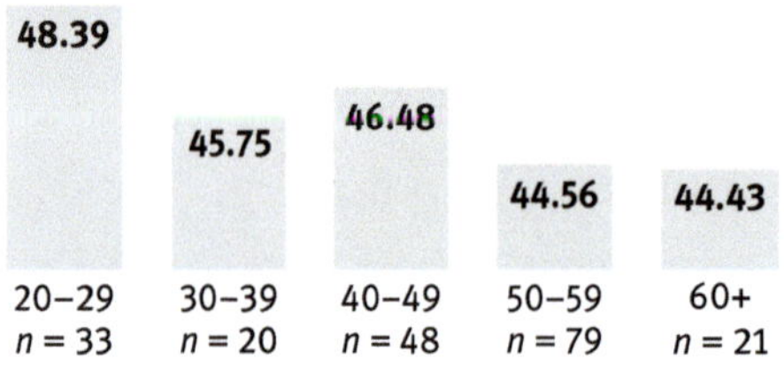

48.39	45.75	46.48	44.56	44.43
20–29	30–39	40–49	50–59	60+
n = 33	n = 20	n = 48	n = 79	n = 21

Figure 6.8: Relationship-specific social decentering by age.

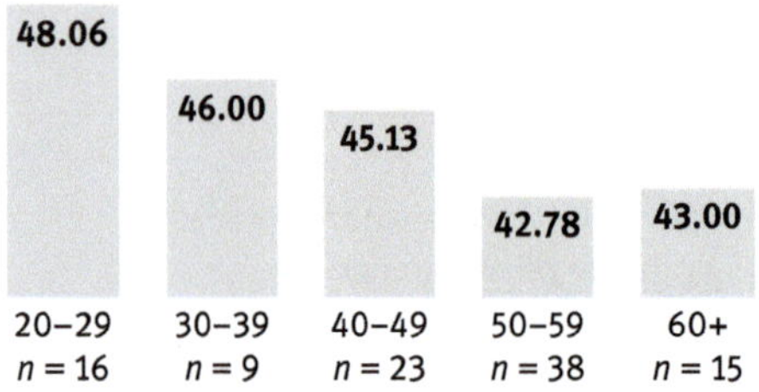

48.06	46.00	45.13	42.78	43.00
20–29	30–39	40–49	50–59	60+
n = 16	n = 9	n = 23	n = 38	n = 15

Figure 6.9a: Husbands' RSSD by age.

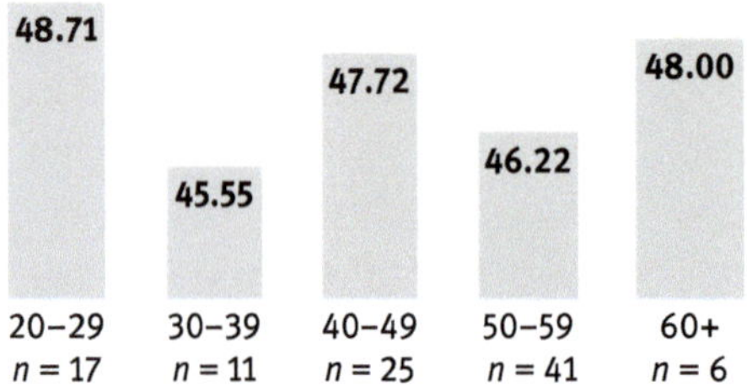

48.71	45.55	47.72	46.22	48.00
20–29	30–39	40–49	50–59	60+
n = 17	n = 11	n = 25	n = 41	n = 6

Figure 6.9b: Wives' RSSD by age.

between the husband age groups, with the RSSD scores from the youngest respondents (ages 20–29) continuing to drop until becoming significantly different from those of husbands who were ages 50–59 years [F (4, 98) = 2.81, p = 0.03]. Wives' scores varied only by 3.15 points across the age groups, resulting in no significant differences between these groups.

The change in RSSD by the length of marriage is notably different from the change associated with age. One reason for this difference is that the average ages associated with the length of marriage are not equally distributed. The average age for each of the four 10-year spans of marriage is 30.8 (0–10), 45.6 (11–20), 51.1 (21–30), and 56.7 (31–40), producing a 14.8 year difference between the first and second groups and differences of only 5.5 and 5.6 between each pair of subsequent groups. While the average age from length-of-marriage group 2 and group 4 is only 16 years, the length of marriage spans 29 years. Thus, the different distributions of respondents by length of marriage and by age results in the analyses of each producing different patterns.

6.4.3 Relationship Between Social Decentering and RSSD

As expected, the same processes underlie both social decentering and RSSD as evidenced in their significant correlation (r = 0.54, p < 0.000, N = 202) and the correlations of r = 0.55 for the wives (p < 0.000, n = 101) and r = 0.48 for the husbands (p < 0.000, n = 101). The magnitudes of these correlations indicate that the two measures are related. But since the overall measures only account for 29% of the variance between them, social decentering and RSSD must be considered two distinct processes. Those who are strong in social decentering would be expected to be strong in RSSD, but no such expectation exists that those who are strong in RSSD would be strong in social decentering. Of the 102 higher social decenterers, 72 were also among the higher scorers in RSSD, and the other 30 fell among those with lower RSSD scores. Of the 100 lower social decenterers, 70 were also in the lower half of RSSD scorers, but 30 scored among the higher half on RSSD. Thus, 70% of the respondents' RSSD scores parallel their comparable social decentering scores, whereas 30% of the respondents' RSSD scores diverged.

Similarly, RSSD scores significantly correlated with each of the three social decentering analysis subscales: specific-other subscale, r = 0.56 (p < 0.000); use of generalized-other, r = 0.42, p < 0.000); and use of self (r = 0.47, p < 0.000). The correlation for specific-other subscale was significantly stronger than that for the use of generalized-other (Fisher z-test, p = 0.06). Since the specific-other subscale is designed to assess a person's general ability to socially decenter using knowledge of specific people, it makes sense that it would be the subscale most highly correlated with RSSD. While this correlation is strong, 69% of the variance between the specific-other subscale and RSSD is still unexplained, which further demonstrates that a special kind of social decentering develops in intimate relationships.

Social decentering and RSSD correlated in three of the four different length-of-marriage groups and in four of the five different age groups (see Table 6.6). The variations in the correlations and the two insignificant correlations provide further confirmation that the measures of social decentering and RSSD assess different phenomena.

Table 6.6: Correlations between social decentering and RSSD by marriage length group and age groups.

Length of Marriage	r	p	Age	r	p
0–10 years	0.58	0.000	20–29	0.63	0.000
11–20 years	0.34	0.19 (ns)	30–39	0.76	0.000
21–30 years	0.53	0.000	40–49	0.42	0.003
31–40 years	0.42	0.03	50–59	0.52	0.000
			60–+	0.39	0.082 (ns)

(ns, not significant, $p < 0.05$)

The results of the analysis thus far provide further insight into social decentering and RSSD. Social decentering seems to be a personal quality that diminishes over time, being affected more by the aging process than by the length of marriage. In contrast, changes in RSSD seem to be linked more to changes in the relationship over the course of marriage. Some possible influences have been discussed in this chapter, but additional research into how changes over the course of marriage (addition of children, children leaving home, illness, job stress, retirement, etc.) affects RSSD is needed. Some specific relational and communication factors are discussed in the following sections.

6.4.4 Social Decentering and Marital Satisfaction

This study found no significant correlation between marital satisfaction and social decentering for either the respondents overall ($r = 0.09$, $p = 20$) or the husbands and wives analyzed separately.[1] And the social decentering scores of the individual spouse did not correlate with the satisfaction reported by their partner. In addition, none of the social decentering subscales (e.g., experience-based information, use of self, cognitive response) were significantly related to the marital satisfaction of wives or husbands or their partner.

To examine the degree to which spouses' similarities and differences in their social decentering affected their marital satisfaction, the respondents were divided at the mean into two groups – higher social decenterers and lower social decenterers. Since there is a significant difference between the means of the wives and husbands

---

[1] Following Kenny's (1996) suggestion for dealing with interdependent scores from spouses, structural equation modeling was used to assess the interactions.

(11.7 points higher for wives), each spouse was classified as a higher or lower social decenterer relative to those in their same sex group. Pairing the high versus low groups in a 2 × 2 matrix created four groups: two symmetrical relationships, one in which both spouses were lower in social decentering ($n = 52$) and one in which both spouses were higher ($n = 54$); and two complementary relationships, one in which the husband was higher and the wife lower ($n = 48$), and one in which the wife higher and husband lower ($n = 48$). Classifying respondents relative to others of their sex meant that some wives were classified as low even though they had a higher score than that of their husband, who was classified as high. Nonetheless, 36 of the 48 husbands in the husband high/ wife low quadrant had higher social decentering scores than that of their wife.

ANOVA of the four groups indicated a significant difference in their levels of marital satisfaction [$F(2, 198) = 2.97, p = 0.033$]. Post hoc comparison of the groups using Tukey HSD found that the only significant difference was between the complementary group with both spouses as high social decenterers and the symmetrical group with husbands high and wives low ($p = 0.039$; see Table 6.7). While not significantly different, the two highest means were for couples in symmetrical relationships supporting the premise that compatibility in social decentering positively affects marital satisfaction, particularly when both partners are strong in social decentering. Of the four quadrants, the one representing the group with complementary relationships in which the husband is high in social decentering and the wife is low probably the most socially abnormal. Such a relationship involves the husband being more sensitive to the wife than she is to him. Apparently, such an arrangement works against marital satisfaction.

An ANOVA of marital satisfaction conducted on just the husbands and then on just the wives between the four groups found no significant differences among either the husbands or wives. In addition, no significant difference was found within each of the four groups between husbands' and wives' marital satisfaction. Marital satisfaction of both husbands and wives appears equally affected when the husbands' social decentering is higher than that of the wives. Marriages appear to be negatively affected when the husband is stronger in social decentering compared to other men

Table 6.7: Satisfaction means for pairs of high and low social decentering spouses.

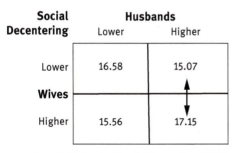

Social Decentering	Husbands	
	Lower	Higher
Wives Lower	16.58	15.07
Wives Higher	15.56	17.15

Arrow indicates significant difference ($p = 0.039$).

and the wife is weaker compared to other women. Husbands appear to look less favorably on their relationship if they are the one who is being more understanding, perhaps having a negative response to having to be accommodating. Wives' diminished satisfaction might emerge from their feeling that their husband is being too intrusive in wanting to know more from them or feel they are inadequate because of their inability to reciprocate his understanding or sensitivity.

To confirm the decision to use social decentering scores relative to each respondent's sex group, an ANOVA was run comparing the four groups on the basis of the degree of difference between each spouse's social decentering score (see Table 6.8). Within each quadrant, the scores of the spouses were significantly different ($p < 0.01$). These numbers can be compared to the overall mean difference between all the husbands' scores and all the wives' scores (11.66). The symmetrical groups (wife low/husband low and wife high/husband high) were not significantly different from each other and were fairly close to the overall mean difference. But the two complementary groups (wife high/husband low and husband high/wife low) were each significantly different from the other three groups. The mean of the wife high/husband low couples was significantly higher by 25.17 points than the overall mean difference ($t = -9.58$, df = 23, $p < 0.000$), and the mean of the husband high/wife low group was significantly higher by 23.95 points ($t = 10.1$, df = 23, $p < 0.000$). These results suggest that, on average, each group's social decentering scores differed as expected and that dividing spouses into high and low decenterers relative to their own sex group did not bias results.

Table 6.8: Mean differences in social decentering between each social decentering couple.

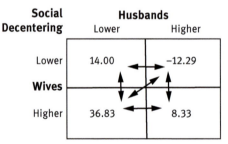

Positive numbers: wives' scores > husbands'
Negative number: husbands' scores > than wives'
Arrows indicate significant difference ($p < 0.05$)

6.4.5 RSSD and Marital Satisfaction

RSSD provides a foundation on which spouses can adapt in an appropriate and effective ways within the constraints discussed in Chapter 2. A positive relationship was expected and found between RSSD and reported marital satisfaction overall ($r = 0.22$,

$p = 0.001$, $N = 202$) as well as in separate analyses of husbands ($r = 0.20$, $p = 0.04$, $n = 101$) and wives ($r = 0.24$, $p = 0.02$, $n = 101$) Husbands' RSSD scores did not correlate with wives' reported marital satisfaction, but the wives' RSSD scores correlated with their husbands' satisfaction ($r = 0.22$, $p = 0.03$, $n = 101$). Husbands appear to be affected by variations in their wife's demonstration of other orientation, whereas wives are not. Perhaps women's relationship, marital, and sex role expectations are such that they don't expect their husbands to engage in RSSD. In contrast, husbands appear to be the opposite of their wives, possibly leading husbands to feel less satisfaction when their wife does not adapt to them.

As in the social decentering analysis, couples were classified as high or low in RSSD relative to other respondents of the same sex. Couples were then placed into a 2 × 2 matrix creating four groups: two symmetrical groups, one in which both spouses were lower in RSSD ($n = 50$, $m = 40.9$) and one in which both spouses were higher in RSSD ($n = 52$, $m = 51.1$); and two complementary groups, one in which wives were higher in RSSD and husbands were lower ($n = 50$, $m = 45.4$) and one in which husbands were higher in RSSD and wives were lower ($n = 50$, $m = 45.4$). Table 6.9 lists the resulting marital satisfaction means for each group. An ANOVA found significant differences between the groups [F (3, 198) = 6.29, $p < 0.000$]. A post hoc analysis using Tukey HSD found that couples in the symmetrical relationships with high RSSD scores were significantly more satisfied than were each of the other three groups, whereas the other three groups did not significantly differ from each other. Low or imbalanced RSSD appears to diminish spouses' marital satisfaction. Couples strong in RSSD are more likely to be in tune with each other's thoughts, feelings, and dispositions and thereby more likely to effectively adapt to each other and confirm each other's value.

Table 6.9: Satisfaction means for pairs of high and low RSSD spouses.

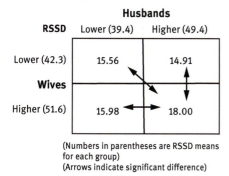

(Numbers in parentheses are RSSD means for each group)
(Arrows indicate significant difference)

An examination of the differences between the four groups according to age and length of marriage revealed significant differences between the groups in terms of the respondent age [F (3, 197) = 7.53, $p < 0.000$]. The high/high RSSD couples were significantly younger on average than the other three groups ($p < 0.01$), with an average age of 40.0 years compared to the low/low couples ($m = 51.5$), wife high/husband low couples ($m = 48.1$), and husband high/wife low couples ($m = 48.9$). While not significant, the results for length of marriage followed a similar pattern with the high/high group being married the shortest ($m = 16.2$ years).

Significant differences between the four RSSD groups were also found when marital satisfaction was analyzed separately for the group of husbands and the group of wives: husbands [$F (3, 97) = 3.05$, $p = 0.032$] and wives [$F (3, 97) = 4.10$, $p = 0.009$]. Post hoc analysis (Tukey HSD) revealed one pair of significant differences for each spousal analysis (see Tables 6.10 and 6.11). For husbands the significant difference was between the symmetrically high and low RSSD couples. That is, husbands in the high RSSD symmetrical group were significantly more satisfied ($p = 0.032$) than were husbands in the low RSSD symmetrical group. On the other hand, wives in the high RSSD symmetrical group were significantly more satisfied ($p = 0.004$) than were wives in the complementary group in which they were low in RSSD and their husband was high. One interpretation of the husbands' results would be that, in general, husbands are more satisfied when their wife has a strong understanding of them. The wives' results suggest that when wives cannot reciprocate their husband's strength in understanding them, they feel less satisfied. These results parallel the social decentering findings and reinforce the prospect of an overarching attitude among women that when men are stronger decenterers, women feel less adequate or put off by a husband who appears more capable in reading their minds.

Table 6.10: Husbands' marital satisfaction for high and low RSSD spouses.

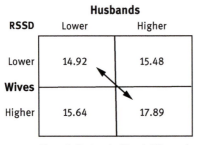

(Arrow indicates significant difference)

Table 6.11: Wives' marital satisfaction for high and low RSSD spouses.

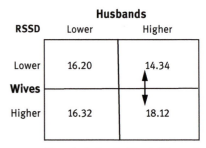

(Arrow indicates significant difference)

6.4.6 Social Decentering, RSSD, Relationship Attitudes, and Relational Communication

An examination of whether skill in social decentering and RSSD would, as expected, enhance positive relational behaviors and reduce negative relational behaviors included analysis of (1) how respondents' social decentering and RSSD related to their self-reported relational attitudes and behaviors, (2) how social decentering and RSSD affected respondents' perception of their spouses' relational attitudes and behaviors, and (3) how respondents' perception of their spouses' relational attitudes and behaviors related to their spouse's social decentering and RSSD. For some of the analyses, the high and low decentering groups discussed earlier were used to examine the impact of social decentering and RSSD on respondents' perceptions of their spouse.

6.4.6.1 How Social Decentering and RSSD Related to Self-Reported Relationship Attitudes and Communication Behaviors

Individuals can be expected to be conscious of their use of considering other people's dispositions (to socially decenter) and their decisions to adapt accordingly to their partners. Generally, individuals can also be expected be recognize specific behavioral adaptations by their partners. In an ongoing specific relationship, particularly one that is intimate, development of RSSD should lead individuals to be keenly aware of their efforts to adapt. Respondents' social decentering and RSSD scores were correlated with their scores on the relationship attitude and communication behavior scales (see Table 6.12). The results show that strength in social decentering related to having a greater concern for partner's welfare and engaging in more positive and supportive communication. These behaviors reflect outcomes that we might generally expect from strong social decenterers in any significant

Table 6.12: Correlations between respondents' social decentering and RSSD scores and their self-reported relationship attitudes and communication.

	Couples (*N* = 202)		Husbands (*n* = 101)		Wives (*n* = 101)	
	Social Decentering	RSSD	Social Decentering	RSSD	Social Decentering	RSSD
Relationship Attitude						
Resentment/discontent	0.02	−0.15*	−.02	−0.17	−0.03	−0.17
Concern for partner's welfare	0.14*	0.33***	0.08	0.28**	0.21*	0.40***
Spouse see as friend/confidant	−0.02	0.19*	−0.11	0.19	0.07	0.20*
Relationship Communication						
Positive/supportive communication	0.29***	0.48***	0.20*	0.47***	0.27**	0.44***
Negative communication	0.01	−0.22*	−0.03	−0.19	0.08	−0.24*
Blaming behaviors	−0.03	−0.28*	−0.09	−0.28**	0.04	−0.30**
Ignore/fail to consider Knowledge of partner	−0.11	−0.26***	−0.08	−0.15	−0.12	−0.35***

*p < 0.05; **p < 0.01; ***p < 0.001

interaction. The impact of considering the partner is particularly evident in the results for RSSD, which show significant correlations with all of the relational scales. As with social decentering, the most significant correlations for RSSD were between concern for partner and positive/supportive communication. In contrast, failure to consider knowledge of the partner was negatively associated with RSSD. While both husbands and wives' social decentering significantly related to higher positive/supportive communication, only wives' social decentering significantly correlated with concern for a partner's welfare.

A more pronounced difference occurred between husbands and wives in how their RSSD skills correlated with the relational scales. That is, significant correlations were found with three of the seven scales for husbands and six of the seven scales for wives. The one scale that did not relate to RSSD for either husbands or wives was feelings of resentment. Spouses feelings of resentment appear to arise in those who are strong or weak in RSSD. Indeed, resentment might even be fostered by RSSD producing heightened awareness of a partner's selfish attitudes and behaviors. The greatest difference in the correlations of wives and husbands was for failure to consider knowledge of the partner, with wives much less likely than husbands to ignore such information.

6.4.6.2 How Respondents' Level of Social Decentering Related to Their Spouse's Perceptions of Their Relationship Attitudes and Communication Behavior

Since respondents reported on their own behaviors, it is not surprising that respondents who see themselves as strong decenterers might also see themselves as strong in behaviors that are orientated toward their spouse such as displaying effective listening, concern, and interest. But do spouses' perceptions of their partner's relationship attitudes and communication behaviors correlate with their partner's self-reported scores? Correlations were calculated to determine how spouses' perceptions of the relationship attitudes and communication behaviors of their partner related to their partner's social decentering scores. No significant correlations were found between spouses' perceptions of partner's relationship attitudes or communication behaviors and their partner's level of social decentering. Nor were any correlations found between the husbands' perceptions of their wife's attitudes and communication behaviors and their wife's social decentering. The only correlation found was between wives' perceptions of their husband's negative communication behavior and their husbands' level of social decentering ($r = 0.23$, $p < 05$). This finding, which is contrary to the expectation that social decentering enhances relational communication behaviors, exemplifies an important caveat associated with social decentering: Just because someone can socially decenter does not mean that the person will act in ways that are beneficial or accommodative to their partner. An examination of the scale indicated that the negative relationship between a husband's social decentering score and a wife's perception of negative communication behavior is misleading. Only one of the seven items constituting the measure of negative communication significantly correlated with the husbands' social decentering – "My husband is quick to point out my mistakes or failings" ($r = 0.30$, $p = 0.002$, $n = 101$). While social decentering is likely to contribute to the husband's awareness of his wife's failings, strength in social decentering does not explain a husband's decision to voice such observations.

Since correlations primarily assess linear relationships, t-tests were conducted on the groups of high and low social decenterers. Wives whose husband was in the group of higher social decenterers perceived their husband as displaying significantly more concern for their welfare ($M = 6.2$, $n = 50$) than did wives whose husband was in the group of lower social decenterers ($M = 5.7$, $n = 51$; $t = 2.34$, df = 99, $p = 0.02$). High social-decentering husbands were perceived by their wife as a confidant/friend ($M = 6.1$, $n = 50$) more than were low social-decentering husbands ($M = 5.7$, $n = 51$; $t = 1.70$, df = 99, $p = 0.09$). Despite the wives' perceptions, there was no significant difference between the high and low social-decentering husbands' own self-reports of concern for welfare or being a confidant/friend. Husbands' perceptions of their wife's relationship attitudes and communication behavior were not significantly different between those whose wife was from the high social-decentering group and those whose wife was from the low social-decentering group.

6.4.6.3 How Respondents Level of RSSD Related to Their Spouse's Perceptions of Their Relationship Attitudes and Communication Behavior

The partner-specific nature of RSSD means that it should have a more direct impact on adaptive behaviors in intimate relationships than should social decentering. Respondents' RSSD negatively correlated with their spouse's perception of their resentment and discontent ($r = -0.15$, $p < 0.05$, $n = 202$) and positively correlated with their spouse's perception of their positive/supportive communication ($r = 0.23$, $p < 0.01$, $n = 202$). Husbands perceived three relational qualities that significantly related to their wife's levels of RSSD. First, the higher a wife's level of RSSD, the less resentment and discontent that was perceived by their husband ($r = -0.20$, $p < 0.05$, $n = 101$). Second, husbands' perception of supportive and positive communication behavior related positively to the wife's level of RSSD ($r = 0.27$, $p < 0.01$, $n = 101$). And the higher a wife's level of RSSD, the less negative communication their husband reported perceiving ($r = -0.20$, $p < 0.05$, $n = 101$). But no significant relationships were found between wives' observations of their husband's attitudes and behaviors and their husband's RSSD scores.

Again, analyses were conducted comparing the high and low RSSD groups; this time comparing relational attitudes and communication behaviors. Respondents perceived their spouse as being more resentful or discontent if the spouse was in the low RSSD group ($m = 2.28$) than if the spouse was in the high RSSD group ($m = 2.01$;

$t = 1.92$, df $= 200$, $p = 0.057$). Low RSSD respondents were also perceived by their spouse as being less positive or supportive in their communication ($m = 5.01$) than were respondents in the high RSSD group ($m = 5.48$; $t = 2.90$, df $= 200$, $p = 0.004$). These two effects were probably due to the influence of the husbands' perceptions of their wife since no significant differences were found in the wives' perceptions of their husbands, but five significant differences were found in the husbands' perceptions of their wife.

Husbands whose wife was in the high RSSD group had significantly different perceptions of their wife than did husbands whose wife was in the low RSSD group on five of the seven relational scales (see Table 6.13). Those wives who were strong in RSSD were seen by their husband as being less resentful, concerned for his welfare, a friend and confidant, supportive and confirming, and less confusing, nagging, and critical (negative communication). These results suggest that wives strong in RSSD adapt and display behaviors that are recognized by their husbands.

Table 6.13: Differences in husbands' perceptions of their wife's relationship attitudes and communication behavior grouped by RSSD ability (high and low).

	Lower RSSD Wives ($n = 50$)	Higher RSSD Wives ($n = 51$)	t (df $= 48$)	p
Resentment/discontent	$M = 2.51$	$M = 2.04$	2.19	0.031
Concern for welfare	$M = 5.87$	$M = 6.24$	−1.84	0.068
Confidant/friend	$M = 5.59$	$M = 6.02$	−2.42	0.017
Positive/supportive communication	$M = 4.99$	$M = 5.67$	−3.29	0.001
Negative communication	$M = 2.97$	$M = 2.53$	−2.56	0.012

6.4.6.4 The Impact of Respondents' Social Decentering and RSSD on Their Perceptions of Their Spouse's Relationship Attitudes and Communication

As discussed earlier as a research challenge, the respondents' sensitivity to others as reflected in their social and relationship-specific decentering is likely to impact their perceptions of their spouse's behaviors. Their sensitivity is as likely to enable them to perceive positive attributes as it is negative attributes. No significant differences were found between how high and low social decenterers perceived their spouses. Nor were any differences found in the separate analyses of the wives' and husbands' social decentering. But differences were found for RSSD.

Table 6.14 lists the differences between the scores of respondents in the higher and lower RSSD groups for their perceptions of their spouse's relationship attitudes and communication behavior. No significant differences were found in the perceptions of negative communication or blaming behaviors between any of the groups.

Table 6.14: Significant differences between the scores of respondents' in the low and high RSSD groups for their perceptions of their spouse's relationship attitudes and communication behavior.

	Couples (N = 202)		Husbands (n = 101)		Wives (n = 101)	
	Low RSSD	High RSSD	Low RSSD	High RSSD	Low RSSD	High RSSD
Relationship Attitude						
Resentment/discontent	2.28	2.01*	2.30	2.24	2.25	1.78**
Concern for spouse's welfare	5.73	6.26***	5.82	6.23*	5.65	6.24**
Spouse as friend/confidant	5.66	6.06**	5.65	5.96	5.67	6.15**
Relationship Communication Behavior						
Positive/supportive communication	4.96	5.53***	5.10	5.56*	4.82	5.50**
Negative communication	2.67	2.62	2.70	2.79	2.63	2.46
Blaming behaviors	3.04	3.05	3.17	3.18	2.91	2.93
Ignore/tail to consider knowledge of partner	2.50	2.24*	2.35	2.27	2.65	2.20*

*$p < 0.05$; **$p < 0.01$; ***$p < 0.001$

The lower mean ratings for negative communication and blaming seem to indicate less occurrence of such behaviors, but the negative impact likely makes them apparent to most spouses regardless of their level of RSSD. The negative attitude of resentment/discontent also led to a low mean rating indicating lesser occurrence. Husbands' RSSD did not affect their perception of their wife's resentment/discontent. But wives who were low in RSSD perceived more resentment/discontent in their husband than did those who were high in RSSD. This difference between the two groups of wives led to a similar result at the couples' level. High RSSD wives' understanding of their husband apparently led them to interpret their husband's behavior as less resentful or discontented.

RSSD only affected the husbands' perception on two of the seven scales: concern for partner's welfare and positive/supportive communication. On the other hand, RSSD affected the wives' perception on five of the scales, which appeared to consequently affect those same five scales at the couples' level. Having RSSD appears to have made spouses more sensitive to their partner's concern for their welfare and more apt to see their partner as engaging in positive/supportive communication. Among the possible explanations for such findings are that: (a) RSSD provides a perspective of one's spouse that leads to more positive interpretations of the spouse's behavior, (b) partners respond to spouses who are strong in RSSD in a more positive manner, or (c) spouses with low RSSD inject their own feelings (e.g., insecurity or low self-esteem) into their interpretation of their spouse's behavior. The third explanation is somewhat supported by the finding that low RSSD wives were more likely than high

RSSD wives to perceive their husband as ignoring or failing to consider information about them – a tendency that is inherent in being low in their relationship-specific understanding of their husbands.

6.4.6.5 How the Respondents' and Their Spouse's Levels of Social Decentering and RSSD Affect the Respondents' Perceptions of Their Spouse

The final analysis of the respondents' perceptions of their spouse examin how such perceptions are affected by both the respondents' own level of social decentering and RSSD and their spouse's level of social decentering and RSSD. Low decentering respondents' perceptions of their low social decentering spouse were compared with low decentering respondents' perceptions of their high social decentering spouse. Similarly, high social decentering respondents and perceptions of their low decentering spouse were compared with high decentering respondents' perceptions of their high decentering spouse. Analysis for RSSD was conducted using this same format. Separate analyses were done for wives and husbands. Given the ensuing reduction in sample size to be around 25, a more liberal level of significance was applied to this analysis ($p < 0.10$).

No significant differences were found on any of the scales in the perceptions of high social decentering wives' perceptions of their high social decentering husband compared to high social decentering wives' perceptions of their low social decentering husband. But the low social decentering wives with a high social decentering husband and the low-decentering wives with a low-decentering husband had significant differences in their perceptions of their husbands on four scales: concern for welfare, confidant/friend, positive communication, and negative communication (see Table 6.15). Again, low social decentering wives responded more positively to their husband if he had a similar social decentering level to their own. That is, low-decentering wives with a low social decentering husband viewed their husband as displaying positive attitudes and behaviors more than did low-decentering wives with a high social decentering husband. As with the

Table 6.15: Significant differences in low social decentering wives' perceptions of the relationship attitudes and communication behavior of their husband according to their husband's level social decentering (high or low).

	Low Decentering Husbands Means (n = 26)	High Decentering Husbands Means (n = 24)	t (df = 48)	p
Concern for welfare	6.24	5.25	2.97	0.005
Spouse as confidant/friend	6.26	5.46	2.89	0.006
Positive/supportive communication	5.33	4.66	1.86	0.07
Negative communication	2.31	2.71	−1.84	0.07

earlier satisfaction results, lower social decentering wives married to higher social decentering husbands had a lower level of marital satisfaction, which might bias their perceptions, creating a perceptual horn effect in which positive behaviors are interpreted negatively. For example, a low-decentering wife might interpret her husband's concern about her general welfare as patronizing and displaying a lack of confidence in her ability to take care of herself. Being similar to or stronger than their husband in social decentering appears to prompt wives to have more positive perceptions of their husbands.

Regarding the husbands' perceptions of their wife, social decentering husbands with a low-decentering wife perceived their wife as having more resentment/discontent ($m = 2.76$, $n = 24$) than did high-decentering husbands with a high-decentering wife ($m = 1.94$, $n = 27$; $t = 2.61$, df = 49, $p = 0.012$). No other differences were found between high social decentering husbands' perceptions of their high or low decentering wife. On the other hand, low social decentering husbands rated their high social decentering wife more negatively than husbands with a low social decentering wife on five of the relational scales (see Table 6.16). Apparently, spouses in low-decentering symmetrical relationships viewed each other more positively than did low-decentering spouses in a complementary relationship with a stronger social decentering partner.

Table 6.16: Significant differences in low social decentering husbands' perceptions of the relationship attitudes and communication behavior of their wife according to their wife's level of social decentering (high or low).

	Low-Decentering Wives Means ($n = 26$)	High-Decentering Wives Means ($n = 24$)	t (df = 48)	p
Resentment/discontent	1.99	2.47	−1.72	0.093
Concern for spouse's welfare	6.28	5.81	1.87	0.067
Spouse as confidant/friend	6.04	5.54	2.21	0.032
Blaming	2.79	3.38	−1.88	0.066
Ignore/fail to consider knowledge of partner	2.08	2.54	−1.95	0.057

High RSSD wives married to a high RSSD husband had different perceptions of their husband than high RSSD wives married to a low RSSD husband on two relational factors: positive/supportive communication and ignore/fail to consider knowledge of spouse. The high RSSD wives with a high RSSD husband reported more positive/supportive communication ($M = 5.81$, $n = 26$) than did high RSSD wives with a low RSSD husband ($M = 5.17$, $n = 25$; $t = −2.36$, df = 49, $p = 0.022$). High RSSD wives also saw their high RSSD husband as ignoring or failing to consider the knowledge they had of them ($M = 1.97$, $n = 26$) significantly less than did high RSSD wives with a low

RSSD husband (M = 2.43, n = 25; t = 2.05, df = 49, p = 0.045). Apparently, husbands' RSSD positively influenced their adaptation to their wife and this adaptation was recognized by the stronger RSSD wives.

Low RSSD wives married to a low RSSD husband differed from low RSSD wives married to a high RSSD husband on two perceptions: concern for spouse's welfare and negative communication. As with the findings of low social decentering wives with a high social decentering husband, the low RSSD wives with a high RSSD husband perceived their husband in a more negative light than did low RSSD wives with low RSSD husbands (or perhaps wives saw the low RSSD husbands in a more positive light). Low RSSD wives with a high RSSD husband perceived less concern for their welfare (M = 5.35, n = 25) than did wives with a low RSSD husband (M = 5.95, n = 25; t = 1.69, df = 48, p = 0.098). Low RSSD wives with a high RSSD husband also perceived more negative communication (M = 2.82, n = 25) than did low RSSD wives with a low RSSD husband (M = 2.44, n = 25; t = –1.70, df = 48, p = 0.095).

Perceptions of high RSSD husbands who had a high RSSD wife significantly differed from those of high RSSD husbands with a low RSSD wife on three of the relational scales: resentment/discontent, positive/supportive communication, and negative communication. Specifically, high RSSD husbands with a high RSSD wife perceived their wife as acting less resentful (M = 1.87, n = 26) than did high RSSD husbands with a low RSSD wife (m= 2.63, n = 25; t = 2.18, df = 49, p = 0.034). High RSSD husbands also viewed their high RSSD wife as displaying more positive and supportive communication (M = 5.90, n = 26) than did high RSSD husbands with a low RSSD wife (m = 5.21, n = 25; t = –2.13, df = 49, p = 0.038). And high RSSD husbands viewed their high RSSD wife as displaying significantly less negative communication (M = 2.53, n = 26) than did high RSSD husbands with a low RSSD wife (M = 3.06, n = 25; t = 2.03, df = 49, p = 0.047).

Unlike the findings for low RSSD wives with a high RSSD husband, low RSSD husbands with a high RSSD wife reported two positive behaviors more frequently than did low RSSD husbands with a low RSSD wife. The low RSSD husbands reported that their high RSSD wife regarded them as a friend and confidant (M = 5.87, n = 25) more than did low RSSD husbands with a low RSSD wife (M = 5.44, n = 25; t = –1.82, df = 48, p = 0.075). Low RSSD husbands also reported more supportive and positive communication from their high RSSD wife (M = 5.43, n = 25) than did low RSSD husbands with a low RSSD wife (M = 4.77, n = 25; t = –2.69, df = 48, p = 0.01).

6.4.7 Social Decentering, RSSD, and Positive Relationship Discussions

The positive relationship discussion scale was used to measure whether relationship discussions benefited from partners having a strong understanding of each other and thus from possessing skills in social decentering and RSSD. Positive relationship discussion positively correlated with both social decentering (r = 0.17, N = 202, p = 0.017) and RSSD (r = 0.30, p = 0.03) among the overall respondents. While separate correlation analyses for husbands and wives found no significant relationship between social decentering and positive relationship discussion, RSSD scores did significantly correlate with positive relational discussions for both husbands ($r = 0.32$, $n = 101$, $p = 0.001$) and wives ($r = 0.29$, $p = 0.003$). These correlations indicate that the high RSSD spouses are more inclined to report having frequent positive discussions with their spouse than are low RSSD spouses; these findings do not necessarily mean that RSSD led to that success. If RSSD contributed to the frequency of positive discussions, then one spouse's RSSD should correlate with the other spouse's response to the positive relationship discussion scale. No such correlations were found for either the husbands or the wives. To further explore RSSD's role, the four high and low social decentering and RSSD couple combinations were again analyzed.

An ANOVA indicated that the four social decentering groups significantly differed from each other in their reports of positive relationship discussions [F (3,198) = 2.08, $p = 0.10$]. But the only significant difference ($p < 0.10$) between the four groups as indicated by a Tukey post hoc analysis was the symmetrically high group reporting more frequent positive discussions ($m = 5.05$, $n = 54$) than the symmetrically low group ($M = 4.39$, $n = 48$).

Differences between the four couple types paired by high and low RSSD scores [F (3, 198) = 6.22, $p < 0.001$] were more pronounced than those found for social decentering. The symmetrically high RSSD couples reported a significantly (Tukey b, $p < 0.05$) higher frequency of positive relationship discussions ($M = 5.38$, $n = 52$) than did any of the other three couple groups with means ranging from 4.39 to 4.48. Analyzing just the husbands perceptions of the frequency of their positive relationship discussions produced significant differences [F (3, 97) = 4.35, $p = 0.006$] between the four groups. High RSSD husbands with a high RSSD wife reported significantly more frequent positive discussions ($M = 5.37$; Tukey b, $p < 0.05$) than low RSSD husbands with a low RSSD wife ($M = 4.19$) or low RSSD husbands with a high RSSD wife ($M = 4.29$). But high RSSD husbands with a high RSSD wife were not significantly different from high RSSD husbands with a low RSSD wife ($M = 4.69$). Analyzing just the wives' perceptions between the four groups indicated significant differences [F (3, 97) = 3.77, $p = 0.013$], but only one significant difference was found between the four groups in a post hoc analysis. High RSSD wives with a high RSSD husband reported more frequent positive relationship discussions ($M = 5.40$) than did low RSSD wives with a high RSSD husband ($M = 4.09$; Tukey b, $p < 0.05$).

Generally, the husband's higher level of RSSD has a stronger effect on the perception of positive relationship discussions for the husbands regardless of the wife's level then it does for the wives. For the wives, their husband's high level or RSSD only had a positive effect on how they viewed relationship discussions when they were also strong in RSSD. The imbalance is created when the wives' RSSD was low and the husbands' was high and resulted in those wives perceiving the least amount of positive relationship discussion, which once again shows a marked interaction effect of the spouses' sex and feelings toward their partner's level of understanding and adaptation.

6.5 Discussion and Conclusions

6.5.1 Symmetrical (Similar) or Complementary (Different)

This chapter reports on the study that explored the degree to which married couples established a relationship with spouses who had social decentering skills that were similar to (symmetrically high or low) or complemented their own (one spouse with stronger social decentering than the other). A small but significant correlation was found between the social decentering scores of the spouses and their partners that suggests some impact of similarity in forming or maintaining a relationship. But the fairly even distribution of couples with symmetrical and complementary social decentering skills indicates that the respondents did not form or maintain relationships based on their partner's sensitivity to other people's dispositions. While couples might not have established their relationships based on each other's social decentering skills, other findings in this study indicate that marital satisfaction is affected by couples' symmetrical or complementary social decentering skills.

Obfuscating these analyses is the fact that women generally have significantly higher levels of social decentering and RSSD than men, so in marriage, both husbands and wives might become desensitized to each other's differences in social decentering. But this study showed that the wives were negatively affected when their husband had a higher level of social decentering or RSSD either than them or to the social norm for men.

6.5.2 Age and Length of Marriage

This study found that social decentering and RSSD were strongest in the first years of marriage and generally declined over the course of the marriage, only slightly rebounding in the later years of marriage. Just as previous research found that martial satisfaction declined over the course of marriage, this study found that social decentering and RSSD likewise declined both as a factor of age and length of marriage. The decline was more pronounced for social decentering than RSSD. Various changes throughout couples' lives, such as parenthood, the demands of their marriage, family, and careers, probably affect the ebb and flow of spouses' awareness of and sensitivity to each other. But these factors seem less likely to affect people's general ability to socially decenter. The decline in social decentering that was found implies a decline in the skills associated with understanding and taking into account the dispositions of other people in general. Apparently, marriage and family take their toll on social decentering. Perhaps focusing on the spouse and family leads to being less focused on understanding those outside the family. And in longer marriages, as spouses grow in age, the decline in their social decentering might reflect a decline in social orientation and rise in egocentrism that appears to occur as people grow older.

If social decentering and RSSD can be expected to decline with age but be strong during the first years of marriage, what happens when older people get married or remarried? The answer to this question depends on whether the decline in decentering found in this study was due to respondents' length of marriage or their aging. If age is the determining factor, then the associated decrease in decentering will hinder the formation of new intimate relationships as people age. On the other hand, their motivation to form intimate relationships could be an impetus for them to better understand their partners and thus result in higher RSSD. Unfortunately, this study's sample did not have enough respondents who were older and recently married to test these questions. Besides further investigating those questions, a study is needed to compare the social decentering and RSSD of older single people to married people to determine if marriage is the dominant factor in the changes in social decentering and RSSD.

6.5.3 Marital Satisfaction

Previous studies have found little to no relationship between empathy or perspective-taking and marital satisfaction. The results of this study offer some insights to those previous findings. Although this study found no significant direct relationship between general social decentering and marital satisfaction, RSSD did have a small but significant impact on marital satisfaction. These results parallel those of others such as Long (1994, 1993) in demonstrating that understanding the dispositions of one's spouse is more important to a marriage than having a general ability to consider and adapt to others.

An analysis of how marital satisfaction relates to the symmetrical and complementary levels of social decentering and RSSD found a nonlinear relationship. Couples where both spouses were similarly high or low in social decentering had the highest levels of satisfaction, whereas those in complementary relationships in which one spouse was high and the other was low were less satisfied. Marital satisfaction was significantly greater for couples where both spouses were high social decenterers than for those where when the husband was a high decenterer and the wife was a low one. And differences between spouses paired according to their high and low RSSD scores were more pronounced than they were for high and low social decentering. Marital satisfaction for couples where both spouses were high in RSSD was significantly higher than it was for any of the other three pairings. While the other three pairings were not significantly different from each other in their level of marital satisfaction, the lowest level of marital satisfaction among all pairings was found in couples where the husband was high in RSSD and the wife low. In essence, when both spouses are in tune with each other – sensitive to each other's situation and understanding of each other's dispositions – it can have a significantly positive impact on their marital satisfaction. But the question remains whether marital satisfaction causes spouses to develop a better understanding of each other or whether developing an understanding of each other leads to greater marital satisfaction. In all likelihood, it's probably a combination of both.

Husbands were most satisfied when both they and their wife were strong in RSSD and least satisfied when they were both low. Gender role appears to have some effect because husbands who are less inclined to consider or adapt to their wife still expect their wife to consider and adapt to them. And husbands who consider and understand their wife's dispositions expect their wife to reciprocate. Likewise, wives who are high in RSSD are most satisfied with their husband if he is also high in RSSD. Unlike husbands, the least satisfied wives were those who were low in RSSD but had a husband who was high in RSSD. One expectation for the feminine gender role is to be relationally oriented (Wood, 2001); thus, wives who identify with feminine gender roles might feel threatened by their husband being more other-oriented than they are, perhaps even causing them to feel guilt and dissatisfaction.

6.5.4 Marital Attitudes and Communication

Recall that people who use social decentering or RSSD do not necessarily engage in adaptive behaviors, so their spouse might not know that their partner has decentered. Social decentering and RSSD provide foundations on which people can adapt their communication to their partner, but since they can also choose not to do so, their relationship might not be that strong. This study examined decentering for its impact on seven relationship attitudes (resentment/discontent, concern for spouse's welfare, and spouse as confidant/friend) and communication behaviors (positive/supportive communication, negative communication, blaming behaviors, and ignore/fail to consider knowledge of partner) measuring both the perspective of the decenterers and their spouse's perception of them. Respondents' reports of their own concern for their spouse's welfare and their use of positive/supportive communication positively related to their level of social decentering. All seven of the scales related to respondents' reported level of RSSD, with positive/supportive communication having the strongest relationship ($r = 0.48$), followed by concern for spouse's welfare ($r = 0.33$). As would be expected, negative communication behaviors, blaming behaviors, and failing to consider knowledge of the spouse all had negative relationships with RSSD. The findings were somewhat different for wives than husbands, most notably on the relationships with RSSD. Husbands' level of RSSD only related to three of the seven scales, whereas wives' level of RSSD related to all but the resentment/discontent scale.

Another question examined in this study was whether married people's perceptions of their spouse's adaptive behavior affected by their own social decentering. The results of this study suggest that they are not. Only one significant relationship was found and that was counter to what might be expected; the stronger a husband's social decentering, the more negative his wife saw his communication; most notably her husband pointing out her mistakes or failings. If the wives' observation is accurate, why would their husband make such comments? Perhaps social decentering heightens a husband's awareness of his wife's mistakes and reacts by blurting out his observation (Hample, Richards, & Skubisz, 2013). Social decentering involves analyzing their wife's behavior relative to their own behavior (use of self), to their wife's previous behavior (use of specific-other), and to behavior of people in general (use of generalized-others). The stronger their social decentering, the more cognizant the husbands might become of their wife's divergence from their expectations based on these three comparisons, and thus, view their wife's behaviors as failings. The decision to remark or not to remark on the mistakes rests on factors that go beyond social decentering, such as his marital satisfaction or skill in creating tactful statements.

Essentially, the results suggest that married people's social decentering does not cause their spouse to observe their adaptive behavior if there is any. But there are other possibilities for this result, including faulty methodology, spouse's lack of observational skills, and decisions not to adapt. Another possibility is that strong social decenterers adapt to a myriad of relationships and when they specifically adapt to their spouse, the spouse does not notice, instead seeing such behavior as simply the partner's norm. Or perhaps married people's general social decentering has minimal impact on their perception of their spouse' attitudes and communication behaviors. And since some strong decenterers are likely to have a spouse with more negative qualities while an other has a spouse with more positive qualities, the average impact would offset finding any significant difference. Finding only one significant relationship is in keeping with the earlier finding that spouses' social decentering had minimal impact on their marital satisfaction.

In contrast to their social decentering, married people's RSSD should be more visible to their spouse because it is specifically developed relative to that individual and relationship. This study found that the respondents perceived that their spouse provided more positive and supportive communication and was less resentful and discontent if the spouse was high in RSSD. In addition to perceiving that their wife displayed more positive communication and was less resentful, husbands also reported less negative communication if she was high in RSSD. But no relationships were found between the wives' observations of their husband's relational attitudes and communication behaviors and their husband's level of RSSD – perhaps because wives project role-based attitudes and behaviors onto their husbands regardless of whether he has displayed adaptive behaviors because of his RSSD. Or perhaps, even when strong in RSSD, husbands opt not to adapt their attitudes and behaviors to their wife.

Additional differences were explored by comparing high and low RSSD groups. The study found that husbands perceived their high RSSD wife in a more positive light than did husbands with a low RSSD wife. That is, husbands with a high RSSD wife perceive her as displaying a more positive attitude and engaging more often in supportive and confirming communication. This finding indicated that women make positive behavioral adaptations based on understanding their husband. But this action did not seem to be reciprocated. Wives married to a high RSSD husband did not significantly differ in their perceptions of their husband's relational attitudes and communication behavior from wives married to a low RSSD husband. This is discouraging news for husbands, where their self-reports indicated that those higher in RSSD engage in more positive and supportive communication, less blaming behavior, and more concern for their wife's welfare than do lower RSSD husbands. Yet these efforts by high RSSD husbands in adapting to their wife went either unobserved and/ or unappreciated. This difference in husbands' and wives' perceptions suggests an effect of sex and gender roles, where the respondents might have projected onto their spouse traditional expectations of how to behave based on their sex.

Unlike social decentering then, RSSD did affect the respondents' reported perceptions of their spouse, having a greater impact on the perceptions of the wives than on those of the husbands. High RSSD wives, compared to low RSSD wives, were more likely to see their husband as showing concern for their welfare, being a friend/ confidant, and engaging in positive/supportive communication and being less likely to ignore or fail to consider his knowledge about them, and being less likely to be resentful and discontented. High RSSD husbands saw their wife as having greater concern for their welfare and more positive/supportive communication than did low RSSD husbands. Respondents' RSSD appears to positively increase their valuation of their spouse's relationship attitudes and communication behaviors. In using RSSD, people gain a better understanding of their partner and an increased awareness of the partner's attributes that perhaps leads to a more sympathetic reaction to behaviors that they might otherwise regard negatively.

The final analysis of relationship attitudes and communication determined the interaction effect of both spouses' levels of social decentering and RSSD. To do this, the perceptions of high social decentering respondents married to a high decentering spouse were compared to those of high social decentering respondents married to a low decentering spouse, and the perceptions of low social decentering respondents married to a high decentering spouse were compared to those of low decentering respondents married to a low decentering spouse. This analysis implicitly examines the impact of symmetrical and complementary levels of social decentering on perceptions. The same procedure was used to analyze the impact of RSSD.

This analysis found no significant differences between the perceptions of high social decentering wives with a high decentering husband and those of high decentering wives with a low social decentering husband. Low social decentering wives with a high decentering husband, however, saw their husband in a more negative light than did low decentering wives with a low decentering husband on four of the relational scales. This result confirms the preference of low social decentering wives for a symmetrical relationship with their husbands, but that preference does not hold for high decentering wives. And this result, along with the results for marital satisfaction, supports the impact of symmetrically low social decentering relationships presented in the marital model in Chapter 5. The only difference found for high social decentering husbands with a low social decentering wife was the perception of greater resentment from their wife than was perceived from a high decentering wife. Putting the pieces of these results together leads to a conclusion that wives who are low in social decentering feel resentment toward their higher social decentering husband and that these husbands become aware of that resentment. In this way, social decentering causes both the resentment and contributes to recognizing that resentment. Finally, low social decentering husbands with a high decentering wife perceived their wife more negatively on five of the relational scales than did low social decentering husbands with a low decentering wife. Thus, as with low decentering wives, low social decentering husbands prefer a symmetrical relationship with their spouse.

High RSSD wives married to a high RSSD husband saw their husband as providing more positive/supportive communication and more apt to consider his knowledge of her than did high RSSD wives married to a low RSSD husband. The effect of being in a symmetrical relationship is again apparent in low RSSD wives' responses. Low RSSD wives regarded their high RSSD husband more negatively than how low RSSD wives regarded their low RSSD husband on two of the relational scales (concern for welfare and negative communication).

A symmetrical effect can be seen in the reports of high RSSD husbands, as well; those with a high RSSD wife viewed their wife more positively on three of the relational scales (resentment, positive/supportive communication, and negative communication) than did those with a low RSSD wife. This finding suggests that husbands who are strong in their understanding of and adaptation to their wife appreciate having a wife who reciprocates such understanding and adaptation.

However, a complementary effect can be seen in the reports of low RSSD husbands: those with a high RSSD wife more often perceived their wife as being a confidant/friend and displaying more positive/supportive communication behaviors than did low RSSD husbands married to a low RSSD wife. These results along with those from the marital satisfaction analyses indicate that low RSSD husbands view having a complementary level of RSSD with their wife as being more positive than having a symmetrical level.

Low RSSD husbands do not appear to resent their high RSSD wife as much as low RSSD wives resent their high RSSD husband. Both low and high RSSD husbands reported more positive communication with their high RSSD wife than low RSSD wives reported with their high RSSD husband, which means husbands perceived their wife as asking questions about and showing interest in what they were doing, providing supportive comments, and making confirming statements more than low RSSD wives saw from their high RSSD husband. This finding parallels the significant differences found between the self-reports of high RSSD wives and low RSSD wives on these scales. Confirmation of the wives' self-reports by their husbands' perceptions of them (whether he was high or low in RSSD) suggests that high RSSD wives accurately self-reported their behavior and that their husband's ability to perceive their behavior was unaffected by his level of RSSD.

Despite these analyses, the complexity of possible interactive effects makes it difficult to cull the impact of social decentering and RSSD on the accuracy of perceiving the partner's relational behaviors. Social decentering should lead to being more attuned to a spouse's behaviors, and RSSD should lead to even stronger sensitivity. But comparing a person's perceptions of their spouse with the self-report of that spouse in order to determine the accuracy of these perceptions is not so straightforward. Since part of decentering relies on an individual's sense of self as a source for understanding others, strong decenterers will likely report their own communication attitudes and behaviors more accurately than will weak decenterers. Thus, the differences found in this study between perceptions and self-reports might not be caused by an error in the decenterer's perception but instead be caused by their spouse's inaccurate self-appraisals. Indeed, the decenterers' ratings of their spouse's attitudes and behaviors might be more accurate than their spouse's self-report.

The final question examined in this study was the degree to which social decentering and RSSD affected the frequency of positive and productive relationship discussions. Both social decentering and RSSD correlated with how often couples had such discussions, but RSSD produced a stronger correlation. An analysis of wives' and husbands' scores separately found such a correlation for RSSD but not for social decentering. Both social decentering and RSSD related to the respondents' perception of their spouse's positive relationship discussions. But if social decentering and RSSD had some causal impact, then the respondents' social decentering or RSSD scores should have correlated with their self-report for positive relationship discussions, which was not the case. Pairs of high RSSD spouses reported the highest level of positive relationship discussions compared to the other three pair combinations, suggesting that RSSD has some impact on engaging in positive discussions. Further evidence is provided by the large significant difference found between high RSSD wives with a high RSSD husband and low RSSD wives with a high RSSD husband. The lack of positive relationship discussions for these low RSSD wives with a high RSSD husband is in keeping with the results for lower satisfaction and greater resentment among wives in this RSSD pairing.

Overall, this study indicates that the general ability to understand people as the result of social decentering plays a minimal role in married couples except for instances in which social decentering is symmetrical. Couples similarly high in social decentering reported the strongest marital satisfaction and couples similarly low in social decentering perceive their spouse's relationship attitudes and communication in a more positive light than do those in complementary relationships.

RSSD, however, had a much greater effect on marriage than did social decentering. Having strong RSSD skills played a significant and positive role in the satisfaction, relationship attitudes, and communication between couples. The development of RSSD provides married people with a foundation for understanding the dispositions and behaviors of their spouse and for adapting behavior. Failing to develop RSSD causes them to be more susceptible to projection – to seeing their spouse as more similar to themselves than they might be. In the case of the lower RSSD wives, their lack of RSSD caused them to not perceive their husband's positive relationship attitudes and communication. The positive impact of RSSD is greatest when both partners are strong in RSSD. When the husband is high in RSSD and the wife is low, the effect of RSSD is the weakest and can even be a negative.

6.5.5 Limitations of the Study

The couples who participated in the study are largely functional and satisfied with their marriage. And while differences were found between these couples, they are skewed regarding what occurs in functional marriages. Future research should strive to include couples who are dysfunctional and dissatisfied. Similarly, studying couples who are either in the process of divorcing or divorced would provide further insight into the degree to which social decentering and particularly RSSD are important to the maintenance of marriage. While this study analyzed the length of marriage and age of respondents, it was not a longitudinal study. Longitudinal studies are needed to more definitively examine how couples who are high or low in social decentering or RSSD respond to and manage the typical decline in satisfaction experienced by married couples over time. In addition, specific events over the course of marriage could be identified that contribute to or detract from social decentering and RSSD.

The classification of respondents as either high or low social decentering and RSSD was relative to the sample and not an actual reflection of respondents' lacking a given skill except perhaps the husbands who were low in social decentering. As a result, the high–low analyses actually reflected a comparison between those who are strong and those who are medium but not those who are weak in either. So, the impact of social decentering and RSSD is probably more substantial than the results of this study indicate. A large-scale study is needed to generate a sufficient pool of respondents who actually fall below the midpoint and can truly be considered as weak in RSSD or social decentering.

6.5.6 Lessons Learned: Implications for Counselors and Married Couples

For the respondents in this study, social decentering and RSSD were at their highest in the early years of marriage and generally declined over the course of it, rebounding somewhat in the later years. Why this decline occurs and the impact it has on marriage are unclear, nonetheless, a married person might be expected to become somewhat disenchanted when their spouse no longer displays the same level of understanding, sensitivity, and adaptation as earlier in the marriage. Counselors can explain that spouses' other-orientation naturally declines over the course of marriage. They might also elect to work on restoring couples' efforts to engage in social decentering and RSSD. Improving a state-based ability such as RSSD is more likely to be successful than trying to improve a trait-based quality such as social decentering. As with most counseling, the first issue will be to ensure that the couple is willing to make efforts to improve. A counselor can lead a willing couple in activities that increase their knowledge of each other's current dispositions (an effort that already occurs in many counseling sessions).

Such training has been done with empathy and perspective-taking with a fair amount of success. Long, Angera, Carter, Nakamoto, and Kalso (1999) conducted a 10-hour training program over 5 weeks with couples (66% of them married with an average of 10 years) that was designed to improve self and other dyadic perspective-taking (empathy). Couples were taught about empathy, practiced listening, discussed important issues, learn to use paraphrasing, and shared their understanding of each other. The training program resulted in significant improvement 6 months after the training was completed. General perspective-taking also improved even though that was not a goal of the training. But contrary to findings showing women stronger in empathy, participants' pre-test scores for the male participants in this program were not significantly different from those for the females. The researchers surmised that the men who volunteered were more empathic than the average man is, which raised concern about the training's effectiveness for men who are less empathic to begin with than those in the study.

Increasing couples' awareness of the processes of social decentering and RSSD is another early step to improving both. Because these processes often decline due to lack of motivation and the establishment of relational rituals, bringing couples' attention back to what they had been doing earlier in their marriage might help them rekindle their earlier efforts. For many years, I have introduced students in my introductory interpersonal communication classes to the concepts of social decentering and RSSD and am always pleased to find students embracing these other-oriented processes by the end of the term.

Efforts to have spouses consciously consider each other's dispositions to a given situation can be facilitated by having them reflect on the ten questions listed at the end of Chapter 5. These questions reflect the elements that constitute the theories of social decentering and relationship-specific social decentering including cognitive and affective responses, the use of self, use of specific-other (modified to marital partner), and the use of generalized-other.

6.6 References

Carstensen, L. L. (1998). A life-span approach to social motivation. In J. Heckhausen & C. S. Dweck (Eds.), *Motivation and self-regulation across the life span* (pp. 341–364). New York, NY: Cambridge Press.

Christensen, A., & Sullaway, M. (1984). Communication Patterns Questionnaire. Unpublished questionnaire, University of California, Los Angeles.

Cronbach, L. (1955). Processes affecting scores on "understanding of others" and "assumed similarity." *Psychological Bulletin, 53*, 177–193.

Davis, M. H. (1983). Measuring individual differences in empathy: Evidence for a multi dimensional approach. *Journal of Personality and Social Psychology, 44*, 113–126.

Funk, J. L., & Rogge, D. D. (2007). Testing the ruler with item response theory: Increasing precision of measurement for relationship satisfaction with the Couples Satisfaction Index. *Journal of Family Psychology, 21*, 572–583.

Hample, D., Richards, A. S., & Skubisz, C. (2013). Blurting. *Communication Monographs, 80*, 503–532.

Kenney, D. A. (1996). Models of non-independence in dyadic research. *Journal of Social and Personal Relationships, 13*, 279–294.

Long, E. C. J. (1993). Perspective-taking differences between high- and low-adjustment marriages: Implications for those in intervention, *The American Journal of Family Therapy, 21*, 248–259.

Long, E. C. J. (1994). Maintaining a stable marriage. *Journal of Divorce & Remarriage, 21*, 121–138.

Long, E. C. J., Angera, J. J., Carter, S. J., Nakamoto, M., & Kalso, M. (1999). Understanding the one you love: A longitudinal assessment of an empathy training program for couples in romantic relationships. *Family Relations, 48*, 235–242.

Looft, W. R. (1972). Egocentrism and social interaction across the life span. *Psychological Bulletin, 78*, 73–92.

Mehrabian, A., & Epstein, N. (1972). A measure of emotional empathy. *Journal of Personality, 40*, 525–543.

Murray, S. L., Holmes, J. G., Bellavia, G., Griffin, D. W., & Dolderman, D. (2002). Kindred spirits? The benefits of egocentrism in close relationships. *Journal of Personality and Social Psychology, 82*, 563–581.

O'Brien, E., Konrath, S. H., Gruhn, D., & Hagen A. L. (2012). Empathic concern and perspective-taking: Linear and quadratic effects of age across the adult life span. *The Journals of Gerontology, Series B: Psychological Sciences and Social Sciences, 68*, 168–175.

Schieman, S., & Van Gundy, K. (2000). The personal and social links between age and self-reported empathy. *Social Psychology Quarterly, 63*, 152–174.

Wood, J. T. (2001). *Gendered lives (4th ed.)*. Boston, MA: Wadsworth/Cengage.

7 Social Decentering and Relationship-Specific Social Decentering (RSSD) in Context: Health Care Professionals, Teams, Organizations, and Intercultural Interactions

Whenever we anticipate interacting, interact, or reflect on interactions with other people, we have the option of engaging in social decentering to help us in our planning, understanding, and adapting. We are also affected by the other person's use of social decentering on us. So far in this book the focus has been on interpersonal interactions, specifically those with friends, romantic partners, and spouses. That discussion provides a broad and encompassing understanding of social decentering and relationship-specific social decentering (RSSD) that can be applied to any human interaction. However, some interactions are defined by specific roles and contexts that affect the use, value, appropriateness, and impact of social decentering. For example, psychotherapy is seen as a specific form of interpersonal interaction (Hatcher, 2015), where the roles of the therapist and client guide the interaction. In organizations, managers with strong social decentering abilities are likely to make different adaptations to subordinates who are late to work than they do when their children are late for dinner. The roles that managers play toward subordinates evokes different goals in using social decentering (maintaining a productive workforce) than it does in interacting with their children (teaching responsibility). In this chapter, I will briefly discuss some of the more common contexts in which other-oriented processes have been applied and studied – health care/counseling, teams/ groups, organizations, and intercultural interactions. Rather than providing an extensive review of the literature on empathy and perspective-taking related to each application, the focus of the discussions will be the major role that social decentering and RSSD play in each context. I have chosen not to include a number of research articles that appear to be examining the roles of empathy or perspective-taking in a given context because of methodological concerns (see Chapter 2). For example, I have avoided studies that measure empathy using only Davis' measure of empathic concern which by fiat, are focused more on the empathizer's own emotional reactions (feeling sorry or being soft-hearted) than on feeling what the target is feeling.

7.1 Health Care Professionals

The largest context into which empathy has been applied is the health care professions such as therapists, counselors, nurses, and physicians. For some health care professionals, empathy is one of the primary tools used to accomplish their goals. Indeed, the essence of Carl Roger's (1951) client-centered therapy is the use of

https://doi.org/10.1515/9783110515664-008

empathy by therapists to help clients reorganize their self and adjust to life. Rogers (1975) observed that "a high degree of empathy in a relationship is possibly *the* most potent and certainly one of the most potent factors in bringing about change and learning" (p. 3). Empathy has been identified and advocated as a significant counseling skill for many years (Benjamin, 1969; Carkhuff, 1969; Gladstein, 1983; Rogers, 1957; Truax and Carkhuff, 1967). Rogers (1975) and Carkhuff (1969) saw counselors using empathy to identify and describe client feelings that the client is scarcely aware of or chosen not to express. In this sense, empathy goes beyond using just what is observed by using one's imagination for input, as reflected in the social decentering model. Rogers felt that counselors shouldn't actually experience the client's feelings; likewise, Katz's (1963) fourth and final stage of empathy in the counseling situation involves "detachment from shared feelings" to increase a counselor's objectivity that might otherwise be clouded by empathy.

The notion of detachment contrasts with the conceptualizations of empathy that involve feeling what the other person feels. Nonetheless, experiencing empathy in the sense of sharing the same feelings as a client/patient could be detrimental to the outcomes of a professional health care interaction. Counselors are likely to burn out quickly if they are constantly experiencing the same emotions as their clients. In this sense, health care professionals are well served by that part of the social decentering process that involves recognizing and perhaps even feeling some of the same emotions as their patients, but ultimately turning to their cognitive process of understanding the emotions and developing strategies to address them.

Variations in conceptualizations have led to contrasting measurement emphasis with some studies focusing on the perception of empathy by clients and patients and other studies focusing on the possession of empathy by the health care professional. As a result, research on empathy and perspective-taking among health care professionals is inundated with conceptual and methodological contradictions. Empathy is defined and measured in such a wide variety of ways it undermines the ability to synthesize and combine concepts and results. Sometimes the approaches are too simplified and fail to reflect the complexity of being other-centered. The multidimensional nature of social decentering theory and scale should more completely capture what occurs when health care professionals engage in other-centeredness while analyzing and responding to clients and patients' cognitive and affective dispositions.

A variety of studies have found support for a positive impact of being other-centered on the outcomes of a health care interaction. For example, Anderson, Ogles, Patterson, Lambert, and Vermeersch (2009) found that therapists' interpersonal facilitative skills (such as empathy and developing a therapeutic alliance) were associated with better therapy outcomes. For other professions such as nurses and physicians, empathy plays a less obvious but no less important role. For health care givers, the values of being other-orientated through social decentering or empathy include building helpful relationships, gaining information, gaining and sharing insights, and providing support and comfort. Studies on the impact of physician empathy on patients found "improvement in patient satisfaction and adherence, decrease of anxiety and distress, better diagnostic and clinical outcomes, and more patient enablement" (Derksen, Bensing, & Lagro-Janssen, 2013, p. 78). Research has also shown when nurses have strong empathy they are able to better sense the patient's readiness to talk, create a climate of trust, and understand the patients' responses to health problems (Reynolds & Scott, 2000). Strong empathy in nurses helps patients reach positive health outcomes, reduce physiological distress, improve their self-concept, and reduce their anxiety and depression (Reynolds & Scott, 2000). Unfortunately, Reynolds and Scott (2000) indicate that studies find a substantial lack of empathy among physicians and nurses.

For counseling and therapeutic applications, Rogers (1951) described how other-centeredness applies:

> [...] the counselor's function to assume, in so far as he is able, the internal frame of reference of the client, to perceive the world as the client sees it, to perceive the client himself as he is seen by himself, to lay aside all perceptions from the external frame of reference while doing so, and to communicate something of this empathic understanding to the client. (p. 29)

Rogers' description of therapists' other-orientation suggests that their responses are not truly empathic in the sense of the therapist having the same emotional reactions as the client. Rogers emphasized that a therapist should perceive the hates, hopes, and fears of a client but not actually experience those hates, hopes, and fears. Rogers' main concern is the perception of empathy by the clients rather than the therapists experiencing similar emotional responses to the clients; this lead Rogers (1975) to conclude "clients are better judges of the degree of empathy than are therapists" (p. 6).

In Chapter 2, I discussed the principle that people can engage in social decentering yet not produce any discernable adaptive behaviors. Thus, others' assessment of those individuals' behaviors would lead to the conclusion they have not engaged in social decentering. Of course, in therapy the emphasis has been how the perception of empathy affects a client. This perspective ignores the value of engaging in empathy by therapists even when not observed by the client. The conflicting views of empathy and perspective-taking might be one reason studies often fail to find a correlation between a person's self-report and their partner's observations (see, e.g., Park & Raile, 2010). Social decentering that doesn't produce observable responses (internal responding) still can be valuable to the decenterer, just as social decentering that results in adaptive behaviors (external responding) can be valuable to the recipient. Internal responding includes the development of more complex understanding of others and strategic decision-making (e.g., censorship of certain comments or reactions that are considered detrimental to the client/patient). External responses produce verbal and nonverbal messages that allow clients and patients to feel understood and confirmed. Much of the research and focus on empathy in counseling focuses on producing external empathic responses. Such focus makes sense, since it reflects the primary concern of using empathy to positively affect the client.

External and internal responses are also measured in different ways – self-reports versus observer reports (considered objective). A meta-analysis of empathy training found that training produced a greater impact on objective measures (observational) of empathy than on self-reports, though self-reported empathy did improve (Teding van Berkhout & Malouff, 2016). Often empathy training focuses on modeling behaviors and role-playing which of course is more likely to create change in observable behaviors than in social cognition. Besides training, experience can facilitate improved other-centeredness. Anderson et al. (2009) found that the age of therapists was positively associated with therapy outcomes but that effect appeared primarily due to increases in interpersonal facilitative skills as therapists gained experience (aged).

The following discussion of how social decentering applies to counseling, therapy, and other health care professionals is structured on the dimensions of social decentering presented in Chapters 1 and 2 beginning with what motivates its enactment. The very act of interacting as a health care professional with a client/patient should inherently activate social decentering. Inherent in the role of many care providers is understanding and adapting to the client/patient. While this should happen automatically, some professionals become entrenched in playing out a role divested of sensitivity to others. Physicians are somewhat notorious for failing to adequately consider the patient's perspective (Spiro, 2009). As a result, medical schools often take steps to improve physician empathy and perspective-taking, particularly since medical students' empathy declines over the first 3 years of medical school (Hojat et al., 2009). I once conducted a communication workshop in a hospital that was open to any staff member. A number of nurses and support staff attended and found the training on becoming more other-centered very helpful, but at the end of the workshop several of them commented on how they wish that the physicians would have attended. They recognized that sensitivity to others, both patients and staff, was a quality doctors often failed to display.

Activation: Activation of social decentering requires motivation to engage in social decentering which means health care professionals need to feel there is something they will gain by expending the time and energy needed to understand the dispositions of their clients, patients, and co-workers. An obvious but underappreciated value of social decentering is that it facilitates achieving job goals. Studies indicate that physicians with stronger empathy make more accurate diagnoses, gain greater patient adherence to treatment, elicit greater patient satisfaction, and are sued less for malpractice (Hojat, 2016) – they more effectively accomplish their medical goals. Believing such values accrue from social decentering can be an impetus to be more client/patient-centered. Unfortunately, the demands on a health care professional's time and energy are often to the detriment of the time and energy needed to develop and engage in social decentering, and even more so, for RSSD. For example, the time physicians have for patients in a clinical setting is often barely enough to learn the patient's current medical needs which leaves little, if any, time to learn the more personal information on which to more substantially ground social decentering and

RSSD. Dr. Spiro (2009), an emeritus professor of medicine at Yale University, strongly advocates for physicians to be empathic and wrote:

> Physicians must have the time to listen to their patients. Listening can create empathy – if physicians remain open to be moved by the stories they hear. Empathy has always been and will always be among a physician's most essential tools of practice. (p. 1179)

Ultimately, health care professionals must make the decision to exert a conscientious effort to be client-centered. In presenting his client-centered approach to therapy, Rogers (1951) observed that those who were already motivated and working toward understanding others learned the client-centered techniques more quickly. For Rogers, the right attitude, personality, and philosophical orientation toward respect for others provided the motivation to be client-centered. He saw students able to achieve empathic understanding if they had the desire to understand other's viewpoints. These same motivations and desires lead many health care professionals to engage social decentering.

Input: Once the decision is made to engage in social decentering, the next step is taking inventory of what information is available on which to base an analysis of the client/patient. The information step of social decentering involves using experience-based information (observation and recall) and imagination-based information (extrapolating from experience-based information).

To best examine the role of information to the health care professional, I am going to describe a typical first time medical patient interaction (based and biased primarily on my own experiences). A patient meets with a nurse or aide who asks what the issue is and/or collects other initial information about the patient's visit. Since the patient doesn't know the nurse, the patient provides limited and specific information. Without a preexisting relationship, the patient might not feel sufficient trust to share more. Before seeing the patient, the physician reviews the information collected by the nurse. Upon meeting the patient, the doctor shares her or his understanding of the situation and asks the patient for any additional information. Again, no real relationship exists, and trust is somewhat limited. The physician then conducts an examination, perhaps sending the patient for further tests. The process ends with the physician engaging in or prescribing some course of action. In extended research interviews with 35 patients who had just met with a doctor, 31 did not fully share their concerns (Barry, Bradley, Britten, Stevenson, & Barber, 2000). The failure to fully share concerns was due to doctors not seeking or attending to the relevant information and from patients worried about the appropriateness of disclosing and wasting the doctors' time. An option for health care providers to gain both trust and more personal patient information is for the provider to self-disclose. This takes advantage of the strategy discussed in earlier chapters for gaining information by using the dyadic effect or reciprocity of self-disclosure. Research has found that self-disclosures by counselors lead to self-disclosure by the clients/patients (Henretty & Levitt, 2009; Henretty, Currier, Berman, & Levitt, 2014).

Throughout the medical visit example, the focus was on gaining information pertinent to the physical condition of the patient. Let's consider how social decentering could enter into this process. The focus on medical history and symptoms limits the kind of information contributing to social decentering. In counseling and medical interactions, the health care professionals draw from their extensive experience-based catalog of information that relates to what they are told by the client or patient. A client who expresses feelings of depression leads therapists to access the information they have accumulated. Over time, as a relationship is developed between the health care provider and the patient, more information is learned. Unlike interpersonal interactions, professionals almost always record the information they learn from the client and access that information as needed in subsequent visits. While such records insure accurate recall of information, it might restrict the acquisition of more personal information because the focus is on writing notes and recording symptoms that can undermine empathic listening. How health care professionals can improve the acquisition of personal information is discussed later.

Until more is learned about a patient, imagination-based information has a limited role in health care interactions. But creativity and imagination are seen as important qualities for a physician to have (Altschuler, 2016). Imagination allows the physician or therapist to consider experience-based information in creative ways that can provide both insight and understanding. As a relationship develops, the health care provider can use imagination as a way to consider how the patient or client is likely to respond to new information and treatments. Imagining how a given patient is going to react to a diagnosis of terminal cancer allows a physician to consider how to best share the diagnosis and to prepare support resources adapted to that patient. After reviewing theory and research on perspective-taking, Lobchuk (2006) observed that patient caregivers could attain greater empathic accuracy "by imagining how patients perceive their situations and how they feel as a result" (p. 338). Someone does not need to experience cancer to imagine what someone else might be thinking and feeling. Such use of imagination-based information benefits from being grounded in experience-based information where a caregiver uses previous experiences with patients to imagine a particular patient's thoughts and feelings. But in doing this, health care professionals also need to be sensitive to and incorporate in their imaginings how the particular patient differs from previous patients.

The use of social decentering is not limited to health care providers, but also extends to users. Clients and patients also engage in social decentering during these encounters. Patients' previous experiences with health care professionals serve as the foundation for deciding on how to behave and for interpreting the behavior of the health care providers. Previous experiences can lead to inappropriate and dysfunctional behavior such as the patient mentioned earlier who didn't share information because he or she thought he or she would be wasting the physician's time. Patients' responses to health care professionals are a reflection of their previous experiences and their imagination of the health care professional's dispositions. Patients who have been treated rather impersonally by medical personnel are likely to behave rather impersonally in ensuing visits because that's what they believe the health care provider wants.

Analysis: The theory of social decentering posits three methods by which information is analyzed: use of self, use of specific-others, and use of generalized-others. Each method uses both experience-based and imagination-based information as the foundation for the analyses. The application of each form of analysis is context dependent – the appropriateness of counselors self-disclosing their own drug recovery to a client differs from a nurse sharing her experience of breast cancer with a breast cancer patient. The counselor is trying to gain trust and build a relationship on which to build recovery. The nurse is trying to provide comfort and hope. The following discussion should be read with the understanding that the claims and assertions are contextually bound.

Use of self: In a 1991 movie entitled *The Doctor* (based on a true story), a self-centered physician develops cancer and discovers what it's like to be a patient where medical staff show little concern for patient feelings or emotions. His transformation leads him to develop a program to teach his interns the importance of empathy by having them all "admitted" and treated as nondescript patients in a proxy hospital ward. Such an experience develops physicians' ability to incorporate use of self in their interactions with patients. Considering their own reactions to treatment can be an effective base from which to understand and adapt to others.

In *The Doctor*, sensitivity is raised about how medical personnel behaviors affect patients, but use of self can also develop when the health care professional has experienced similar problems as those encountered by patients and clients. This is the reason a number of drug and alcohol counselors are themselves recovering addicts. In a document published by the U.S. National Institute on Drug Abuse, Mercer (2000) wrote:

> Many counselors in this field are either in recovery themselves or have had a family member who was addicted. An indepth knowledge of addiction and the tools for recovery and ability to empathize with the client are essential for an addiction counselor. One way to develop this knowledge and ability is for the counselor to be in recovery. (p. 85)

Counselors in recovery can draw upon their use of self to more fully understand and relate to the experiences of clients with the caveat that the experience of any given client will also be different. Counselors who themselves have not been addicts can still apply use of self by imagining themselves as addicts and in recovery.

The results of interviews with 36 patients who had experienced mental health issues indicated that learning (often through the Internet) that other people have similar mental health issues made them feel they were not alone and that the other people could understand and empathize with them (Powell & Clarke, 2006). This suggests that, in some instances, the use of self would be an effective option for health care professionals even to the point of sharing their own thoughts and feelings with the clients.

The value of use of self for both providing a foundation for understanding and a model of hope and inspiration is one reason there is extensive use of peer recovery support services including therapy groups. Whether it's an AA meeting or a student support group, interacting in a structured format with others who share similar experiences increases the potential for feeling understood by others, finding that someone is not alone in facing the given issue, and gaining strength from others.

Use of specific-other: Many health care encounters initially center on gaining basic information about the client or patient – age, medical and mental health history, current conditions, etc. Such information provides a foundation onto which use of specific-other process can be applied, to the degree that it provides comparisons between patients or clients. That information allows the health care providers to recognize similarities between a given health care user and a previous client or patient. The information from a previous patient or client can serve as the foundation for making predictions and understanding current patients/clients. The effectiveness of the use of specific-other depends on how well developed the use of specific-other is (did it reach RSSD?), how much information has been gathered about the current client/patient, and how truly similar the two are. As more information is learned and the health care professional identifies more similarities, she or he can feel more confident in applying the use of specific-other, or decide that the application is inappropriate. Indeed, dissimilarity can be as informative and helpful as similarity. Dissimilarity leads to efforts to acquire more information about the current health care user in order to understand the differences and more appropriately adapt.

The more experience a health care professional gains, the larger the number of specific-others he or she has from which to draw. For many years my faculty member responsibilities included academic advising. Early on, if students came to me after the semester to talk about their failing grades, I would think about a student I had advised with a similar problem that proved to be because of a lack of studying. That student served as my specific-other and the foundation for understanding and adapting to other advisees with grade problems. That worked fairly well, since failure to adequately study tends to be a general problem. But later in my advising career I was advising a student who studied hard but was still failing. The experience of my previous specific-others didn't apply and in realizing this, I sought additional information from her. It became clear that college wasn't for her and that she had other aspirations and left school. She then became another specific-other that I drew upon when advising subsequent students for whom aptitude was an issue.

Use of generalized-other: Use of generalized-other is probably the most immediately applied form of analysis that occurs in health care encounters. One reason for this is that a significant part of the education of health care professionals is classification of patients and clients. A therapist draws from a different pool of information with someone identified as having a panic disorder than with someone who is compulsively obsessive. A physician has a different mind-set when dealing with a patient with diabetes than a patient with high cholesterol. Such classifications provide the foundations for the use of generalized-others. The earlier discussion about the lack of empathy among physicians relates to a tendency to primarily rely on and act on the use of generalized-other without utilizing the other two methods. Health care professionals draw on the demographic information, prior diagnoses, and test results as triggers for which generalized-other information to apply. For example, a doctor might simply attribute a 70-year-old patient's vision complaint to aging, but had the doctor conversed with the patient, the doctor might have found out that the patient had considerably increased her needlepointing without the benefit of good lighting. While this is an example of a poor medical exam, it does illustrate how dependence on generalized-others can lead to incorrect conclusions, and stresses how important gaining information is to effective social decentering.

While studying establishes many of the categories applied when dealing with patients and clients, experience leads to their refinement and the creation of the health care professional's own set of generalized categories. Health care professionals need to be keenly aware of applying the use of generalized-other method to understanding and reacting to health care users. Such awareness needs to include comparisons to the use of self and use of specific-other to most fully predict, understand, and adapt to patients and clients.

RSSD: Over time it is possible for a health care provider and a patient to develop an interpersonal relationship that supports the development of RSSD by the health care professional. Developing such relationships is often discouraged particularly because of the possibility of creating dependence and must be balanced with objectively defined roles. The lack of equal power and self-disclosure inherently creates relational inequities. For example, RSSD is more likely to develop for the health care professionals but not for the clients and patients. RSSD can develop in situations where the health care professionals have an ongoing relationship with the health care user and a significant amount of knowledge is learned about the user. But unlike most interpersonal relationships, RSSD in health care relationships represents a unilateral form of RSSD wherein the health care professionals know the clients intimately, but clients have limited personal knowledge of the professionals.

I have had the same general practice physician for 30 years and he knows I enjoy camping and hiking in the national parks and playing basketball, that provides him a degree of RSSD, but I have also learned that he enjoys this things. In my yearly checkups, he not only engages me in discussion of these areas, but uses that discussion as a way of assessing both my mental and physical health. Happily, despite the occasional injuries and aches, he continues to encourage me to play basketball as part of his medical advice. Fortunately, it doesn't take 30 years for a health care professional to learn enough from a patient or client to establish some RSSD, but I have also learned that he enjoys this things. Each piece of new information acquired allows for better understanding and adapting to the health care user. Finding out a health care user's mother died two weeks before, becomes a piece of information specific to that user that allows the health care professional to consider the impact of the mother's death on the user relative to other information already known. If sufficient RSSD has developed, the health care professional should be able to predict and assess the impact on and response of the user based on this new piece of information.

Unlike most of our interpersonal interactions, health care professionals usually review the notes and charts that have been made about their patients or clients before each encounter. Such a review is one way of activating the relationship-specific level of information that has been collected but not committed to memory. Some personal information is not recorded and thus depends upon the health care professionals' recollections, that is particularly challenging for those with a large patient or client lists. Nonetheless, such notes bolster the ability to engage in RSSD. As patients, we feel personally validated by a physician who begins the encounter by asking how we are doing relative to some prior diagnosis or treatment; unlike the feeling we have when a physician begins the encounter and is clueless about who we are or what we need.

Overall, health care professionals need to recognize that they should try as much as possible to develop a schema for each of their patients or clients if they wish to fully and successfully engage in other-centeredness. Once recognized, health care professionals need to make a conscientious effort to create and apply RSSD. The shorter time between encounters the easier it is to develop RSSD, such as in weekly therapy sessions; but at the same time, the health care user's expectation for understanding and adaptation will also increase. Such expectations are akin to those that occur in interpersonal relationships as the provider-user relationship becomes more long-term and intimate. On the other hand, the longer the breaks between user and provider encounters, the more forgiving the patients and clients will hopefully be regarding the health care provider forgetting personal information.

OUTPUT – Cognitive and Affective: The analysis of information leads to both cognitive and affective responses within the social decenterer. The cognitive response includes predictions, understanding, and development of potential strategies. The affective response includes the decenterer's own feelings about the situation that might include sympathy for the other person. The affective response might also include having similar emotional reactions to the situation as the target – what I consider truly to be empathy. On the cognitive side, health care providers develop an understanding of the behaviors and feelings of their clients and patients. Providers can use social decentering to predict the reactions of users to diagnoses and proposed treatments and to develop the most effective strategy for presenting those to the users. On the affective side, health care providers must consider whether to share their own emotional reactions to the health care users' situation. While such expression can potentially build trust, it can also stifle communication because some emotional disclosures by the provider might seem judgmental. When the health care professionals' emotional responses are empathetic, they enhance the cognitive process by providing insights about the user's emotional experience. Providers who express their empathy can confirm the user's own feelings, demonstrate effective listening, and create a supportive climate for further user disclosures.

Unfortunately, there is a downside to the affective experiences of health care professionals – burnout and fatigue. The experience of constant emotional arousal of negative emotions (sadness, anger, frustration, sorrow, helplessness, etc.) as the result of social decentering or empathy can lead health care providers to emotional exhaustion, compassion fatigue, and burnout. In addition, showing empathy and concern while repressing other emotions such as sadness and anger creates emotional labor leading to stress and exhaustion (Wright, Sparks, & O'Hair, 2013). A considerable amount of research has been done specifically on compassion fatigue among health care providers. Compassion involves an awareness of and desire to address another person's suffering (Sinclair et al., 2017). Compassion can be thought of as one of the products of social decentering in which an individual recognizes another person's situation (suffering), feels an emotional response to that perception, and then responds with an effort to help the person manage the suffering. Unlike other social decentering responses that are not expressed or exhibited, an important component of compassion is the action step. The emotions evoked through social decentering in response to other people's suffering are likely to contribute to compassion fatigue. A Portuguese study of 280 nurses found that empathic concern (assessed with the Davis subscale) was a significant predictor of compassion fatigue (Duarte, Pinto-Gouveia, & Cruz, 2016). In a review of research on compassion fatigue, Sorenson, Wright, and Hamilton (2016) found that a variety of similar conditions fall under different labels such as compassion fatigue, compassion stress, secondary traumatic stress, and burnout. Their review of studies across the spectrum of health care provider roles found that compassion fatigue and related conditions produced negative physical, emotional, and work-related effects, reduced the ability to feel empathy, and affected interactions with co-workers and patients. Additional effects of compression fatigue, burnout, and emotional fatigue include negative impact on personal life, heightened concern for one's own health, reduced job satisfaction, and quitting one's job.

Among the methods Sorenson et al. (2016) identified to counter compassion fatigue were educational interventions, supportive working environment and management, and compassion satisfaction (feeling positive about one's contributions). Duarte et al. (2016) found that self-compassion moderated the effects of empathic concern and personal distress on compassion fatigue. Self-compassion involves the ability of people "to be caring, supportive, and understanding toward themselves, particularly when faced with suffering or failure, and who feel interconnected with other people" (Duarte et al., 2016, p. 8). In terms of social decentering, individuals can choose not to engage in an analysis of the client's or patient's situation. However, such decisions can move the provider back to the impersonal, clinical treatment of others. Health care providers need to recognize those situations that will benefit from their engaging in social decentering and those for which it is less consequential.

In so doing, the level of emotional exhaustion can be reduced. A social decenter-er's sense of self-worth can also be bolstered by applying social decentering to an analysis of their own contributions toward helping and comforting others and the positive impact that they had.

As in other contexts, the issue of whether empathy and perspective-taking are cognitive or affective is debated within the health care context. In applying empathy to health professionals, Hojat (2016) defined empathy as a cognitive process that results in understanding a patient's perspectives and experiences and communicating that understanding to the patient for the purpose of helping the patient. Hojat equates emotional empathy with sympathy and warns that excessive sympathy can be detrimental to health care professional decisions.

Hojat (2016) emphasized understanding emotions by health professionals over actually experiencing emotions. In the model of social decentering, the line that connects the cognitive response to the affective response reflects Hojat's thinking about emotions. While we can "think" about another person's emotional disposition, we should also recognize that almost all humans will also have an emotional reaction to the information they are processing. Hojat's concern appears primarily to be that the health care provider's emotional responses not interfere or undermine subsequent treatment.

Rather than denying the emotional reaction, health care professionals need to recognize their reaction and determine the degree to which it is affecting them. One rule for dealing with emotions in conflict is deciding whether to express that emotion to the other person (Beebe, Beebe, Redmond, 2017). Similarly, health care professionals might choose to share their emotional reactions to the patients or clients as a genuine demonstration of concern and empathy. For example, it might be appropriate for a physician telling a long-time patient that he has terminal cancer to also express her or his own feelings of sadness and loss while providing comforting messages.

STRATEGIES/RESPONSES: Recall that individuals often engage in social decentering without displaying apparent adaptive behaviors. One reason for not displaying adaptive behaviors is a lack of responsive skills in the social decenterer. A nurse might feel ill at ease giving a patient a hug even though the nurse recognizes it would be comforting to the patient. Much of the interpersonal training of health care professionals is designed to overcome this limitation by providing training in responsive and empathic behaviors. A second reason for not displaying adaptive behaviors is strategic; displaying understanding might actually create stress for the recipient. Most of us don't like it when someone declares that they know what we're thinking – we don't like people reading our minds. Health care professionals are often in the position of having to repress their empathic impulse when they realize it would be detrimental to a user's health care or therapy. Elliott, Bohart, Watson, and Greenberg (2011) saw such a need for therapists to tailor their empathic responses to the clients:

> Therapists therefore need to know when – and when not – to respond empathically. When clients do not want therapists to be explicitly empathic, truly empathic therapists will use their perspective-taking skills to provide an optimal therapeutic distance in order to respect their clients' boundaries. (p. 48)

Elliott et al. implicitly identify the production of both affective and cognitive output; such output is part of the social decentering process. Social decentering by health care professionals includes the emotional reactions experienced by the health care professional and the cognitive analysis of how various different responses might impact the patient or client, including the therapists' expression of their own emotions. Such skill is critical to the success of most health care interactions. In writing about therapists' responsiveness skills, Hatcher (2015) wrote: "Responsiveness may be continually informed by new experiences with others, and enriched by strengthening and modifying existing interpersonal skills" (p. 748). For such strengthening to occur, health care professionals need an awareness and openness to the information afforded in new experiences and adding it to their experience-based information archive.

Bylund and Makoul (2005) examined the actual communicative behaviors of 20 academic primary care physicians in response to patients' explicit statements of emotion. They found that 30.3 % of the time, physicians acknowledged the emotion, 28.2% of the time, they pursued the emotion with questions or advice, and 26.5% of the time, they confirmed the legitimacy of the emotion. Rarely did physicians express a shared feeling or experience, give an implicit or perfunctory reply, or deny the emotion. While such responses demonstrated effective listening and confirming responses, they do not really prove the physicians engaged in empathy, perspective-taking, or social decentering. Statements that reflect an understanding of the emotion within the terms of who the other person is would be stronger indices of the physician actually being other-centered. Interestingly, Bylund and Makoul found patients didn't provide physicians many opportunities to respond to the patients' emotions, with 40% of the patients making no emotional statements and 60% averaging only two and a half statements regarding their emotions. While not the intent of the study, it does reinforce the point made earlier that patients are reluctant to self-disclose, thus limiting the ability to socially decenter. In addition, patients were more likely to share negative feelings while physicians were more likely to respond empathically to patients' positive feelings. The authors suggest that physicians might either be trying to remain calm and thus neutralize the negative feelings or feel ill-suited to address the negative feelings. The second suggestion is in concert with the notion that people can engage in social decentering yet lack the wherewithal to appropriately respond.

Suchman, Markakis, Beckman, and Frankel (1997) also examined missed empathic opportunities and developed an interactional model that reflects how patients' emotions come into play when interacting with physicians. First, they observed that patients rarely articulated their emotions initially but provide indirect verbal and nonverbal clues. Next, empathic clinicians pick up these clues and invite exploration of what the patients are feeling. Once expressed by the patients, clinicians provide confirming responses that convey understanding of the patients' feelings. Suchman et al. also observed that when patients re-introduce an emotion to the conversation that was not initially acknowledged, they likely are signaling that the emotion is important to them and needs to be acknowledged and explored. Suchman et al. also noted that clinicians need to continue to invite their patients to elaborate on their feelings before the clinicians state their understanding. If a health care professional expresses understanding before the patients have fully shared their feelings, the professional implicitly signals an end to the discussion and thus subverts full exploration of the patient's emotions.

7.1.1 Training Health Care Professionals to Socially Decenter

Teding van Berkhout and Malouff (2016) reviewed extant studies and concluded "empathy training programs tend to be effective in increasing empathy levels. The present overall results suggest that it could be worthwhile to train individuals in empathy and to evaluate, at least informally, the effects" (p. 39). An examination of a recent training study provides an example of what often occurs in empathy training. Ruiz-Moral, Pérula de Torres, Monge, García Leonardo, and Caballero (2017) implemented and successfully tested a training program for third-year medical students that was organized as a sequential "empathic process." Students first learned to identify affective and contextual cues, then they learned communication skills to more deeply explore the patients' illness experiences, and finally they were taught to make empathic statements. As in the definition of social decentering, their training began with an observation of some trigger (e.g., nonverbal emotional cues) and the consideration of the context. Response to these cues led to collecting more in-depth information. This training program like many others focuses on identifying an emotional marker, seeking elaboration from the patient, and providing confirming empathic statements such as "I understand you feel frustrated." This program recognized the need for the students to understand the patients' experience but that was only measured in terms of empathic statements. Such training moves from activation triggers to empathic statements without necessarily engaging in social decentering, empathy, or perspective-taking. Students need to consider the patient's thoughts, how the patient differs from other patients, and how they would feel in the patient's situation, which perhaps the training included. The challenge of training is teaching students to understand the patients or clients' dispositions and when appropriate, genuinely convey their sense of understanding and feelings.

For health care professionals, to socially decenter means more than just recognizing, acknowledging, and sympathizing with patients or clients' emotions; it involves a broader understanding of who the patient is and how the patient thinks. Training needs to include developing mental schemas of patients and clients and using those schemas to interpret, understand, and respond to their statements and behaviors. But the health care professional must seek a balance between the sensitivity/connection achieved through social decentering and the objectivity/detachment needed to make sound decisions. One format for training that I have used with students involves briefly interacting with another person who provides a minimal description of a personal issue. The decenterer is then asked a series of questions that encourage them to first consider the information they have about the situation and the person, what additional information they might need, and how they might acquire that information (e.g., additional background information, probing questions, and use of dyadic self-disclosing). Next, they are asked to consider the person and his or her situation using each of the three methods of analysis: "What would they think and feel if faced with a similar situation?," "What do they believe this other person is thinking and feeling?," and finally, "What would most people in general think and feel?" (a full set of social decentering reflection questions appears at the end of Chapter 5). Finally, the target person provides feedback about the accuracy of the assessment. The goal of the activity is to have students consciously engage in social decentering and assess the degree to which they understand the thoughts and feelings of another person. Additionally, trainees should consider, and practice response strategies based on their analysis including the use of confirming and supportive statements when appropriate.

7.2 Groups/Teams

Groups represent "interpersonal communication among three or more people who view themselves as a group and who are working toward a shared purpose or goal" (Redmond, 2000a, p. 256). Thus, groups include such entities as families, committees, workgroups, and project teams. The terms groups and teams are used interchangeably in the following discussion. Group and team goals and interactions have two orientations: task and social (relational/emotional) (Redmond, 2000a). Teams with goals of policy-making, decision-making, or problem-solving tend to be highly task-oriented. Groups that exist primarily to satisfy needs for companionship, belonging, and personal confirmation are highly social and relationally oriented. Task-oriented groups are not devoid of social/relational goals nor are social groups devoid of tasks. Other-oriented processes such as social decentering can contribute to successful completion of both task and social/relational goals. Tompkins (2000) argued that for teams to develop well-functioning relationships they need, "The ability to empathize and listen to team member's ideas and the ability to respond" (p. 214). In identifying qualities needed for effective teams, Borrill and West (2005) wrote, "Team members must be able to 'decentre', to take the perspective of others into account in relation to both their affective and cognitive position" (p. 145).

Empathy, particularly when conceptualized as an affective process, has an obvious connection to the socioemotional factors that contribute to group process. Perspective-taking, on the other hand, appears more connected to understanding other group members, and could help improve task and leader efficiency. As both a cognitive and affective process, social decentering facilitates both the social and task goals. Kellett, Humphrey, and Sleeth (2002) found a positive correlation between group members' perception of another member's empathy ("shows sensitivity and understanding" p. 531) and their perception of his or her leadership. Kellett et al. felt there were two behavioral routes to being perceived as leaders: empathic behaviors and mental abilities. Empathy was seen as important to leaders because "perceiving others' feelings and empathizing with them is likely to establish an affective bond or relationship that offers benefits for leadership" (p. 536). While they emphasized the emotional part of empathy, their measure included items focused on a member's level of understanding and, as such, is similar to the social decentering measure.

Pescosolido (2002) and Wolff, Pescosolido, and Druskat (2002) present a case for a type of emergent leader who manages both the group's task and the emotional state. Such leaders display emotional reactions that cue other members' emotional reactions and thus influence group performance. Such management occurs because strong empathic skills allow these leaders to better understand and identify the needs of the group members. Such understanding has task implications by contributing to improved problem-solving. Empathy allows leaders to develop strategies that are adapted to the emotional states of the members and thus, to the degree that management of emotions is relevant, improve group productivity (Wolff et al., 2006). Wolff et al. don't limit empathy's impact to emotional processes but instead argue that empathy also strengthens effective perspective-taking by the leaders. Their combination of empathy and perspective-taking constitutes the same social cognition process that makes up social decentering. Social decentering can thus be expected to aid emerging leaders in successfully adapting to the emotions and thoughts of the group members.

Other-orientation has an impact on the emergence and effectiveness of team leaders. Dugan, Bohle, Woelker, and Cooney (2014) argued that social perspective-taking (concern for others) contributes to self-understanding relative to others, thus fostering social bonds and less in-group favoritism, which in turn enhances one's ability to function in groups. Textbooks on effective decision-making groups and leadership often advocate learning about and adapting to other group members. For example, Young, Wood, Phillips, and Pederson's (2001) guide to group discussion emphasizes the need for a leader to recognize and appreciate the diversity among group members – leaders need to "adapt their actions not just to the group as a whole, but also to the needs and preferences of individual members – a challenging task" (p. 50). They also emphasize the need to analyze and adapt to the situation, a key component of social decentering. To apply social decentering to groups, leaders need to learn about and adapt to group-specific member variables. These variables include members' reasons for participating in the group, members' stakes in the issues facing the group, the skills members bring to the group as well as their limitations, and members' involvement in and commitment to the group (Young et al., 2001). Analysis of these variables benefits from the application of social decentering but also contributes to social decentering.

One of the main reasons groups are utilized for decision-making and problem-solving is the value that accrues from tapping a diverse set of perspectives and skills. But, that diversity is also problematic because it can block effective inter-actions and the establishment of productive relationships, as well as become a source of tension and conflict. A focus on differences can foster bias, disrespect, and intol-erance. Members might find it difficult to carry on conversations with other members who hold contrasting perspectives preventing them from seeing each other's view-points (as demonstrated for example, in the US Congress, the British Parliament, and the German Bundestag). Hoever, van Knippenberg, van Ginkel, and Barkema (2012) identified perspective-taking as a significant way to offset the problems associated with diverse perspectives. They argue that through reciprocation, perception-taking emerges as a team process that "helps teams to capitalize on their diversity on crea-tive tasks by fostering the sharing, discussion, and integration of diverse viewpoints and information" (p. 984). Further, they argue that efforts to understand a teammate's perspective leads to both active and passive information seeking. Hoever et al. also point out that in homogenous teams, perspective-taking would not be particularly beneficial. In essence, homogenous perspective-taking would be akin to the use of self method of social decentering. Contrary to Hoever et al., the harm of such homo-geneity is not in undermining perspective-taking but in creating groups that lack the benefits of diverse perspectives. Hoever et al.'s study found that perspective-taking in diverse groups had a positive effect on information elaboration and creativity. Just as social decentering requires cognitive effort and thus motivation to do so, Hoever et al. noted that one role of a transformational leader would be to motivate diverse members to make the effort to consider their teammates' perspectives.

Besides the use of social decentering, group members can also develop and apply RSSD. The depth of RSSD that is developed with each of the other members is dependent on self-disclosing, the behaviors exhibited by each group member, and additional interactions outside the team. The knowledge learned about each member provides a foundation for adapting to each member's unique characteristics. Such skill is particularly valuable to team leaders who need to effectively interact with all members. But adapting to members who are quiet and fairly inactive obviously limits both the use of social decentering and the development of RSSD.

Just as RSSD can be developed with each of the group members, a form of social decentering can be developed based an understanding of the group as a whole – in essence, group-specific social decentering. We develop a sense of how a certain group of people behave, think, and feel. For example, you might consider a work project team that you're in as dysfunctional with too many egos and everyone trying to outdo the others. This understanding of the group should help you accomplish your goals by selecting strategies adapted to this group. Seeing the group as a single entity for which we have a positive regard is likely to lead us to describe the group as a team or family. Think about the groups or teams in which you have been a member. Do you have a mind-set that describes those groups as a whole? Do you compare and contrast the groups you are or have been in? To form such group-specific social decentering, members need to have shared their thoughts and feelings. Since members are likely to vary in terms of how much they are willing to share, group-centered social decentering will be incomplete and its effectiveness limited. Rico, Sanchez-Manzanares, Gil, and Gibson (2008) identify trust as a significant factor leading to members opening up about themselves, "trust promotes the information exchange between team members necessary to integrate their different perspectives on the situation into a common understanding" (p. 172). In turn, perspective-taking enhances understanding of other members' messages, intentions, and interpretations (Rico et al., 2008).

Social decentering can impact groups and teams in terms of the effectiveness of task and social leaders and in terms of the social decentering skills of the group members. To examine these issues, I conducted a study in which 74 students from three upper-level communication courses worked in 16 problem-solving groups of three to six members for two to four weeks. Each group produced a paper and made a presentation to the class. At the completion of their project they completed the social decentering questionnaire, the Group Attitude Scale (Evans & Jarvis, 1986), a measure of perceived quality of discussion (adapted from Gouran, Brown, & Henry, 1978), and a measure of the quality of group behavior dealing with relevant and systematic discussions and healthy interpersonal relationships (Gouran et al., 1978). Each member identified who they felt had been (1) most influential, (2) provided the most guidance/ direction, (3) showed the greatest concern, and (4) was the overall leader. Members identified by 40% or more of the other members on a given item were considered a leader on that item. Social decentering scores were used to divide those leaders into two groups: high and low social decenterers. Social decentering did not impact the emergence of task leaders; the social decentering scores of members identified as leaders for influence, guidance, and overall leader were not significantly different from nonleaders. Those identified as showing the most concern for other group members were significantly stronger in social decentering than other members ($t = 1.68$, df = 65, $p = 0.04$). The skills needed to manage the task aspects of group activity appear unaffected by the level of social decentering held by task leaders or overall leaders. Apparently, the emotional component of social decentering comes more into play in helping strong social decentering leaders' effectively convey feelings of concern to other members.

While social decentering did not impact the emergence of leaders, it did impact the perceived quality of the interactions. Members reported greater team attraction in those groups with high social decentering task leaders (influence, guidance, and overall leader). Members perceived higher quality of discussion in groups with high social decentering influential leaders and guidance/direction leaders. No such impact on interactions was found for high social decentering/high concern leaders.

As in previous studies, quality of interaction was more related to effective task management than to social-emotional management.

Besides the impact of a leader's level of social decentering, the overall members' level of social decentering among the group members is also likely to impact their interaction and success. Groups where all the members are strong at developing an understanding of the other group members should produce a more positive climate than groups where members are less sensitive and adaptive to each other. In the above study, the average social decentering scores were calculated for each of the 16 groups and the groups divided into the eight highest and eight lowest social decentering groups. Members in groups with the higher social decentering averages reported stronger attraction ($t = 1.43$, df $= 70$, $p < 0.10$), higher quality discussion ($t = 2.84$, df $= 70$, $p < 0.01$), and more positive group behaviors ($t = 1.32$, df $= 70$, $p < 0.10$). While this study is limited in both the number of groups examined and in controlling the social decentering composition of the groups, the results support the overall contention that the social decentering levels of leaders and team members impact the member's perceptions and feelings about the group.

Another study that examined how member qualities affected the group process was conducted by Falk and Johnson (1977). They created 30 groups of students who engaged in the NASA decision-making task. Half the groups were given perspective-taking instructions that explained several steps to follow in order to better understand and convey understanding of the other member's viewpoints and information. The other half of the groups received egocentric instructions that emphasized pushing for their own solutions. Compared to the egocentric groups, the perspective-taking groups produced better and more creative solutions, utilized member resources better, felt more commitment and satisfaction with the solution, had less conflict over the ideas presented, and reported greater trust in one another.

The influence of social decentering on fostering positive climates should result in social decentering having a positive indirect effect on decision-making and outcomes as found in the Falk and Johnson study. Such influence is likely to be the strongest when the group task is one that requires the leader and group members to understand and appreciate each other's perspectives and goals. In many ways, groups are sets of interpersonal relationships and thus the factors that influence the success of interpersonal relationships also affects the success of groups and teams. Thus, the application of social decentering and RSSD in teams is an extension of what occurs in interpersonal relationships.

7.3 Organizations/Managers/Leaders

Interactions and relationships in organizations fall into the two broad categories – personal and professional – which are not mutually exclusive. On the personal level, members of organizations form friendships and romantic relationships and in general apply social decentering and RSSD in the manner discussed earlier about such relationships. Since personal relationships occur within an organizational context, decentering includes the added focus and sensitivity about how one's partners are affected by the organization itself. These relationships provide members with social support and organizational support, and help in managing organizational change (Beebe, Beebe, Redmond, 2017), which in turn, are enhanced by social decentering and RSSD.

Co-workers are in a position to more readily relate to and understand the impact of common organizational problems and issues on each other (e.g., a difficult boss, changes in company policy, or issues of scheduling or pay). Co-workers are often in a better position to socially decenter with other co-workers than their friends and romantic partners who work elsewhere. The commonality of their experiences makes the use of self method of social decentering a fairly effective option as co-workers commiserate or celebrate organizational events that have a similar impact on both.

Parker, Atkins, and Axtell (2008) broadly defined perspective-taking as both an affective and cognitive process of understanding others as they examined its application to organizations. They noted that "Given its effect on communication and other fundamental interpersonal processes, perspective-taking is likely to enhance the performance of all roles within organizations that have a strong interpersonal requirement" (p. 159). Parker et al.'s review of perspective-taking research identified such benefits in organizations as messages framed for others to more easily understand, fostering self-disclosure by others, improved interpersonal problem-solving, greater trust, and less interpersonal aggression.

The professional relationships in organizations are formal relationships defined by the positions that individuals hold, most notably, those of supervisor and subordinate. Each position usually includes a set of expectations to whom and how individuals communicate and behave toward each other. For example, communication from managers and supervisors to subordinates usually revolves around providing instructions, rationales, policies, appraisals, and information to help develop and fulfill the organization's mission/vision (Beebe, Beebe, & Redmond, 2017). Formal organizational relationships are often grounded in who has power or decision-making responsibility over other employees. Even among peers, communication and responsibilities are tied to seniority and status. Power can have a negative effect on people's enactment of social decentering and RSSD by increasing egocentrism and self-interest.

The structure that dictates the formal communication within organizations falls into specific directional categories: downward – superior to subordinate; upward – subordinate to superior; horizontal – peer to peer; and outward – internal to external (customers/suppliers). For each of these, social decentering and RSSD can enhance both the personal and professional interactions. On the other hand, the nature of organizations and their culture might inhibit the development and/or application of social decentering and RSSD. The managerial culture of an organization might discourage managers from seeking to understand subordinates' personal problems and feelings.

Within downward communication, social decentering and RSSD center primarily on managers' performance of their responsibilities with their subordinates. For leaders, social decentering and RSSD can be significant tools that allow them to emerge as leaders and foster followership. The terms, managers and leaders, are sometimes treated as interchangeable. But in this discussion, I will treat these as two separate roles. You can have managers who are not leaders and leaders who are not managers. Managers are assigned to play a particular role and perform particular tasks and whom subordinates follow because the manager controls resources (e.g., pay and work schedule) wanted by the subordinates. Leaders are people to whom others turn for guidance and direction and who inspire others to follow them. Ideally, managers are also leaders, while leaders often emerge among nonmanagers.

Managers are given position power that allows them to influence and direct others. Having power provides both assets and liabilities. Research suggests that power tends to undermine perspective-taking and empathy. Within organizations, this means that the more power individuals have the less likely they will be to engage in social decentering. Robert Sutton (2009) wrote in the *Harvard Business Review* that "people who gain authority over others tend to become more self-centered and less mindful of what others need, do, and say" and that "bosses tend to oblivious to their followers' perspectives" (p. 44). Similarly, Galinsky, Jordan, and Sivanathan (2008) observed that "The powerful appear to be particularly poor perspective-takers. Indeed, power appears to reduce social attentiveness, placing a blind spot on considering the unique vantage point of others" (pp. 289–290). Galinksky et al. add that powerful people fail to recognize that others don't share their privileged perspectives and that they are less perceptive of and influenced by others' emotions. Managers appear susceptible to these limitations in contrast to the impact on leaders. Galinksky et al. contend that power and leadership are separate constructs and that effective leaders are "able to harness the positive psychological effects of power while mitigating the negative ones" (p. 283). Thus, leaders are distinguished from managers in that, despite their power, they continue to engage in social decentering toward those around them. To maintain social decentering, leaders and managers need to offset the negative influence of power.

The impact of power can apparently be mitigated through the use of perspective-taking. Galinsky, Magee, Rus, Rothman, and Todd (2014) conducted three studies in which they primed participants to take another's perspective. In one study that involved solving a murder mystery, pairs of students were randomly assigned to be the subordinate or the boss. The boss was described as directing, evaluating, and rewarding the subordinate. Each partner received shared clues and one received several more unique clues, including key information needed to solve the mystery. Primed participants were instructed to perspective-take by considering their partner's perspective. Nonprimed participants were instructed to consider a time where they successfully took another person's perspective. Pairs were given 10 minutes to solve the mystery. Bosses primed to perspective-take discussed their unique clues more with their subordinates than did nonprimed bosses. Subordinates discussed more of their unique clues to their bosses who had been primed to perspective-take more than subordinates with nonprimed bosses. No effects were found in discussing clues by subordinates who were primed to perspective-take and those who weren't. Similarly, pairs with primed bosses picked the correct suspect 63% more often than the pairs with nonprimed bosses. The perspective-taking of the subordinate had no such effect on accuracy. These differences between the boss and subordinate supported the claim that perspective-taking mitigated the tendency of those in power to be egocentric and controlling.

Galinsky et al.'s study should not be taken to mean that everyone who is primed can engage in perspective-taking. Individuals vary in their perspective-taking and social decentering abilities, and priming is unlikely to radically improve a person's ability. Priming might act as a trigger that reminds and motivates those with perspective-taking or social decentering ability to tap those resources. The average of primed skilled and unskilled participants is likely to produce greater positive impact over a nonprimed group but not all of the primed participants necessarily engaged in perspective-taking. Two factors appear to affect the engagement in other-centeredness – priming and power. Both factors appear to affect the motivation needed to activate perspective-taking or social decentering.

Power also seems to affect motivation of those low in power who might feel it is not worth their time and energy to engage in social decentering. Engaging in social decentering might even lead to the decision not to act. For example, social decentering subordinates' analysis of their bosses could lead to a decision not to share certain information because they know the boss will disregard it (this construct is often reflected in the *Dilbert* cartoon). Power can thus inhibit the open flow of information from subordinates to managers. Milliken, Morrison, and Hewlin (2003) found that being silent was a common experience for 85% of the employees they interviewed; primarily, because they felt the managers did not want to hear about problems or that the managers would react negatively. In other words, the social decentering ability of subordinates led to conclusions about negative managerial response that rested in the power the manager possessed. To offset this, managers need to foster relationships that minimize the negative impact of their position power, demonstrate their openness to input from subordinates, and develop and engage in social decentering.

Upward communication involves efforts by subordinates to interact and influence their managers. Despite the negative impact of power, subordinates are likely to be motivated to socially decenter with their managers when they have strong personal reasons for doing so. Seeking approval for a project, asking for a pay raise, or requesting time off might motivate subordinates to use their understanding of their managers to develop the most effective and appropriate compliance-gaining strategy. Employees who know their managers well are in a better position to develop and apply social decentering than newer employees or employees who have not garnered sufficient information about their managers. Such information is accrued by personal interaction and observation of the managers as well as from co-workers. New employees often turn to current employees to find out what the manager is like.

Gregory, Moates, and Gregory (2011) examined the relationship between managers' level of dyad-specific perspective-taking and the transformational and transactional styles of leaders. Dyad-specific perspective-taking is like RSSD, in that the focus is on how well managers feel they know a particular employee. RSSD's balance between the cognitive and emotional sensitivity makes it a broader measure of orientation than the dyad-specific perspective-taking measure created by Gregory et al. Two qualities of a transformational leader that seem most strongly related to other-orientation are inspirational motivation (accurately communicating a vision to followers) and individualized consideration (concern with followers' developmental needs and willingness to provide support toward the followers' goals) (Gregory et al., 2011). Perspective-taking and social decentering provide a foundation for managers to develop strategies to inspire and effectively adapt to subordinates' professional and personal needs and goals. Accomplishing these contributes to the perception of the manager as a transformational leader. Gregory et al. had 23 supervisors rate their dyad-specific perspective-taking with up to five subordinates and had the 83 subordinates rate the supervisors' leadership. They found that managers' dyad-specific perspective-taking positively influenced the subordinates' ratings of their bosses' transformative leadership but not for transactional leadership. The researchers found variation in subordinates' ratings of the same manager which meant managers developed dyad-specific ratings with some subordinates and not with others. Variations in the manager's use of dyad-specific perspective-taking suggests dyad perspective-taking is not the same as the trait behavior associated with general perspective-taking. This is congruent with the proposition that individuals who are not necessarily strong in general social decentering can nonetheless develop RSSD. Managers' knowledge and understanding of their subordinates varies and thus their development of RSSD varies. As a result, managers are more adept at adapting to some employees than to others which creates variation among the subordinates' perceptions of their managers' leadership style. Perhaps your perception of a given manager has differed from your co-workers' perceptions – where you have felt inspired and supported and your colleagues did not (or vice versa). Managers with strong RSSD are aware of the thoughts and feelings of a given employee and are able to develop an effective strategie tailored to inspire and motivate that subordinate.

Leader-member exchange (LMX) theory centers on explaining how supervisor-subordinate relationships vary in type and quality. High-quality relationships are characterized by mutual trust, respect, and support while low-quality relationships stay within assigned roles and task responsibilities (Beebe, Beebe, Redmond, 2017). Those in high-quality relationships are found to be more satisfied, more committed, and more productive. But research by Fix and Sias (2006) indicates that subordinates' perception of supervisors' person-centeredness apparently mediates the effect of LMX. Person-centeredness can be thought of as the degree to which one's communication reflects adaptation to another, as such, it represents the output of the social decentering process. Fix and Sias had employees write out what they felt their supervisor would say to them if their unit was restructured and their job redesigned. Participant responses were coded for the degree to which they reflected person-centeredness on the part of their supervisor. Perception of supervisor person-centeredness positively impacted the perception of the quality of the leader-member relationship and was more strongly related to job satisfaction than LMX. Fix and Sias concluded that person-centeredness has benefits both for the employees (satisfaction, commitment, and autonomy) and for the supervisors (lower turnover and higher productivity). Supervisors who are strong social decenterers and those who have developed RSSD with a subordinate are in a position to produce person-centered messages that result in stronger LMX relationships and thus acquire its accompanying benefits.

Besides improving the relationships, the ability of managers and leaders to engage in social decentering and RSSD should be an asset to their ability to manage subordinates. Understanding the dispositions of employees provides a foundation for developing and applying effective management strategies. After reviewing extant research, Kellett et al. (2002) concluded that empathy provides leaders with knowledge and understanding that enables "leaders to influence follower's emotions and attitudes in support of corporate goals and objectives [...]" (p. 528). Remember, however, that there is one set of skills for understanding and analyzing strategies and another set of skills to enact strategies. Ku, Wang, and Galinsky (2015) thoroughly reviewed perspective-taking research in developing a model of perspective-taking in organizations. The model identifies the numerous benefits of perspective-taking by managers and leaders such as increasing liking, reducing stereotyping, improving distributive and integrative negotiations, and increased helping behavior. Parker et al. (2008) suggest that organizations interested in reducing stereotyping among all employees would benefit from enhancing employee perspective-taking rather than their efforts to suppress stereotyping.

Ku et al.'s (2015) model also identified factors that can lead to unintended negative consequences of managers and leaders use of perspective-taking; for example, giving preferential treatment, making negative inferences (among managers with low self-esteem), developing a less positive view of stereotypically positive targets, and engaging in egotistical and unethical behaviors when the target is perceived as competitive. Their identification of negative consequences of perspective-taking coincides with my observation that being other-centered and engaging in social decentering can intentionally be used not just to benefit others, but also for personal and selfish gains with possible negative consequences for others. Parker et al. (2008) recognized that perspective-taking could be used for personal gain to the detriment of others such as sales staff getting buyers to purchase things they don't need or managers manipulating subordinates.

Another negative repercussion of social decentering and RSSD is leading managers and leaders to make decisions that are detrimental to the organization. Social decentering and particularly RSSD can lead managers to not only empathize but also to sympathize with subordinates' personal life challenges. Knowledge of a subordinate's problems might result in a decision that supports the subordinate while undermining the goals and productivity of the organization. For example, letting an employee continue to arrive late to work because of problems at home reduces productivity, and the special treatment might lower the morale of other employees. Payne and Cooper (2001) observed that acting "negatively toward an employee, even when justified, requires that supervisors set aside or distance themselves emotionally from the tendency to empathize" (p. 73). They point out that some people are unable to detach themselves from empathizing and thus represent a person-job misfit. Indeed, constantly having to make dispassionate decisions with subordinates with whom a manager has developed strong RSSD can create stress and even burnout. Making decisions that favor the organization over the individual becomes another challenge created by social decentering. Decisions favoring the organization might reflect the path most likely taken by a manager while standing behind decisions favoring the individual is the path taken by a democratic leader.

Ku et al. (2015) identified factors that are likely to elicit the more selfish application of perspective-taking, including low moral concern and strong drive for personal success. Strong social decentering managers/leaders with low moral concern and strong personal success drive might be more inclined than others to utilize their understanding of others to develop and apply strategies for personal gain, sometimes at the expense of others. Because I recognized these dangers, over my years of teaching, I explained the power and influence that students could gain by becoming effective in social decentering, but I also stressed the need to be ethical in its use – not using it to exploit others.

The popular people styles inventory (Bolton & Bolton, 2009) classifies workers according to four styles: analytical, driver, expressive, and amiable. In examining the role of people styles in the workplace, Bolton and Bolton see empathy as a key quality associated with the amiable style. Amiables are people-oriented, friendly, and personal. Bolton and Bolton explain that in applying empathy, amiables are:

> [...] concerned about what other people think and want. They're often more interested in hearing your concerns than in expressing their own. Amiables are especially sensitive to other people's feelings. They're more likely than people of other styles to be able to vicariously put themselves in another person's shoes. (pp. 54–55)

Interestingly, no real connection has been made between perspective-taking and the four styles. But one of the major themes of Bolton and Bolton's book is for people to recognize the styles of their co-workers and adapt to them. They provide advice for people in each style about how to adapt to other styles. In other words, they are promoting perspective-taking and social decentering as critical skills for working with others. For example, amiables are advised to "be more task oriented," "de-emphasize feelings," "be systematic," and to "be well organized, detailed, and factual" (pp. 156–158). They are suggesting that amiables turn down their empathy and adapt a more analytic style. Inherent in social decentering is the ability to reach such conclusions about adapting your style to others in the workplace. Use of self gives insight of how your style affects your responses and then to recognize the different styles and responses of others, thus providing a foundation for strategic adaptation. Understanding the effects of co-workers' styles can help in managing a variety of organizational interactions such as negotiation.

Negotiation is one form of organizational behavior that seems particularly influenced by participants' levels of empathy and perspective-taking but in different ways. Perspective-takers are seen gaining an edge on their partners by providing insight into the other party, thus improving the appeal of their arguments and offers (Ku et al., 2015). In addition, when perspective-taking is used to determine the lower bounds of acceptability to the other party it can offset the anchor effect and distributive advantage the other party gains in making the first offer (Galinksy & Mussweiler, 2001). On the other hand, the emotional reactions evoked through empathy, such as sympathy, are seen as diminishing the negotiator's position (Ku et al., 2015). Another set of studies found that negotiations that involved a perspective-taker resulted in greater success than those involving empathy (the study actually measured empathic concern using the Davis scale) (Galinsky, Maddux, Gilin, & White, 2008). Galinsky et al. concluded that "understanding the interest and motives of opponents in competitive decision-making interactions appears more valuable than connecting with them emotionally" (p. 383). But, in one of their studies, sellers were most satisfied when they dealt with an empathic buyer, leading the researchers to suggest that empathy could be helpful in building interpersonal capital that would benefit future negotiations. In addition, empathy was seen as being valuable in certain types of negotiation, such as those that are emotionally charged.

Mnookin, Peppet, and Tulumello (1996, 2000) studied empathy's impact on negotiation as it related to assertiveness. Empathy and assertiveness are often viewed as competing approaches to negotiation. For example, highly assertive negotiators would use competitive styles while highly empathic negotiators would be accommodative (Mnookin et al., 1996, 2000). Mnookin et al. argued that the strongest negotiators are strong in both empathy and assertiveness. Such a combination involves a negotiator engaging in listening and demonstrating a nonjudgmental understanding of the other's needs, interests, and views without a statement of agreement but with an expectation for reciprocation from the other when the negotiator asserts her or his own needs, interests, and views. Social decentering allows a negotiator to appreciate the needs, interests, and emotions of the other party while analyzing the appropriateness and effectiveness of various strategies. A strong application of social decentering helps negotiators separate their own thoughts and feelings (use of self) from those of the other party (use of specific-other or RSSD). Such awareness helps in selecting strategies that reflect an understanding and appreciation of the other negotiator's stand. Such awareness also involves recognizing how one's own level of unrelenting assertiveness is counterproductive to negotiation. And, as Mnookin et al. (2000)

contend about empathy and assertiveness, social decentering enhances negotiation when both parties skillfully engage in it.

External communication in organizations deals with employees' interactions with customers and clients. Empathy is seen as having a positive influence on customers. But the studies tend to focus on customer perception of empathy without regard for whether the employee is actually empathic. In other words, customers feel happier when they perceive positive, confirming behaviors from people like the sales staff or company representatives. For example, Weißhaar and Huber (2016) operationalized empathy as a multidimensional construct and had 215 customers of a German consulting firm complete questionnaires assessing the perception of salespeople's perspective-taking and emotional concern. Perception of perspective-taking had a strong positive relationship to customers' trust and commitment to the salesperson, and to a lesser degree, the perception of emotional concern. One study that directly assessed employees' empathy was conducted by Wieseke, Geigenmüller, and Kraus (2012). Not only did they assess employee empathy, they also assessed customers' empathy. Agents from 93 German travel agencies and their customers completed a multidimensional measure of their empathy that included items regarding perspective-taking, empathic concern, and emotional contagion (feeling the same feelings as the other). Employees' empathy positively related to customers' reported satisfaction and loyalty. Employee empathy had an even stronger impact on customer satisfaction when customers themselves were higher in empathy. Interestingly, customers' emotional empathy sustained their loyalty even when satisfaction fell. The authors argue that the more empathic customers appear to be more sensitive to frontline employees' emotions, and thus more inclined to forgive dissatisfying service encounters. Wieseke et al. suggested that employers should "hire service employees capable of sensing customer expectations" as well as "offering opportunities for frontline employees to learn and develop their abilities to sense customer thoughts and feelings" (p. 326).

But there is a toll taken on frontline employees for being other-centered. Varca (2009) found that the more service personnel at a call center engaged in emotional empathy with callers, the more they experienced stress and role conflict. The conflict was caused by their effort to form an emotional attachment with the customer while at the same time having little authority to meet the customer's demands, leading to such service personnel responses as, "I feel as frustrated as you do, but there isn't anything I can do about it." Such a situation provides one explanation for high employee turnover at call centers and why the frontline employees you reach at a call center might seem detached – it's their way of reducing role conflict. Varca suggested that call centers that want their employees to be other-centered need flexible policies that include giving more authority to the frontline employees.

Despite creating possible role conflicts, service companies would do well to seek employees with strong affective and cognitive social decentering skills. Social decentering training could include an awareness of their use of generalized-other in understanding and responding to customers and the need to develop more RSSD with ongoing customers and clients. Such skill development is inherent in sales approaches that emphasize an other-orientation, such as personal selling, relationship selling, and adaptive selling. Sales performance, loyalty, and satisfaction benefits from a sales staff who are able to gain enough information about customers to effectively apply social decentering in the development of sales strategies.

Social decentering and RSSD can take their toll on managers who become burned out from engaging in a significant amount of emotional work with subordinates. As discussed earlier, emotional work is inherent in some professions such as counselors, social workers, and nurses. But such burnout can also happen wherever a close relationship exists between an employee and a customer or client such as financial advisors (Miller & Koesten, 2008) and real estate agents (Snyder, Claffey, & Cistulli, 2011). Actually, any manager whose role involves significant interpersonal contact with subordinates can experience burnout (Cordes & Daugherty, 1993). Managers with strong social decentering and RSSD are susceptible to emotional exhaustion and depersonalization that result from frequent intense discussions with subordinates about the subordinates' personal difficulties. The impact would be most likely to occur in situations in which managers experience the emotional burdens of multiple subordinates over extended periods of time. Miller and Koesten (2008) noted that their sample of financial planners managed emotional attachment by being able to "feel with" their clients, while also "feeling for," and thus create "detached concern." In other words, being able to engage in social decentering and RSSD but also being able to disengage, perhaps moving from affective responses of empathy to more cognitive response of analysis and perspective-taking.

A subtle but important feature of Wieseke et al.'s (2012) study was the inclusion of the customers' level of other-orientation. The results of my studies reported in the relationship and marriage chapters confirmed the transactional nature of social decentering in relationships such that both parties affect and are affected by each other's social decentering and RSSD. Both partners' levels of social decentering and RSSD interact with the other, whether the relationship is between employees and customers, managers and subordinates, or co-workers. A subordinate who is strong in social decentering interacting with a manager who is strong in social decentering will produce more positive outcomes than a subordinate and manager who don't understand or appreciate each other's dispositions.

Parker et al. (2008) provide an extended examination of the factors that inhibit perspective-taking in organizations and how perspective-taking can be enhanced. As with social decentering, one of the most critical factors identified was the need to be motivated to perspective-take or at least to try:

> A person who is highly motivated to understand where another is coming from will try harder, will engage in a wider range of cognitive, emotional, behavioral strategies, and will persist longer in order to learn the perspective of another. (p. 171)

Parker et al. point out that in some instances professional roles don't seem to have perspective-taking as necessary or valued. Organizations would do well to expand the expectations for all personnel to more consciously engage in social decentering – take time to think about the dispositions of co-workers, managers, subordinates, customers, clients, and suppliers. Motivation stems partially from the belief that there is value in understanding others. The degree to which another person in the organization is important, either on a personal level (liking and friendship) or professional level (power and ability to reward), affects the degree to which people are motivated to engage in social decentering with co-workers. Organizations that foster a culture of considering other's dispositions and adapting accordingly are likely to be more productive and enhance satisfaction with the work environment thus reducing stress and turnover.

7.4 Intercultural Interactions

Effectively engaging in social decentering is easiest when the two interacting individuals are very similar and most difficult when the two individuals are very different. When someone is different, the use of self is less relevant (though not altogether) and the use of generalized-others can become more valuable particularly if people have built meaningful group schemas that apply to the other person. Everyone is different from everyone else to some degree but there are degrees of difference. At one end are differences in sex and age, and at the other end are differences in religion, ethnicity, and culture. Each difference limits the ability to effectively socially decenter until we acquire sufficient information. The ability to socially decenter will be minimally affected by the age difference of a 40-year-old person talking to a 46-year-old person. But a 20-year-old man from Iowa talking to an 80-year-old woman from Malaysia would only be able to socially decenter in very broad terms – a young man to an older woman. The first step in socially decentering with diverse others is mindfulness of the differences. The second step is considering the effect those differences have on our perceptions and behaviors toward the other person. We need to realize when our perception is distorted or biased and thus undermining our ability to effectively engage in social decentering. The third step is to begin applying social decentering toward understanding how the dispositions of the other person are different from our own. We quickly recognize when someone is a different sex than us, but do we really think about how that other person's life is affected because of their sex. Do men understand the demeaning way women are often treated by men and how that affects the women? Is a woman, who believes all men are misogynistic, able to set that view aside in her initial interaction with a man? Regardless of the level of difference, social decentering is an important tool to use in appreciating, learning, understanding, and adapting to those differences. Social decentering is only one skill that individuals need when engage in intercultural interactions. Scholars have identified various sets of skills needed to successfully manage intercultural interactions, that are often labeled intercultural competence or intercultural communication competence. One of the more consistently identified skills that contributes to intercultural competence is empathy (see review by Matveev, 2017). But cultural differences and a lack of information often make it difficult to empathize.

Intercultural interactions are among our most challenging interactions due to potential differences in language, nonverbal cues, values, beliefs, attitudes, customs, and world views. In intracultural conversations there is a rather large level of intrinsically shared information that makes the interaction much more manageable. But in intercultural conversations there can be a significant amount that is unknown about the other which hampers the interaction and social decentering.

Social decentering in initial intercultural interactions generally relies heavily on the use of generalized-others method of analysis. We draw upon whatever preexisting classifications and stereotypes we have of people based on country of origin. For some people only one category might be used – foreigners. In other words, these people categorize anyone not from their country as alien or foreign. Such an encompassing category is an ineffective basis for social decentering since it produces little understanding or ability to predict. Some people have a multitude of categories, even to the point of having several categories in which to place people from the same country. For example, rather than just a category of Iraqi, an individual might instead categorize Iraqis as Sunni, Shite, and non-Muslim with an appreciation for the beliefs and values of each group. But as discussed in Chapter 1, having many categories can be unwieldy and defeat the purpose of creating easily accessible groupings of information. Our cultural categories are likely to be limited to those cultures with which we have the most experience or exposure.

The cultural categories we create and access in the use of generalized-other analysis provide initial information that we can use to understand and predict someone we have just meet from a given culture. Gudykunst (1995) observed that:

> The categories in which we place strangers also provide us with implicit predictions of their behaviors. When we categorize strangers, our stereotypes of the groups in which we categorize them are activated. Our stereotypes provide predictions of strangers' behavior and our interactions will appear to have rhythm if strangers conform to our stereotypes. (p. 22)

For Gudykunst, use of generalized-other allows us to coordinate our initial conversation to the degree that our expectations align with the actual behavior of the other person. But no one totally fits a stereotype, so it becomes important to recognize and adapt to differences between categorical expectations and the observed behaviors of the other person. Gudykunst (1993) identified the need to be mindful as an important element toward intercultural communication effectiveness. Three factors identified by Langer (1989) that contribute to mindfulness were incorporated into Gudykunst's (1998) description of a plan for intercultural adjustment training. These factors are imbedded in successful intercultural social decentering. The first factor is a need to create new categories; categories that are more specific to each culture rather than relying on broad categories. The second factor is openness to new information, that is used in creating and refining the new categories. Inherent in this factor is a motivation to learn, as well as awareness and sensitivity to cultural differences. The third factor is recognition that there is more than one perspective, which Langer observed, gives more choices for responding. Essentially, Langer reminds us that the way we see the world is not the same as the way other people see the world and that we need to be sensitive to that in how we think, what we say, and what we do. Such awareness of other perspectives and consideration of multiple responses are intrinsic elements of the social decentering process. Social decentering is again the tool that, in concert with mindfulness, allows us to recognize different perspectives, be open to information we learn about others' perceptions, and create new categories that facilitate successful intercultural interactions. Over time, we gain idiosyncratic information about the other that allows us to develop RSSD that incorporates relevant cultural knowledge and cultural nuances.

The social decentering scale was designed to assess individuals' tendencies to form and use categories as part of the use of generalized-others analysis. Four of the 12 items that constitute the use of generalized-other subscale specifically assess people's intercultural sensitivity:

1. *I have wondered what people in some foreign countries think about various world problems.*
2. *I take into consideration both the situation and a person's cultural and ethnic background when I'm trying to understand the behavior of someone I don't know very well.*
3. *I can imagine how some of my attitudes, beliefs, and values might be different than they are if I had been raised in a different country's culture.*
4. *I know some of the values, attitudes, and thoughts associated with different cultural and ethnic groups.*

Interacting with those who are different from us creates uncertainty, stress, and anxiety. Gudykunst and Hammer (1988) extended uncertainty reduction theory to initial intergroup/intercultural interactions and added anxiety as a factor affecting people's thoughts and behaviors. Gudykunst (1988) recognized that people feel anxious about interacting with others whose culture differs from their own. Gudykunst's (1993, 1995, 2005) theory sought to identify the aspects of intercultural interactions that affect and are affected by uncertainty and anxiety. The aspects of his model most related to social decentering include ability to empathize, ability to adapt communication, knowledge of similarities and differences, and the ability to create new categories into which we place groups of people. Possessing such attributes reduces uncertainty and anxiety which in turn results in more effective intercultural communication.

On the other hand, Gudykunst (1993) claimed that when we exceed our maximum threshold for uncertainty or anxiety, we are unable to communicate effectively. The combination of anxiety and ineffective communication results in an inability to accurately interpret or predict the other person through social decentering. Use of self proves ineffective because of the significant differences between decenterers and their intercultural partners. The maximum threshold reflects a circumstance in which we have no specific-others or generalized-others to provide a foundation for interpreting or predicting.

Social decentering heightens our awareness that our interactions with someone from another culture differs from what we are used to and from what we expect. Such awareness results in increased stress and anxiety because of an inability to effectively understand and predict the behavior of the other person. Thus, social decentering contributes to the stress experienced by sojourners. On the other hand, travelers low in social decentering are likely to be somewhat oblivious to the cultural differences and therefore inclined to feel less stress. In a study of 644 international students attending Iowa State University conducted by myself and my colleague, Judith Bunyi (Redmond & Bunyi, 1993), the effect of social decentering was confirmed by a positive correlation between the students' level of social decentering and their reported stress. Respondents were consolidated by countries and regions to produce 14 similar size samples. Analysis of variance of the 14 samples indicated no significant differences in their average social decentering scores. But significant differences were found among the countries/regions in students' ability to adapt, socially integrate, and communicate effectively. One possible explanation for the stress can be found by examining the level of difference between countries of origin and the host country. The similarity of social decentering scores among international students indicates that social decentering is skill that occurs across cultures unlike more culture-dependent skills such as communicating effectively. Some skills like language acquisition and knowledge of the host culture limit intercultural competence to interactions within specific cultures. On the other hand, social decentering is a transcultural quality in which people recognize similarities and differences in each culture they encounter and have the capabilities to observe, learn, analyze, and understand the people with whom they interact in each culture.

Geert Hofstede (1980, 1983, 1997, 2001) identified four central values that he found varied among cultures: power distance, uncertainty avoidance, individualism/collectivism, and masculinity/femininity. In a follow-up analysis of the data from the previous study, I conducted regression analyses for students whose cultural values were closest to the US values; and an analysis for students whose values were furthest away (Redmond, 2000b). Social decentering significantly contributed to the prediction of greater stress associated with differences and similarities for each of the four cultural values for both those close and far away in value. The following beta weights for social decentering for students coming from cultures most similar to the United States are listed in order of value: 0.31 – uncertainty avoidance, 0.23 –masculine/

feminine, 0.15 – power, and 0.14 – individualism/collectivism. Beta weights for students least similar to the United States were, in order of value: 0.30 – individualism/collectivism, 0.26 – power, 0.22 – masculinity/femininity, and 0.12 – uncertainty avoidance. For students coming from cultures high in uncertainty avoidance similar to the United States, the issue of similarity is probably less consequential than the value itself. Possessing the cultural value of intolerance for ambiguity is likely to produce stress regardless of the host country's value. Social decentering is likely to exacerbate the stress for those with intolerance for ambiguity by increasing the respondents' awareness of that ambiguity. Sojourners can expect that certain cultural differences between themselves and theirs host countries along with their engagement in social decentering will compound their initial stress.

Social decentering was not found to directly relate to the ability to cope with stress as they related to differences in the four values. One reason for this might be that social decentering did not relate to the countries of origin and thus did not differ relative to other communication competence differences between the native culture and the United States, as for example, language did. Communication effectiveness, ability to adapt, and the ability to integrate into the social network of the United States positively contributed to a student's ability to cope with stress. Social decentering contributes to these three intercultural communication competencies and thus has an indirect impact on handling stress. For example, social decentering provides an understanding of host culture members that enhances the ability to adapt. Social decentering also helps sojourners predict a host member's reactions to various behaviors and thus improve strategic choices. For example, through social decentering, a male student from Spain might forego his cultural norm of kissing females on the cheeks as a greeting and instead offer to shake hands when meeting a female student from the United States, predicting that she would back away if he tried to kiss her on the cheeks. Such awareness improves the likelihood of successfully integrating into the host culture's social network.

Another term introduced to reflect intercultural other-orientation is cultural empathy, which Kim (1988) conceptualizes as the ability to be flexible in ambiguous and unfamiliar situations. Two dimensions of cultural empathy that were identified by Cui and Van Den Berg (1991) are empathizing with cultural norms and awareness of cultural differences. They found cultural empathy contributed to the intercultural effectiveness of US business people working in China. Unfortunately, the conceptualization and measurement of cultural empathy is inconsistent. For example, one measure of cultural empathy is the Multicultural Personality Questionnaire (Van der Zee & Van Oudenhoven, 2001), that appears to be a general measure of empathy that does not include cultural contexts. Part of its validation consisted of comparing the respondents' self-reports to reports about them from a partner, close friend, or family member. This measure has been used by other researchers as well (see review by Arasaratnam, 2014). The use of *cultural* to describe empathy is misleading and by default implies that there isn't anything unique about empathizing with people from the same or different cultures. In contrast, the measure of social decentering includes use of generalized-others analysis, that assesses individuals' ability to draw on their knowledge of other cultures in the process of understanding and predicting diverse others.

The term cultural empathy is also used to describe a special form of empathy utilized by counselors when dealing with clients from different cultures (Ridley & Lingle, 1996; Ridley & Udipi, 2002). Ridley and Lingle defined cultural empathy as "the learned ability of counselors to accurately gain an understanding of the self-experience of clients from other cultures" (p. 32) and to communicate that understanding with an attitude of concern. Several of the characteristics they associate with cultural empathy are also characteristic of social decentering, such as being multidimensional, being an interpersonal process, the similarity between counselors and clients helping to establish understanding, and the ability to learn the skill. The inclusion of communicating understanding as part of cultural empathy differentiates it from social decentering. As discussed earlier, social decentering and empathy are valuable tools for effective counseling. But contrary to Ridley and Lingle, I would argue that just as social decenterers might choose not to disclose their understanding or predictions, culturally empathic counselors might choose not to reveal their understanding or predictions when they think such revelation would undermine the relationship or therapy.

Ridley and Lingle (1996) identify counselors' tendency "to impose their cultural values onto their clients" (p. 38) as a significant problem in multicultural counseling. This problem is similar to relying on the use of self analysis for making sense of clients' cultural dispositions. Such an error comes from the incomplete application of social decentering. Use of self can be an effective tool in intercultural interactions by accentuating how the decenterer's thoughts and feelings differ from those of the targets, leading to a keener understanding and appreciation of other people's cultural experiences. But use of self without attending to how the self differs from others undermines intercultural communication. To effectively socially decenter in intercultural interactions, egocentrism (use of self while ignoring differences) and ethnocentrism (imposing our cultural values on others) must be avoided.

Building off Ridley and Lingle's notion of cultural empathy as it applies to counseling, Wang, Davidson, Yakushko, Savoy, Tan, and Bleier (2003) developed the concept and measure of ethnocultural empathy. Ethnocultural empathy is conceptualized as "empathy directed toward people from racial and ethnic cultural groups who are different from one's own ethnocultural group" (p. 221). The concept was initially operationalized as having three components, but four emerged from their data analysis: intellectual empathy (understanding racially or ethnically differences), empathic emotions (attention to and feel the other's emotional condition), communicative empathy (expressing empathic thoughts and feelings), and empathic awareness (social and media treatment of racial and ethnic groups). As operationalized, the scale appears to have limited application to interactions between people from different countries, since its focus is on intracultural interactions that cross race and ethnicity. Many of the scale items revolve around attitudes on racism, hate crimes, discrimination, etc. But such awareness is also pertinent to intercultural interactions, for which there is a need to be sensitive to cultural biases held against various ethnic groups within other cultures.

The ethnocultural empathy scale does highlight an important application of social decentering to interactions among diverse citizens in the same country who differ in terms of race and ethnicity, to which I would add, differ from each other in religion, sex, sexual orientation, mental and physical abilities, and even social economic status. Each of these reflect groups within a given culture for which there might exist biases, prejudice, discrimination, conflict, and social mores. The ethnocultural empathy scale brings attention to these intracultural contexts and defines ethnocultural empathic individuals as those who are aware of how their shared culture treats people differently depending upon group identification. The definition of social decentering ends with the phrase "within a given situation." Given situation is meant to reflect the specific circumstances that currently surround the person with whom we are socially decentering. But those circumstances go beyond what is occurring at a given moment and include the broader social-cultural context in which the other person lives. For social decentering to be effective, a white university student from London would need to consider the social climate and prejudices that a black student from Sweden has experienced. A consideration of the ethnocultural influences on each person is important if we are to truly understand their thoughts and share their feelings. In some ways, we create a category or stereotype of a particular group of people that is an amalgam of information about how members of that category are treated by the culture and society. As with any category, individual members of these ethnocultural groups do not all share the same experiences and for that reason, it is particularly important for individuals to listen and acquire information that allows them to develop and access the use of specific-other level of social decentering analysis and RSSD. In their discussion of cultural empathy in counseling, Ridley and Lingle (1996) emphasize the need for counselors to explore a particular client's cultural group experience, particularly in terms of how it deviates from the normative.

Stereotypes and perceptions of outgroup members (other cultures) are often tainted with bias and prejudice that can then undermine effective communication (Beebe, Beebe, & Redmond, 2017). While contact leads to learning about outgroup members which in turn can reduce prejudice, Pettigrew (2008) observed that "empathy and perspective-taking are far more important" (p. 190). He noted that contact facilitated empathy and perspective-taking with the outgroup. Empathy as an affective process was seen as having a stronger effect on reducing prejudice than did the cognitive process associated with perspective-taking. Pettigrew and Tropp (2008) conducted a meta-analysis of extant research on prejudice, empathy, and anxiety that indicated that: anxiety had a negative mediating effect between contact and prejudice; empathy had a positive effect; and empathy and anxiety were negatively related. These findings led them to postulate that "initial anxiety must first be reduced with intergroup contact before increased empathy, perspective-taking, and knowledge of the outgroup can effectively contribute to prejudice reduction" (p. 929).

As applied to social decentering this means that when people are anxious about interacting with someone from another culture that anxiety is going to inhibit their ability to socially decenter. Positive intergroup contact can reduce that anxiety (Pettigrew, Tropp, Wanger, & Chirst, 2011), which leads to increased information exchange and a reduction in the emotions that were blocking socially decentering.

Intercultural business interactions combine the impact of the organizational factors discussed earlier with issues of cultural differences. The earlier discussion of managers, employees, and organizations has a definitive western bent to it. While there is similarity in the roles and expectations of managers across cultures, there are also differences. For example, employers in France create very family-like relationships with employees, and subordinates in Saudi Arabia tend to avoid eye contact with superiors (Blacharski, 2008). Matveev and Nelson (2004) described the benefits of empathy in multicultural business teams:

> A culturally empathetic team member has the capacity to behave as though he or she understands the world as team members from other cultures do, has a spirit of inquiry about other cultures and the communication patterns in these cultures, an appreciation for a variety of working styles, and an ability to view the ways things are done in other cultures not as bad but simply as different. (p. 258)

The broad description of cultural empathy imbedded in the above list is a better description of what occurs through social decentering than empathy. Social decentering provides a foundation for understanding, requires motivation, involves examining and comparing general categories of people including cultures and working styles, and the ability to learn by recognizing similarities and differences in cultures between oneself and others.

Matveev and Nelson (2004) hypothesized that coming from a more collectivistic culture, Russian managers would have higher cultural empathy than American managers coming from an individualistic culture, but the results of their study found no significant difference. They argued that the American managers were driven to perform and achieve individual growth that motivated them to be culturally empathic. This means individuals are likely to engage in social decentering when their individual motivations exceed the cultural value of self-orientation. Social decentering is an effective tool for accomplishing personal goals, and in that way, being other-oriented allows individuals to accomplish self-goals, which means it is of value in both collectivistic and individualistic cultures, albeit, for different reasons.

7.5 Other Contexts

While the focus of this text has been on social decentering in interpersonal interactions, it can also be applied in less interactive contexts. For example, in writing this book I have tried to consider who will be reading it and what they might most want to know. I've also tried to consider how they will react to what I have written. I've relied upon my use of generalized-other in making that assessment as well as use of self. Use of self is sometimes problematic though because one's ego and face come into play. I often experience negative reactions to re-reading something that I wrote a year earlier when I now find that I originally failed to notice its errors and weaknesses.

Most media involves some degree of audience analysis, which is a type of other-orientation that involves considering the dispositions of some general audience rather than a particular individual. But in today's world of technology, more and more websites collect information about each user and then target ads and other information to that information; essentially, computers are being programmed to socially decenter, though inclusion of an emotional component is still a work in progress. I remember in the 1980s that there was a computer program that acted as a counselor. Essentially, the program simply sent back what the user typed and added a question mark or displayed a message "Tell me more," or "How do you feel about that?" Obviously, the computer had no understanding or empathy but used counseling catchphrases to get people to explore themselves. Rather than simply providing robotic responses, it is important to convey the depth of understanding that you developed when you considered the other person's dispositions and given situation.

Being audience-centered is a notion shared by public speakers, authors, producers, marketers, and entrepreneurs. Considering the dispositions of the targets can facilitate accomplishing one's goals with live or mediated audiences, readers, or consumers. The process of social decentering applies here because people collect and analyze information that allows them to evaluate and predict the effectiveness of the messages or products they create. Marketing surveys are attempts to collect information about a target audience to create messages that can be adapted to that audience and thus be most effective. You have probably watched a TV commercial that you thought was senseless and wondered why it was ever created. In those instances, the creators either failed to understand you and predict your reaction, or more likely, you were not their target audience. But if your friends agree with you, that the commercial was senseless, that still might not mean the commercial failed since you and your friends are similar and perhaps none of you are the target audience. For example, in the United States, TV shows and commercials target 18- to 34-year-old viewers the most, which means in the US, that if you and your friends are over 40, the ad probably wasn't aimed at you. Prandelli, Pasquini, and Verona (2016) found that having graduate management students consider the perspective of a potential user resulted in enhancing their creativity in considering and addressing the user's needs while applying their own expertise. The experimenters activated the students' social decentering efforts using the information provided about the user/consumer to evaluate and predict the user's preferences thus enhancing their entrepreneurial success.

Audience adaptation is often a core principle taught in public speaking textbooks. Its role was explained by my colleague, Denise Vrchota and myself (2007), "Adaptation involves using your understanding of the audience and the situation to select strategies tailored to the audience's needs and interests" (p. 11). Funny how this definition reflects my principles of social decentering, isn't it? Even the questions we suggest readers answer are similar to the questions asked when social decentering, for example, "If I were sitting in this audience, what would I want to hear?" (use of self), "How is this audience different from me?" (use of self and use of specific-other), and "What does *this* audience want?" Interactions with audiences are somewhat akin to intercultural encounters in that they vary from speaking with audiences about whom very little information is known, to speaking to audiences with whom the speaker has an ongoing relationship and in-depth information.

For authors, social decentering not only allows them to consider their audience, it serves as a method of creating and expanding characters. One piece of advice from children's literature editor Mary Kole (2012) to authors reflects the use of self as a way to write more effectively: "When you know the teen experience and can place yourself in your target readers' experience, you're that much more likely to write a book that resonates with them on a deeper, thematic level." Authors of young adult fiction draw from their memories of their own teenage experiences, listen in to conversations among teens while riding the bus, and interact with teenage relatives as a foundation for adapting their writing to their readers (*The Guardian*, 2015). Such practices reflect authors' efforts to gain information either from observation and memory, and by imagining life as a teenager, and then writing in a way that reflects that appreciation and understanding. Such authors utilize the use of self in both recalling and imagining their thoughts and feelings, extrapolate from their knowledge and experiences with specific teenagers (use of specific-others), and significantly employ use of generalized-others by creating categories of teenagers on which to build and develop characters. Strength in social decentering allows authors to create relatable and believable characters. Failure to effectively socially decenter has probably undermined the success of many an author.

Any communication that is directed to a specific person or target audience can be enhanced through the use of social decentering. Besides books, speeches, and advertising, social decentering plays a significant role in today's world of electronic communication. For example, knowledge of another person allows us to "encrypt" text messages with references, abbreviations, or idioms we know the other person will understand. A number of studies have examined the impact of social media on empathy but with mixed results. Concerns have been raised about the negative impact of the Internet on people's social skills with some studies finding a negative impact on face-to-face interactions and empathy among those spending considerable time online including social media and gaming. But a longitudinal study of 942 Dutch adolescents (10–14 years of age) found that the initial reports of social network use were positively related to higher cognitive and affective empathy a year later (Vossen & Valkenburg, 2016). The researchers concluded that frequent use of social media improved adolescents' "ability to share and understand the feelings of others over time" (p. 123) by providing them opportunities to practice.

Another survey with over 1,000 respondents between the ages of 18 and 30 asked about their "time behind the screen" use (TV, computer, and phone) and used the basic empathy scale to assess their cognitive empathy (essentially thoughts about other people's feelings) and affective empathy (feeling or not feeling what others feel) (Carrier, Spradlin, Bunce, & Rosen, 2015). Other assessments included virtual cognitive and affective empathy (the basic empathy scale revised to apply to an online context), and social support. No significant correlation was found between time online and either cognitive or affective empathy for men. For women, no significant relationship was found for time online and affective empathy, but a small negative relationship was found with cognitive empathy ($r = -0.09$). The kind of online activity appears to mediate the relationship between time online and empathy. Video gaming significantly reduced cognitive and affective empathy for women and cognitive empathy for men. Regression analysis indicated that the use of a computer for such activities as e-mailing and instant messaging lead to more face-to-face communication and that lead to improved affective and cognitive empathy. But such computer use did not directly affect empathy. The results of the study led the authors to speculate that social connections might result in more arranged face-to-face meetings or increased the chances of seeing the person off-line, which then increases the opportunities to hone empathy skills. Carrier et al. found that empathy significantly correlated with virtual empathy, but virtual empathy was not as strong. Cognitive empathy and affective empathy strongly related to social support ($r = 0.37$ and 0.24, respectively). Virtual cognitive empathy and affective empathy positively related to social support, but to a much smaller degree than general empathy ($r = 0.15$ and 0.10, respectively). The overall implication of Carrier et al.'s study is that people who are empathic maintain their empathy regardless of how much time they are online. While a high amount of video gaming was related to less empathy, those inclined to spend hours upon hours gaming are generally less empathic than the general population and their video gaming becomes a replacement for social engagement.

We can expect that the findings from Carrier et al.'s study applies equally well to social decentering. People who are strong in social decentering are likely to maintain that strength regardless of how much time they spend online. The relationship between social decentering and online activity is twofold: first, the degree to which individuals apply social decentering while online, and second, the degree to which online activity informs or influences social decentering. Imagine you are checking your Facebook page and see a post and picture from a close friend at a party looking sad and uncomfortable as several people crowd around trying to get in the picture. Because of your RSSD with your friend, you know that must have been an awkward moment since your friend dislikes being crowded and touched. So, you send your friend a personal message expressing your understanding and concern. In this instance, social decentering that exists outside the online universe is applied to understanding another's online communication. On the other hand, the photo could be an indication that your friend is trying to be more social and that might prompt you to confirm that with your friend. As a result, you add to your knowledge of your friend and thus improve future application of RSSD. This example illustrates how social decentering can be used in social media to both understand and predict the communication of others and as a source of information to help develop further social decentering.

Our online experiences fall into two broad categories: passive and interactive. Passive experiences are those where we simply observe or consume without any direct interaction with the source. Watching an online video reflects this passive experience and responding to text messages and posting likes or commenting on someone's Facebook post represent interactive experiences. Social decentering plays a different role in each. For the passive experience, social decentering is primarily activated to provide understanding. You might receive a text message from your boss and use social decentering in considering the meaning and intent without replying. When engaging interactively in social media, one of our prime concerns is the maintenance of our relationships. In these social-mediated instances, the application of social decentering is utilized as with any interpersonal relationship. Social-mediated experiences can also include reacting to strangers about whom we have limited information. We can engage in social decentering with these individuals, but are limited to what we observe, imagine, relate to, or use from our understanding of people in general.

Remember that the first thing that has to happen for social decentering to occur is for it to be triggered. Our detachment with people online is likely to reduce the likelihood of engaging in social decentering. If you have a lot of Facebook friends, you are likely to skim quickly through their posts and pictures with little in-depth analysis. A posting by a stranger is unlikely to stimulate social decentering if you perceive little consequence. The level of relational intimacy with the sender/poster, the relevance of what is sent/posted, and the importance you associate with a given online message are factors that mediate the decision to socially decenter. Once trigged, we attend to the information at hand, in memory, and imagined. A unique aspect of mediated communication is that we have records such as old text messages or Facebook posts that can be reviewed. For example, you could scan pictures on your friend's Facebook page for confirmation of your belief that your friend is uncomfortable in crowded social situations and thus feel more confident about your social decentering and RSSD. The use of any of the three social decentering methods for analyzing and adapting to another person in the social media network is dependent on how much information is available about the person and the person's situation. If we know a lot about the person we encounter on social media, then we are apt to apply use of specific-other or RSSD. If we only know a little about the person who texted or posted, we are likely to apply use of generalized-other to consider the thoughts and feelings associated with the message/post – what do most people mean by such a post? The more we know about the situation, the more effectively we can apply use of self for analysis. Reading a detailed story online about the police mistakenly raiding the wrong address and arresting the resident provides enough information for you to apply the use of self analysis as your recall any similar incident happening to you or imagining it happening to you and how you might react. Next comes your internal response, the thoughts, and feelings that are aroused as a result of what we observe on social media. In instances where we are simply a passive observer, the accuracy of our understanding and emotional responses is fairly unimportant. When we engage in interactive social media experiences, usually within the context of ongoing relationships, social decentering plays a more critical role in helping us consider the person and their situation as we develop our response. Another advantage of some mediated interactions is the ability to take time to consider the person and the situation before responding. I've had to remind myself over the years when I'm irritated by someone's email not to immediately send a response, but instead take time to consider how the other person will react to the various messages I might send. My response after waiting a day is almost always a lot more constructive. Which brings us to the last part of social decentering – to act. Sometimes, my analysis of the email and person who sent it results in a decision to do nothing. Of course, that makes it appear to outsiders that I did not engage in social decentering, but in reality, social decentering led me to conclude that taking no action was smart thing to do. As introduced in Chapter 1, social decentering is not a personality trait and not an unconscious reaction, but is social cognition. Such a distinction is not meant to diminish or deny the occurrence of truly empathic emotional responses or altruistic acts. It is meant to clearly identify the cognitive process presented in this book by which humans thoughtfully consider the thoughts, feelings, and dispositions of other people and in so doing successfully navigate their social worlds.

7.6 References

Altschuler, S. (2016). The art of medicine: The medical imagination. *The Lancet, 388*, 2230–2231.
Anderson, T., Ogles, B. M., Patterson, C. L., Lambert, M. J., & Vermeersch, D. A. (2009). Therapist effects: Facilitative skills as a predictor of therapist success. *Journal of Clinical Psychology, 65*, 755–768.
Arasaratnam, L. A. (2014). Ten years of research in intercultural communication competence (2003–2013): A retrospective. *Journal of Intercultural Communication, 35*, 5–5.
Barry, C. A., Bradley, C. P., Britten, N., Stevenson, F. A., & Barber, N. (2000). Patients' unvoiced agendas in general practice consultations: Qualitative study. *The BMJ, 320*, 1246–1250.
Beebe, S. A., Beebe, S. J., & Redmond, M. V. (2017). *Interpersonal communication: Relating to others (8th ed.)*. Boston, MA: Pearson.
Benjamin, A. (1969). *The helping interview*. Boston: Houghton Mifflin.
Blacharski, D. (2008). *The savvy business traveler's guide to customs and practices in other countries*. Oscala, FL: Atlantic Publishing Group.
Bolton, R., & Bolton, D. G. (2009). *People styles at work – and beyond (2nd ed.)*. New York: American Management Association.
Borrill, C. S., & West, M. A. (2005). The psychology of effective teamworking. In N. Gold (Ed.), *Teamwork: Multi-disciplinary perspectives* (pp. 136–160). New York: Palgrave Macmillan.
Bylund, C. L., & Makoul, G. (2005). Examining empathy in medical encounters: An observational study using the empathic communication coding system. *Health Communication, 18*, 123–140.
Carkhuff, R. R. (1969). *Helping and human relations, Vol. II*. New York: Holt, Rinehart, Winston.

Carrier, L. M., Spardlin, A., Bunce, J. P., & Rosen, L. D. (2015). Virtual empathy: Positive and negative impacts of going online upon empathy in young adults. *Computers in Human Behavior*, *52*, 39–48.

Cordes, C. L., & Dougherty, T. W. (1993). A review and an integration of research on job burnout. *The Academy of Management Review*, *18*, 621–656.

Cui, G., & Van Den Berg, S. (1991). Testing the construct validity of intercultural effectiveness. *International Journal of Intercultural Relations*, *15*, 227–241.

Derksen, F., Bensing, J., & Lagro-Janssen, A. (2013). Effectiveness of empathy in general practice: A systematic review. *British Journal of General Practice*, On-line: http://bjgp.org/content/63/606/e76.short.

Duarte, J., Pinto-Gouveia, J., & Cruz, B. (2016). Relationships between nurses' empathy, self-compassion and dimensions of professional quality of life: A cross-sectional study. *International Journal of Nursing Studies*, *60*, 1–11.

Dugan, J. P., Bohle, C. W., Woelker, L. R., & Cooney, M. A. (2014). The role of social perspective-taking in developing students' leadership capacities. *Journal of Student Affairs Research and Practice*, *51*, 1–15.

Elliott, R., Bohart, A. C., Watson, J. C., & Greenberg, L. S. (2011). Empathy. *Psychotherapy*, *48*, 43–49.

Falk, D. R., & Johnson, D. W. (1977). The effects of perspective-taking and egocentrism on problem solving in heterogeneous and homogeneous groups. *Journal of Social Psychology*, *102*, 63–72.

Fix, B., & Sias, P. M. (2006). Person-centered communication, leader-member exchange, and employee job satisfaction. *Communication Research Reports*, *23*, 35–44.

Galinksy, A. D., Jordon, J., & Sivanathan, N. (2008). Harnessing power to capture leadership. In C. L. Hoyt, G. R. Goethals, & D. R. Forsyth (Eds.) *Leadership at the crossroads* (pp. 283–299), Westport, CT: Praeger.

Galinsky, A. D., Maddux, W. W., Gilin, D., & White, J. B. (2008). Why it pays to get inside the head of your opponent. *Psychological Science*, *19*, 378–384.

Galinsky, A. D., Magee, J. C., Rus, D., Rothman, N. B., & Todd, A. R. (2014). Acceleration with steering: The synergistic benefits of combining power and perspective-taking. *Social Psychological and Personality Science, 5*, 627–635.

Galinsky, A. D., & Mussweiler, T. (2001). First offers as anchors: The role of perspective-taking and negotiator focus. *Journal of Personality and Social Psychology*, *81*, 657–669.

Gladstein, G. A. (1983). Understanding empathy: Integrating, counseling, developmental, and social psychology perspectives. *Journal of Counseling Psychology*, *30*, 467–482.

Gregory, B. T., Moates, K. N., & Gregory, S. T. (2011). An exploration of perspective-taking as an antecedent of transformational leadership behavior. *Leadership & Organization Development Journal*, *32*, 807–816.

Guardian (2015). How do you write for teenagers? Retrieved online: https://www.theguardian.com/childrens-books-site/2015/oct/23/how-do-you-write-for-teenagers.

Gudykunst, W. B. (1988). Uncertainty and anxiety. In Y. Y. Kim and W. B. Gudykunst (Eds.), *Theories in intercultural communication (Vol. 12)* (pp. 123–156). Newbury Park, CA: Sage.

Gudykunst, W. B. (1993). Toward a theory of effective interpersonal and intergroup communication: An anxiety/uncertainty management (AUM) perspective. In R. L. Wiseman & J. Koester (Eds.), *Intercultural communication competence* (pp. 33–71), Newbury Park, CA: Sage Publications.

Gudykunst, W. B. (1995). Anxiety/Uncertainty management theory (AUM) theory: Current status. In R. L. Wiseman (Eds.), *Intercultural communication theory* (pp. 8–58). Thousand Oaks, CA: Sage.

Gudykunst, W. B. (1998). Applying anxiety/uncertainty management (AUM) theory to intercultural adjustment training. *International Journal of Intercultural Relations*, *22*, 227–250.

Gudykunst, W. B. (2005). An anxiety/uncertainty management (AUM) theory of effective communication: Making the mesh of the net fine. In W. B. Gudykunst (Ed.), *Theorizing about intercultural communication theory* (pp. 281–322). Thousand Oaks, CA: Sage.

Gudykunst, W. B., & Hammer, M. R. (1988). Strangers and hosts: An uncertainty reduction based theory of intercultural adaptation. In Y. Y. Kim & W. B. Gudykunst (Eds.), *Cross-cultural adaptation: Current approaches (Vol. 11)* (pp. 106–139). Newbury Park, CA: Sage.

Hatcher, R. L. (2015). Interpersonal competencies: Responsiveness, technique, and training in psychotherapy. *American Psychologist, 70*, 747–757.

Henretty, J. R., Currier, J. M., Berman, J. S., & Levitt, H. M. (2014). The impact of counselor self-disclosure on clients: A meta-analytic review of experimental and quasi-experimental research. *Journal of Counseling Psychology, 61*, 191–207.

Henretty, J. R., & Levitt, H. M. (2009). The role of therapist self-disclosure in psychotherapy: A qualitative review. *Clinical Psychology Review, 30*, 63–77.

Hoever, I. J., van Knippenberg, D., van Ginkel, W. P., & Barkema, H. G. (2012). Fostering team creativity: Perspective-taking as key to unlocking diversity's potential. *Journal of Applied Psychology, 97*, 982–996.

Hofstede, G. (1980). *Culture's consequences: International differences in work-related values.* Beverly Hills, CA: Sage Publications.

Hofstede, G. (1983). Dimensions of national cultures in fifty countries and three regions. In J. B. Deregowski, S. Dziurawiec, and R. C. Annis (Eds.), *Explications in cross-cultural psychology* (pp. 335–355). Netherlands: Swets & Zeitlinger.

Hofstede, G. (1997). *Cultures and organizations: Software of the mind.* New York: McGraw-Hill.

Hofstede, G., & Bond, M. H. (1984). Hofstede's cultural dimensions. *Journal of Cross-Cultural Psychology, 15*, 417–433.

Hojat, M. (2016). *Empathy in health professions education and patient care.* New York, NY: Springer.

Hojat, M., Vergare, M. J., Maxwell, K., Brainard, G., Herrine, S. K., Isenberg, G. A., Veloski, J., & Gonnela, J. S. (2009). The devil is in the third year: A longitudinal study of the erosion of empathy in medical school. *Academic Medicine, 84*, 1182–1191.

Katz, R. L. (1963). *Empathy: Its nature and uses.* London: The Free Press of Glencoe.

Kellett, J. B., Humphrey, R. H., & Sleeth, R. G. (2002). Empathy and complex task performance: Two routes to leadership. *The Leadership Quarterly, 13*, 523–544.

Kole, M. (2012). Writing for the young adult audience. *Writer's Digest.* retrieved from: http://www.writersdigest.com/editor-blogs/there-are-no-rules/writing-for-the-young-adult-audience.

Ku, G., Wang, C. S., & Galinksy, A. D. (2015). The promise and perversity of perspective-taking in organizations. *Research in Organizational Behavior, 35*, 79–102.

Langer, E. J. (1998). *Mindfulness.* Reading, MA: Addison-Wesley.

Lobchuk, M. M. (2006). Concept analysis of perspective-taking: Meeting informal caregiver needs for communication competence and accurate perception. *Journal of Advanced Nursing, 54*, 330–341.

Matveev, A. V. (2017). *Intercultural competence in organizations.* Cham, Switzerland: Springer.

Matveev, A. V. & Nelson, P. E. (2004). Competence and multicultural team performance: Perceptions of American and Russian managers. *Intercultural Journal of Cross Cultural Management, 4*, 253–270.

Mercer, D. (2000). Description of an addiction counseling approach. In *Approaches to drug abuse counseling* (pp. 83–92). Washington, D.C.: National Institute on Drug Abuse.

Miller, K. I., & Koesten, J. (2008). Financial feeling: An investigation of emotion and communication in the workplace. *Journal of Applied Communication Research, 36*, 8–32.

Milliken, F. J., Morrison, E. W., & Hewlin, P. F. (2003). An exploratory study of employee silence: Issues that employees don't communicate upward and why. *Journal of Management Studies, 40*, 1453–1476.

Mnookin, R. H., Peppet, S. R., & Tulumello, A. S. (1996). The tension between empathy and assertiveness. *Negotiation Journal, 12*, 217–230.

Mnookin, R. H., Peppet, S. R., & Tulumello, A. S. (2000). *Beyond winning: Negotiating to create value in deals and disputes*. Cambridge, MA: Belknap Press.

Park, H. S., & Raile, A. N. W. (2010). Perspective-taking and communication satisfaction in co-worker dyads. *Journal of Business and Psychology, 25*, 569–581.

Parker, S. K., Atkins, P. W. B., & Axtell, C. M. (2008). Building better workplaces through individual perspective-taking: A fresh look at fundamental human process. In G. P. Hodgkinson & J. K. Ford (Eds.). *Industrial and organizational psychology (vol. 23)*. Hoboken, NJ: Wiley & Sons, 149–196.

Payne, R. L., & Cooper, C. L. (2001). *Emotions at work: Theory research and applications in management*. New York, NY: Wiley & Sons.

Pescosolido, A. T. (2002). Emergent leaders as managers of group emotion. *The Leadership Quarterly, 13*, 583–599.

Pettigrew, T. F. (2008). Future directions for intergroup contact theory and research. *International Journal of Intercultural Relations, 32*, 187–199.

Pettigrew, T. F., & Tropp, L. R. (2008). How does intergroup contact reduce prejudice? Meta-analytic tests of three mediators. *European Journal of Social Psychology, 38*, 922–934.

Pettigrew, T. F., Tropp, L. R., Wagner, U., & Christ, O. (2011). Recent advances in intergroup contact theory. *International Journal of Intercultural Relations, 35*, 271–280.

Powell, J., & Clarke, A. (2006). Information in mental health: Qualitative study of mental health service users. *Health Expectations, 9*, 359–365.

Prandelli, E., Pasquini, M., & Verona, G. (2016). In user's shoes: An experimental design on the role of perspective-taking in discovering entrepreneurial opportunities. *Journal of Business Venturing, 31*, 287–301.

Redmond, M. V. (2000a). *Communication: Theories and applications*. Boston, MA: Houghton Mifflin.

Redmond, M. V. (2000b). Cultural distance as a mediating factor between stress and intercultural communication competence. *International Journal of Intercultural Relations, 24*, 151–159.

Redmond, M. V., & Bunyi, J. M. (1993). The relationship of intercultural communication competence with stress and the handling of stress as reported by international students. *International Journal of Intercultural Relations, 17*, 235–254.

Redmond, M. V., & Vrchota, D. A. (2007). *Everyday public speaking*. Boston, MA: Allyn & Bacon.

Reynolds, W. J., & Scott, B. (2000). Do nurses and other professional helpers normally display much empathy? *Journal of Advanced Nursing, 31*, 226–234.

Rico, R., Sanchez-Manzanares, M., Gil, F., & Gibson, C. (2008). The implicit coordination processes: A team knowledge-based approach. *Academy of Management Review, 33*, 163–184.

Ridley, C. R., & Lingle, D. W. (1996). Cultural empathy in multicultural counseling: A multidimensional process model. In P. B. Pedersen, J. G. Draguns, W. J. Lonner, & J. E. Trimble (Eds.), *Counseling across cultures (4th ed.)* (pp. 21–46). Thousand Oaks, CA: Sage.

Ridley, C. R., & Udipi, S. (2002). Putting cultural empathy into practice. In P. B. Pedersen, J. G. Draguns, W. J. Lonner, & J. E. Trimble (Eds.), *Counseling across cultures (5th ed.)* (pp. 317–336). Thousand Oaks, CA: Sage.

Rogers, C. R. (1951). *Client-centered therapy*. Boston: Houghton Mifflin.

Rogers, C. R. (1975). Empathic: An unappreciated way of being. *The Counseling Psychologist, 5(2)*, 2–10.

Ruiz-Moral, R., Pérula de Torres, L., Monge, D., García Leonardo, C., & Caballero, F. (2017). Teaching medical students to express empathy by exploring patient emotions and experiences in standardized medical encounters. *Patient Education and Counseling, 100*, 1694–1700.

Sadri, G. (2015). Empathy in the workplace. *Industrial Management, 57(5)*, 22–25.

Sinclair, S., Beamer, K., Hack, T. F., McClement, S., Raffin Bouchal, S., Chochinov, H. M., & Hagen, N. A. (2017). Sympathy, empathy, and compassion: A grounded theory study of palliative care patients' understandings, experiences, and preferences. *Palliative Medicine, 31*, 437–447.

Snyder, J. L., Claffey Sr., G. F., & Cistulli, M. D. (2011). How similar are real estate agents and human-service workers? *Journal of Business Communication, 48*, 300–318.

Sorenson, C., Wright, K., & Hamilton, R. (2016). Understanding compassion fatigue in healthcare providers: A review of current literature. *Journal of Nursing Scholarship*, *48*, 456–465.

Spiro, H. (2009). Commentary: The practice of empathy. *Academic Medicine*, *84*, 1177–1179.

Suchman, A. L., Markakis, K., Beckman, H. B., & Frankel, R. (1997). A model of empathic communication in the medical interview. *Journal of the American Medical Association*, *277*, 678–682.

Sutton, R. I. (2009). How to be a good boss in a bad economy. *Harvard Business Review*, *87(6)*, 43–50.

Teding van Berkhout, E., & Malouff, J. M. (2016). The efficacy of empathy training: A meta-analysis of randomized controlled trials. *Journal of Counseling Psychology*, *63*, 32–41.

Tompkins, T. C. (2000). Developing mature teams: Moving beyond team basics. *Advances in Interdisciplinary Studies of Work Teams*, *7*, 207–222.

Truax, C.B., & Carhuff, R. R. (1967). The meaning and reliability of accurate empathy ratings: A rejoinder. *Psychological Bulletin*, *77*, 397–399.

Varca, P. E. (2009). Emotional empathy and front line employees: Does it make sense to care about the customer? *Journal of Services Marketing*, *23*, 51–56.

Van der Zee, K. I., & Van Oudenhoven, J. P. (2001). The multicultural personality questionnaire: Reliability and validity of self- and other ratings of multicultural effectiveness. *Journal of Research in Personality*, *35*, 278–288.

Vossen, H. G. M., & Valkenburg, P. M. (2016). Do social media foster or curtail adolescents' empathy? A longitudinal study. *Computers in Human Behavior*, *63*, 118–124.

Wang, Y., Davidson, M. M., Yakushko, O. F., Savoy, H. B., Tan, J. A., & Bleier, J. K. (2003). The scale of ethnocultural empathy: Development, validation, and reliability. *Journal of Counseling Psychology*, *50*, 221–234.

Weißhaar, I., & Huber, F. (2016). Empathic relationships in professional services and the moderating role of relationship age. *Psychology & Marketing*, *33*, 525–541.

Wieseke, J., Geigenmüller, A., & Kraus, F. (2012). On the role of empathy in customer-employee interactions. *Journal of Service Research*, *15*, 316–331.

Wolff, S. B., Pescosolido, A. T., & Druskat, V. U. (2002). Emotional intelligence as the basis of leadership emergence in self-managing teams. *The Leadership Quarterly*, *13*, 505–522.

Wright, K. B., Sparks, L., & O'Hair, H. D. (2013). *Health communication in the 21st century*. Malden, MA: Wiley-Blackwell.

Young, K. S., Wood, J. T., Phillips, G. M., & Pederson, D. J. (2001). *Group discussion (3rd ed.)*. Prospect Heights, IL: Waveland Press.

Appendix A: The Social Decentering Scale

The Social Decentering Scale is a 36-item multidimensional scale where each item includes three dimensions: input, process, and output. Summing specific groups of items produces measures of the seven components that make up the social decentering theory. Respondents are presented with the 36 items and asked to rate each item in terms of how well that item describes their own thoughts and behaviors on a five-point Likert scale.

Researchers interested in assessing just the cognitive dimension of social decentering (perspective-taking) can use just the 18 items constituting the cognitive subscale listed at the end of this section.

Researchers interested in assessing just the affective dimension of social decentering (empathy or affective perspective-taking) can use just the 18 items constituting the affective subscale listed at the end of this section.

Sample Instructions

The following items deal with a person's ability to relate to others. Read each item carefully and think about how true the statement is in **describing you** and your experiences. Please be as honest and objective as you can in responding. Use the following scale:

1----------------------------2----------------------3----------------------------4----------------------5

Strongly Disagree   **Disagree**   **Agree/Disagree**   **Agree**   **Strongly Agree**

Write the number that reflects how much each statement applies to you in the space provided each tem

Social Decentering Scale Items

__1. I get emotional over almost anybody's crisis.
__2. I would be likely to feel a rush of excitement and enthusiasm while trying to guess what was making someone I didn't know shout with joy.
__3. When I hear about other people's problems that I've never personally faced, I imagine what my thoughts would be if I were in their situation.
__4. I have wondered what people in some foreign countries think about various world problems.
__5. Sometimes when I daydream about situations I've never experienced before, my daydreams evoke strong emotional reactions in me.
__6. I feel the pain my closest friends feel when they are in trouble.
__7. There are times when I become quite emotional while watching TV shows or movies, though what I feel may not necessarily be the feelings portrayed by the actors.
__8. Sometimes when I'm considering how to react to a person, I plan out what to do, and then imagine how I would feel if someone acted towards me the way I was planning to act.

https://doi.org/10.1515/9783110515664-009

__9. (Think of a particular close friend.) I try to anticipate and "second guess" what my friend will say in reaction to alternate ways I might phrase a problem I want to discuss with them.

__10. When I watch a news story where a child has just suffered the tragic loss of their parents, I feel some of the same feelings the child is probably feeling.

__11. Sometimes I can understand what others are thinking by recalling the thoughts I have had when I experienced a similar situation.

__12. If I thought about it, I could guess what people one hundred years from now will think about various major events that are occurring now.

__13. I am likely to carefully consider what I know about a friend when planning on how to best approach them for something they might be reluctant to give or lend to me.

__14. I would feel some of the same feelings as a close friend (think of a particular friend) if both his/her parents were killed in an automobile accident; my friend would probably have some feelings I would not feel, as well.

__15. The way I think and behave serves as my general basis for understanding how people in general think and behave.

__16. I would feel some of the feelings that a senior citizen I was talking to might have upon learning of the death of his/her spouse of 50 years.

__17. I think about how I would handle situations that I hear or read about confronting other people.

__18. When I hear about a person's problem that is similar to a problem I've experienced, I usually recall what I thought and did about my problem.

__19. I usually get as excited as my best friend (think of a particular friend) when I find out something exciting has happened to him/her.

__20. I get emotionally involved in news stories about the tragedies and joys of other people.

__21. I take into consideration both the situation and a person's cultural and ethnic background when I'm trying to understand the behavior of someone I don't know very well.

__22. My emotions are easily aroused when I am imagining myself in another person's predicament.

__23. (Think of a particular friendship that you have recently developed). I have tried to understand how this person thinks by considering their background, personality, maturity, etc.

__24. I can imagine how some of my attitudes, beliefs, and values might be different than they are if I had been raised in a different country's culture.

__25. I know my closest friend (think of a particular friend) so well, that I even know how he/she thinks most of the time.

__26. My emotional state sometimes seems determined by my best friend's emotional state; when he or she is down, I become down; when he or she is up, I become up.

___27. I know some of the values, attitudes, and thoughts associated with different cultural and ethnic groups.
___28. I have learned about some of my feelings and emotional reactions by putting myself in situations confronting characters in movies and books, and other people in general.
___29. I often think about what it would be like for me to be in other people's shoes; what I would say and what I would think.
___30. My closet friend and I would probably experience some of the same feelings in reaction to the news that he/she suddenly had come into a large sum of money though my feelings would be different in a few ways.
___31. I tend to feel some of the same pain a parent must feel about the accidental death of one of their children when I read about such a tragedy in the news.
___32. (Think of a close friend who has never been in trouble with the law.) This friend and I would probably have the same emotional reaction to he/she being mistakenly arrested.
___33. I can tell a lot about a stranger's attitudes, beliefs and values, after talking to him/her for just a minute or two.
___34. I pay attention to the things I learn about acquaintances as we become closer, so that I can better understand how they think.
___35. I try to guess what the circumstances might be surrounding a stranger's public emotional outburst (crying, cheering, etc.) and my speculations would arouse an emotional reaction in me similar to the stranger's reaction.
___36. I sometimes think about how my closest friend will think about a controversial subject even before we start to discuss it.

Scoring the Social Decentering Scale Measure

Add the responses to the 36 items to get an overall social decentering score. Scores for subscales are calculated by totaling the appropriate list of designated items (the means of each subscale can be used instead of totals to allow for easier comparisons across subscales).

Overall Social Decentering Scale: Sum all 36 items.

Input Subscales (means = total/18)
Experience-Based Subscale: 1, 6, 7, 10, 11, 15, 18, 19, 20, 21, 23, 25, 26, 27, 28, 31, 33, 34
Imagination-Based Subscale: 2, 3, 4, 5, 8, 9, 12, 13, 14, 16, 17, 22, 24, 29, 30, 32, 35, 36

Process Subscales (means = total/12)
Use of Self Subscale: 1, 3, 5, 7, 8, 11, 15, 17, 18, 22, 28, 29
Use of Specific Other Subscale: 6, 9, 13, 14, 19, 23, 25, 26, 30, 32, 34, 36
Use of Generalized Others Subscale: 2, 4, 10, 12, 16, 20, 21, 24, 27, 31, 33, 35

Output Subscales (means = total/18)

Cognitive Subscale: 3, 4, 9, 11, 12, 13, 15, 17, 18, 21, 23, 24, 25, 27, 29, 33, 34, 36
Affective Subscale: 1, 2, 5, 6, 7, 8, 10, 14, 16, 19, 20, 22, 26, 28, 30, 31, 32, 35

Appendix B: The Relationship-Specific Social Decentering (RSSD) Scale

In administering this measure, the researcher needs to specify in the instructions who the target person is such as spouse, boyfriend, best friend, or mother. The term "partner" can be replaced by the target person you are interested in studying. Respondents should be asked to think about this one person and the relationship they have with that person as they respond to each of the items.

Instructions: Answer each of the following items in terms of your _____ and the relationship you have with this person at this time.

Write the number that reflects how much each statement <u>applies to you</u> in the space provided in front of each item using the following scale:

1	2	3	4	5
Strongly Disagree	**Disagree**	**Agree/Disagree**	**Agree**	**Strongly Agree**

__1. I feel the pain my partner feels when he or she is in trouble.

__2. I try to anticipate and "second guess" what my partner will say in reaction to alternate ways I might phrase a problem I want to discuss with him or her.

__3. I am likely to carefully consider what I know about my partner when planning on how to best approach my partner for something he or she might be reluctant to give or lend to me.

__4. I would feel some of the same feelings as my partner if both his/her parents were killed in an automobile accident; my partner would probably have some feelings I would not feel, as well.

__5. I usually get as excited as my partner when I find out something exciting has happened to him/her.

__6. I have tried to understand how my partner thinks by considering his or her background, personality, maturity, etc.

__7. I know my partner so well, that I even know how he/she thinks most of the time.

__8. My emotional state sometimes seems determined by my partner's emotional state; when he or she is down, I become down; when he or she is up, I become up.

__9. My partner and I would probably experience some of the same feelings in reaction to the news that he/she suddenly had come into a large sum of money though my feelings would be different in a few ways.

__10. My partner and I would probably have the same emotional reaction to his or her being mistakenly arrested.

__11. I pay attention to the things I learn about my partner, so that I can better understand how he or she thinks.

https://doi.org/10.1515/9783110515664-010

__12. I sometimes think about how my partner will think about a controversial subject even before we start to discuss it.

Scoring: The total or average of the 12 items represents the respondents' RSSD score.

List of Figures

https://doi.org/10.1515/9783110515664-011

List of Tables

https://doi.org/10.1515/9783110515664-012

Index

https://doi.org/10.1515/9783110515664-013